HUMAN RISING

THE PROHIBITIONIST PSYCHOSIS AND ITS CONSTITUTIONAL IMPLICATIONS

ROAR A. MIKALSEN

For Liv

"May this Great Monument, raised to liberty, serve as a lesson to the oppressor, and an example to the oppressed."

Contents

Part Two:
The Social Experiment of Drug Prohibition

Part Three:
Power Politics

Part 4
The Legal Perspective

INTRODUCTION

"Once society shifts from a world view of taking drugs as one of victimization, helplessness, and aberration to one of conscious regulation of a natural drive, the drug enforcement enterprise will cease to have validity . . . Its very premise will have been crushed. The need for the Government's 'protection' from an external enemy will vanish. The War on Drugs will emerge in its true character—a war on one-third of the American people, or more accurately, a stupid and futile attack on their satisfaction of a fundamental human drive."[1]

—Steven Wisotsky, Professor of Law—

FOR MORE THAN a century, the drug laws have had their effects on society. In pursuit of the drug-free ideal, we have given authorities more and more powers, but still we are no closer to the utopia our leaders had in mind when they adopted the prohibition experiment. On the contrary, many will say that things have gone from bad to worse and some will even claim that the costs of pursuing a drug-free world are so great that the fabric of society cannot bear them much longer.

This may seem hyperbole. However, it is uncontroversial that power to authority always comes at a cost to individual liberty, and so it should come as no surprise that more and more are sceptical of a crusade whose rewards are—at best—elusive and whose costs are evermore apparent.

I say "apparent", for in a debate on drug policy it is no longer possible to deny that, despite good intentions, prohibitionism has

---

[1] STEVEN WISOTSKY, *BEYOND THE WAR ON DRUGS: OVERCOMING A FAILED PUBLIC POLICY* (1990) 214

had a series of unfortunate side-effects. These include, on the individual level, increased poverty, health-problems, and death, while on the collective level the enforcement of drug laws has led to large-scale social, ecological, legal, and moral distress. Some of these side-effects are officially recognized.[2] Even so, most remain unaware of the extent to which prohibition has undermined society and it is commonly understood to be a decent endeavour, one without which we would be much worse off.

This is what prohibitionists will say. According to this view, the criminalization of certain drugs is necessary to protect society, but this assumption is refuted by data. We now have several examples of societies, even countries, that live in peaceful relationships with drug users and the evidence shows exactly what we could expect: (1) That the more we normalize relations between drug users and society, the more also the problems associated with drug abuse go away, and (2) that the harder we persecute drug users and distributors, the worse are the implications for the individual and society.

It is therefore the subject of this book to present an argument for the legalization of all drugs. While controversial, it is my assertion that the ideology of prohibition is a sinister threat to values that we hold most dear and that we cannot blossom as a society without its repeal. Not only that. I shall go as far as to say that the War on Drugs represents a crime against humanity and show why it is incompatible with fundamental principles of law.

Yes, it is unheard of. Even so, the reason for the former is that, after reviewing the data, we can say that every year prohibition continues another 400,000 die needlessly; another five million are wrongfully deprived of liberty; another $400 billion in profits are

---

[2] To quote the UNDP: "evidence shows that in many countries, policies and related enforcement activities focused on reducing supply and demand have had little effect in eradicating production or problematic drug use. As various UN organizations have observed, these efforts have had harmful collateral consequences: creating a criminal black market; fueling corruption, violence, and instability; threatening public health and safety; generating large-scale human rights abuses, including abusive and inhumane punishments; and discrimination and marginalization of people who use drugs, indigenous peoples, women, and youth." UNDP, *Perspectives on the Development Dimensions of Drug Control Policy* (2015) 2

given to organized crime syndicates (and laundered in Western banks); another staggering but unimaginable amount of pain and misery is inflicted on individual human beings; and another ridiculous amount—we are talking hundreds of billions—is spent on law-enforcement and bureaucratic manoeuvring that has had little impact on drug use or supply, but whose only effective function is restricting a people's free will.

In short, unless prohibitionists can show this argument wrong, they are responsible for a policy that has left mass graves and mass suffering in its wake, and it is here drug prohibition comes into trouble with first principles—i.e., our constitutional heritage.

Now, as these principles remain absent in the public debate, most have neglected them. Even so, adherence to these principles is the only thing that separates a legitimate democracy from a tyrannical government, and without a proper understanding of them and their importance we remain impotent against injustice.

I shall therefore, with this book, remind the reader of our political custom. As citizens of the West, we build our society from a set of principles that is not only to protect us from the harmful behaviour of others, but the destructive force of arbitrary government. These are what we call first principles. In our world, they give rise to systems of justice and government; they are all obvious to reason, they are all intuitively recognized, and they are all interconnected.[3]

In fact, if history has been rough on humanity, it has been our own fault, as most—if not all—of our misfortune has been due to our neglect of first principles. At the very least, in following them, we would have avoided all that injustice done to individuals and population groups as a result of false authority and moral panics— and if we are to erect a more perfectly ordered society, there is no

---

[3] As Alexander Hamilton wrote on first principles: "In disquisitions of every kind there are certain primary truths, or first principles, upon which all subsequent reasonings must depend. These contain an internal evidence which, antecedent to all reflection or combination, commands the assent of the mind." (Federalist no. 31) More shall be said on this moral platform, but principles such as autonomy, equality, proportionality, non-arbitrariness, dignity, and the liberty presumption are its primary sources of justice, while principles such as individual sovereignty, separation of powers, limited government, and so on, are at the heart of government.

controversy as to the necessity of us abiding by their light. Not only that, but our constitutional order demands that they are respected and so I shall argue from such a perspective. It is, after all, the only way to ensure that one's argument remains rooted in reason, not prejudice, and it is also the only way to ensure basic human rights protection.

The Contents of the Book

We shall soon see what this means. Throughout these pages, the extent to which the prohibition ideology has corrupted Western society and core values shall be documented and its problem with constitutional constraints illuminated. In the first part, the basic parameters of the social contract are laid out: I explain the political theory from which modern states draw legitimacy and why, according to human rights activists, there is a problematic relationship between the drug law and the Constitution.

It will take the rest of the book to prove why. However, drawing upon a century of experience, a solid case shall be made that the drug law does restrict the violators' inherent right to life, liberty, and the pursuit of happiness—and that it does so in a disproportional, arbitrary, and discriminatory manner.

Such a case rests on the premise that the now illicit drugs pose a lesser threat to society than is formally acknowledged by government; that the law has proven to be an ineffective means of dealing with this threat; and that there are less restrictive means better suited to deal with the problem. Because of this, a claim is made that the law is incompatible with key human rights principles; that this has been obvious for decades; and that, in fact, only a moral panic now sustains the prohibition argument.[4]

---

[4] This has been evident to law professors for a long time. Already in the 1960's, there were increasing concerns, and by the 1970's, there was no longer any meaningful debate on the topic. By then there were overwhelming evidence that the political process behind the 1937 Marijuana Tax Act was motivated by racism, ignorance, and empire-building; that government did not care about its unconstitutional nature; and that Americans, because of this, would keep suffering the illegitimate consequences of cannabis prohibition. As Professors Bonnie and Whitebread summarized the status quo: "The source of the law is

While controversial, the evidence is in. And the implication of living in times of moral panic is not only that there will be a distance between the morality of the Constitution and that of contemporary society, but there will also be a collective psychosis ensuring that this distance remains unseen.

This is the prohibitionist psychosis, and in this book we shall study its impact as it plays out in the Western world. Building upon the social dynamics generated by the enemy image of drugs, we shall see that the drug war has turned former democratic countries into tyrannies; that the morality of prohibition is really one of thugs; that in accepting its enemy image, we become part of the problem; and that its morality is the exact opposite of the Constitution.

In the second part, we shall provide more factual grounding for this thesis. Looking at the evolution of drug policy, the enemy image of drugs will not only be dispelled, but we shall study the impact of moral panic and its destructive course. As shall be seen, there is no denying that our society remains in the thrall of collective psychosis, and in part three we shall discuss the dark, unmentionable aspect of drug policy—the link between drug barons and government.

As shall be seen, there is a difference between theory and practice and the corrupting influence of the drugs economy is such that the status quo depends upon it to survive. Hence, not only have trillions of dollars been laundered in Western banks with no one being arrested, but those drug warriors who have tried to investigate this link have been punished. If this is shocking to consider, the double dealings and hypocrisy that comes with drug prohibition extends well beyond this. Indeed, the connection between politics and organized crime cemented long ago, and looking behind the scenes, we find that wars have been waged to

---

now its defense—ignorance. Even though independent researchers have disproved all of the old assumptions, the status quo is maintained on the ground that the evidence is not yet in on long-range effects of repeated use." Richard Bonnie & Charles Whitebread, *The Forbidden Fruit and the Tree of Knowledge: An Inquiry into the Legal History of American Marijuana Prohibition*, Virginia Law Review Vol. 56:971 (1970) 1170

control profits and that secret services have structured the illicit economy toward their own ends.

For reasons that shall become obvious, the drugs economy is an important tool of power-politics, and to prove it once and for all—in what will most certainly be an eye-opener—we shall follow the trail of witness testimony and see how the Reagan administration, to launch an illegal war in Nicaragua, coordinated for a nefarious plot of intrigue, making the U.S. government the biggest drugs and arms smuggler of the Western hemisphere.

In this period, due to government orchestrated drug smuggling, the imports of cocaine to the United States more than doubled, ensuring a vast fortune for the Vice President and his friends. This fortune would accommodate the agenda of a power-political faction that had a strong penchant for despotism and to hide the truth hundreds were murdered, arrested, or pressured into silence. This is why the big media networks did not report the story as it should have been told. For reasons of national security, the press would disregard the vicious gang of war profiteers that had taken over the White House and when investigative journalists tried to break ranks the government and media would unite in effort to quench them. The story of Gary Webb was just one example of what happened to those who departed from the heard; others lost their lives trying to expose high treason and in this continuing fashion reality did not make it into the news.[5] Even so, the truth always outlasts a lie. And despite a stringent regime of oppression and self-censorship, sufficient evidence has come to light to make a definitive case against top officials. The story of high crimes shall be presented here—and as we shall see, it is no longer possible to believe in the prohibitionist fairy tale of good guys versus bad guys.

Recognizing the impact of the drugs economy, we should understand why it must be stopped. If it has corrupted the rule of

---

[5] The Vice President, George Bush Sr., is now dead and his power network is in competition with others. In exposing the dirty dealings of power in the Reagan Era, therefore, my hope is that we can find the courage to learn from history. If it happened in the Reagan administration, there is no reason to think that it cannot happen again—or that it is not a common enough practice.

law to the point where drug dealing and murderous cover-ups have become policy, not only can we have no expectations of winning the War on Drugs, but to the extent that it is fought, it will encourage the tyrannical aspects of the state.

This book will leave no doubt about this, and so the folly of the drug war should be self-evident. Indeed, as seen from the perspective of the collective psyche, it is revealed to be a symptom of unconsciousness; it is a testimony of the extent to which we have abandoned the responsibilities of autonomous living, and to the extent that we believe in the propaganda offered by state servants, we will set course for a different destination than that staked out by our founding fathers. We will then set sails for the same terrorizing waters that the citizens of Pol Pot's Cambodia, Mao's China, Hitler's Germany, and Stalin's Soviet Union came to experience. In a misguided attempt to rid the world of evil, we will abandon all pretence of civility and society becomes an open theatre of war—as we shall see, not so unlike today, but potentially much worse.

This comparison between drug prohibition and historically recognized despotisms may seem unfair. Nevertheless, we have reached that stage of moral panic where the citizenry, protected by the law, murder, and oppress for no good reason; we have passed that stage where the masses accept as granted the legitimacy of state-run terror campaigns; and we have crossed that stage where the servants of state, to protect the status quo, systematically ignore the duty to protect the wrongfully persecuted. Hence, constitutional ground is well behind, and all it takes is an escalation of fear before murder and mayhem rockets.

Indeed, if we compare social dynamics from the perspective of enemy images and their effects, there is only one difference: that the enemy image of drugs has not reached the height as that of the Jew in Nazi-Germany. That, however, is not to say that it cannot, as the power of enemy images is always fluctuating, and the citizenry is easy prey for those who profit from their existence. Thus, all it takes to increase the level of fear is a well-orchestrated propaganda attack, and in the War on Drugs this has been frequently deployed. Because of this, there is a death penalty in more than 30 countries, and while western politicians normally settle for less, they support such tactics both directly and indirectly by praising hard-line policies and funding anti-drug efforts in such countries. Not only that. We just heard President Trump argue that drug dealers should be applicable for the death penalty, and he is not alone. Building on deranged reasoning, such fear-mongers claim that drug dealers are the cause of thousands of people dying and so capital punishment is required to protect society. We shall later expose the fallacy of such an argument. As we shall see, drug dealers are guilty of no worse crimes than the average salesperson, but as such hysteric jabber is officially accepted everything is set for an Orwellian nightmare.

Indeed, as we shall see, there is a connection between power and fear that does not bode well for the individual and the drug war speaks all about it. In our attempt to rid the world of evil, we have come to embrace the same totalitarian tactics as any of the above-mentioned dictatorships would deploy—and while this is not commonly understood, part four explains how drug prohibition is in violation of basic human rights.

As we shall see, there is a direct relationship between our faithfulness to the Constitution and our tendencies to stray into troubled waters. In times of moral panic, the damage that has been done will be proportional to the enemy image; there is a direct connection between this phenomenon, scapegoating, arbitrary persecution, and human rights violations, and as soon as the moral climate allows for a principled look at policy, the Constitution must come to the rescue. Correctly interpreted, it provides the solution to the problem of moral panics and authoritarian governments, and those who have the fortitude to guide by its principles will find a way back to constitutional shores.

Part four elucidates upon this process discussing human rights, the connection between law and morality, as well as the implications of taking constitutional law seriously. Because of the link between moral panic and human rights violations, a truth- and reconciliation commission is the proposed mechanism for moral recalibration. We are dealing with a crisis of law, one that has yet to be seen or understood by most, but the link is obvious. As more and more reports recognize moral panic as the engine behind drug prohibition, therefore, our obligation to ensure an effective remedy is plain. In fact, from the perspective of a constitutional scholar, we are either heroes, cowards, or traitors; these are the only options, and this book provides a basis for those accepting the social and legal commitment to change.

With that, all is ready for an adventure that is set to broaden our horizons. As we shall see, no one is served by the status quo— and redemption is found in making the darkness conscious.

Part One:
The Psychological Perspective

1

MORAL PANICS—PAST AND PRESENT

"The loud little handful will shout for war . . . . Then the handful will shout louder. A few fair men on the other side will argue and reason against the war with speech and pen, and at first will have hearing and be applauded; but it will not last long; those others will out shout them and presently the anti-war audiences will thin and lose popularity. Before long you will see the most curious thing: the speakers stoned from the platform, and free speech strangled by hordes of furious men. And now the whole nation will take up the war-cry, and shout itself hoarse, and mob any honest man who ventures to open his mouth; and presently such mouths will cease to open.

Next the statesmen will invent cheap lies, putting the blame upon the nation that is attacked, and every man will be glad of those conscience-soothing falsities, and will diligently study them and refuse to examine any refutations of them; and thus he will by and by convince himself that the war is just, and will thank God for the better sleep he enjoys after the process of grotesque self-deception."[6]

—Mark Twain—

THE IDEA THAT we are living in times of moral panic may be a controversial—even intolerable—assertation. For one, there is the problem that moral panics are never recognized by contemporary society—that is why they endure. Secondly, if a moral panic has

---

[6] MARK TWAIN, *THE MYSTERIOUS STRANGER* (1916) 135

spread, this means that irrational fear has overcome society to the point where reason cannot be consulted, and it is hard to imagine that a campaign which has been collectively embraced for so long can be entirely without merit. If this were the case, those in power would not only have no authority, but the moral compass of the nation would be a wreck. Indeed, the law would be a tool for oppression rather than liberation, and it is difficult to accept this premise.

To do so entails nothing short of a reorganization of our moral universe, one that will be psychologically painful to the extent that one's identity is rooted in the prohibition paradigm—and one that few are prepared to embrace.

Even so, during times of moral panic, this is the only way out of the psychosis that has society in its spell, and so this is what I will ask. I want the reader to embrace integrity, question authority, and look at the data. As shall be seen, it unambiguously favours reform, and those willing to lay prejudice aside will find that drug prohibition is truly a beast of biblical proportions.

As a matter of fact, considering the evidence, the controversy and language surrounding current policy is not merely strange but indicative of a moral panic and the psychological trauma that comes with the territory. I say this because the taboo surrounding drug policy speaks for itself and because, realistically, there should be no more debate as to the pros and cons of prohibition. Indeed, after a hundred years of letting it influence policy, we know its dynamics through and through and we have not only learned that the more we fear drugs, the more inhumane and harmful will our policies be but that the opposite is equally true.[7]

---

[7] "The policy that we have called punitive drug prohibition is rooted in the assumption that illicit drugs are so dangerous that most illicit drug users will likely become abusers or addicts. Ironically, much of the behavior cited to support this assumption stems from the mind sets and social settings of use that are shaped by punitive prohibition itself. By making drug users deviants, our laws marginalize them in deviant subcultures. In a kind of self-fulfilling prophecy, their contact with criminal worlds is maximized while the potentially moderating influences of "normal" society are minimized. Informal social controls, on the other hand, approach users as people who are full citizens of society and who have a self-interest in getting and using information about the risks of the drugs they use. Of course, self-regulating drug use and informal social controls are more likely among those who have balanced lives, who can look forward to a decent life in the future, and who therefore have some stake in conventional life and society. Just as marginalizing drug use into deviant

In other words, evidence is in that the problem is not drugs per se but the enemy image of drugs. It is important that we separate between the two, for when it comes to drugs and drug policy there is a difference between truth and perceived reality. In times of moral panic this is always the case, and the bigger the enemy image the more its destructive power will infiltrate society, corrupting the basis of our constitutional order—that human connection which ensures rational solutions, equal treatment, and proportionality in law.

No matter time and place, this process is the same. The engine of moral panics can always be traced back to the influence of exaggerated enemy images, and this is a clue that begs attention. Indeed, those who study the phenomenon will not only find it at the heart of any mass-movement gone wrong: When it comes to the social dynamics, they will discover that campaigns as seemingly different as the Spanish Inquisition, Hitler-Germany's Nazism, and modern drug prohibition are identical—and that those who pursue them are suffering from the same psychological condition.[8]

That the reasons for prohibition can be found in a diseased psychological condition may come as a blow.[9] However, proof of

---

subcultures increase the likelihood of abuse, so does socioeconomic marginalization increase the likelihood of mind sets and social settings that increase the likelihood of drug problems." Harry G. Levine & Craig Reinarman, *The Transition from Prohibition to Regulation: Lessons from Alcohol Policy for Drug Policy*, in JEFFERSON M. FISH (ED.), HOW TO LEGALIZE DRUGS (1998) 289

[8] This is the essence of the prohibition mentality: Just like Nazis, they are fighting phantoms due to the influence of an exaggerated enemy image; they are therefore engaged in an endless war against human nature, against autonomy and free will, but because the enemy image dictates logic, not otherwise, they do not perceive their mistake. Instead, blinded by the power of this image, they will justify any transgressions towards fellow citizens, thinking it a service to humanity.

[9] A psychosis is the condition of having two conflicting ideas while accepting both and the prohibitionist psychosis can be encountered every time an informed individual meets an agent of the prohibition regime. We know from before that they have sworn an oath to the Constitution and to its people and that they are bound by law to take human rights concerns seriously. Even so, whenever they are presented with logic or evidence that reveals a dissonance between their policy and human rights law, they will reject it out of hand. Thus, we observe the workings of their defense mechanisms (denial and projection) ensure some dissociative-ego state, where they can continue to boast of being representative of wholesome values, while they at the same time live in denial of the disconnect that exists

the cognitive dissonance which ensures the perceived credibility of this experiment will be presented, along with documentation showing the extent to which prohibitionists will disregard the truth. As we shall see, this evidence has never been refuted and accepting it is as easy as putting two and two together. Nevertheless, when confronted, those responsible for policy will space out into an incoherent state of mind where reason does not compute.

While unfortunate, this is the very hallmark of moral panics, as the collective consciousness will be too vibrant with fear for most to oppose the unconscious forces that ensure their survival.[10] Denial being the only way to avoid the responsibility that comes with knowing better, this is the preferred option, and it can be observed on a daily basis due to the psychological condition behind drug prohibition.

Indeed, as human rights organizations have carefully described the disconnect between constitutional law and the War on Drugs, this is the only reason why drug prohibition continues.[11] Social engineers have offered solutions to the problem of moral panics[12] and had public officials acted on responsibilities, this misguided and misunderstood war would have been subjected to scrutiny and declared unconstitutional long ago.

Make no mistake about it: This is what the Constitution demands—this is their official duty. However, due to the conditions of moral panic, whenever officials are asked to

---

between prohibitionists' morale (which is informed by an enemy image) and a more fundamental morality, that which they apply to those they love.

[10] As psychologists have noted, it is psychologically painful to let go of collectively shared prejudice and the more widespread, the greater is the integrity needed for it to be overcome. To understand this pressure, our officials are faced with the same difficulties as potential whistleblowers working in criminal organizations or soldiers fighting in immoral wars, and they can expect much the same treatment as dissidents who oppose them. Should they act on their conscience, they will be hounded by lesser peers for not embracing the lie to which others have devoted their lives—and depending on the extent to which they oppose oppressive tendencies, the system's force of inertia will ensure that they are punished.

[11] See for instance: www.arodpolicies.org

[12] For more on social engineering, see ROAR MIKALSEN, *TO RIGHT A WRONG: A TRANSPERSONAL FRAMEWORK FOR CONSTITUTIONAL CONSTRUCTION* (2016)

consider the problematic relationship between the Constitution and the drug law, they can be counted upon to ignore their obligation towards the former. This clearly states that the laws of the nation are subject to human rights analysis, but this is never done. Instead, due to the influence of collectively shared prejudice, they will side with prohibition and ensure that the law escapes scrutiny.

Those who try to connect the world of human rights with that of drug policy have witnessed this phenomenon for several years. As we shall see, it has been brought to the attention of public officials many times, but even when confronted with their own reports that policy is a result of moral panic they dissociate and deny constitutional implications. As it stands, therefore, the impact of the moral panic has gone so far as to empirically invalidate the rule of law in several countries. What we see is not merely a systemic disregard for the rights of hundreds of millions of people, but proof that the prohibitionist psychosis has taken society to a whole other level, one where leaders openly side with tyranny.

1.1. Morality and Constitutional Ground

"The lesson is clear. Moral regulation perpetuates fear, not morality. . . . At the core of the effort to regulate morality lies the desire of "us" to regulate "them." With each prohibition, a socially dominant group burdens a weaker class of citizens with its notion of propriety. And notwithstanding the moral justifications used to support them, moral regulations only succeed in exacerbating existing social rifts. . . . As we enter a new century, it is abundantly clear that it is time to free ourselves from the idea of prohibition. . . . We should understand, like never before, that the idea is inherently flawed."[13]

—Charles H. Whitebread, Professor of Law—

That the Western tradition of open societies, due to the War on Drugs, has become a tradition of open tyranny is not yet officially recognized. This, however, does not mean much (other than that the masses have lost their sanity) and a reminder of constitutional ground will expose the true nature of this crusade.

I say "crusade," for as economist Thomas Sowell stated: "Policies are judged by their consequences, but crusades are judged by how good they make the crusaders feel."[14] In this case, there is no doubt that we are dealing with the latter. A closer look exposes the War on Drugs as an endless war against human nature waged by hypocrites, and if history should teach us one thing, it is that whenever enemy images are embraced on such mass scale, there is a strong possibility that governments become tyrannical.

As I have said, adherence to constitutional principles is the only thing that separates a legitimate democracy from a tyrannical government and when it comes to drugs and drug policy, there is

---

[13] Charles H. Whitebread, *Us and Them and the Nature of Moral Regulation*, Southern California Law Review Vol. 74:361 (2000) 362-63,70

[14] THOMAS SOWELL, *COMPASSION VERSUS GUILT AND OTHER ESSAYS* (1987) 74

a difference between truth and perceived reality. The morality of the drug war, therefore, is not merely different from the morality of the Constitution; as we shall see, the two are as opposite as could be, for while the ideological foundation of the former rests on state power and zero-tolerance, the ethics of the latter are those of autonomy rule and the presumption of liberty.

If the difference is not yet clear, this is explained by the influence of moral panic. During such times humanity will be guided by a diseased morality, one that is hazardous to health and safety but deceptively taken to be consistent with the morality of the Constitution. Even so, we are talking about two fundamentally different ethics, one based upon totalitarian premises and another on libertarian—and while this is not recognized by most, the Constitution provides the tools to separate one from the other.

1.2. THE STATE AND INDIVIDUAL POWER

"Laws: We know what they are, and what they are worth! They are spider webs for the rich and mighty, steel chains for the poor and weak, fishing nets in the hands of the government."[15]

—Pierre-Joseph Proudhon—

Considering that we are born into a world where contemporary morality is hailed as being equal to that of the Constitution, it may seem like a leap to accept this premise. Nevertheless, we know that historically the state has had a tendency towards despotism. The first law of politics reminds us that rulers want to rule and to rule they need subjects, and so the state apparatus has always been opposed to liberation movements.

---

[15] Pierre-Joseph Proudhon, *General Idea of the Revolution in the Nineteenth Century, Fourth Study. The Principle of Authority* (1851)

While authority will want to deny this, this trend is confirmed by historical precedent. No matter time and place, those who govern have been a threat to the evolution of human rights; what we have gained has been hard won, and the relationship between state power and personal liberty explains why. Those who pry find that there is a dichotomy between the two in that one can only expand at the expense of the other. This means that the more powerful the state becomes, the less room for the individual to flourish, and that authority will be threatened by empowered individuals. Authority, after all, will have a natural inclination towards protecting its sphere of influence.[16] And because rulers are psychologically predisposed towards control-oriented patterns,[17] they do not want a nation of self-governing individuals. This would put those who excessively meddle in the affairs of others out of business—and so, while values such as integrity, autonomy, responsibility, etc., are praised, those in positions of authority are systematically inclined to detest their content.

---

[16] Hence, there will be a competition between the departments/agencies of state and these agencies will have interests that do not necessarily conform with those of the people. From a perspective of self-preservation, these institutions will be driven by a momentum towards greater budgets, more power and influence, and when it comes to war-profiteers, their interests are in direct opposition to those of the people.

[17] Psychology teaches that that the more we are inspired by fear, the more a certain segment of the population—those we call sociopaths or psychopaths—will aspire to positions of control and power. Hence, those people who are the most interested in ruling others are those least fit to guide humanity onwards. Roughly one percent of the population proscribe to these criteria, but contrary to popular lore psychopaths are often found at the top of the power-structure. Recognizing this, we understand why the second law of politics dictates that power will expand until it meets effective resistance and why rulers, most of all, fear integrity. For some academic research on this subject, we have Jim Kouri, vice president of the National Association of Chiefs of Police, who did a study showing that leaders possess the exact same traits as serial killers. These are traits such as superficial charm, an exaggerated sense of self-worth, glibness, lying, lack of remorse and manipulation of others. As he said: "While many political leaders will deny the assessment regarding their similarities with serial killers and other career criminals, it is part of a psychopathic profile that may be used in assessing the behaviors of many officials and lawmakers at all levels of government." (Malcolm, *Oh-oh! Politicians share personality traits with serial killers*, L.A. Times, June 15, 2009). That psychopaths are overrepresented in leadership positions is recognized by other psychologists. Hare and Babiak estimate that psychopaths are 3-4 times more common, and Brooks et al. reckon that it could be as much as 21 times—i.e., the same percentage found among the prison population. BABIAK & HARE, *SNAKES IN SUITS* (2007). Brooks, N. & Fritzon, K, Psychopathic Personality Characteristics amongst High Functioning Populations, Crime Psychology Review, Vol 2 (1) 2016 (22-44) (retracted)

Again, authority will want to deny this. Nonetheless, the record speaks for itself, and this book will document how public officials have arrested the advance of human rights by ensuring a culture of impunity. If it were not for the naïveté of the people, the systematic disregard for first principles would be plain to see. However, because constitutional interpretation is interlinked with human psychology—and because politics and law will mirror the quality of our collective psyche—we find, in times of moral panic, that there is not much interest in first principles nor their repercussions. Neither officials, academics, nor the public, therefore, will have much awareness of the extent to which contemporary morality departs from constitutional ground. Secondly, because ignorance is bliss to the common man when constitutional treason prevails, there will not be among the general population any inquisitiveness into the nature of authority nor their own psychology. For this reason, few will have begun to understand the basics of human experience; they will be moved by consciously unacknowledged forces, they will be ignorant of political reality, and they will have no idea of how it violates the greater morality of our Constitution.

No doubt, our civilization has arrived in dire straits because of this. Due to our neglect of first principles, we are living in hierarchical, control-, and competition-oriented structures, places where trauma is being inflicted, endured, and passed on at such regular basis that it is hardly noticed. Under these circumstances few have any idea that the Constitution provides the solution to our problems. Even so, as shall be seen, in drawing upon its powers, we will not only ensure the dynamics that bring out the best in us, but we will never let the state project stray. This means that problems such as war, poverty, illegitimate persecution, etc., will become extinct. We will, in fact, as a society, be on our way to enlightenment—all due to an enlarged vision of what it means to be human.

I say "enlarged", for if this is the power of the Constitution, we have clearly failed to draw upon its potential. And because we live in a world where neither the populace nor politicians have any idea that they have lost constitutional ground—or that the Constitution, rightly interpreted, would invite harmony back into the world—our society continues without the proper use of this moral compass. This is unfortunate. As we shall see, we would have been much more successful as a society had the founders' vision been allowed to prevail, and so let us begin with a reminder of what this grand project of civilization building entails.

1.3. CONSTITUTIONAL GROUND: THE LIBERATION OF MIND

"Prohibition goes beyond the bounds of reason in that it attempts to control a man's appetite by legislation and makes crimes out of things that that are not crimes. A prohibition law strikes a blow at the very principles upon which our government was founded."[18]

—Abraham Lincoln—

When it comes to constitutional construction, it is only logical that the status quo will interpret the Constitution according to the needs and wants of society's power structure. This has been the case until today and the troubled relationship between state and individual power explains why. On the political spectrum, tyranny and autonomy are mutually exclusive, and this makes it no coincidence that, for those with a perceived interest in the status quo, the spirit of the Constitution will be difficult to grasp. As we shall see, it was designed to protect the individual against the tyrannical tendencies of the State and so, as seen from the perspective of authority, it is preferably read as a directionless

---

[18] JAMES P. GRAY, *WHY OUR DRUG LAWS HAVE FAILED AND WHAT WE CAN DO ABOUT IT* (2001) 122

piece of paper, one that can be taken to mean whatever power says.

In siding with the status quo, however, magistrates and officials are not only ignoring the ideological framework that brought Western Civilization into being; they are depriving us of societal growth that is needed, and we would do well to remind ourselves that the Constitution, at its core, is a deeply spiritual endeavour.

We see that from its origin. It began with the Enlightenment Era, and our constitutional heritage is the result of an intellectual trend which saw the character of historical motion as dialectical and driven by necessity. The founders, in other words, believed in a God of reason, one that had a plan with the world, and history was perceived as a preordained path—one where humanity, as it learned from its mistakes, would be released from the clutches of tyranny.

It is important to note that tyranny, in this sense, was not just a political status but a state of mind. As shall be shown, the two are connected, and according to the founders' vision, the world was in a woeful state due to incomplete understanding.[19] This incomplete understanding would result in ethics that were self-contradictory, ill-advised, and hurtful to others. Nevertheless, an innate knowing which centred around those values, ideals, and principles that follow from the Wholeness perspective was constantly at work. This intrinsic knowing would be described as connected to a system of Higher law,[20] and because of this

---

[19] The founders, of course, were a motley crew. They were men of many colors and some more than others represented the Spirit of Freedom. Nonetheless, it is uncontroversial that this spirit was the driving element behind the French and American revolution, and the French Declaration of the Rights of Man and of the Citizen, the American Declaration of Independence, the first State Constitutions, etc., remain testimony to this fact. Furthermore, as this spirit continuously anchor all legitimate government, I shall not debate the extent to which each and every founder were committed to its ideals; we know that, despite their professed loyalty to First principles, there were definitely agents of power involved, and it is unquestionable that these agents, over the course of centuries, would come to dominate the interpretation of law. In this part, however, I focus on the theory behind our constitutional order, not the smallness of men's minds. And when I speak of the founders, therefore, I speak of the spirit that pushed through their reasoning.

[20] This intrinsic knowing was not available to anyone. To the extent that people were limited by contemporary morality, they would be blind to the bigger picture, but to those who had

mystical feature our ignorance of the greater reality was destined to give way; as it did, a morality of love and spirit of freedom would command ever greater resources—and by the time of the French and American revolution, this force had become sufficiently powerful to build a new political foundation for the world.

Thus, while political theory before this time argued that the State was absolute and that kings had a divine right to rule, the founders rejected this as nonsense. Instead, from this point onwards, sovereignty rested with the individual and the idea behind our constitutional order was to secure optimum conditions for individual growth, conditions that rested upon the assumption of autonomy rule—of freedom under responsibility. The founders knew that only if this code was honoured could utopian societies arise. And the purpose of the social contract, therefore, (that which gave rise/legitimacy to the state) was to provide a mutual assurance that pre-existing natural rights—i.e., the inalienable rights to life, liberty, and the pursuit of happiness—would be respected.

The details shall be elaborated upon. However, being anchored in Higher law and that greater morality which exists independent of contemporary understanding, the founders understood that the integrity of law was intimately connected to its origin and that only a resonance between the two could ensure that the law fulfilled its function as a tool for liberation. Thus, a system of principled law was constitutionalized, and the State was given a monopoly on force to ensure that no one violated the rights of others to live free and productive lives. Because of this,

---

learned to see through collective prejudice and personal bias this greater recognition would make itself known. As Locke said: "I admit that all people are by nature endowed by reason, but from this does not necessarily follow that it is known to any and every one. For there are some who make no use of the light of reason but prefer darkness and would not wish to show themselves to themselves. . . . There are also others, brought up in vice, who scarcely distinguish between good and evil, because a bad way of life, becoming strong by lapse of time, has established barbarous habits, and evil customs have perverted even matters of principle. In others, again, through natural defect, the acumen of the mind is too dull to be able to bring to light those secret decrees of nature." JOHN LOCKE, *ESSAYS ON THE LAW OF NATURE* (1954) 113

activities like stealing, murdering, raping, and pillaging were rightfully frowned upon—and this police power, correctly construed, would ensure that society became a just and decent venture where autonomy was the name of the game.

We must keep in mind that this project was the result of an intellectual trend that perceived time as a purposeful progression of events, one where a greater Spirit of Freedom would manifest. The appreciation of autonomy can be seen as a testimony to this drift, as the idea of human rights, of equal privilege and worth, would have been unheard of a century before. As Europe arose from the Dark Ages, however, there was a spirit of upliftment; the thinkers of the Enlightenment sought far and wide for ideas and the printing press ensured a revolution in the sharing of information. Drawing upon all of this, the founders considered themselves fortunate to be living in a time when the collective wisdom of humanity was available for a new political structure to be designed.[21] They were among the most advanced thinkers of their age, and while hopeful for the future, they did not trust the state to bring in utopian societies. In fact, they all shared a deep suspicion of authority. The founders knew that if the regimes of the Old World were called aristocracies, theocracies, monarchies, democracies, or republics did not matter. The only difference was the mechanism by which a few would control the rest and understanding the need for a higher reason, they looked to principles to define the limits of law.[22]

---

[21] As Washington wrote: "The foundation of our Empire was not laid in the gloomy age of Ignorance and Superstition, but at an Epocha when the rights of Mankind were better understood and more clearly defined, than at any former period, the researches of the human mind after social happiness have been carried to a great extent, the Treasures of knowledge, acquired by the labours of Philosophers, Sages, and Legislators, through a long succession [of] years, are laid open for our use, and their collected wisdom may be happily applied in the Establishment of our Forms of Government, the free cultivation of Letters, the unbounded extension of Commerce, the progressive refinement of Manners, the growing liberality of sentiment, and above all, the pure and benign light of Revelation, have had a meliorating influence on Mankind and increased the blessings of Society; At this auspicious period, the United States came into existence as a Nation, and if their Citizens should not be compleatly Free and Happy, the fa[u]lt will be entirely their own." George Washington to John Hancock (Circular), 11 June 1783

[22] As Thomas Paine would say: "Man is not the enemy of man, but through the medium of a false system of Government. Instead, therefore, of exclaiming against the ambition of kings, the exclamation should be directed against the principle of such governments; and

These limits follow as a result of reason. Ever opposed to it, however, is passion, and the founders recognized this threat to liberty. They knew that when society is troubled by fear-based beliefs, and these are accepted without further deliberation, there is the likelihood that moral panics arise. The citizenry, then, will imagine that they are under the attack of some great, imminent evil, and state-run campaigns towards its eradication will be popularly embraced. The Inquisitionist- and the Nazi state are well-known examples and even though the lawyers of Hitler-Germany failed to recognize this fact, our Constitution is put together to safeguard the individual from the dangers inherent in every government. I say every government, because the Nazi State was a mere reminder of what happens when we leave constitutional ground behind. In fact, if the Germans had respected first principles, there would be no problem to begin with and rather than see the good intentions of a nation make way for a nightmare, they would have built from this foundation to create utopian societies.

In the course of this book, why shall become evident. Even so, from the perspective of self-preservation, we already know that the relationship between the state and the individual is troubled by conflicting interest; while the state, from the perspective of power, stands to benefit from any law, nothing is more damaging to society than disserving laws, and to guard against moral panic and totalitarian government there was a presumption of liberty in the Constitution. Thus, any state-directed campaign had to abide by principles of law and reason.[23] To deprive the individual of liberty, there had to be weighty reasons—and these reasons, if contested, had to be proven valid, not merely the delusion of ignorant minds.

---

instead of seeking to reform the individual, the wisdom of a nation should apply itself to reform the system." THOMAS PAINE, *RIGHTS OF MAN* (1791) part 1.7

[23] They are called principles of law and reason because, being derived from the Wholeness, these are eternally valid and self-evident. Once superstitions are left behind, they prove to be the basis of all constructive social organization and, according to the founders' school of thought, they are our guiding lights through trial and errors. To access their realm (and connect with the greater morality) there must be a willingness to challenge the authority of collective prejudice, and the founders knew that utopian societies could not arise until sufficiently many had the courage to connect.

1.4. THE RAMIFICATIONS OF MORAL PANIC

"Necessity is the plea for every infringement of human freedom. It is the argument of tyrants; it is the creed of slaves."[24]

—William Pitt—

The need to document good reasons is important. As shall be seen, historically speaking, a majority of the population has been under the spell of collectively held but limiting and erroneous beliefs. This group can be counted upon to use the law as a moral compass and in times of moral panic this will generate confusion. In such times, the law will no longer be bound to proper morality; even so, the masses will use it as a barometer of reason, and as overcoming this bewilderment requires a psychological realignment that will be painful to the extent that one's identity is rooted in the current paradigm, the majority will resist the temptation of even trying.

Consequently, no matter time and place, most people will live their lives convinced that they are on the side of good; society's moral climate dictate that this is so, and it is psychologically difficult to see beyond this belief. To do so necessitates an expansion of our moral universe, one where a more comfortable, but naïve and childlike, acceptance of authority is left behind for a more mature version. This more mature version has the power to question authority; this questioning builds integrity, but truth is never rewarded in times of moral panic. In such times the masses will be swayed by fear, not reason, and those who go against the grain will suffer the contemporaries' discontent. Being committed to the status quo, the masses, after all, must reject the implications of principled reasoning and to the extent that a society is driven by fear those who point to the difference between theory and

---

[24] GRAY, *WHY OUR DRUG LAWS HAVE FAILED AND WHAT WE CAN DO ABOUT IT* (2001) 97

practice will be ignored, hounded, persecuted, or killed. There is simply no way for the collective psychosis to endure without this mechanism and so the status quo preserves itself by a constant infliction of trauma.

The founders were aware of this. They did not need the example of Nazi-Germany to understand the problems of a philosophy founded upon state power and collective notions of the common good. The problems attached to power and the psychology of fear was evident already, and so they devised a constitution that would provide an effective remedy against injustice. In this manner, even one voice—if it was the voice of reason—was given the power to command all others; and this was the solution to arbitrary rule.

Or perhaps "solution" is too optimistic. After all, when persecution has become policy, not only will a culture of fear provide the momentum to continue, but agents of state will be accustomed to powers they want to keep. It goes without saying, therefore, that this mechanism will be tempting for power to ignore and the founders feared the worst. Even so, thanks to their legacy, public officials remain not only morally but legally bound to defend the Constitution against all enemies, foreign and domestic—and if a citizen can prove that they are engaged in policies of destruction, it is their duty to act. This means that an independent, impartial, and competent tribunal must be erected, one that is fit to deal with matters of constitutional importance—and if this tribunal should conclude that the campaign of violence is based on fallacious grounds, the state is not only obliged to stop its harassment but to ensure compensation.

In the tradition of the Enlightenment, that was the gift of the Constitution. It established, for all posterity, the sanctity of the individual, granting absolute freedom from oppressive tendencies, while offering a frame of ethics which defined the perimeters of justice. Since then, this model has become recognized as western civilization's greatest contribution to world culture and progressive states build their charter on the Global Model of Human Rights.[25]

Hence, whether we look to Norway, England, Canada, India, South Africa, the United States, or Mexico, constitutional courts are ready to decide upon the merits of an argument—and the merits of this argument can always be traced back to first principles. The founders were merely the first to recognize their impact, for America was not only an assembly of states; as we have seen, it was the vision of an enlightened realm, one where reason trumped passion, and where the values, ideals, and principles connected to the Wholeness would be reflected not merely in words but action.

From this follows the spiritual foundation of the Constitution. It was the result of a long and painful road, one where humanity after sufficient oppression would become formally pledged to Freedom. And to initiates of mystery schools (which included many of the founding fathers), the founding was the culmination of an ancient prophecy, one that templars, freemasons, Rosicrucian's, and other secret societies had been working for centuries to see achieved.[26] The Old World, however, had proved too plagued control-oriented elites to accept a rule of reason and only with the discovery of America did an opportunity arise. Now, finally, the experiment of a government dedicated to the Spirit of Freedom could begin—and even though totalitarian forces would endeavour to undermine the rule of law, the architects of the Constitution composed a document that, through the integrity of the human being, linked the law of the land to the law of the Heavens.

In doing so, they provided us with a tool for submitting existing standards to the dictates of a superior reason, and as humanity wised up this reasoning would gradually penetrate and be reflected in our institutions.[27] Thus, slavery and racist

---

[25] KAI MÖLLER, *THE GLOBAL MODEL OF CONSTITUTIONAL RIGHTS* (2012)

[26] MANLY P. HALL, *THE SECRET DESTINY OF AMERICA* (1944)

[27] As President Lincoln said: "[The Founders] set up a standard maxim for free society, which could be familiar to all, and revered by all, constantly looked to, constantly labored

legislation slowly but surely subsided—and while we are yet to arrive at utopian societies, they remain the promise of the Constitution.

---

for, and even though never perfectly attained, constantly approximated, and thereby constantly spreading and deepening its influence and augmenting the happiness and value of life to all people of all colors everywhere." Gerber, *Liberal Originalism* (2014) 10

2

PSYCHOLOGICAL, MORAL AND CONSTITUTIONAL EVOLUTION

"Our world is ruled by inflexible laws which control not only the motions of the heavenly bodies, but the consequences of human conduct. These Universal motions, interpreted politically, are impelling human society out of a state of autocracy and tyranny to democracy and freedom. This motion is inevitable, for the growth of humans is a gradual development of mind over matter, and the motion itself represents the natural and reasonable unfoldment of the potentials within human character."[28]

—Manly P. Hall—

WE HAVE SEEN that according to the founders' vision, it is the destiny of humanity to attain ever loftier insight. The values, ideals, and principles that follow from Wholeness represent our moral compass, and as humanity matures there is a movement towards greater levels of coherence between contemporary morality and Higher law. Thus, contemporary law becomes ever more calibrated to resonate with a Spirit of Freedom and a morality of love.

Now, while key to the integrity of law, the bond to Higher law is rarely noticed among lawyers. Being educated in law schools dedicated to the status quo, they are as lost to contemporary trends as the average man and few have any idea that they are participators in a greater process, one that predictably will lead to

---

[28] HALL, *THE SECRET DESTINY OF AMERICA* (1944) 5

the supremacy of principled law. Even so, among the more perceptive lawyers, the progression of law towards a higher state of equilibrium is clearly seen:[29] From century to century, law has rid itself of many inadequacies, and we are drawing near to that point where first principles can become recognized as a frame for societal growth.

In the spirit of the founders, therefore, we can see the evolution of law as confirmation of their historical thesis. And while society have yet to awaken from our forgetfulness, human experience can be perceived as a learning curve where we reach ever higher into the destiny of our stars. These stars, the inner moral compass that guides us, are the first principles of human interaction and government, and to the extent that we stay the course our salvation is assured. Indeed, the values, ideals, and principles behind the Constitution are the same guiding lights that motivated the prophets of religion, and in this respect the founders' project was similar to that of spiritual teachers such as Jesus, Mohammed, and Buddha.

2.1. OUR CURRENT CONFUSION

This comparison between the prophets and the founders may come as a surprise. Even so, in the course of this book we shall see that their mission, for all intents and purposes, was one and the same in that they all pointed to an enlightened realm—one where the greater morality, that which is our inherent potential, would become the norm.[30] Not only were they agents of autonomy, but they represented the most morally advanced men of their age, those who accepted a rule of principle rather than

---

[29] Metaphors such as "Law works itself pure", "There is a higher law within and yet beyond positive law, toward which positive law grows", and "Law has its own ambition", is testament to their intuitive recognition of this greater process.

[30] As Thomas Jefferson wrote: "Enlighten the people generally, and tyranny and oppressions of body and mind will vanish like evil spirits at the dawn of day," Letter to Éleuthère Irénée du Pont de Nemours April 24, 1816

their own subjective passion. From this point onwards, connection with the Spirit of Freedom (and the Law of One) is assured and there will be a movement towards integrating all that follows.

As a matter of fact, the common denominators between the founders and the prophets remain unknown only because we are born into societies of lesser ethics. The trauma that comes with living in our type of society provides a barrier against growth and we shall see how contemporary trends are coloured by confusion. Nonetheless, while we as a society remain committed to ignorance, modern psychology has confirmed that development is not static; the experiment of human consciousness is truly going somewhere, and the founders of religion were merely more psychologically advanced than their contemporaries—indeed, more than most people today.[31] Hence, we can all aspire to their heights, and as more and more findings indicate that consciousness is not merely a biproduct of matter but the fundamental substance of the Universe,[32] we would do well to rethink the present paradigm.[33]

2.1.1. Introducing the Power of Thought

If we look beyond the current paradigm, miraculous things become possible. We find, then, that our thoughts are not mere figures of imagination but that they contain a certain energy which

---

[31] The concept of personality development is discussed at length in other works. For a general introduction, see ROAR MIKALSEN, *REASON IS: ON THE NATURE OF CONSCIOUSNESS AND HOW EVERYTHING IS CONNECTED TO EVERYTHING* (2014). Regarding its implications for law, see MIKALSEN, *TO RIGHT A WRONG* (2016)

[32] For more on the science that confirms this hypothesis, see MIKALSEN, *REASON IS* (2014)

[33] While disproved by quantum physics, the Newtonian worldview continues its undue influence and the ideas and actions that follow from accepting its implications are tearing society apart. As authority will have us believe that we are worthless beings, helplessly adrift on a planet doomed for extinction, wonder that many have given into despair; our political, academic, and religious institutions are clogged by its debris and the suffering that results from accepting fragmented, fear-oriented beliefs is plain to see. If we would let go of the cultural prejudice that continues to ravage our souls, however, a greater reality awaits, one firmly established on a morality of love and a Spirit of Freedom.

will have a definite impact upon the world. At the level of society, this energy will have a positive effect to the extent that it is motivated by love and it will have a detrimental effect to the extent that it is motivated by fear. We can see this in our personal relations as well as our collective interactions—and while the former is the force that provides growth, the latter preserves and regenerates trauma. Trauma is the result of energetic information of such impact that the mind cannot rise above. As psychologists are aware, what we cannot integrate we will dissociate, and so defence mechanisms such as projection and denial come to our aid.

Due to their misdirecting efforts, reality and (most importantly) responsibility can be avoided for some time. However, while society usually recognizes this phenomenon in those instances when individual citizens are going through a personal crisis, it is much more difficult to spot when it is culturally inflicted. In those cases, a psychosis is not merely collectively shared, but the state will be committed to policies of destruction—and projection and denial will ensure a steady escalation of mayhem, both internally and externally, until we wake up and take responsibility for our creation.

Indeed, collectively speaking, these two can be found lurking behind every moral panic; it is denial and projection that ensures its survival, and drug prohibition is just another example of how these mechanisms ensure a morality that is twisted to its core.

2.2. Drug Prohibition: Unconsciousness Writ Large

"Law may be rooted in fiction as well as fact. Indeed, a public policy conceived in ignorance may be continuously reaffirmed, ever more vehemently, so long as its origins remain obscure or its fallacy unexposed. Yet once a spark of truth ignites the public opinion process, the authority of time will not stay the flames of controversy. . . . So it has been with Marijuana."[34]

—Richard Bonnie & Charles Whitebread,
Professors of Law—

The fact that drug prohibition, just like the Spanish Inquisition and Nazism, on the collective level is no more than the savage attempt of a torn psyche to understand, rearrange, and complete itself is not commonly recognized. However, psychologists, judges, criminologists, and professors of law have all noted scapegoating as its driving engine,[35] and it is all the evidence we need.

2.2.1. Scapegoating

This psychological phenomenon arises from our inability to integrate experience and put responsibility where it belongs. Psychologically speaking, it can be construed as the antithesis to

---

[34] Bonnie & Whitebread, *The Forbidden Fruit and the Tree of Knowledge*, Virginia Law Review Vol. 56:971 (1970) 974

[35] THOMAS SZASZ, *CEREMONIAL CHEMISTRY: THE RITUAL PERSECUTION OF DRUGS, ADDICTS, AND PUSHERS* (2003); DOUGLAS HUSAK, *DRUGS AND RIGHTS* (1992); RICHARD L. MILLER, *THE CASE FOR LEGALIZING DRUGS* (1991) 109-24; Susan Stuart, *War as Metaphor and the Rule of Law in Crisis* (2011); Levine & Reinarman, *The Transition from Prohibition to Regulation: Lessons from Alcohol Policy for Drug Policy*, in FISH (ED.), *HOW TO LEGALIZE DRUGS* (1998); Somerville: *Stigmatization, Scapegoating and Discrimination in Sexually Transmitted Diseases: Overcoming "Them" and "Us"* (1994)

the vision of the founders (that of an enlightened realm) because it provides the illusion of purification by the creation of a vilified outgroup, one that is to atone for the sins of others.[36]

Historically, it is this predisposition that has troubled mankind. As we shall see, it is a common way for societies of low self-esteem to vindicate their failures, and this trend manifests as a tendency to blame politically weak minorities for troubles that are a collective responsibility.[37] In persecuting this group, the citizenry becomes convinced of their own moral superiority, for they have identified evil and attained a moral standard that puts them beyond reproach. Thus, they can continue their life, feeling good, while ignoring that they are living on their knees, having accepted a social contract built upon lies, deceit, and oppression.

The importance of the scapegoating mechanism can hardly be overestimated. It has been the generator of a vast proportion of humanity's suffering, and René Girard, the French philosopher, not only describes how prohibitions derive from this phenomenon, but considers it to be the very foundation of cultural life. He claims that "Natural man became civilized, not through some sort of rational deliberation embodied in a social contract, (as it was fashionable to think among 18th century philosophers) but rather, through the repetition of the scapegoat mechanism."[38]

---

[36] Psychologist Neel Burton describes it thus: "The ego defense of displacement plays a role in scapegoating, in which uncomfortable feelings such as anger, frustration, envy, and guilt are displaced and projected onto another, often more vulnerable, person or group. The scapegoated target is then persecuted, providing the person doing the scapegoating not only with a conduit for his uncomfortable feelings, but also with pleasurable feelings of piety and self-righteous indignation. The creation of a villain necessarily implies that of a hero, even if both are purely fictional." Neel Burton, *The Psychology of Scapegoating*, Psychology Today, December 21, 2013

[37] "Labeling drug users as evil may be factual nonsense, but serves a strong psychological need. If users are bad, non-users can see themselves as good. That self-concept helps reduce guilt experienced by non-users who fear autonomy; the unpatriotic anti-American bums are those pot smoking peaceniks, not churchgoers who relinquish traditional freedoms upon command from government officials. No hard thinking is required to find the moral path; just follow the rules in order to be moral, obedience is goodness. Such a philosophy appeals to people who view the world in black and white contrasts. Everything else may be changing in the world, but at least anti-drug zealots can be certain that they are good and that drug users are bad." MILLER, *THE CASE FOR LEGALIZING DRUGS* (1991) 112

[38] http://www.iep.utm.edu/girard/#H3

His perception is keen. As it is powered by projection and denial, this mechanism relies upon unconsciousness to survive, and to the extent that it is present society will be retarded from reaching the destination set out by the founding fathers. Rather than the bliss of utopian societies, we will then experience a hellish circle where the psychology of fear runs amuck, and modern academics have written shelves on this topic. We can find them in any library, describing the dynamics of Pol Pot's Cambodia, Mao's China, Stalin's Soviet Union, and Hitler's Germany, and how they drove otherwise law-abiding citizens to commit mass-atrocities. Yet, as a society, we have failed to see the parallels to our time and our great social experiment.

This is unfortunate. Indeed, from a constitutional perspective, the taboos of drug policy are exactly where its bodies are buried. And to those who look closer, the drug war is not only exposed as identical to other historical mass-movements gone wrong, but its ideology is a blueprint for tyranny.

2.3. DRUG WAR: A BLUEPRINT FOR TYRANNY

"An addiction to drug laws is caused by an inadequate understanding of individual rights and the vital role such rights play in deciding matters of legality. As a result, policies are implemented that cause serious harm to the very individuals whom these policies were devised to help and to the general public."[39]

—Randy E. Barnett, Professor of Law—

Now, to most people, the drug war is a crusade for decency, and it is difficult to see how the prohibition formula for liberty is really one for tyranny. Nevertheless, the map that connects psychology

---

[39] Randy E. Barnett in JEFFREY SCHALER (ED.), *DRUGS: SHOULD WE LEGALIZE, DECRIMINALIZE OR DEREGULATE?* (1998) 172

and politics is rather specific and no matter where we are born into this universe, we will experience either the weight of our surroundings or their light, all according to time and place and where society exists on its path towards a greater understanding—that which includes an ever more refined insight into the mind of God.

In societies of advanced understanding, we will experience the light of our surroundings and we will grow into its radiance and beyond. Not so, however, in fear-filled societies. Here, where the play of duality makes life tough, we will have a harder time finding the light. The collective consciousness will be too charged with fear for most to resist its influence, but even so love is there, growing upon us, enriching each generation, while patiently awaiting our discovery.

As humanity comes of age, therefore, we learn to connect with the implications of Wholeness. As we evolve, society is transformed, and the quality of this structure mirrors the degree to which we collectively honour the law of One. This is the universal language, the moral code of enlightenment. Whenever times are hard, therefore, it will be because we collectively fail to honour our commitment to sound principles and values, and if we want the world to improve it is the responsibility of the individual to set an example.

The only way to do so is a steady commitment to those values everyone else endorse, but whose implications they ignore in their own lives. We must effectively be the change we want to see, for this brings integrity. It is integrity that connects us to the greater, timeless morality, and just as there is a link between responsibility and liberty, so there is a connection between defence mechanisms and tyranny. Thus, the connection to first principles shines through. It is, after all, incontestable that only integrity can prevent the rise of moral panics and that only integrity can overcome them. And so, while the road to salvation may be paved politically with principled law, it is the responsibility of the individual to free him/herself from collective prejudice. Only to the extent that this is done can society become a more harmoniously functioning body, and it begins with a willingness to question authority.

On the psychological map integrity and autonomy is interrelated, for if we put the authority of others before our own the result is a loss of control over our moral and psychological evolution. We become absorbers of collectively shared prejudice, unfounded enemy images, and premature—even contradictory—beliefs. We let existence be defined by the repressed psychological material that humanity en masse has ignored, and we take part in a mostly unconscious mass-movement, one guided by passion rather than reason. This is the prohibitionists' problem.

2.3.1. THE COSTS OF NOT THINKING THINGS THROUGH

"Current drug laws are the product of society's fears and prejudices and would certainly strike an unbiased observer as irrational, if not insane."[40]

—Andrew Weil. M.D. —

We have seen how the scapegoating phenomenon results from our inability to place responsibility where it belongs, and to the extent that we are troubled by this affliction, the world will be in chaos. On the national level, suppressed fear and shame will translate into a need of blaming others for problems that are a collective responsibility; this brings fertile ground for enemy images, which results in a steady escalation of state-orchestrated violence. On the personal level, the indignity of having accepted a social contract based upon lies, deceit, and oppression ensures a steady state of denial. This denial provides food for projection, and the ordeal continues. We have seen it before. As a matter of fact, it is the

---

[40] ANDREW WEIL & WINIFRED ROSEN, *FROM CHOCOLATE TO MORPHINE: EVERYTHING YOU NEED TO KNOW ABOUT MIND-ALTERING DRUGS* (2004) 205

same story that unfolds in any authoritarian society, and the hunt for witches, Jews, or drug fiends are historically similar in that they represent humanity's quest to overcome sin. Sin, correctly understood, represents that which separates us from Wholeness and comes in many forms. To psychologists, it is understood to be those fear-based belief structures that keep us from seeing the greater reality and, through therapy, people can overcome the suffering.[41]

In its proper form, then, the ridding of sin means going within; it means overcoming the habit of dualistic thinking through a steadfast commitment to those values, ideals, and principles that follow from Wholeness, but that is not how most know the process. Because our society has come to embrace the tenets of organized religion and established science, we are convinced that we must be sinful, depraved beings abandoned by a vengeful God, or mere matter organizing into form left to witness our extinction in a universe that does not care. As seen from such perspectives, there is no real point in self-exploration and our authorities mirror the extent to which we collectively have ignored the call to do inner work. Indeed, the spiritual truth "as above, so below", translates into politics; the policies of a nation, therefore, will mirror the extent to which citizens value autonomy, and we get exactly the leaders that we deserve.

In looking at the status quo, this does not bode well. We know that our authorities will lie, cheat, threaten, and murder to get what they want, while at the same time refusing to take responsibility for their actions. With such people at the helm, we ought not be surprised that problems arise. Nor should we complain when they

---

[41] This is done by providing a reliable set and setting for psychological growth. We shall have more to say on this subject, but as we live in a society that has fallen prey to psychosis, it is no coincidence that the drugs that have proven the most efficient at eliminating trauma is also those prohibited by authority. As seen from a perspective of self-preservation, as authority does not like the idea of a direct connection with God nor a true brotherhood of humanity, this only makes sense. Nevertheless, while the most powerful tools remain legally prohibited, there are other methods of healing, and the quest of all true psychology is to help people access that enlightened state of which the prophets spoke. For more on this, see MIKALSEN, *REASON IS* (2014)

do, as those who elect corrupt politicians are not victims but accomplices.

After all, if we want a better world, all we need to do is hold public officials to their oath and, if they do not comply, make sure that they never hold public office again. This is what a responsible people would do. However, as previous generations, we are not really that keen on accepting the responsibility that comes with being adults. We prefer to think of authority as some sort of benign father-figure when it is a wolf in sheep's clothing, and this is our mistake.

2.3.2. THE STATE: A WOLF IN SHEEP'S CLOTHING

"The twentieth century was the century of governmental power expanded to a maximum. It is perhaps no coincidence that it was also the century that saw more war, and more governmental-sponsored genocide and slaughter, than any other in memory. As Assistant Secretary of State for Human Rights John Shattuck notes, in the twentieth century 'the number of people killed by their own governments under authoritarian regimes is four times the number killed in all this century's wars combined.' As Neil Stephenson reminds us the twentieth century was one in which limits on state power was removed in order to let 'intellectuals run with the ball, and they screwed everything up and turned the century into an abattoir.'"[42]

—Professors Glenn Reynolds and David Kopel—

We have seen that the interests of governments and individuals are directly opposed. The basic antagonism in political theory, therefore, is not between fascism or socialism, capitalism, or

---

[42] *Glenn H. Reynolds & David B. Kopel, The Evolving Police Power: Some Observations for a New Century, Hastings Constitutional Law Quarterly, Vol. 27:511 (2000) 536*

communism, or any of the great ideologies of the 20th century: These ideologies have all been embraced due to an unprincipled opposition to state power, and if we wonder what the state truly fears it is the fully autonomous human being.[43]

Because the state apparatus, at this point, is no more than a representative of the collective unconscious, we find that it remains opposed to the idea of an enlightened realm. Due to the social dynamics inherent in fear-oriented societies, these structures are inhabited by people more interested in power than to realize the inherent potential of humanity. Hence, just as organized religion, to build its power structure, would twist the message of the prophets beyond recognition, so state officials, to present as acceptable their idea of government, would sabotage the founders' mission.

While unfortunate, the dynamics between the individual and the collective made this inevitable. The state is a most formidable apparatus and so special interest groups, gangsters, war profiteers, and ambitious sociopaths have used it as a means of exerting influence. Psychologically speaking, these are the people least fit to govern. We already know that accepting the status quo means accepting a social contract built on deceit, duplicity, and coercion, and it follows not only that unconsciousness is needed to prevail, but that the people in charge will be those most prone to the trauma-based thinking that keeps the system afloat.

Without it, integrity would grab hold and we would begin to represent a healthy expression of human potential rather than some diseased, split psyche at war with itself. Even so, as taking part in the system demands an unhealthy commitment to

---

[43] Psychiatrist Thomas Szasz has written eloquently on this subject: "Why is self-control, autonomy, such a threat to authority? Because the person who controls himself, who is his own master, has no need for an authority to be his master. This, then, renders authority unemployed. What is he to do if he cannot control others? To be sure, he could mind his own business. But this is a fatuous answer, for those who are satisfied to mind their own business do not aspire to become authorities. In short, authority needs subjects, persons not in command of themselves—just as parents need children and physicians need patients. Autonomy is the death knell of authority, and authority knows it; hence the ceaseless warfare of authority against the exercise, both real and symbolic, of autonomy—that is against suicide, against masturbation, against self-medication, against the proper use of language itself!" SZASZ, *CEREMONIAL CHEMISTRY* (2003) 175

ignorance, those who have successfully climbed to positions of power will be those most eager to leave integrity behind—and so enlightened rule is not on their agenda. Far from it. Instead, to the extent that leaders are coloured by fear, they will be predisposed towards control-oriented behavioural patterns rather than the liberation of the human mind—and while they will not admit to it, they create trauma to succeed.

2.3.3. THE CONNECTION BETWEEN POWER AND FEAR

"The whole aim of practical politics is to keep the populace alarmed (and hence clamorous to be led to safety) by menacing it with an endless series of hobgoblins, all of them imaginary."

—H. L. Mencken, 1918—

We may not like to think about the link between power and fear. However, just as there is a natural limit to the criminal sanction, there is a natural limit to the growth of government. Consequently, the officials who want more than to be of service must find a way to increase in scope and powers. Only to the extent that this is done can budgets and powers be maintained vis a vis other factions and agencies, and so fear becomes a mighty ally.

As philosopher Eric Hoffer noted, "it is when power is wedded with fear that it becomes formidable,"[44] and to the elites' social engineers this is the most effective way of subjugating a population. They know that the shape of society will be a direct reflection of our average consciousness—and while the psychology of love heals trauma, provides for personal growth and results in healthy interaction, the psychology of fear does the opposite: It produces trauma, which again provides for the

---

[44] Zimbardo, THE LUCIFER EFFECT (2009) 11

defence mechanisms that give rise to moral panics and totalitarian government.

In the world of power-politics, therefore, the application of trauma has been used with great fervour. Since Machiavelli's book on advice to rulers the amorality of power has become established lore, and knowing that the ability to subjugate is proportional to the level of fear, agents of power have spun tales of enemies abroad and within. This is the only way to thrive. And traditionally, to make us accept their solutions, the orchestration of false flag events, fabricated narratives, and enemy images have been used with great efficiency. These tools of power-politics ensure that environment which is most conducive to dominance, as a fearful citizenry will not reflect upon the nature of authority, nor want the responsibility that comes with autonomous living. They have come to see the world as a treacherous place and rather than cope with this perceived reality, they want a knight in shining armour to save them from their troubles. Hence, they tend to accept the authority of state without thinking and have no idea that there is a correlation between the promise of the Constitution and their integrity.

Even so, this correlation remains, and it is seen in the shame that comes with accepting false authority. It is no coincidence that the more a society departs from Higher law, the more explosive the situation will be. The psychological pain of accepting a social contract on false premises generates a passion for scapegoats while reality must be ignored. It goes without saying that this is a recipe for disaster. Indeed, to the extent that we let enemy images inform our reasoning, we will go into the night along with any authoritarian regime, and only an open mind can reorganize the world and make it whole again. I say, "make whole again", for whether the enemy image be witches, Jews, drugs, or terrorism, the divisive social dynamics are the same. The more power of the enemy image, the more it separates the world into 'us' versus 'them', and the more it dehumanizes 'the other', paving way for persecution and atrocities.

This is always the effect of an enemy image—and to the extent it is fed, the panic escalates. Not only will it make us intolerant and insensitive to the suffering of others; the enemy image feeds on fear and the more powerful it becomes, the more it empowers those who agitate for dominance and control. Thus, when moral panic has reached a certain momentum, laws will be written down to legitimize the way that the ingroup deals with the outgroup and from this point on those with a vested interest in the enemy image, whether it be emotional, financial, or political, will embrace it mindlessly.

I say "mindlessly", as the enemy image will define our morality. As soon as it is accepted, it will inform our reasoning, and because the enemy image dictates logic (and not the other way around) it is difficult for those in its grip to see beyond its horizon.

Whether intentionally or not therefore, during such times, most civil servants will feed the flame that keeps the moral panic alive—and so it is that the sins of our fathers come back to haunt us. What started out as a moral quest based on ignorance and fear becomes a holy crusade for generations to follow, for as soon as the enemy image is sanctioned by law, the law seems to justify the atrocities that follow.

This trend of moral panics never fails. Once an enemy image has come to influence policy, agents of power will feed on its energy and to the extent that the citizenry have faith in authority, no one will notice the departure from constitutional ground. Even so, a departure there will be, and while the morality of the Constitution is that of autonomy rule, equality and proportionality in law, limited government and the liberty presumption, the totalitarian momentum of the drug war has reversed this basis, making us accept the same means to an end as authoritarian states would employ.

2.3.4. The Prohibitionist Psychosis Revisited

"The real problem in this area actually is not the drugs themselves. The real problem is that our citizens and our leaders simply will not look at the evidence, even though it is all around us. Our present policies are exacerbating the problems and will not stand up to scrutiny. What we really need to do is to open the subject to rigorous public debate. This is our best and perhaps our only hope for moving forward to a better strategy, and to adopting programs that will actually work. The advocates of the status quo stand firmly against any full or open discussion of federal drug policy, but what we really need to do is explore our options realistically, and tell each other the truth."[45]

—Judge James Gray—

Now, to the extent that the world is run by control-oriented elite factions, the state will have no intention of fulfilling the social contract. As shall be seen in part three, this is empirically the case, and to hide a distance between theory and practice social engineers are dedicated to altering our perception. Somehow, the citizenry must be made to think that their government represents a healthy expression of human potential and that all is well in the relationship between the individual and state. To succeed in this quest enemy images become extremely helpful. As we have seen, not only will they provide momentum for an expansion of power, but they will make the population rally around the state.

In the history of man, therefore, our rulers have constantly painted the world as a hostile place. In so doing, they have made us accept a social contract built upon unwholesome premises, but it was not until the 20th century that authorities found a way to make civilized men so lame as to think that they, on the penalty

---

[45] GRAY, *WHY OUR DRUG LAWS HAVE FAILED AND WHAT WE CAN DO ABOUT IT* (2001) 15

of death or imprisonment, needed the state to control their access to consciousness-altering substances.[46]

In the enemy image of drugs, however, disciples of state not only found a way to relieve the masses from the burden of autonomous living, but to make society attack those who departed from the heard. As historian Richard Lawrence Miller wrote, drug scapegoats would "perform the function of Christ."[47] And while it is difficult to see the parallels between the prohibition regime and other mass-movements gone wrong, we must not forget that the means by which this crusade has been fought are those of finding ever more ingenious, ever more effective ways, of undermining free choice. This is the basis of the prohibition ideology: Even though it is believed to be for the common good, prohibitionists are in the business of eradicating plants, chemicals, and other substances which are popular in demand—and unless there be good reasons to abstain, this can only be done by totalitarian tactics. The authority of government will then be built on a lie, and this will ensure a social dynamic where the state, to preserve its prestige, powers, budgets, and authority, will become an enemy of the people.

Integrity, after all, must be fought every step of the way, and so authority will have to use propaganda, brute force, and deceit. These are the only tools available for an out-of-bounds state machinery. To justify its existence, the state must maintain a level of fear compatible with its treason—and as fear is the only thing that can keep the truth from bursting through psychological defences, those in authority will use it to protect officially-sanctioned lies. During a moral panic, this is the only way for the

---

[46] As an Editorial in *the Oregonian*, a U.S. newspaper, commented on the government's first big seizure of smuggled opiates in 1886: "Of all serious crimes . . . smuggling . . . least violates the consciences of men. It is a crime against law and government, but not against morality. The smuggler robs no man. He buys his goods honestly in one market and sells them honestly in another. His offense is against an arbitrary regulation of government . . . he simply fails to pay its demands. Many men otherwise honest are unable to see any moral turpitude in smuggling   . . . government, in exacting toll, plays the part of the highwayman." Mandel, *The Opening Shots of the War on Drugs*, in JEFFERSON M. FISH (ED.), *HOW TO LEGALIZE DRUGS* (1998) 218

[47] MILLER, *THE CASE FOR LEGALIZING DRUGS* (1991) 118

status quo to maintain credibility: Those in power must feed the panic to ensure its momentum and if the level of fear is sufficient, authority can move forward, running roughshod over our liberties.

Historically, this is always the case, and drug prohibition is no different. As we shall see, the tactics are the same as those used by authoritarian states in times of war, and in pursuit of the drug-free ideal prohibitionists have gone from armed home invasions to murdering innocents—even executing children along the way.[48]

---

[48] In the Philippines' current drug war, the government has murdered more than 20,000, including many children. Since 2016, in an embarrassing exposure of the totalitarian force inherent in prohibitionism, more than 100,000 "drug personalities" have been arrested and more than 1,3 million have surrendered to authorities. The police have gone on a rampage, terrorizing the inhabitants, and President Duterte has been a most vocal advocate of extra-judicial killings. It comes as no surprise that human rights groups have observed that many of the "criminals" are political activists, union leaders, and others who oppose the totalitarian force of their government. Nor does it come as a surprise that the president has covered up evidence that his brother is linked to drug smuggling and undeclared multi-million-dollar bank accounts. This is the way it goes; the drug war is tool for social control, one that makes it possible for authority to subject the citizenry to a reign of terror while painting itself as a moral savior—and, as we shall see, the government of the United States is no different.

2.3.5. DENIAL AND PROJECTION: PRESERVERS OF THE STATUS QUO

"Many people are shocked at the idea that pushers should not be punished at all. Their reaction to this suggestion is much like that of people after the Inquisition and the Nazi program were well established: there could be no question then—even in the minds of the most 'liberal' and 'well-meaning' persons—that 'something had to be done' with or to witches and Jews. 'Reasonable' people could debate only what that 'something' ought to be."[49]

—Thomas Szasz, Professor of Psychology—

While we do not think about such tragedies, they happen every day. In America alone, because of the drug war, 50.000 homes are stormed by military-like police squads every year and reporting friends and family to police has become a widespread activity. The enemy image of drugs has poisoned human relations, ensuring a rise in tensions, while encouraging the will to dominate. This year more than a thousand U.S. citizens will be murdered by a police force that has become accustomed to seeing the population as its enemy, and as a result of the prohibitionist psychosis a mighty apparatus of war profiteers has taken control of policy.

Not only is there is an enormous industry devoted to the forceful rehabilitation of drug users; the prison population has expanded dramatically and America, a former beacon of liberty, now incarcerates a greater percentage of its population than most known villains from history. Due to the drug war, between 6 and 7 million are currently under correctional supervision—and for those with eyes to see, it should have been a clue that the U.S. prison complex has grown beyond that of Stalin's Gulag Archipelago. It should also have been a clue that, despite

---

[49] SZASZ, *CEREMONIAL CHEMISTRY* (2003) 70

totalitarian tactics, we have arrived no closer to the drug-free utopia and that the means used to get there have brought us closer to hell.

Important stuff like this should have told us that something was amiss. However, not even the loss of moral sway has made prohibitionists question their crusade. We all agree that laws prohibiting murder, rape, etc., make sense—and yet, increasingly, segments of the population have lost respect for the rule of law. Notwithstanding the state's determined efforts, these people think drug use is a personal matter, and they continue using illegal drugs or let others do them without interfering. Why?

One answer could be that humans have enjoyed consciousness-altering states for millennia[50] and that their lure is such that it supersedes the threat of all punishment prohibitionists can muster. Today, many countries have death penalties for drug law violations and even in these places individuals will risk everything for the experience offered by their drugs of choice. Could it be that these users have valid reasons for seeking them out? Could it be that they provide relief from grief, anxiety, and the stress of living in societies so far beneath our potential? Could it be that some of these drugs even provide a way out of the ordinary consciousness span, allowing access to greater aspects of our psyche—our more godlike potentials? And could these drugs be of assistance for humanity in rediscovering its true heritage, our connection with spirit and the soul of the universe?

Legitimate questions like these have never been asked. Instead, when new drugs arrived at our shores and the youth began to experiment, society would go into panic mode. It certainly did not help that these drugs had a prior history with frowned-upon classes; as we shall see, the early drug laws originated as a tool of social control and when authority understood that the use of substances like cannabis and LSD did not inspire confidence in the status quo, our leaders pronounced them to be public enemies.

---

[50] For more on the historical use of drugs, see ANTONIO ESCOHOTADO, *A BRIEF HISTORY OF DRUGS: FROM THE STONE AGE TO THE STONED AGE* (1999)

Since the beginning, therefore, prohibitionists have denied free choice any merit. Instead, following the scapegoater's recipe, they have blamed drugs for society's problems and persecuted those who did not comply. To succeed in this quest, they painted drug users as victims of some terrible plague, people with no will of their own, and those involved with the drugs economy came to represent the embodiment of evil. They were now the pushers, the ones that lured gullible kids into a life of sin, sickness, and reckless abomination, and the only decent thing to do was to put them down or behind bars.

To this day, this has been the only dispute. Convinced of their own moral virtue, prohibitionists have never doubted the validity of their quest and have only differed on two subjects: (1) whether drug users should be forcefully rehabilitated or imprisoned, and (2) whether drug dealers should be incarcerated or killed.

The enemy image of drugs makes any other option appear naïve, even unthinkable. Indeed, to the drug warriors, all talk of human rights, limited powers, etc., has been a nuisance, and they have quickly expelled those from their ranks who cared to think things through. Being on a mission, they were not about to let second-guessers deprive them of ambition, and as society fell into totalitarianism, prohibitionists demanded more powers while they blamed the victims.

In this fashion, the drug war would continue from decade to decade. Even so, as the deficiencies of their plot become more apparent with time, prohibitionists had to erect greater and greater barriers against truth.[51] To this day, therefore, this has been a price that they are willing to pay and to preserve a sense of

---

[51] As others have noted: "The most ominous proposal comes from the United Nations. The UN's International Narcotics Control Board's 1997 report called on member states to criminalize opposition to the war on drugs. Citing the 1988 UN Convention Against Illicit Trafficking in Narcotic Drugs and Psychotropic Substances, the INCB claimed that all governments are obligated to enact laws that prohibit 'inciting' or 'inducing' people to use illegal drugs. If such a vague restriction on freedom of expression were not odious enough, the INCB contends further that member governments are also obligated to ban speech that 'shows illicit drug use in a favorable light' or any advocacy of 'a change in the drug law.'" Ted Galen Carpenter, *Collateral Damage: The Wide-Ranging Consequences of America's Drug War*, in TIMOTHY LYNCH (ED.), *AFTER PROHIBITION: AN ADULT APPROACH TO DRUG POLICIES IN THE 21ST CENTURY* (2000) 157

righteousness, they twisted the dynamics of demand and supply into one of victim and aggressor. In so doing, it became possible to justify sentences that exceeded those of rapists and murderers—and to keep at it, prohibitionists detached from Moral ground.

Even so, denying constitutional and moral obligations becomes easy when a collective effort is made and the rejection of autonomy rights ensured a modern reign of terror which was intended to make life as hard as possible for those involved with the illegal drugs. If they only could stop more drugs, arrest more pushers, and convince the rest of society that drugs were bad, prohibitionists imagined that the battle would be won. Victory would be assured, and the prohibitionist mindset rule supreme. No matter that humanity would be locked in a culture that was designed to make people feel worthless, that would make them work in trades that did more harm than good and whose values were designed by a weak and fear-filled ego, disconnected from emotion, spirituality, and a more wholesome psyche. The problem was not war-profiteers, bankers, corrupt politicians, guilt-ridden religion, loneliness, or a status quo which suppressed the human spirit; prohibitionists could not think that the illicit substances were anything but a plague that had to be stopped, for they had sufficient faith in the system to embrace scapegoating.

Thus, because prohibitionists did not know that the crime, sickness, and overall state of misery among drug users was a result of prohibition,[52] they mistook symptom for cause. It was, after all, plain to see that the different drugs made youth rebellious and disrespectful of authority. Drug cultures evolved that made youth

---

[52]Andrew Weil MD., an advisor to the Carter administration, put it this way: "When ordinary people look at heroin addicts, what they mostly see are victims of grinding social forces. Visible addicts tend to be in trouble, involved with crime, in poor health, purposeless, psychologically damaged, unhappy, and unable to get out of their grim predicament. Many of these conditions are more the result of society's blunders in trying to control the abuse of drugs than of heroin itself. . . . By making heroin illegal, a society ensures that its heroin addicts will all be criminals. It is clear that drug laws have done nothing to discourage people from becoming addicts. There are more addicts than ever, and the kinds of addiction are worse than before those laws were passed." WEIL & ROSEN, *FROM CHOCOLATE TO MORPHINE* (2004) 101

misbehave, turn to crime, addiction—or inwards. In any way, these rebels questioned the status quo, and as the status quo relied on flawed premised, the system could not risk having dirty laundry exposed.[53]

So the drug war became an outlet for all that could not be faced—and the drug warriors embraced psychosis. They did not want to acknowledge that the problems associated with drug abuse could be attributed to the psychological pain of living under the duress of hierarchical, competition-, and control oriented structures.[54] The secret shame of accepting a social contract built on flawed premises was simply too much to face, and so prohibitionists would go to work, terrorize others, and ignore that the problem was a fundamentally unjust social structure—one just made worse. Instead, the drug war provided an outlet for unacknowledged shame, anger, and regret, and the more people shied away from the responsibilities of autonomous living, the more vindictive they were towards those who threatened to destabilize their worldview.

Hence, not even robbers, rapists, or murderers would be hated as much as drug users. And the minimum penalties imposed by U.S. Federal law illustrate this level of fear, as well as the insanity that results: Burglary with a gun—2.0 years; kidnapping—4.2 years; rape—5.8 years; attempted murder—6.5 years; possession of LSD—10.1 years![55]

We can see that the idea of a well-adjusted, intelligent drug user is not only an oxymoron in our society, but that false

---

[53] It is no coincidence that there is a clash among cultures. If we divide the population into those most prone to autonomy and those most prone to tyranny, we find that the former are naturally driven to experiment with drugs and that the latter are driven towards positions of power. As seen from the perspective of the collective psyche, then, everything is set for disaster, for there will be a civil war between two different moralities, and the state will be the mechanism that ensures a continuing plot to destroy truth and a greater wisdom.

[54] The numbers of Americans on antidepressants increased from 13.3 million in 1996 to 27 million in 2005. Currently more than 600 000 American kids are diagnosed with a psychological disease and one in four adults have had a psychological breakdown they call "severe". These are all symptoms of living in societies dedicated to lies and confusing moralities. For more on this, see RICHARD G. WILKINSON AND KATE PICKETT, *THE SPIRIT LEVEL: WHY MORE EQUAL SOCIETIES ALMOST ALWAYS DO BETTER* (2009)

[55] SZASZ, *CEREMONIAL CHEMISTRY* (2003) 188

authority does not like being questioned. As a matter of fact, it is no coincidence that the less we know about something (whether it be communists, Muslims, drugs, homosexuals, paedophiles, etc.), the easier it becomes to believe in the demonizing traits that we ascribe to the other; the more impact the enemy image will have on our mind; the more we will despise and fear the perceived enemy; and the more efficient this enemy image will provide its psychological function, which is to absolve us from sin.

Prohibitionists, therefore, remain committed to ignorance for a reason, and to succeed they have built their case on lies and misdirection.[56] They have relied on fear, ignorance, and propaganda to propagate a cultural environment responsive to their demands,[57] and authority intuitively knows this. Indeed, it is the story of the emperor's clothes all over again, but we have not yet reached that point where public officials have the courage to face reality.

As it stands, the enemy image of drugs has the power to ensure their continued psychosis and while there are voices whispering among the public, increasingly laughing at the folly of drug policy, the majority has not yet found the courage to question authority. This is unfortunate, for had reason been consulted the

---

[56] Randy Barnett, a professor of law, summarized this enduring neglect: "In war, it is said, truth is the first casualty. To be blunt, many committed prohibitionists inside and outside of government who profess to care so much about the morals of others routinely lie or willfully mislead the public about nearly every aspect of both drugs and the policy of prohibition. Our consistent experience with drug prohibition—from marijuana, to heroin, to cocaine— is that when careful empirical studies are eventually performed, they reveal the initial official accounts to be either false or wildly exaggerated. Rarely, if ever, does law enforcement then reverse itself or even moderate its rhetoric." Randy Barnett, *Bad Trip: Drug Prohibition and the Weakness of Public Policy* (1994) 2603

[57] As former U.S. Senator Joseph L. Galiber stated: "criminalization of . . . drugs has fostered—indeed, even required—not enlightenment, but enforced public ignorance of the true nature of the perils of drug use. One of the more conspicuous accoutrements of our futile coercive tactics is what has been euphemistically labeled drug 'education.' There is nothing remotely educational about the hyperbole publicly expounded about drugs, which is little other than a medieval attempt to suppress, not reveal, knowledge. It is no more educational than Victorian efforts were to educate young males about masturbation. The metaphors have merely changed from impotence, blindness, and hairy palms to fried brains. The design is the same: terror and fright replace information. Our drug educators act as shrill propagandists instead of cultivators of inquisitive minds." Joseph L. Galiber, *A Bill to Repeal the Drug Laws: Replacing Prohibition with Regulation* (1990) 14

psychosis could have ended and remedies been made. However, as in other times and places, we find a systemic fear of integrity and those who buy into the psychosis will go to great lengths to see it eradicated.[58]

The current trend of threatening or firing officials who speak the truth and of denying drug users their constitutional rights is all the proof that we need, and the fact that it has yet to be publicly recognized is a testimony to the unhealthy relationship between us and authority. We are, after all, in a situation today where most cannot compute that there is exactly the same law of supply- and demand involved when it comes to licit and illicit drugs, and that the vast majority of drug users are functional and well-behaved citizens who would much rather deal with their local drug dealer than the local police. While evident everywhere, simple facts like these do not register. To speak bluntly, they cannot register because they contradict a necessary premise of prohibition: that these are victims of a plague who either (1) are thankful for prohibitionist intervention or (2) are corrupted by the enemy.

To preserve the prohibitionist paradigm, therefore, these people have been ignored, even though there is evidence that they exist and that they represent roughly 90 percent of the drug-using population. It is quite a feat to ignore. We are talking about the lives of hundreds of millions, but this is what it takes to preserve a fundamental premise of prohibition, that all illegal drug use equals abuse. Hence, this is what we do. Psychologically speaking, we have seen that there are good reasons. Even so, if we could see past the prohibitionist propaganda, it would become obvious that legitimate autonomy interests were involved—and that, unless prohibitionists can show good reasons for singling out these people for persecution, they are the real criminals.

---

[58]After completing his legal studies on prohibition, policy analyst James Ostrowsky noted the totalitarian prohibitionist mindset: "The only civilized way to deal with irreconcilable conflicts in ultimate values is to declare freedom of religion and let each go his or her own way. That is the last thing the prohibitionists have in mind. Rather, their solution to the problem of irreconcilable conflict of values over drugs is to inflict on those who disagree with them all the force and violence they can muster." James Ostrowski, *Drug Prohibition Muddles Along*, in Jefferson M. Fish (ed.), *How to Legalize Drugs* (1998) 366

The criminal law, after all, to be moral and just, remains anchored in the principle of autonomy. It is merely a subcategory of constitutional law and to ensure that no one violates our private space, whether it be mind, body, or property. When it comes to this, prohibitionists have not only failed to show how the drug consumption of others violates their right to live free and productive lives but how the drug laws protect anything except the interests of war profiteers.[59] All we have is their assurance that they have done this in the name of all things good, but if the drug law fails the test of reason it fails to serve society; and if it fails to serve society, then the persecution of violators can hardly be presented as a decent venture. Instead, it is obvious that it is (and has always been) an immoral and despicable act, and that the enforcers of the law—not the drug dealers—are the real traffickers in human misery.

This, at the very least, is the implication of our Constitution. As seen from its perspective, autonomy and tyranny will always be opposed and while drug dealers have provided people with a service they want, the drug warriors have done so much worse. In their enforcement of these laws they have discriminated, stigmatised, demonised, and terrorised. They have tapped people's phones, opened their mail, spied on them, searched their houses, stripped them naked, performed cavity searches, fined them, confiscated and destroyed their property and their valuables, forced them into "rehabilitation", jailed them, taken their children from them, destroyed their education and work possibilities, threatened them, humiliated them, beaten them, shot at them, and killed them. Not only that, but when drug users have come forward, demanding constitutional rights and an end to

---

[59] Professor Steven Duke speaks to it thus: "The costs of drug prohibition are undeniably huge. But what of the benefits? Sadly, there probably are none to the society at large. Drug dealers owe their livelihoods to prohibition, as do thousands of drug warriors. Prison builders benefit, as do politicians who owe their careers to their opposition to demon "drugs." Inner-city morticians who dress bodies of victims of drug war turf battles, car dealers and jewelers who sell their goods to drug distributors, and other satellite entrepreneurs benefit from drug prohibition, but only those who make money from the drug war benefit from it. Everyone else suffers greatly." Steven B. Duke, *Drug Prohibition: An Unnatural Disaster*, Faculty Scholarship Series 812 (1995) 598

unjust persecution, the prohibitionists have set aside the rule of law to perpetuate unlawful policies.

Thus, looking at the relationship between the drug law and the higher law, the moral disconnect between the two becomes plain: The drug law is revealed to be of the exact same nature as other historical mass-movements gone wrong—and as always, the reason why the nature of this particular crusade does not stand out is the power of an exaggerated enemy image.

2.3.6. The Power of Enemy Images

"The fact that drug use can be discussed at the highest levels of government only in metaphorical terms with mythological demonic imagery constitutes an unmistakable warning to us that something is seriously wrong."[60]

—Judge Robert Sweet & Edward Harris—

If it were not for the enemy image of drugs, the disparity between prohibition and the morality of our Constitution would be disconcerting. It would become obvious that while the former advocates a denial of drug users' autonomy and liberty interests, the latter not only proposes equality and proportionality in law but sets principled boundaries, thus revealing whatever gap there may be between theory and practice.

It is for this reason that prohibitionists will want to forget about their constitutional oath whenever the subject comes up. Their identity remains too entwined with the prohibition quest to accept that this crusade has no merit, and so—to keep up appearances—the gap must be denied.

---

[60] Sweet & Harris, *Moral and Constitutional Considerations in Support of the Decriminalization of Drugs*, in JEFFERSON FISH (ED.), *HOW TO LEGALIZE DRUGS* (1998) 432

Reality, however, does not simply disappear; it will come back to haunt us until we correct our vision—and that there is a gap remains for certain. As we have seen, the morality of the Constitution is synonymous with embracing the values, ideals, and principles that follow from Wholeness, whereas the morality of the drug law is built on an exaggerated enemy image. This is our cue that something is wrong, for whenever enemy images are accepted the world is turned from a state of wholeness into one of fragmentation.

Social engineers recognize this process as the source of our troubles, for as soon as irrational fear takes control, we set course on a path that separates us from our inner moral constitution. The morality we would apply to everyone else is then obliterated: In its place arises some version of the-ends-justifies-the-means thinking, and the greater the power of the enemy image, the more we will rationalize aggressive and intolerant attitudes.

No matter time and place, this process is always the same. The only difference is the enemy image, and to the extent that it is embraced the predictable result is more cycles of turmoil. I say "predictable", as our thoughts are infused with a certain energy and to the extent that we let fear guide us, we cannot appreciate that web of significance, beauty, and dignity which infuses every living being. We cannot truly sense the humanity of others, as we will be cut off from love and this is a most terrible affliction to bear. Not only will it make us susceptible to immoral behaviour and psychological distress; it is love that connects us with the implications of first principles, and without drawing upon its depth we will not have a true system of justice.[61]

We simply cannot, because connecting with the implications of those values, principles, and ideals that follow from Wholeness is crucial for maintaining the integrity of law. Without this

---

[61] In its place will be a system of arbitrary justice, one where collectively shared prejudice, ignorance, and strong-armed lobbyists define the limits of the criminal sanction. It will be a system of law intended to dominate rather than liberate, for in these types of societies lawyers have little understanding of what is beyond their immediate horizon—that which pays their salary. For more on the difference between principled and arbitrary systems of law, see MIKALSEN, *TO RIGHT A WRONG* (2016)

connection, we will be forced to draw upon another morality, that defined by contemporary culture, and this is no reliable standard. After all, we know that in times of moral panic there will be repressive regimes, wanton persecution, ethnic cleansing, genocide, and other atrocities; there will also be lawyers willing to defend the legality of all this, and so—if we are serious—we need a frame of ethics that can help us put matters of liberty and tyranny into perspective.

Our Constitution provides us with this. It is the moral ground of society for a reason but while the power of love is connected to its vision, integrity is needed to connect.

2.4. INTEGRITY: THE KEY TO THE FOUNDERS' VISION

"Honesty is the first chapter in the book of wisdom."[62]

—Thomas Jefferson—

It is uncontroversial that the progression of society, at any given time, is arrested by collectively shared prejudice and that only a show of integrity can improve upon things. Hence, in places where integrity is plentiful, there will be sufficient momentum to do away with this great force of ignorance and society will become calibrated towards truth and a higher functioning.

Not so, however, in societies where the level of integrity is too insignificant to connect with first principles. In these type of societies, collectively shared prejudice will have the momentum to overcome any resistance, and so they continue unguided by reason. As there is not enough integrity to connect with the bigger picture—nothing to anchor truth—they are caught in a sleep-like state where policy is set by unconscious fears rather than fully reasoned considerations, and it is no coincidence that such

---

[62] THOMAS JEFFERSON, *THE WRITINGS OF THOMAS JEFFERSON* (1854) 112

societies are frightful places to live. The health of the nation will be mirrored in the health of the individual and while integrity is needed to connect with the greater morality, in these types of societies the pressure to betray values is enormous. Because the state, no matter how tyrannical, will see itself as a representative of all things wholesome, there will be a gap between theory and practice that cannot be admitted by public servants, and which confuses the citizenry. Being born into a world where fear has taken control of reasoning, it is difficult to overcome the spiritual lethargy that follows, and the greater the level of fear, the greater is the integrity needed to connect with the implications of Wholeness.

In fact, thoughts are like matter. Just as objects, the greater their mass have greater gravitational pull, so ideas, the more they are accepted, become truisms. To think independently, the integrity needed is directly proportional to their attractive force, and so people take for granted that the culture of society represents a healthy expression of human potential. To reflect upon the possibility that this is not so makes people uncomfortable. Indeed, the psychological pain of giving up deeply held, widespread, and much cherished beliefs is too upsetting—and so the masses remain under a spell where they will salute the values, ideals, and principles that follow from Wholeness, while they ignore implications.[63]

No matter time and place, this has always been the case. Due to the power of the collective consciousness, there has always been a distance between the two that the majority have not been able to bridge—and to be good citizens, they accept authority's version of events.

Considering that the state, for its part, can be counted on to claim the moral high ground, no matter how oppressive its regime, the problem should be evident. On the one hand, history reveals

---

[63] Thomas Jefferson observed this trend: "departure from principle in one instance becomes a precedent for a second; that second for a third; and so on, till the bulk of the society is reduced to be mere automatons of misery, and to have no sensibilities left but for sinning and suffering." Letter to H. Tompkinson (AKA Samuel Kercheval), 12 July 1816.

that we will have conniving and deceitful officials who equal the apparatus of state as being representative of all things good and decent, while on the other, we will have citizens who cannot think to question premises. Because they have adopted the worldview of their peers, people presume that the moral code of society is representative of the greater morality, and they ignore all evidence to the contrary. Thus, everything is set for disaster. Whether they go to war, persecute others, inform on political enemies, or stand by those who do, the majority will justify it as necessary to protect wholesome values—and this mentality persists to the point where murdering children becomes justified.

We see it in every country. When an enemy image has gained sufficient weight, people will go to any length thinking that the ends justify the means, and very few will question this premise. If they did, however, they would find that the ends can never be more glorious than the means, and that the only reason why they thought so in the first place was that they underestimated the power of love.

2.4.1. The Powers of Love and Fear

Love, after all, is the quality/universal force that social engineers recognize as all-important if we are to erect more perfectly ordered societies. Not only is it the most powerful force in the universe, the one that gives meaning to life and explains the purpose of being; it is this force that binds us together and the social fibre can only heal to the degree that we embrace it. If we would but recognize this, the world would be in a whole different shape. Its resources are infinite, free, and available to each and every one, and to the extent that we draw upon its powers miraculous things become possible.

Hence, the Constitution is built on the morality of love for a good reason: It is this force that cultivates all successful human development, and whether we are talking self-help, personal relationships, or societal organization, love is the connection that provides further growth. To the extent that we draw upon its powers, therefore, we will—with mathematical certainty—create a heaven on earth. We will live in autonomy-enriching places where community spirit prevails, and where the dynamics between the individual and the whole ensure an ever-higher vision of what it means to be God's children on planet earth.

Not so, however, in fear-filled societies. To the extent we are governed by fear, we will be drawn to another kind of morality, one that sees the world as a treacherous place, and where the defence mechanisms of denial and projection will define the perimeters of our understanding. Being the psychological component that separates us from love, therefore, fear is recognized by social engineers as that which we must overcome to blossom, as the dynamics of society will follow exact parameters in either direction. While the psychology of love paves the way for enlightened minds and societies, the psychology of fear generates and preserves trauma, which again leads to totalitarian government. Consequently, to the extent that the collective psyche is filled with fear, we will live in violence-, deceit-, and dominance-oriented structures, places where trauma is constantly inflicted, endured, and passed on—and again we can say this with 100 percent certainty.

From this simple set up, and from what we have seen so far, we find that behind all our trials and tribulation there has been one reoccurring theme. If we look at the world, humanity has prospered to the extent that we have committed to the ideals, values, and principles that follow from Wholeness and we have regressed to the extent that we have abided by any other moral code. We also know that our society is struggling with grave problems and we should accept the possibility that we, comparatively speaking, may not be much better than our ancestors. From this point of departure, we can make immense progress if we dare to look at ourselves—and the answer to our problems always will be more love for self and others.

This is the key to evolution, and if we want a better world the principles of our Constitution are there to help us move forward whenever we commit. As they remain intricately bound with the timeless morality, they have the power to correct any errant ways, and to the extent that we honour its implications, we have that map which will ensure "a more perfect union."

Knowing this, the comparison between the founders and the prophets should no longer be unheard of. Indeed, once superstitions are left behind, we find that we are all one and that the values, ideals, and principles connected to the Wholeness have always been pointing us towards salvation. The founders of religion merely dealt with their spiritual connotations, while the founders of government focused upon the political. Even so, they were all disciples of the greater morality—and they all, in their own way, sought to remind humanity that behind all apparent fragmentation, there is but one Wholeness complete in itself, and that in tapping into this Oneness we can overcome appearances and rejoice in its light.

In part four we shall have more to say on the spiritual connotations of the Constitution, as well as the legal matters concerning moral panic. Even so, we have seen that drug prohibition, from the greater perspective, is a symptom of unconsciousness and the solution to the drug problem is self-evident. Building upon what we have learned, therefore, we shall now study the impact of the prohibitionist psychosis. We shall follow its destructive path and see how the enemy of drugs has informed development in Western societies. Needless to say, it is not a pretty picture; moral insentience most certainly has its price, but we can take comfort in knowing that exploring the darkness is a prerequisite for enlightenment. If we are to overcome our difficulties, we must first understand our ailments, and we all have a stake in leaving the prohibition ideology behind—agents of government included.

Part Two:

The Social Experiment of Drug Prohibition

3

THE BASIS OF THE INTERNATIONAL DRUG CONTROL REGIME

"It is of great importance to observe that the character of every man is, in some degree, formed by his profession. A man of sense may only have a cast of countenance that wears off as you trace his individuality, whilst the weak, common man has scarcely ever any character, but what belongs to the body; at least, all his opinions have been so steeped in the vat consecrated by authority, that the faint spirit which the grape of his own vine yields cannot be distinguished. Society, therefore, as it becomes more enlightened, should be very careful not to establish bodies of men who must necessarily be made foolish or vicious by the very constitution of their profession."[64]

—Mary Wollstonecraft, 1790—

THE BASIS OF the prohibition regime is the UN Single Convention. Signed in 1961, it codified all existing treaties on drug control and the idea was to rid the world of frowned-upon drug use. The problematic aspect of drug addiction was well-known, and our leaders assumed that a transnational system of cooperation would lessen its social impact. No doubt, there was some basis for concern. However, a strong cultural bias, coupled with power-political pressure, ensured that the most problematic substances, were excluded, while others—i.e., those deemed threatening to

---

[64] MARY WOLLSTONECRAFT, *A VINDICATION OF THE RIGHTS OF MEN* (1790) 17

Western leaders and Big Pharma's profit margins—were targeted for persecution.

Moreover, as is often the case among authorities, there was a strong belief in authoritarian solutions. Hence, the state's law and order apparatus would be the chief means by which the enemy was fought and to this day prohibitionists have relied on ever-increasing budgets and powers to "win" the War on Drugs.

I say "win", as our leaders did not understand that this was a war on human nature and that it could only be lost the harder it was fought. This was evident only to a few,[65] and politicians believed that within a period of twenty-five years all non-sanctioned drug use would be eliminated. With the progression of time, however, the prohibition regime did not go according to plan; not only did drug use persist, but the persecution made matters worse.

In this period, therefore, there would be increasing conflict between those who stood by the prohibition paradigm and those who would reconsider fundamental premises. The system elevated the former to positions of power, but as the problems became more obvious the latter become more plentiful. This resulted in a movement towards policies that recognized the inherent appeal of drugs. Putting human concerns first, these countries would abandon the drug free ideal under a model of "harm reduction." According to its vision, the idea is not to get rid of drugs but to remedy the harm that comes with drug use—and, as we shall see, these policies have been much more successful at achieving their stated aims.

Even so, despite the failure of prohibition to achieve a drug free world, hardliners have remained committed to this ideal; due to the psychological condition behind prohibition, the dream of a drug-free society makes persecuting violators an integral part of their moral code and they are disappointed with political trends. According to them, the movement towards a less hostile world is

---

[65] Already in 1964, scholars pointed out that our drug policy "confounds a relatively minor symptom with the disease." ISIDORE CHEIN ET AL., *THE ROAD TO H: NARCOTICS DELINQUENCY, AND SOCIAL POLICY* (1964) 133

in breach of the UN drug control conventions and they are not shy about expressing their discontent.[66]

As we shall see, however, prohibitionists have it all backwards, and the countries that are dedicated to the drug free ideal have done so at a cost of great human suffering. Attacking the countries that attempt to remedy the side-effects of drug prohibition, therefore, is just another predictable result of the prohibitionist psychosis. As the prohibitionists' discontent is not rationally based, it is merely the preconceptions of a spoilt ego, and if prohibitionists looked closer the signatories to the UN drug control conventions made no other commitment than to protect the welfare of humanity. That was it.

It is only due to the influence of an exaggerated enemy image, not to mention the power it provides, that this has been interpreted as a commitment to the prohibition experiment. Bureaucracies, after all, tend to remain faithful to the ideology that feeds them, and it is difficult to find examples of a more blatant disregard for evidence-based policies. At the very least, since the 1960s, experts, NGOs and concerned citizens have opposed its destructive dynamics and yet politicians have opposed meaningful debate. Not only has the law been shielded from meaningful review, such as cost-benefit or human rights analysis, but in those instances where people opposed the drug war before going into office, they tend to embrace it when in position of power.[67]

The drug war, therefore, is another proof that no bureaucracy dies willingly.[68] As soon as the ideology set roots, the institutions

---

[66] In annual reports, UN treaty bodies have become notorious for commending countries such as Saudi Arabia and China on murderous drug policies while at the same time reprimanding countries that provide access to medical and recreational cannabis, hemp products, etc. These bodies also claim that states such as Paraguay, Canada, Colorado, California, etc., who have regulated cannabis for recreational purposes, are in breach of international law.

[67] Examples include former British Prime Minister Nick Clegg and Donald Trump, the current U.S. President. Before taking office, they discussed the failures of drug prohibition, calling for an end to dysfunctional policies. Even so, as so many others, as soon as they came into office, they became loyal soldiers in the War on Drugs.

[68] Professors David Rasmussen and Bruce Benson: "In a representative democracy there is a tendency to expect that public opinion drives drug policy. This is not the case, as every

that had an interest in the enemy image seized on the opportunity to profit—and knowing that the war would provide privileges, prestige, and income only to the extent that they could convince the world of its merits, prohibitionists at the UN and elsewhere made sure to elevate it beyond rational debate.

With policies so appalling, the enemy had to be painted worse; prohibitionists would look good only to the extent that they could convince the world that drugs were bad, and they did a respectable job at maintaining the panic. Indeed, looking back, not only have the UN drug control bodies refused to reconsider the wisdom of their quest, but to the extent that individual countries have sought new ways, they have been punished.

3.1. NEGLECTING HUMAN RIGHTS IMPLICATIONS

While controversial, all this will be documented. As we shall see, institutions like the International Narcotics Control Board (INCB) were established to oversee progress and to address overall concerns. Their treaty-based function is to ensure that the drug war is fought by the most efficient methods, and within the limits of international law, but they have done the opposite. Despite evident problems, they have kept drug policy firmly entrenched in the prohibition paradigm[69] by refusing any inquiry into the relationship between human rights and drug control conventions.

---

detailed study of the emergence of legal norms has consistently shown the immense importance of interest-group activity, not the public interest, as the critical variable. Drug war, the excessive application of enforcement that aggravates rather than mitigates the social consequences of drug use, is waged because it is in the interests of particular politically influential groups, including law enforcement bureaucracies and public officials. According to this view, legislators can act as moral entrepreneurs, but they are more generally 'middle-men' whose actions are largely determined by interest groups, including those engaged in the law enforcement process—police chiefs, sheriffs, and prosecutors." David W. Rasmussen & Bruce L. Benson, *Rationalizing Drug Policy Under Federalism*, 30 Fla. St. U. L. Rev. (2003)

[69] A group of 770 academics wrote to the UN Secretary General in 1998, declaring that "the global war on drugs is now causing more harm than drug abuse itself", and asking the bureaucrats "to initiate a truly open and honest dialogue regarding the future of global drug control policies; one in which fear, prejudice and punitive prohibitions yield to common

This resilience has already been explained. Because of the drug war, law and order has become corrupted and the collective psyche is split between allegiance to the prohibition quest and a deeper, more unifying morality which sees humanity as one and the world as Whole. Those who look beyond appearances, therefore, will discover that there is a civil war going on: We have a situation where, on the one hand, the ideal of the drug free society makes believers justify any action as necessary, while on the other, the brotherhood of spirit dictates "do not harm". The social fabric, therefore, is being torn due to the moral disconnect between these value systems, and as psychological health is connected to the latter drug prohibition has produced bureaucracies whose services we could do better without.

Nevertheless, while our system is addicted to the prohibition ideology, we have individuals committed to reason, and the dynamic between the two has defined the evolution of drug policy. Thus, while pressure from above has ensured an enduring state of psychosis, some countries have been more receptive to evidence-based policies and these are those in which the harm-reduction approach has become popular. Foremost among them are Holland and Portugal[70]—and, as we shall see, the differences are notable. Building on the examples of zero-tolerance societies and health-oriented cultures, therefore, it shall be shown that the latter have to a much greater extent let reason guide policy.

In these places, the moral panic that has ensured horrendous atrocities elsewhere has not had the same impact. Consequently, in these nations, rulers do not persecute drug users; they only persecute drug dealers and producers, but not with the fervour of zero-tolerance countries. In this way, they are somewhat better.

---

sense, science, public health and human rights". (http://www.drugpolicy.org/ publications-resources/sign-letters/public-letter-kofi-annan/ungass-public-letter-kofi-annan-signato)
For more letters of information and condemnation, see correspondence from the Alliance of Rights-oriented Drug Policies (AROD) to the UN drug control bodies. Found at: www.arodpolicies.org/ungass-2016

[70] Today, several countries have more advanced drug policies—Canada, Uruguay, Mexico, and several U.S. states, to name a few. Traditionally, however, these two countries have led the way and their examples are telling.

Even so, when constitutional principles are applied, this is not much to brag about. After all, if drug users are not persecuted, society recognizes that there are autonomy rights involved. It means that we have begun to take seriously the implications of wrongful persecution—and from the constitutional perspective, if drug use is compatible with the choice of responsible adults, the state not only has no business interfering, but there must be a correlative right to purchase such materials for personal use or else the underlying autonomy right becomes meaningless.[71] Indeed, as seen from this perspective, it is a "rule of law as well as reason that if the principal in any act is not punishable, the accomplice cannot be."[72]

It is no better, then, to put drug dealers behind bars than other salesmen. Even so, we have seen that the psychological appeal of this quest is found in scapegoating, and that prohibitionists, to spread their demon mythology, have turned the dynamics of demand and supply into one of victim and aggressor. Hence, there is a powerful psychological incentive to ignore reality and only a minority have the courage to think things through.[73]

---

[71] "Unless the State can point to a compelling government interest, the right to privacy is infringed upon by the prohibition against the sale of sexually explicit adult material. Since a person has the right to view pornographic items at home, there necessarily follows a correlative right to purchase such materials for this personal use, or the underlying privacy right becomes meaningless." Kam, 69 Haw. at 487-96, 748 P.2d at 375-80 *Quoted in State v. Mallan*, 86 Haw. 440, 950 P.2d 178 (1998) 241 (Levinson J. Dissenting)

[72] Lysander Spooner, *Vices Are Not Crimes* (1875) 11

[73] Despite the influence of moral panic, a few judges have had the integrity to speak truth to power. See e.g. *People v. Lorentzen*, 194 N.W.2d 827 (1972) 182 (Kavanagh J,.concurring in part, dissenting in part) ("I [have] stated the conviction that the government has no constitutional authority to proscribe possession and private use of marijuana. The right to possess and use something, however, has little meaning unless one also has the right to acquire it, and hence *proscription* of sale cannot be reconciled with a right to possess and use. It may be that some legitimate public interest may be served by the *regulation* of traffic in marijuana, but a statute which absolutely forbids the sale of marijuana is as offensive to the right of privacy and the pursuit of happiness as a statute which forbids its possession and use."); *State v. Baker*, 56 Haw. 271, 535 P.2d 1394 (1975) (Majority opinion) ("An assured right of possession would necessarily imply some adequate method to obtain not subject to destruction at the will of the State."); *Crane v. Campbell*, 245 U.S. 304 (1917) 308 ("An assured right of possession would necessarily imply some adequate method to obtain not subject to destruction at the will of the State."); Hindes, *Morality Enforcement Through the Criminal Law and the Modern Doctrine of Substantive Due Process* (1977) 383 ("It is absurd to talk about a right to use a product when it remains illegal to purchase the product and illegal to transport it to the place where it may rightfully be consumed.");

In fact, as we shall see, even the most advanced countries have not evolved to the point where it is possible to apply reason to drug policy. Thus, even though the era of decriminalizing drug use has begun and we think of consumers as worthy of basic human rights protection, drug distributors are not that fortunate. When it comes to this group, the principles of law remain reversed, as they must bear the brunt of society's intolerance.[74] Without the myth of the drug fiend, prohibitionists would no longer be so sure of the merits of their crusade, and the injustice that is done in the name of law will continue until we wise up.

Indeed. Looking ahead, what is before us is a psychological process, a cleansing of the collective psyche on par with South-Africa post-Apartheid and Germany after the Second World War. When we recognize the costs of the drug war will be a healing moment, a catharsis of the soul, but the enemy image of drugs weights too heavily on the collective mind. As a result, the ideology of prohibition muddles along, and we shall now have a look at the problem of moral panic as it unfolded with the evolution of drug policy.

The point is not to offer a comprehensive or definitive history, but rather a high-speed and selective tour, focusing on those sites that hold particular interest from a perspective of rights adjudication. It shall be shown that a century of drug prohibition has had a devastating impact on our morality and that, contrary to prohibitionist lore, the taboos have ensured a dissociative state.

Grosman, *Drugs under the Constitution* (2011) 14 ("If we believe there is a right to use drugs as part of our autonomy, we cannot prosecute drug provision, which is instrumentally necessary to perform the conduct protected by such right. The fact that drugs can be found all the same is no valid answer for the State, since that is so despite its attempts to prevent it. Moreover, it could not be claimed that the State adequately protects this right if it pushes the user to the illegal market as the only way to access the drug.")

[74] It is a principle of law and reason that the more a law infringes the basic right to liberty, the stronger is the presumption against it and the greater the justification required to vindicate its use. Even so, society does not think twice about imprisoning this group and not before constitutional principles are applied can we claim to be a functional democracy under the rule of law. We will have a rule of arbitrary law—a rule of tyranny—and the sooner we recognize this the better.

We will start off with a worst-case scenario, which happens to be Norway.

4

NORWAY

"After a few decades studying the development of our drug polices, I have become more and more sceptical. Speaking bluntly, I have stated that we someday may see it as the 20th Century's greatest misapplication of the criminal law. With this, I speak not only for us, but for the entire world."[75]

—Johs. Andenæs, Professor of Law—

NORWAY, TOGETHER WITH neighbouring Sweden, is known for its zero-tolerance drug policy. True to the UN drug control apparatus, these Scandinavian counties have remained faithful to the ideal of a drug free society—an ideal that seems evermore illusive, but with consequences that are difficult to ignore.

The reason is that the criminalization of drug users was a mistake from the beginning. This, however, has not been a subject for review, and to pursue an ideal end, Norwegian officials have embraced evermore authoritarian means. "Authoritarian means" is not an exaggeration. In fact, when it comes to the corruptive influence of enemy images and the moral panic that accompany them, it is difficult to find a better example than Norway.

The country has positioned itself as a poster boy for the rule of law. Internationally, Norway is strong human rights advocate and respected for its tradition of peaceful diplomacy; it is found among the top countries on quality-of-life surveys; it is a strong believer in equal rights; and it was chosen by Alfred Nobel as the most appropriate candidate for the Nobel Peace Prize. In short, it is difficult to find a country officially more committed to human

---

[75] WILLY PEDERSEN & HELGE WAAL, *RUSMIDLER OG VEIVALG* (1996) 68

rights—and yet a closer look reveals that Norway can no longer be said to be a functional democracy under the rule of law.

4.1. EVOLUTION OF DRUG POLICY

Looking back, Norway's policy of zero tolerance has had a strong cultural foundation. Like the United States, it was one of very few countries that enacted a prohibition on alcohol in the 1920s, and like the United States it has a strong puritan tradition. Unlike the United States, however, the country is not blessed with a solid libertarian tradition to balance out unhealthy moralist trends. Instead, Norway is a strongly socialist country, one where the nation's psyche is defined by thinking in terms of collectivism.

At a first glance, this may not seem so bad. As I have said, the country is consistently found among the top-most popular places to live, and citizens are protected by reliable welfare- and healthcare services. Even so, the collectivist-trend in Norway has ensured policies that has become a tragedy for its people—at the very least the drug using population, their friends and loved ones. To this group, the Norwegian system is not so nice. These people have no rights other than those accepted by prohibitionists, and this has led to large-scale human rights violations.

4.1.1. PERSECUTION BEGINS

The problem began with the adoption of the UN Single Convention. While alcohol had a strong cultural foundation, Norwegians knew next to nothing about the new drugs, and they could not think that there were important parallels from a rights-oriented perspective. Not only did people miss out on the similarities between traditional and non-traditional drugs, but as in other countries, it was unthinkable that the rebellion of youth mirrored problems related to society. Thus, Norwegians did what prohibitionists asked them to do: they blamed the internationally proscribed drugs and relying on upon a Swedish psychiatrist who advocated indoctrination and punishment to stop the plague,[76] the Norwegian government committed to zero tolerance policies in 1964.

While this may seem rash, national legislation followed an international pattern: As in other countries, the problem was in its infancy and few that had any knowledge, let alone any experience, with these drugs.[77] Nevertheless, to protect society against this supposed threat, the liberty presumption was reversed and hasty legislation put in place. This was to assure the legal paperwork for the new campaign, and ever since it has been taboo to reconsider fundamental premises.

It did not matter if this legislation came into being without any real debate; that opposition was punished or ignored; and that the prohibitionists have relied on misconceptions, even untruths, to ensure the continuation of policy.[78] As in other countries, Norwegians would shy away from the responsibilities of autonomous living. They would embrace a zero-tolerance approach to drugs, and this not only meant fertile ground for war profiteers but that the masses, looking for scapegoats, embraced propaganda.

Thus, everything was prepared for a nightmarish ride. To justify this state of emergency, the status quo had to make the most of the enemy image—and to make plausible a moral distinction

---

[76] NILS BEIEROT, *NARKOTIKA OCH NARKOMANI* (1965) 164 ("Against drug abuse, however, much more important than information is indoctrination: This means the management of opinion, attitudes, and public morals in a way that makes experimentation with these drugs more unlikely. As Evang [the Norwegian Minister of Health] has said: it is very important to ensure that drug abuse does not become tolerated or socially accepted; unless this remains so, many more lives will be ruined by addiction")

[77] Drugs like cannabis and opiates were available at pharmacies before this period, and there was little public attention towards the new legislation. As in other places, the political process was informed by the testimony of police and teetotalers and the criminalized drugs had no pressure groups to bring reason to the table.

[78] CHRISTIE & BRUUN, *DEN GODE FIENDE* (1985); PEDERSEN & WAAL, *RUSMIDLER OG VEIVALG* (1996); Brorson, Hovedfagsoppgave, kapittel 5.2.1: *Alt du får vite om narkotika er bare bøff* (2002); Hauge, *Narkotika—Landeplage eller syndebukk?* NORDISK TIDSSKRIFT FOR KRIMINALVITENSKAB (1982); Syse, *Hva er galt med norsk narkotikapolitikk?* (2011); Träskman, *Drug Control and Drug Offences in the Nordic Countries* (2005); PEDERSEN, *BITTERSØTT—NYE PERSPEKTIVER PÅ RUS OG RUSMIDLER* (2015)

between alcohol users and other drug users, prohibitionists defined all illegal drugs as hard drugs and all illegal drug use as abuse. That was the basis of Norwegian policy. From this point on, drugs were simply "bad" and as ignorance became the norm, a culture of fear developed.

Being downgraded to the lowest rank of society, drug users would not be heard from in this debate—not for decades to come. Instead, they came to depend upon the political influence of those that understood their faith, but these people were few and far between. Hence, the moral panic associated with drug prohibition would only spiral and to set an example, prohibitionists put down a maximum of 6 months imprisonment.

Drug use, however, did not go away. It would continue to spread and so prohibitionists escalated punishment to 2 years, 6 years, 10 years (1971), 15 years (1981), and, at last, 21 years, the most severe punishment authorized by the Norwegian constitution (1984). To make good on its promise of penalties, the state expanded its drug fighting machinery. In 1966, 12 policemen were working narcotics, but by the 1980s, as measured per capita, Norway had the greatest law enforcement apparatus in Europe to persecute those who did not conform to prohibitionist demands.

4.1.2. Moral Confusion

So what was the result of this escalation? Not surprisingly, the situation went from bad to worse. Because the moral virtue of prohibition was beyond reproach, the government could not admit to a legitimate demand for these drugs. These users, therefore, were portrayed as a morally depraved, powerless, and naive flock and the enemy image of the drug fiend made society flock together.

With this trick, in reversing the law of supply and demand into one of victim and aggressor, prohibitionists provided a sense of righteousness to their quest. This led to a firmness of resolve and politicians would continue to insist on the necessity of strict legislation. Hence, those less enthusiastic were threatened with budget cuts, and when the Norwegian Penal Code Commission in 2002 recommended a decriminalization of drugs, politicians refused to listen.

According to politicians, decriminalization would send the wrong signal. On these terms, drug policy was elevated beyond a position of fruitful discussion and Norwegian policy continued unguided by constitutional constraints. Even so, more perceptive people understood that the expanding drug war came with a price.[79] The moral fibre of society could not endure the demands of the drug free ideal, and as the hunt for drug fiends accelerated, the visible result was more death, disease, and misery.[80]

In this manner, the Norwegian society went from a place where crime was rare and communal relations were strong, to resemble that of a dystopia. As time progressed, the situation became more and more ominous, but the problems remained. The enemy image of drugs ensured a steady state of psychosis where people mistook symptom for cause, and so the side-effects of prohibition provided more fuel for the drug war. By the 1970s, Norwegian society was already infected by the cancerous growth,

---

[79] As Ragnar Hauge, the grand old man of Norwegian drug policy said: "the manner in which the Norwegian judicial system treats substance users is nothing about which we have reason to be proud. But drugs policy is such a sensitive issue in Norway, no Norwegian politician hoping for re-election has dared suggest milder legal reactions or decriminalization. Instead, drugs policy has been pushed forward by parties clamoring to outbid each other in a manner unparalleled in Norway. The reaction to the majority recommendation of the Penal Code Commission is typical. The Commission worked from 1980 to 2002 to draft a new penal code. That the proposition to decriminalize use and possession of drugs for own use would be rejected was no surprise. It was a response we had anticipated, but we could not let such considerations deflect us from recommending what we believed was right. More surprising, however, when the report was submitted to the Minister, that was the only recommendation he bothered to comment upon publicly— and even before he had read it—despite the fact that the final report sets out a number of politically controversial recommendations." *Conversation with Ragnar Hauge*, Journal Interview, Society for the Study of Addiction 101 (2006) 798

[80] Criminologist Evy Frantzen: "Decades of drug dependency has not gone unheeded, and together with the harsh policy that these people have been met with, the consequences are apparent. The common denominator is destruction." CHRISTIE & BRUUN, *DEN GODE FIENDE* (1985) 212, 223

and as the enemy image of drugs became more powerful, few complained about the powers taken by the state.

Nevertheless, as the Norwegian people one day will discover, it is impossible to embrace enemy images on such mass-scale without preparing for totalitarianism. To win the fight against drugs, the police would arrest violators, prosecutors would build their case on inadequate evidence, judges would accept no constitutional constraints, politicians would offer stronger sentencing, and the people would endorse ever more tyrannical precepts. In the failure to question authority, they did not complain when drug users were put away, when police dogs began appearing at schools or apartment buildings, when drug using parents lost their children, or when officials and magistrates denied human rights. Hence, while the enemy image made sure that no one really noticed the slow transition, the descent into tyranny was evident.

4.1.3. FORCE AND OPPOSITION

"Current policy is strongly contradicted by our knowledge of these drugs and their users. It causes harm to people who are already fragile, and it strengthens tendencies in the state's control apparatus that should not be encouraged. Worst of all, it distracts us from discussing issues of principal and practical concern, issues that needs attending.
. . . The next generation will wonder how we, especially in Norway, could be led astray to embrace policies so damaging to a group of society's most vulnerable."[81]

—Nils Christie, Professor of Criminology, 1985—

Looking back, we have seen that the enemy image of drugs would poison human relations, leading to increased tensions. As drug

---

[81] CHRISTIE & BRUUN, *DEN GODE FIENDE* (1985) 131

users become more despised, society become crueller, and the outcasts suffered more terribly. By the 1980s, Norwegians had fought this war harder than any other European country and yet drugs were winning: Despite combined efforts, drugs had become cheaper, better in quality, and more easily obtained. The social condemnation, however, ensured drug cultures where death, disease, crime, and psychological problems were more likely than not to prevail, and the moral poverty of the state corrupted family relations.

That drug-experimenting youth could no longer trust their neighbour, or their teacher, was one thing; that former friends would incriminate them was another; and as even parents would report them to the police, we can understand that there was a predisposition towards "dropping out". Violators now belonged at the bottom of the social hierarchy. They would be vilified by law and the idea that they had rights did not occur. Instead, they continued to see themselves through the eyes of their oppressors—and in so doing, drug users contributed to their own demise.[82]

To incarcerate these individuals, more prisons were built, and in playing the role that society had provided, many became frequent visitors. As in other places, therefore, there was a trend of increasing prison populations and the ramifications of moral panic—a moral degradation—began to become more clearly seen.

---

[82] In depriving drug users recognition of their choice, we are telling them to buy into the myth of the demon drugs; we are signaling that their will is of little importance, that we are better than them and just in our persecution. This not only makes the drug user more prone to become an addict and to stay an addict, but it provides him/her with an excuse to put blame for bad lifestyle choices elsewhere. Many problem users jump on this opportunity as the rewards are considerable. After all, to the extent that users accept this premise, they will grant prohibitionists their elixir of life; it makes it possible for prohibitionists to feel righteous in their quest and to forget the nagging tension that, perhaps, they are on the wrong side of the moral equation, and in return the drug user is offered leniency or forgiveness. We see this process every day in courtrooms, in prisons, and outside. The myth of the demon drugs is so well-established that we are all touched by it—and this makes lucid thinking on the subject rare to find.

4.1.3.1. Moral Degradation

Moral degradation was found on both sides of the law. As pertaining to drug users, their new identity as enemies of society took an ever increasing toll and it mattered less whether they were inside or outside of prisons.[83] In any way, they would be subjected to the whims of arbitrary codes, and the humiliation that comes with being denied autonomy was deeply felt.[84] Not only were users forced to buy their goods at a market where quality and peaceful relations was difficult to ensure; they were under the domain of people who would persecute, while refusing to think— and so the respect for law and order suffered.

On a daily basis, drug users would endure the role of the social outcast and the drug warriors had little empathy. They saw drug prohibition as a decent venture, necessary not only to keep the children safe but to keep criminal enterprises from taking over, and it was easy to justify transgressions. Thus, drug warriors would enjoy their alcohol or their cigarettes without recognizing that illegal drug users were the same. Instead, the law provided an opportunity to let their own deepfelt discontent find an outlet, and in targeting violators they felt reassured of their own moral superiority.

In this manner the situation in Norway continued to spiral. Society was entrapped by a law that only hurt relations, and as the despair of drug users became more deeply felt, drug-related death continued to rise.[85] It was impossible to subject a vulnerable

---

[83] I have interviewed subjects who, after serving long prison sentences, are so psychologically damaged, so morally disillusioned, that they are afraid to open their mail but not to carry around kilos of illegal products.

[84] Imagine only the absurdity of living on an island with two other people; there are plants on this island making possible the enjoyment of alcohol and cannabis, and suddenly the two people that happen to like the former begin to persecute the one that preferred the latter. The absurdity is plain, and yet the Norwegian drug users found themselves in this exact situation. What were they to make of the world?

[85] In criminalizing their drugs of choice, society is telling users that they are enemies of the state and to the extent that they accept the perspective of the moral majority, it will have a crushing impact upon their psyche. It will derange their sense of self, making sure that they

population to such a debasing treatment without inflicting further damage. Prohibition generated psychological, economical, emotional, and physical problems which resulted in social distress—and by the 1980s, opiates had become the prime reason for young people (15-41 years) dying.[86]

When it comes to these destructive dynamics, Norwegian doctors, criminologists, and jurists have spoken on the subject and it is estimated that 90 percent have died because of drug policy.[87] Even so, discussing the premises of prohibition remained taboo. The problem of scapegoating, therefore, continued with hundreds of young Norwegians dying every year for no good reason, and the authority of state suffered.

---

are much more likely to continue on a destructive path—and this is taken by prohibitionists as evidence of their beliefs.

[86] Since the 1980s, as measured per capita, 2-3 times as many Norwegians have been dying as in the rest of Europe. And while countries with a health-oriented approach have had the best results, Norway has consistently been found at the top of Europe's overdose statistics. To be more specific, in 1976 there were eight drug-related deaths; in 1978 there were 24; and in 1980 there were 32. However, as the persecution of youth escalated, so did deathrates, and according to the police, there were 478 drug-related deaths in the period between 1980-89; 1471 between 1990-99; and more than 2000 between 2000-09. Annually, some 300 Norwegians are dying, while health-oriented countries like Portugal and Holland have nearly eliminated this problem.

[87] "We forgot the lessons from the vagrancy legislation the minute it was abolished—and what is worse, it could be abolished because a minority of this population, through drug legislation, would be vilified and subjected to even harsher punishment. In this way, society's need for scapegoats is sustained. The level of control, however, puts its unmistakable mark on the persecuted groups, and this is well known within criminology. Every day an army of untouchables are reborn. This is the real problem with drug policy. . . . And to the question of the day. Are we killing drug addicts: Yes, we are—as well as we can." Evy Frantzen, *Are We Killing Drug Addicts?* January 9, 2002 http://www.uib.no/sites/w3.uib.no/files/   attachments/dreper_vi_de_narkomane_-_evy_frantzen_-_09.01.2002.pdf.

When it comes to professors of law, Aslak Syse concluded that the consequences of drug policy have been (1) excessive incarceration, (2) more death and disease among drug users, (3) dysfunctional government programs, and (4) making it difficult to advance better alternatives. As he says: "Rather than appreciating harm-reduction and openness and considering drug use as equal to other conditions/illnesses, the Norwegian state has appeared as a reason why we are found at the top of Europe's overdose statistics." Syse, *Hva er galt med norsk narkotikapolitikk?* Särtryck ur Festskrift till Lotta Vahlne Westerhäll, Santérus Förlag (2011) 426 see also LARSEN, *MELLOM ALLE STOLER* (2008) 15; CHRISTIE & BRUUN, *DEN GODE FIENDE* (1985) For more on the failure of Norwegian policy, see Per Ole Träskman, *Drug Control and Drug Offences in the Nordic Countries: A Criminal Political Failure too often Interpreted as a Success*, Journal of Scandinavian Studies in Criminology and Crime Prevention Vol 5 (2005) issue 2

4.1.3.2. INCREASING DISSIDENCE

As time passed, it became increasingly difficult to ignore the destructive course of Norwegian policy. More and more academics began to jump ship and Nils Christie, a professor of criminology, was an early critic. Not only did he warn about exaggerated enemy images and scapegoating; he noted that there was a presumption of liberty in the Constitution, one that dictates that prohibitionists show good reasons, but that this had been reversed in drug cases.[88] Having spent his formative years interviewing Norwegian executioners who worked for the Nazis, he recognized the problems of moral panic, and together with a handful of others was on to the folly of prohibition from its inception.

Opposing these criminologists and sociologists was a powerful apparatus dedicated to the status quo, and the state found scientific validity for its campaign through the Norwegian Institute for Alcohol and Drug Research (SIRUS). When politicians needed an expert, they could rely on someone from this institute to say that all was well with drug policy, and the rising tide of opponents was presented as a dubious breed—people undermined the fabric of society.

This went on for years and principled debate remained off-topic. Those who knew better feared the mentality of the mob and while they privately would speak with frustration on the problems related to prohibition, they were sensitive about stepping on prohibitionists' toes. This was considered politically unwise. Those who did were painted as apologists for the plague, and in upholding a momentum of fear, prohibitionists successfully stalled debate.

As the problems with prohibition became more apparent, however, relying on this procedure turned out to be tricky. In 1982, Ragnar Hauge, the leader of SIRUS, wrote an article that

---

[88] CHRISTIE & BRUUN, *DEN GODE FIENDE* (1985) 131

questioned if drugs were a scapegoat.[89] It was difficult to deny, but the moral panic ensured that those who wanted a career had to stand firm with the prohibition quest.[90] There was no shortage of scientists willing to trade integrity for a salary, and SIRUS would continue its role as a side-kick to government policy while more progressive-oriented interest groups were shunned.

Despite this trend, it would only become more embarrassing to defend the status quo, and with the new millennium tensions could no longer be kept under the rug.

4.1.3.3. INTEGRITY SHINING THROUGH

By this time, the moral climate had matured and prohibitionists had seen better days. It had been evident for 30 years that the emperor had no clothes, and if integrity was rare Norwegians got a display in 2008, when a professor of sociology, who had previously defended the drug law, rejected his former position. Prohibitionists were quick to express emotions over this deepfelt betrayal, but they could no longer elevate above others simply by questioning their position.

As more and more international scientists came forward, the data overwhelmingly favoured an argument for the regulation of drugs and a resistance had formed that was sick of policies that did more harm than good. Consisting of professionals and activists from a varied background, this opposition was weary of being dismissed as frauds whenever they spoke against prohibition—and one was Svanaug Fjær, a former board member of SIRUS. Coming to the professor's defence, she mentioned how

---

[89] Ragnar Hauge, *Drugs—Plague or Scapegoat*, Nordic Journal of Criminal Science (1982) 47

[90] This point was made loud and clear when Hauge testified "too liberally" in front of the standing committee on social affairs in 1992. Professor Hauge himself did not consider his lecture controversial, but in any event "it aggravated those committee members so much they went back to the Storting and tabled a motion to cut the Institute's budget so drastically it would be tantamount to axing the Institute altogether." *Conversation with Ragnar Hauge*, Journal Interview, Society for the Study of Addiction 101 (2006) 798

former leaders had been punished for questioning basic premises and wrote the following on the politicization of science:

"As scientists have accepted a role as guardians of state-policy, evidence-based drug policies have become a taboo for SIRUS. Because of this, researchers find themselves in a situation where the focus remains technically advanced epidemiological studies. Tough questions must be avoided. . . . The demand for scientific neutrality has resulted in a special kind of loyalty which in turn has made it difficult to study objectively the premises of prohibition. Serious research into alternative forms of regulation is virtually non-existent. [As seen in this instance of the Norwegian professor,] the psychological need to conform to the status quo is so great that researchers will attack their own whenever they question the party line. Rejecting his argument as being 'oversimplified' and 'seducing', the article from the researchers at SIRUS . . . shows how they are part of an environment that is dominated by the will to continue a certain kind of policy. The study of the premises of this policy is neglected."[91]

Being an accomplished researcher of Norwegian policy, Fjær had some years previously noted these difficulties. As she said in 2005, after studying the development of Norwegian policy:

"For those who study drug policy, it is easy to be dragged into a common understanding of the problem, one that demands clear answers. It has been difficult to establish an independent, inquisitive position without becoming alienated. . . . It has been difficult for researchers to find any other role than as a supplier of politicalized data. If you question the premises, they will question your professionality as well as your moral constitution. This has

---

[91] Ibid.

*been evident for a long time, even though it has become
more obvious over later years. . . . [Norwegian] drug policy
is not rational but the result of public opinion.*[92]

According to Fjær, Norwegian policy was reminiscent of a
"totalitarian solution,"[93] and she was right. After moral panic had
reached its zenith in the 1980s, Norwegian experts knew very well
that policy had been informed by unconsciousness,[94] and more
and more drug warriors were getting the picture. Even a former
Justice of the Norwegian Supreme Court, Ketil Lund, went public,
calling Norwegian policy "a reality-resistant transgression," one
that had had "seriously destructive consequences," and added: "It
has been horrifying coming to understand and acknowledge my
participation in this—and, unlike those who only now begin to
grasp the drug war's massive and pointless expenditures, I cannot
claim that I did not know any better."[95]

According to this Justice, the zero-tolerance approach had not
only succeeded in the creation of organized crime, nationally and
internationally; it had "had a dehumanizing impact en masse, and
its most reprehensible result was all those lives that has been
destroyed because of prohibition."[96]

Some year later, when the Norwegian chapter of Law-
Enforcement Against Prohibition (LEAP) was born, also the
police would speak out. Until then, the Norwegian Narcotic
Officers Association (NNOA) had been representative of the
police force, and they had been a major influence on policy. In
hyping up the enemy image of drugs, they had not only built

---

[92] Kveim, *Narkotikapolitikk og folkelig fornuft*, 12. desember (2005)

[93] Gjengedal, *Narkotika og straff*, 26. februar (2003)

[94] As Professors Waal and Pedersen wrote in 1996: "After more than a decade of research,
one can conclude that Norwegian polices went somewhat amuck in the 1970s and 1980s.
We know that drug use rates were dropping and still there was a period where those in
congress outdid themselves as exponents of harsher punishment until the Constitution made
it impossible to aim higher." PEDERSEN & WAAL, *RUSMIDLER OG VEIVALG* (1996) 22

[95] Strøm-Gundersen & Foss, *Vil avkriminalisere narkotika*, Aftenposten, February 14, 2010

[96] Id.

positions of power, but they would defend this position by relying on propaganda. This had been their working model since the early days of the drug war. In a series of articles and interviews, however, Bård Dyrdal, the leader of LEAP, easily picked their logic and analyses apart, and finished off with a parting shot: "Such bullshit argumentation is increasingly being seen through, and when people recognize that they have been deceived, we can expect them to become angry. We ought not be surprised if this anger is directed at the police."[97]

As Dyrdal noted, being profiteers of war, the Norwegian police had an unhealthy relationship with the truth,[98] and there was "a reason why prohibitionists now had retracted from the debate." They were "scared to death that everyone should see that they were wearing the 'Emperor's new clothes'. In the social media, however, their deceptions are immediately exposed—and this is why the Narcotics police and their leaders are currently staying away from these media of communication."[99]

It goes without saying that moments like these were instructive. For every warrior that turned, the collective psychosis would become increasingly difficult to ignore. More and more would depart from the prohibition quest, but despite such exposure of integrity the collective consciousness remained too filled with fear to consider constitutional implications.

Norwegian society, therefore, would continue to persecute those involved with illicit drugs. Unbeknownst to its people, however, this could no longer be done under the cloak of law— for while the media failed to report this, drug users no longer bowed their heads when authority came to invade their homes.

---

[97] Bård Dyrdal, *Norsk ruspolitikk i endring*, Politiforum, September 5, 2017 (https://www.politiforum.no/artikler/norsk-ruspolitikk-i-endring/405079)

[98] "Lately, prohibitionists have not even cared if there are dealing with facts. Anything goes, as long as it can delay change." Id.

[99] Id.

4.1.4. ENDORSING TOTALITARIANISM

As I have said, for more than 30 years it had been evident that the drug law did more harm than good and that it continued as a result of moral panic. Academics had all the data to pursue a different course, but drug warriors did not listen and people did not care.

It was with this picture in mind that drug users began to read up on their rights. They discovered, then, that not only did principles of the Constitution invalidate the drug law, but that the justice system provided a possible solution. By now, it was clear that politicians would never willingly let the drug law endure principled scrutiny. Even so, because there was a separation of powers, violators could use the courts to reform the system, as the law clearly stated that they had a right to an effective remedy.

It is a principle of law that the judiciary shall intervene in constitutional matters and say no whenever other branches of government violate the rights of citizens. Consequently, drug users wanted the courts to prepare an independent, impartial, and competent tribunal where the issue of the drug law and its constitutionality could be reviewed.

While uncommon, it was not unheard of.[100] The right to an effective remedy is at the core of our constitutional heritage, and the Norwegian Supreme Court has recognized this a number of times. Showing well prepared, therefore, drug users were hopeful that the feud against them could end—but the Court would not hear of it. In fact, when it came to the autonomy, equality, and liberty rights of drug users, they were denied even an evidentiary hearing, and when John Christian Elden, the defendant's lawyer,

---

[100] This procedure, a citizen's right to challenge the law, has been described as a cornerstone of Western Civilization. Norway's most renowned jurist, Johs. Andenæs, spoke warmly in these terms, calling it the discipline of law's "greatest contribution to the world", and the Norwegian Supreme Court had recognized this before the drug users went to court. What happened was that the Norwegian shipowners filed a complaint against the constitutionality of a law. As the Constitution, according to the principle on 'ex post facto' laws, frowns upon legislation that punish individuals for violations that took place before its enactment, they claimed that the new law violated their economic rights and the Supreme Court agreed, relieving them of this unconstitutional burden.

pushed for a more direct answer during proceedings, he was met with a cold, hard stare.[101]

Thus, ended the rule of law in Norway. The system had become too corrupted by the prohibition ideology to rethink its ways and the state would be free to continue its regime of persecution without showing good reasons. A year later, the Court had a chance to redeem itself, but the moral climate had not changed. For the second time, the justices rejected the drug users' request for a fair trial and the argument would go on to be declined by the European Court of Human Rights.

In another travesty of justice, the European Court accepted this complaint on behalf of 40 million European drug consumers, but the issue would be too controversial. Even though the Court has stated many times that individuals shall have access to an independent, impartial, and competent tribunal, one where a proper analysis can be done on the relationship between human rights and contemporary legislation, this was too much. In a single judge decision, therefore, the Court noted its lack of competence and left drug users hanging.

In this manner, the rule of law suffered internationally. The Court received hundreds of support letters asking the President of the Court and the Secretary General to intervene—but to no avail. The enemy image of drugs made sure that moral panic prevailed, and European drug users would suffer needlessly many more years.

We shall have more to say on the international aspect of this situation. For the people of Norway, however, the betrayal of the European Court meant that authority was free to persecute unchecked—and persecute authority did. To correct the situation, NGOs were founded not only to inform drug users, politicians, and concerned citizens on the rights of drug law violators, but on the responsibilities of officials. Hence, Norwegian politicians, ministries, and departments all received information sufficient to correct the situation—but no one cared.

---

[101] I was there to witness these events at the Norwegian Supreme Court.

Despite an obligation to investigate alleged human rights violations, every institution responsible for policy has failed to respond to questions posed by human rights activists. With the passing of time, therefore, the respect for the rule of law has dropped to a minimum and one can surely say prohibition has taken the Norwegian people on a strange ride. On the one hand, we have officials who endorse human rights principles but actively undermine them, while on the other we have criminals standing up for these principles, trying to protect the people from the blow of arbitrary government.[102]

This has been the situation for nearly a decade. It has been escalating in seriousness since 2009, when the Supreme Court denied drug users access to human rights protection, and the Alliance for Rights-Oriented Drug Policies (AROD) has held several prime ministers, ministers of Health, and ministers of Justice responsible.[103] So far, to no avail, but there are interesting times ahead.

Since the 1980s, moral panic has been slowing, and there is a possibility that Norway will go from its present, post-constitutional state to become a leader on the international stage. Time will tell. At the very least, by 2018, the international trend of decriminalizing drug use had won sufficient appeal for Norwegian politicians to discuss the framework for a regime where drug users were brought under the "care" of the Department of Health, while drug dealers remained under the "care" of the Department of Justice.[104]

---

[102] For example, a former drug dealer (yours truly) has written letters to police and justice minister since 2012, asking to persecute him for his involvement with 2 tons worth of drug-related crime. All he asks in return for his testimony is the right to an independent, impartial, and competent court, one where the constitutionality of drug prohibition can be carefully reviewed, but no one has accepted this offer. For more, see: http://free.roarmikalsen.info/?page_id=60. In 2021, another example occurred when the police confiscated some money that the suspect claimed was to be used for financing a case against the state on behalf of the persecuted groups.

[103] See correspondence at: http://arodpolicies.org

[104] As we see from this, because Norwegian prohibitionists still refuse to reconsider the merits of their argument, they insist on keeping drug policy anchored in a state of unconsciousness, one where the scapegoating mechanism remains their driving engine.

To help with this, the Norwegian government established a Royal Commission. To politicians, thinking about a regulated regime was not acceptable. Nevertheless, the mandate of the Commission included a review of the relationship between human rights and drug policy, and NGOs pushed on for general human rights analysis. They insisted that the Commission not only look at the human rights implications of decriminalization but of prohibition. It was, after all, evident that the proposed legislation included a prohibition—and that the obligation to human rights law, therefore, was to secure an effective remedy to the persecuted groups.

4.1.5. THE ROYAL COMMISSION ON DRUG LAW REFORM

In December 2019, the Royal Commission released its report. To placate politicians, the Commission did not consider the human rights of drug dealers and producers. Even so, it showed how moral panic had informed the evolution of drug policy,[105] used principled reasoning to reject prohibition, and dedicated a chapter to human rights.

As the commission explained, due to pressure from civil society, there had been a shift from interpreting drug control conventions in light of a drug-free ideal, where prohibition was seen as a proper tool, to emphasizing realities on the ground and the intention to promote health and welfare. As such, there was increasing demand from international bodies to ensure legislation compatible with human rights so that drug control policy did not

---

However, as most drug users also sell to friends from time to time, trouble naturally arises and the problem for politicians is how to sort out some legal difficulties.

[105] See the report of the Royal Commission, NOU 2019: 26 Chapter 3.2. and 3.3. Words such as "public panic", "unbalanced views", "misleading perceptions", "misapplication of punishment", and "reality-resistant iniquity" summarize the development of drug policy. According to the report, we are dealing with a debate characterized by "stereotypical representations", "moral indignation and revenge urges", one in which "scientific understanding of the drug problem has played a minor role". "Panic" is used several times.

aggravate problems.[106] The Royal Commission elaborated on this in its review of human rights obligations. The report showed why decriminalization was in keeping with international obligations and why criminalization was seen as an evil.[107] As the commission concluded:

"These international recommendations indicate that changing the orientation of national drug policy from punishment to health, through decriminalization of use and possession and the introduction of health-oriented measures in response to drug use, will make Norway better respect the citizens' right to health."[108]

The Committee elaborated on this bit. It also demonstrated that decriminalization was in keeping with a right to privacy,[109] as well as obligations to the Convention on the Rights of the Child.

---

[106] See WHO, UNDP, UNAIDS and International Centre on Human Rights and Drug Policy; International Guidelines on Human Rights and Drug Policy (2019), Council of Europe, Parliamentary Assembly: Drug policy and human rights in Europe: A Baseline Study. Also see the report of the Royal Commission, NOU 2019: 26, chapter 7.

[107] "How a state's drug policy should be designed to promote the right to the highest attainable health standard depends on what, to the best of our knowledge, is considered to be the actual impact of the policy. Several bodies in the UN system have stated that criminalization of possession of drugs for their own use impedes the fulfilment of the right to health. The WHO has recommended decriminalizing drug use, as this will be a "critical enabler" to improve the situation for HIV-infected people. The UN Special Rapporteur on the right to health has recommended states to remove sanctions or decriminalize the use and possession of drugs. The United Nations High Commissioner for Human Rights has recommended states to consider the decriminalization of drug use and possession as punishment in several ways prevents the right to health. Again, several entities in the UN system have stated that criminalizing the use of drugs and possession for their own use constitutes an obstacle to providing good health care to vulnerable groups, see discussion in paragraph 7.2.3 above. See also statements of the same opinion from the United Nations High Commissioner for Human Rights and the UN Committee on the Rights of the Child presented in paragraph 7.4.1". NOU 2019: 26, Chapter 7.4.2., p. 180

[108] NOU 2019: 26, Chapter 7.4.2., p. 180

[109] "In several countries, including Mexico, South Africa and Germany, criminal prosecution of adult persons for possession of cannabis for their own use has been found to be inconsistent with constitutional provisions on the right to respect for privacy or related provisions on the individual's right to autonomy, which is naturally seen in context with the right to privacy under Article 8 of the ECHR and the right to free development of personality under the United Nations Universal Declaration of Human Rights Article 22. In Georgia, legislation authorizing civil penalties for a prohibition on cannabis was declared unconstitutional and invalid in 2018, because it entailed a disproportionate interference with the autonomy of the citizenry, see discussion in Chapter 6. Interference with the exercise of

It was evident that had the rights analysis been complete, prohibition would have been found incompatible with human rights. NGOs therefore wrote a letter to the Minister of Health,[110] explaining how an otherwise excellent work had been informed by unnecessary acrobatics, abdications of responsibility, and inconsistent reasoning—all to give politicians what they wanted. They noted the scapegoating phenomenon behind drug policy, that moral panic had been detected; that there was a connection between this problem and human rights violations, and that a more solid constitutional debate was required.

Politicians, after all, did not predict a report so far-reaching. The Commission referred to "a summation of knowledge prepared or obtained by UN agencies over the past ten years, published by the UN in March 2019, where it is accepted that policies based on punishment does not appear suitable to combat the illegal use of drugs." And as the premises of prohibition have proved false, the burden of proof falls to the state.[111] According to human rights

---

the right to privacy, etc. can only happen 'when this is in accordance with the law and is necessary in a democratic society for the sake of national security, public security or the country's economic welfare, to prevent disorder or crime, to protect health or morality, or to protect the rights and freedoms of others', cf. Article 8 (2). In order to be compatible with ECHR Article 8, infringement of the right to respect for privacy, etc. the intrusion must promote a legitimate purpose and be necessary in a democratic society. . . . [Although] the states have a wide margin of discretion in assessing whether infringement of the right to privacy and family life is compatible with Article 8 of the ECHR, the requirement of necessity [implies]. . . that it must be demonstrated that the intervention corresponds to a 'pressing social need'. It must also be shown that the intervention is proportional to the purpose of the intervention, taking into account relevant interests that must be weighed in the assessment. It is primarily the responsibility of the state to do these assessments, but the ECHR may review whether the arguments alleged to justify the intervention are relevant and proportionate and whether the rights were adequately respected in the decision-making process leading up to the adoption of the intervention". NOU 2019: 26, Chapter 7.4.3., p. 181

[110]All communication can be found at: https://www.arodpolicies.org/norwegian-authorities

[111] As the report makes clear: "In contemporary Norwegian criminal policy, punishment is generally regarded as a means and not an end in itself. For the sake of clarity, "means" also denotes those cases where actions are punished with the aim of influencing the attitudes of the population or expressing basic values. Punishment, which means that the state is prepared to inflict an intentional suffering on its citizens, must therefore have a "sound justification". Consequently, the individual punishment must have an identified purpose, and it must be shown how punishment is suitable to achieve this purpose in such a way as to justify the human and financial costs of the punishment. This means that the burden of using punishment must be proportionate to the intended effects of the punishment. Hence, it is the expectation of the total intended and unintended consequences of the use of punishment—and that the benefits sufficiently outweigh the disadvantages of

law, it makes no sense to go from criminalization to a system of forced intervention without examining if there is a right to self-determination. Not when the rationale for continuing persecution is missing.[112] Instead, politicians must accept responsibility. Constitutional obligations come into play, and there is a duty to ensure an effective remedy.

When the Norwegian state will conform to constitutional obligations is difficult to say. According to NGOs, only a Truth and Reconciliation Commission can do justice to the persecuted, as this is the normal set-up when moral panic is detected and the ethics of society must be calibrated towards a more wholesome state. The response from the Ministry of Health has been to acknowledge that there is no way around a human rights analysis. The Ministry also recognizes state obligations, but time will tell when the nation has matured to a point where the psychosis can come to an end. As of summer 2021, a year after the Ministry of Health passed on the responsibility for the persecuted groups to the Ministry of Justice, the Ministry of Justice has sent it back to the Department of Health. Hence, no one wants to face the evidence of moral panic and the connection to human rights violations. No one wants a debate on principled terms, and policy continues askew.

---

punishment—which may justify society's use of punishment. Since the immediate costs of punishment, both in the economic and human terms, are almost inextricably linked to our concept of punishment, the burden of argument and evidence lies on those who want the state to punish its citizens for a particular type of action." NOU 2019: 26, Chapter 12.2., p. 247-48

[112] The epidemic model that governed early understanding of drug addiction has been disproved, the fallacy of twisting the dynamics of supply and demand into one of aggressor and victim has been exposed, and the hypothesis that removing criminal liability for drug users necessarily leads to increased use in the population is found wanting (3.2, 3.3). Instead, the Royal Commission finds that "the available data weakens what has been a prevailing hypothesis that removing criminal liability for drug users necessarily leads to an increase in population use". NOU 2019: 26, Chapter 6.4.2., p. 160 The Commission concludes "that factors other than legislation and legislative amendments as such are of great importance for the use of drugs in the population" (1.3.1), and that it is for the State to show that "the intervention corresponds to a pressing social need. The intervention must also be shown to be proportional held up to the purpose of the intervention, taking into account relevant interests that must be weighed in the assessment." (7.4.3) See especially sections 3.2.2.3., 3.2.2.4., 3.2.2.5, 3.2.3. and 3.3. where it is noted that the "'drug fiend' was primarily a political figure, with no empirical evidence".

5

GREAT BRITAIN

"Our MP's role in the national debate on drugs policy has been a disgrace. For 40 years they have said nothing, heard nothing, noticed nothing, acknowledged nothing, understood nothing, done nothing. Those who have departed from the herd have been trampled by the herd. Something stale in the air at Westminster has stupefied not only dissent but even inquiry."[113]

—Matthew Parris, former Member of Parliament—

AFTER REVIEWING NORWEGIAN policy, there is evidence that drug legislation has had a terrible effect on the country. In examining the international community, however, things are not much different, and we shall now have a look at Great Britain. In this country debate has been more informed than in Norway. Even the police have a tradition of speaking up, and the government has released several documents that testify to the problems related to prohibition. As we shall see, there is now no way to defend the basis of Britain's drug policy, the ABC system that categorize classified drugs. Even so, moral panic has ensured the same

---

[113] *Just a whiff of mind altering substances*, The Times, 7. June 2001.

dynamics as in Norway,[114] and the government has consistently ignored human rights implications.[115]

5.1. THE ABC SYSTEM

"[The ABC system] is antiquated and reflects the prejudice and misconceptions of an era in which drugs were placed in arbitrary categories with notable, often illogical, consequences."[116]

—Professor Colin Blakemore, Chief Executive of the Medical Research Council—

The ABC system is the basis for Great Britain's drug laws. Separating licit from illicit substances, it has provided the legal basis for persecution since 1971, when the Misuse of Drugs Act was passed. The criminalized drugs are the same as those defined by the UN drug control conventions and not only is it claimed that these drugs have no value, but that it is necessary to persecute those who do not obey the law.

---

[114] Today, there are 4 million British drug users (involving some 350,000 opiate-addicts). The government annually spends £1.5bn on battling drugs and drug users have faced the same trend of increasing estrangement, persecution, punishment, and overdose-death as in other hard-hit countries. More than a 100,000 are arrested annually on drug charges and many go on to become imprisoned in institutions that are troubled by corruption and inhumane conditions—more so, than in Norway.

[115] As in Norway, organizations have formed that see policy from a rights-oriented perspective. The Drug Equality Alliance, for example, has informed government on the problematic human rights aspect related to the prohibition regime, but authority refuses to respect its civic duty. See Casey William Hardison, *Letter to Leslie Iversen*, February 10, 2010. http://www.drugequality. org/files/Casey_Hardison_Leslie_Iverson_Letter.pdf

[116] Quote taken from *SCIENTIFIC ADVICE, RISK AND EVIDENCE: HOW GOVERNMENT HANDLES THEM*, House of Commons Minutes of Oral Evidence Taken before the Science and Technology Committee (1 Mars 2006) 118 (Note: The transcript is not yet an approved formal record of these proceedings. Any public use of, or reference to the contents should make clear that neither Members nor witnesses have had the opportunity to correct the record.")

The Misuse of Drugs Act, however, did not tell us why the drugs were placed in different categories; as in other countries, the omittance of alcohol and tobacco would only become more problematic, but the Advisory Council on the Misuse of Drugs (ACMD) was created to make sure that the list was updated according to scientific findings and reasonable criteria. In this regard, ACMD officials have failed, and having served as a political rather than a scientific instrument, they have filled the same function as SIRUS in Norway. Because of their neglect of duty, therefore, the authority of state has suffered—and while perhaps not so much as in Norway, the prohibitionist psychosis is no less obvious.

The ABC system, then, is interesting because it provides more evidence of how drug policy has been informed by forces of unconsciousness and how war profiteers have come to inform systems of government. The critique raised against it is applicable to other nations and a look will have more to say on how prohibitionists have left reality behind.

5.1.1. ITS CRITICS

Just as the Single Convention and any other list naming substances for prohibition, the ABC system will not stand up to scrutiny. Such lists ignore substances like alcohol and tobacco for no other reason than that they are culturally accepted, and this is even officially admitted.[117]

---

[117] In a report initiated by the former Home Secretary Charles Clarke, the following advice was given to ministers: "The classification system under the Misuse of Drugs Act is not a suitable mechanism for regulating legal substances such as alcohol and tobacco. The distinction between legal and illegal substances is not unequivocally based on pharmacology, economic or risk benefit analysis. It is also based in large part on historical and cultural precedents. A classification system that applies to legal as well as illegal substances would be unacceptable to the vast majority of people who use, for example alcohol, responsibly and would conflict with deeply embedded historical tradition and tolerance of consumption of a number of substances that alter mental functioning [...]. Legal substances are therefore regulated through other means. [...] However, the Government acknowledges that alcohol and tobacco account for more health problems and deaths than illicit drugs. CM 6941, *The Government Reply to the Fifth Report from the House of Commons Science and Technology Committee Session 2005-6 HC 1031 Drug*

At the present, therefore, we are at that stage of moral panic where the drug war's irrational and destructive character is impossible to contest, but where our leaders—rather than act on this information—attempt to hide it.[118] In countries like Norway, debate has successfully been stalled by keeping scientists from investigating difficult issues, but the British system was put through independent supervision in 2000, when the Home Affairs Select Committee put together a commission. Named after its head, Ruth Runciman, this commission concluded that there was no scientific basis for the ABC system and that changes needed to be made.[119]

The British Government not surprisingly rejected its recommendations. Even so, more trouble came. In 2002, the Home Affairs Select Committee printed its third report which evolved on the arbitrary nature of the system.[120] The range of expert witnesses who provided evidence was unprecedented; difficult accusations informed their testimony, and more evidence was forthcoming.[121] In 2006, the House of Commons Science and

---

classification: making a hash of it? (13. October 2006) 24. In 1997, the United Nations also released a report that recognized the inherent contradiction. It added: "The cultural and historical justifications offered for this separation may not be credible to the principal targets of today's anti-drug messages—the young." United Nations World Drug Report (1997) 9

[118] The British Government, for instance, fought for three years to keep secret its admittance that legal drugs posed a greater threat to society than illegal drugs. The Drug Equality Alliance had to use the freedom of information Act before the document was released.

[119]*Drugs and the Law, The Report of the Independent Inquiry into the Misuse of Drugs Act 1971*, The Police Foundation (2000)

[120] *The Government's Drug Policy: Is It Working?* Count the Costs (2002)

[121] On 14 September 2006, the ACMD itself published a report in which the Council declared unequivocally that the artificial divide in drugs policy lacks rationality. As it said: "We believe that policy-makers and the public need to be better informed of the essential singularity in the way in which psychoactive drugs work. . . . At present, the legal framework for the regulation and control of drugs clearly distinguishes between drugs such as tobacco and alcohol and various other drugs which can be bought and sold legally (subject to various regulations), drugs which are covered by the Misuse of Drugs Act (1971) and drugs which are classed as medicines, some of which are also covered by the Act. The insights summarized indicate that these distinctions are based on historical and cultural factors and lack a consistent and objective basis. . . . For the ACMD to neglect two of the most harmful psychoactive drugs simply because they have a different legal status no longer seems appropriate." ACMD, *Pathways to Problems: hazardous use of tobacco, alcohol and*

Technology Committee released a report which addressed the improper relationship between evidence, scientific advice, and the classification of drugs. It concluded that the current system of classification, being arbitrary and unscientific, was "not fit for purpose", and that a more scientific measure of harm should be used for classifying drugs. As it summarized the need for changes:

"With respect to the ABC classification system, we have identified significant anomalies in the classification of individual drugs and a regrettable lack of consistency in the rationale used to make classification decisions. In addition, we have expressed concern at the Government's proclivity for using the classification system as a means of 'sending out signals' to potential users and society at large—it is at odds with the stated objective of classifying drugs on the basis of harm and the Government has not made any attempt to develop an evidence base on which to draw in determining the 'signal' being sent out. We have found no convincing evidence for the deterrent effect, which is widely seen as underpinning the Government's classification policy, and have criticized the Government for failing to meet its commitments to evidence based policy making in this area. More generally, the weakness of the evidence base on addiction and drug abuse is a severe hindrance to effective policy making and we have therefore urged the Government to increase significantly its investment in research.

Finally, we have concluded that the current classification system is not fit for purpose and should be replaced with a more scientifically based scale of harm, decoupled from penalties for possession and trafficking. In light of the serious failings of the ABC classification system that we have identified, we urge the Home Secretary to

---

other drugs by young people in the UK and its implications for policy, 2006 (Paragraph 1.13, 22, introduction, 14)

*honour his predecessor's commitment to review the current
system, and to do so without further delay."[122]*

The critique raised against ACMD was unprecedented and more
and more demanded that authority apply reason to policy.
Prohibitionists, however, would not listen. They had one mission
alone: to offset any movement towards a new regime, and to do
so they tried to stop more damning papers from being released.
The government's policy of suppressing the truth, however, had
insignificant effect and while the Drug Equality Alliance used the
Freedom of Information Act to get access to documents revealing
that state officials knew that they could not explain their policies
by any measure of reason, another report came out that left no
doubt as to the system's flawed basis. As the RSA Report
concluded:

> *"The law as it stands is not fit for purpose. The principal
> statute, the Misuse of Drugs Act 1971, is now more than
> thirty years old. It is unwieldy, inflexible and at some points
> addresses problems that no longer exist. It fails to embrace
> alcohol, tobacco, and other harmful substances. It is driven
> more by 'moral panic' than by a practical desire to reduce
> harm. It relies too heavily on discretion in its enforcement.
> It sends people to prison who should not be there. It forces
> people into treatment who do not need it (while, in effect,
> denying treatment to people who do need it). Efforts to
> implement the law as it stands waste a great deal of money.
> Not least, the law as it stands embodies a classification of
> illegal drugs that is crude, ineffective, riddled with
> anomalies and open to political manipulation. We
> recommend that the Misuse of Drugs Act 1971 and the*

---

[122] *Drug classification: Making a hash of it?* Government reply to the fifth report from the
House of Commons Science and Technology Committee, session 2005-06, HC 1031,
October 13, 2006, 3

subsequent legislation associated with it be repealed and be replaced by a comprehensive Misuse of Substances Act."[123]

Moral panic being already established, the commissioners' recommendations for a more wholesome and consistent drug policy should have inspired politicians to pursue changes. However, the connection between this phenomenon and human rights violations was not pursued and the commission went on to be ignored. This should no longer come as a surprise. The British psyche depends as much on the scapegoating phenomenon as any other nation and thinking seriously about drug policy is out of the question. The commissioners themselves noted this tendency. As they said, throughout their investigations, they were "concerned and disappointed by the attitudes of the ACMD and the police towards the classification system."[124] Thus, also in this country drug policy is driven by unconsciousness and as elsewhere the drift towards tyranny remains a substantial problem.

---

[123] *Drugs–Facing facts*: The report of the RSA Commission on Illegal Drugs, Communities and Public Policy (March 2007) 15

[124] Id.

5.1.2. ISSUES OF CONTROVERSY

"The key problem is the total illogicality of the current list of controlled drugs, and their classification within the list; this problem is so great as to render the list scientifically 'arbitrary' and therefore impossible to defend on other than political grounds—not good if one truly desires an evidence-based strategy."[125]

—Richard Brunstrom, Chief Constable of North Wales—

Building on a three-tier system the British government has categorized controlled substances. As seen, they have been relying upon political prejudice rather than scientific criteria, and one problem is that vastly different versions of these substances have been classified as the same, leaving agents of the state free to persecute opium smokers and coca leaf users with the same vengeance as it bullies users of cocaine and heroin. As is easy to prove, it is a great difference between these substances in their natural form and their more potent derivatives and this makes the entire system arbitrary. Nevertheless, there are more pressing concerns, and the biggest problem is that the system fails to include alcohol and tobacco, substances that clearly are more dangerous than those put-on display. Because no one wants to return to a prohibition on traditionally accepted drugs, principled debate has been difficult to muster, and we shall have more to say on how the national and international drug control system is incompatible with basic human rights.

For now, however, we shall concentrate on the problems that arise whenever constitutional implications is denied. And as focus has been on bits and pieces rather than the whole picture, the collective psychosis is best explained by looking at more "trivial" stuff. To elucidate upon our authorities' commitment to ignorance, therefore, we shall have a look at psilocybin.

---

[125] Richard Brunstrom, *Drugs Policy–A Radical Look Ahead* (2007)

5.1.2.1. PSILOCYBIN

Being the active ingredient in psychoactive mushrooms, the UN outlawed this substance due to its hallucinogenic properties. That such substances could be beneficial was unacceptable, and so it was placed in Schedule 1, together with heroin and cocaine. This was to signal the dangers attributed to the drug, as well as its lack of medical properties. In Britain, therefore, the drug is classified category A, which has given prohibitionists some explaining to do.

It is, after all, difficult to rationalize why, as Sir Michael Rawlins, the Chairman of ACMD admitted to the House of Commons Science and Technology Committee. As he told his inquisitors: "I have no idea what was going through the minds of the group who put it in Class A in 1970 and 1971 . . . It is there because it is there."[126]

The committee had an interest in psilocybin because until this point it had been legal to buy fresh mushrooms with this ingredient. It was only when they were dried that psychedelic mushrooms qualified as a class A drug, and the government now wanted to close this loophole. After looking into the matter, however, the committee found that the government had not put forward any explanation for criminalizing this substance (other than that it was a mind-altering drug), and its members were not pleased with the ACMD's indifference. As they put it:

"We were . . . surprised and disappointed to hear Sir Michael Rawlins, Chairman of the ACMD, tell us that 'it was not a big issue' whether magic mushrooms were in the right Class. In Sir Michael's view: 'there are bigger, more important issues to worry about than whether fresh mushrooms join the rest of the other things in Class A.' The Chairman of the ACMD's attitude towards the decision to place magic mushrooms in Class A indicates a degree of

---

[126] *Drug Classification: Making a Hash of it?* Fifth Report of Session 2005–06.

complacency that can only serve to damage the reputation of the Council. . . . The ACMD should have spoken out against the Government's proposal to place magic mushrooms in Class A. Its failure to do so has undermined its credibility and made it look as though it fully endorsed the Home Office's decision, despite the striking lack of evidence to suggest that the Class A status of magic mushrooms was merited on the basis of the harm associated with their misuse. "[127]

The Science and Technology Committee concluded that psilocybin did not fulfil the criteria as a class A drug. The government, however, did not care and the new law, as well as ACMDs position, made Richard Brunstrom, the police chief of Wales, renounce the status quo. As he said:

"I must disagree in the strongest possible terms [that it is 'not a big issue'], and I share the opinion of the Select Committee that Sir Michael's comments damage the reputation of the Council. The upshot of this is that UK criminal law now allows a citizen to go to prison for life for possessing magic mushrooms with intent to supply, for no reason at all other than 'It is there because it is there.' This is just not an acceptable state of affairs in a civilized society. The law in this regard is a disgrace, and as a professional police officer I am ashamed of it. "[128]

As we can see, there is no good reasons why this drug was put in class A, and yet none of this mattered to politicians or the ACMD. The same situation applies to drugs like MDMA and LSD, and the neglect of duty is considerable. Indeed, it is due to misinformation that the enemy image associated with these drugs survive,[129] and

---

[127] Ibid.

[128] Richard Brunstrom, *Drugs Policy–A Radical Look Ahead* (2007)

[129] As Professor Nutt noted: "A telling review of 10-year media reporting of drug deaths in Scotland illustrates the distorted media perspective very well (Forsyth, 2001). During this

114

there is research that they hold great promise not only for medicinal but recreational and spiritual purposes.[130]

5.1.2.2. CANNABIS: FROM B TO C, AND BACK AGAIN

The classification of cannabis is another contested issue. It was a class B drug until 2004, when politicians followed up on a petition to deescalate the persecution of cannabis users. Cannabis, therefore, became a class C drug with no drama whatsoever—except from prohibitionists. For no good reason, therefore, the drug was upgraded to class B in 2008.[131] To justify this decision, the British prime minister, Gordon Brown, explained that

---

decade, the likelihood of a newspaper reporting a death from paracetamol was 1 per 250 deaths, for diazepam it was 1 in 50, whereas for amphetamine it was 1 in 3 and for ecstasy every associated death was reported." David Nutt, *Equasy—an overlooked addiction with implications for the current debate on drug harms*, Journal of Psychopharmacology 23(1) (2009) 5

[130] Clinical research on psychedelic drugs has yielded positive results in the following areas: Criminal recidivism, relationship counseling, treatment of substance abuse and addiction, PTSD, depression, end-stage psychotherapy with the dying, and obsessive-compulsive disorder, as well as being unique tools for stimulation of the meditative state and elicitation of mystical experience See WINKELMAN & ROBERTS (EDS.), *PSYCHEDELIC MEDICINE* (2007); Grob, et al., *Pilot Study of Psilocybin Treatment for Anxiety in Patients with Advanced-stage Cancer* (2011) 71-78; Mash, *Ibogaine Therapy for Substance Abuse Disorders* in BRIZER & CASTANEDA (EDS.), *CLINICAL ADDICTION PSYCHIATRY* (2010) 50-60; MIKALSEN, *REASON IS* (2014) Vollen-weider & Kometer, *The Neurobiology of Psychedelic Drugs: Implications for the Treatment of Mood Disorders* (2010) 642-651. Anthropologists generally agree that the use of these psychedelic drugs is beneficial to the cultures that use them. See Ibid. and SZASZ, *CEREMONIAL CHEMISTRY* (2003) 126.

[131] The *UK Drug Policy Commission* said this in their 2008 report to the ACMD: "In terms of 'sending a signal' to young people, the evidence suggests classification is a very ineffective vehicle for doing this. For instance, the view that downgrading cannabis from B to C sent out the 'wrong message' is not supported by drug use prevalence statistics—the number of young people using cannabis in the UK has continued to decline. Furthermore, according to a major government survey the number of secondary school children who think it is 'ok' to try cannabis has almost halved since reclassification from B to C. A wide range of international evidence indicates that changes in drug laws do not have a direct effect on prevalence. The ACMD has also advised that 'criminal justice measures—irrespective of classification—will have only a limited effect on usage' and instead it has pressed for a public health approach to any strategy aimed at minimising drug use. *The use of the classification system to send messages was strongly criticised by the House of Commons Science and Technology Select Committee which found no persuasive evidence of a deterrent effect from classification.* The evidence suggests there are more effective ways of communicating to young people and reducing drug use." (my emphasis)

cannabis was more dangerous than before, that it was a gateway drug, and that putting it back in class B was necessary or else youth would get the wrong message.

5.2. The Prohibitionists' Faulty Premises

Again, we return to the deterrent-effect, which is embraced as an excuse not to discuss alternatives. On this basis politicians continue to justify their contempt for the rule of law, as nothing mentioned by Brown made plausible the decision to upgrade cannabis. Indeed, contrary to official reasoning, problems related to cannabis were reduced between 2004 and 2008 and even the ACMD opposed the decision. It is also uncontested that the deterrent effect rests upon faulty assumptions,[132] and the only message politicians could send by upgrading cannabis was one of disgrace.

After all, being a symptom of unconsciousness, our drug policies can only be defended by encouraging fear and ignorance, and Brown as much as any other British Prime Minister was willing to trade integrity for power. That is why he made sure to keep a safe distance to reality, even posing as proud to ignore the advice of experts.[133] Without it, there was simply no other way for

---

[132] The oral session of the House of Commons Science and Technology Committee speaks to this. As the committee summarized their attempt at getting hard evidence for this effect: "we have found no solid evidence to support the existence of a deterrent effect, despite the fact that it appears to underpin the Government's policy on classification. In view of the importance of drugs policy and the amount spent on enforcing the penalties associated with the classification system, it is highly unsatisfactory that there is so little knowledge about the system's effectiveness. . . . The Government's desire to use the Class of a particular drug to send out a signal to potential users or dealers does not sit comfortably with the claim that the primary objective of the classification system is to categorize drugs according to the comparative harm associated with their misuse. It is also incompatible with the Government's stated commitment to evidence-based policy making since it has never undertaken research to establish the relationship between the Class of a drug and the signal sent out and there is, therefore, no evidence base on which to draw in making these policy decisions." House of Commons Science and Technology Committee *Drug classification: making a hash of it?* Fifth Report of Session 2005–06. http://www.drugequality.org/files/Making_a_Hash_of_It_2006.pdf

[133] *Gordon Brown: I'm Right to Overrule Drug Advisers*, Evening Standard, November 3, 2009

such a decision to be made and so he had to rely on the retarded reasoning, bureaucratic fear-mongering, and tragic small-mindedness that has kept the War on Drugs going.

Contrary to popular lore, however, the prohibitionists in charge cannot hide behind "the will of the majority" without incriminating themselves; nor can they appeal to the deterrent effect without basing their claim on biased preconceptions, and this is why the fear of sending mixed signals is inherently flawed. As we have seen, the only message politicians have sent by subjecting drug users to an arbitrary regime of violence is that the system presents a wretched deal—one where crooks, charlatans, and traitors consistently ignore the citizenry's constitutional rights. Hence, if we wonder why the theory of classification as a deterrent does not work, the answer is simple: It is the fact that the average youth is not only more knowledgeable, but more aligned with integrity than the average politician—and that the authority of state has suffered.[134]

In this situation, it is no solution to uphold or escalate a regime of persecution. As long as the regime is built on flawed premises, it can only bring contempt, pity, or compassion from those who know better—and in our day, it is more often than not the former. This only comes naturally. After all, while it is understandable that people have a family to take care of and that they are eager for a salary, it is difficult to see decade after decade go by and the drug warriors being committed to psychosis. Throughout this ordeal, the most vociferous opposition has come from free thinkers and retired drug warriors. And because people, whenever they are brought into positions of power, will go from opposing the drug war to embracing it—and then to renounce it when they

---

[134] As Bill Masters, a U.S. Sheriff, noted: "If you want to know the "message" politicians are sending to our children with the drug war, here it is: it's okay for armed enforcers to kill innocent children . . . if they believe drugs to be present. It's okay for police to bust down doors in the middle of the night with submachine guns locked and loaded, if some drugged-up, paid informant said there might be drugs around. It's okay for police to take your property without even charging you with a crime. It's okay for politicians to wipe their feet on the Bill of Rights, as long as they are doing it in the name of getting tough on drug dealers. That's the 'morality' of the war on drugs," BILL MASTERS, *DRUG WAR ADDICTION: NOTES FROM THE FRONTLINES OF AMERICA'S NO. 1 POLICY DISASTER* (2001) 61

leave office—we know that a driving engine of prohibition is hypocrisy.

This has been confirmed many times. And that prohibitionists have a problem with integrity was made clear when the Government sacked David Nutt, its chief advisor on drugs policy. As so many professionals, Nutt was embarrassed to be identified with policies that did more harm than good and used his position to speak out against irrational and dehumanizing policies. Not only did he oppose the groundless separation between licit and illicit substances, but he stated that cannabis and ecstasy was less harmful than activities such as horse riding and advised society to consider the implications.[135]

This was too much for those dedicated to psychosis and Professor Nutt was sacked in 2009. The decision itself created an uproar and three other scientists immediately resigned. After several more meetings between the ACMD and the government four more advisors left—and with that, what was left of any alleged link between reason and drug policy.

Since those days, policy has continued very much the same, only with increasing tensions. As we have seen, it is not easy being part of a system that hates individual integrity, and the police have spoken out. In 2007, the North Wales Police Authority produced a report which argued for the legalization of all drugs. In this report Richard Brunstrom, the Chief of Police, finally put the bar where it belongs—with the rights of the citizenry, as expressed through the state's contractual obligations. As he said:

> *"Until only a few decades ago, the law of the UK treated problematic drugs users for what they largely were— vulnerable people in need of help. Prohibition now turns those without substantial means into social outcasts. Large numbers of people, otherwise law abiding, are being criminalized in a way that has already been demonstrated*

---

[135] Nutt, *Equasy—an overlooked addiction with implications for the current debate on drug harms*, Journal of Psychopharmacology 23(1) (2009) 3–5

to be 'arbitrary', and it seems to me in conflict with the principles underlying the European Charter of Human Rights. . . . If policy . . . in the future [is] to be pragmatic not moralistic, driven by ethics not dogma, then the current prohibitionist stance will have to be swept away as both unworkable and immoral, to be replaced with an evidence based unified system (specifically including tobacco and alcohol) aimed at minimization of harms to society. Such a strategy leads inevitably to the legalization and regulation of all drugs. "[136]

5.3. INCREASED OPPOSITION

As we shall see, there are no holes in this argument. His reasoning is even confirmed by professors of law,[137] and British politicians with integrity have gathered under a single banner to ensure that human rights law is applied to drug policy.[138] Even so, as in other countries, people remain eager for scapegoats and authority has become so corrupted that principled debate remains off the table. For this reason, the drug war has continued its destructive course on the British Islands, and the result is that more and more are awakening to the disgrace that has become of authority. Because authority must rest its power on either deception or truth, false authority will have to use totalitarian means to preserve its

---

[136] Richard Brunstrom, *Drugs Policy–A Radical Look Ahead* (2007)

[137] Alex Stevens, *Drug policy, harm and human rights: A rationalist approach, International Journal of Drug Policy* 22 (2011). See also MIKALSEN, TO RIGHT A WRONG (2016) for many other professors.

[138] As the All-Party Parliamentary Group for Drug Policy Reform says: "interpretation of the Drug Control Conventions must take full account of the Universal Declaration of Human Rights, and the impact of current policies in human terms. This applies fully to the response to the production, trafficking and sale of controlled drugs. When the existing unbalanced prohibitionist response to drug market activities breaches human rights, then adjustments must be made," The All-Party Parliamentary Group for Drug Policy Reform *Guidance on Drug Policy: Interpreting the UN Drug Conventions* (2015) 15

powers, and it is plain to see that the enemy image of drugs has brought Western civilization to its knees. The only rise is through integrity, and this means policies dedicated to the ideals, values, and principles of the Enlightenment.

Truth, then, being a good place to begin, leaders would be wise to anchor policy on such basis. If they fail, they must continue to rely upon ever more totalitarian means to subdue those that agitate for change, and their values, ideals, and principles will become ever more corrupted. This is the way the machinery of political-social interaction works, and British drug policy speaks volumes. Hence, while civil rights activism has not yet reached the level of Norway, where NGOs are selling cannabis outside police stations to liberate rights and hold those in charge responsible for high treason, organizations have formed that are catching on. As in Norway, drug policies have ensured escalating death and three times more than the European average is dying. With the mounting evidence that these are harms related to prohibition, more and more NGOs place the responsibility on officials; those with integrity have long since begun to jump ship, and with the resignation of Julian Critchley it was evident for all to see.

In 2000, he had quit his job as director of the UK Anti-Drug Co-Ordination Unit because, as he said, "I was sick of having to implement policies that I knew, and my political masters knew, were unsupported by evidence". Eight years later, as British policy continued its dismal slope, he wrote an article in the media that explained the corruption of authority, leaving those involved with drug policy in a tight spot. As he said:

"Unfortunately, evidence is still not a major component in our policy . . . I think what was truly depressing about my time in the civil service was that the professionals I met from every sector held the same view: the illegality of drugs causes far more problems for society and the individual than it solves. Yet publicly, all those people were forced to repeat the mantra that the Government would be 'tough on drugs,'

even though they all knew that the policy was causing harm."[139]

With good reason prohibitionists were upset. The article sparked debate in the country's biggest newspapers and all the government could respond was the mantra that the citizenry had heard so many times, only now more hollow. As Danny Kushlick, the director of the Transform Drug Policy Foundation went on to write:

"Critchley is to be congratulated for speaking out with such candour on the issue. I have met many former and current civil servants who are of the same opinion, but haven't gone public. What Critchley makes absolutely clear is that many, if not most of those working in the drugs field are knowingly colluding with a regime that actively causes harm. Their silence is not based on ignorance but is tacit support for one of the great social policy disasters of the last 100 years.

. . . In 2003 at a press conference, I asked the then drugs spokesperson at the Home Office, Bob Ainsworth MP, whether the government would support a cost benefit analysis of drug law enforcement. Quick as a flash his reply came back: 'Why would we want to do that unless we were going to legalize drugs?' Does that sound like a man ignorant of where that audit trail would lead?

It is the candour of the likes of Critchley and others that exposes the hypocrisy of those failing to speak out and makes prohibition untenable in the long term. As Joseph McNamara, former police chief of Kansas City and San Jose put it: 'The drug war cannot stand the light of day. It will collapse as quickly as the Vietnam war, as soon as people find out what's really going on.' Tragically and despicably,

---

[139] Julian Critchley, *All the experts admit that we should legalize drugs*, The Independent, August 13, 2008

the government's commitment to populist posturing means that the collapse will come far too late for many."[140]

---

[140] Danny Kushlick, *Drug prohibition–An untenable hypocrisy*, The Guardian, August 13, 2008.

6

DUTCH DRUG POLICY

"Those who have built their careers in the U.S. drug control complex fear Dutch drug policy like the Catholic Church feared Galileo: they must believe the Dutch model is a disaster, for if it is not their whole cosmology shatters."[141]

—Craig Reinarman, professor of sociology and legal studies—

AS IN THE countries reviewed, also the government of Holland was troubled by the 1960's rebellion and the new drugs. The different direction of Dutch policy, therefore, is found in a slightly more sensible approach as two independent commissions were created to look into policy issues (the Hulsman- and Baan Committee)—and, unlike the other nations, Holland would listen to its advisors.

Unfortunately, neither of these committees would investigate the human rights perspective. The idea that the prohibition per se was unconstitutional was too controversial even to consider, and as this questionable basis was omitted, the focus was to find that strategy which would remedy the damage of drugs without straying too much from the demands of hard-line countries. When it came to the conclusions, both committees denounced the gateway hypothesis, the idea that cannabis users naturally become opiate addicts. They also denounced the notion that drug users were a threat to society and that all drug use was abuse. Instead, they recognized that there was a difference between soft drugs

---

[141] Craig Reinarman, *The Dutch Example Shows that Liberal Drug Laws Can be Beneficial,* in SCOTT BARBOUR (ED.), *DRUG LEGALIZATION: CURRENT CONTROVERSIES* (2000) 102-108

(cannabis, magic mushrooms) and hard drugs (cocaine and heroin) and that separating these markets was advisable—or else, users of soft drugs would become more likely to go on to harder drugs.

Hence, it would make sense to regulate this market in the same way that government regulated alcohol and tobacco. However, because of prohibitionist pressure, a full legalization of the cannabis trade was perceived as unworkable, and to comply with prohibitionist demands the Dutch created the coffee shop. This was an arrangement where consumers could buy their products legally, while the owner of the store had to buy from the illegal market. For sure, it was a contradiction in terms. But as a solution to its unprincipled position, the government would pursue a policy of looking the other way, meaning that the law enforcement apparatus would focus on harder drugs and other crimes.

The Dutch model, then, together with Portugal's, is the closest to a health-oriented regime a country can get without leaving the tenets of prohibition behind. And while it has proven to be a much more humane approach, the in-between solution is not without problems. On the one hand, it has provided improved quality of life for drug users and the reputation of the police is not as tarnished as in hard-line countries; on the other, criminalization is propelling the drugs economy and it does nothing to stop the international cartels that operate with impunity. As in other countries, therefore, Holland is struggling with drug-related crime and corruption—or prohibition-related, to call it what it is.

Because of this, there are forces who want to push further. As we shall see, however, these forces have been struggling against the same collective lack of integrity as in other countries, and as nothing threatens the advocates of tyranny as much as a good example, the promising direction of Dutch policy has been a nuisance to prohibitionists. The way they have tried to present this country as a failure is further evidence of their criminal negligence—and so, before we go on to describe the opposition, let us look at the lies and deception.

6.1. THE THREAT OF A GOOD EXAMPLE

Because Holland for 50 years has had more successful drug policies than hard-line countries, those with a vested interest in prohibition must paint it as a failure—and to do so, they have relied on deception or outright lies. We saw an example in 1998, when Barry McCaffrey, the US Drug Czar, visited the country. Coming from a former position in the military, he had no other relevant background than the war crimes he had committed while serving in Iraq and elsewhere. As the man in charge of the Office of National Drug Control Policy (ONDCP) and President Clinton's drug war, however, he was now to visit a far worse place—the drug infected city of Amsterdam.

Before going, McCaffrey could not withhold his judgement. In the week leading up to his European tour, he assured Americans that Holland's policies were "an unmitigated disaster", and that the murder rate was twice as high as that of the United States. Drugs, of course, were to blame, and because of liberal drug policies the crime rate in Holland was 40 percent higher than in the United States. In addition, he told that while 30,2 percent of Dutch youth had tried cannabis, only 9,1 percent of American kids had done the same. He conveniently forgot to mention that the number attributed to the Dutch was representative of lifetime prevalence, while the US statistics represented last month's use. If McCaffery had compared lifetime prevalence for Americans, however, he would have found that it was at 49,6 percent in 1997—and that the United States, with its hard-line policy, not only had a greater prevalence of use, (nearly double that of the Dutch) but that its murder rates were four times that of Holland. Researchers quickly noticed the deception and exposed the bluff. McCaffrey and ONCDP promised to correct the situation, but nothing happened and the prohibitionist psychosis endured.[142]

---

[142] Rober J. MacCoun has told the story of how ONCDP twice abused statistics presented by him and Peter Reuter—and how they promised to correct their mistake, but never did. As he noted: "We wrote a correction letter to the Los Angeles Times, and faxed a copy to ONDCP as a courtesy. They immediately contacted us to apologize, and we negotiated an arrangement whereby we would withdraw our correction letter and ONDCP would correct

While telling, this story is not unique. It is part of a pattern of deceit and denial that has been key to the triumph of the prohibitionist quest—and a more honest look reveals that Holland, as far as it goes, has been a success story. After implementing the coffee shop system, not only is the country below the European average in drug use, but the Dutch have been more effective at curbing drug abuse and mitigating its ramifications. They have done so without resorting to the same fear-based belief-structure and tactics that other nations have relied upon, and recognizing the difference between soft drugs and hard drugs has been important. Another crucial factor has been the recognition that not all drug use equals abuse; this has led to more realistic insights, and because the enemy image of drugs has carried less weight, problem users in Holland have been few and with a better quality of life.

6.1.1. UN Bias

The fact that liberal and more humane policies have shown better results, however, is difficult for prohibitionists to accept. For this reason leading drug warriors, while vilifying and reprimanding the country on a regular basis, have sought to hide the reality of Holland from the rest of the world. We have already seen how Clinton's Drug Czar went about this and another example is found in the 2000 UN World Drug Report. To prohibitionists, it has been a nuisance trying to explain why Holland consistently has been

the error themselves. We received a copy of that letter but it never appeared in the Times. Some months later, the Houston Chronicle ran the McCaffrey essay in its uncorrected form. A call to ONDCP elicited another agreement that they would send in a correction. Again, no correction letter was ever published." Rober J. MacCoun, *American Distortion of Dutch Drug Statistics*, 12. December (2000). Because of this, the Dutch Departments of Justice, Health, and Foreign Affairs produced a message for the press, stating: "The impression had been gained that Mr. McCaffrey was coming to the Netherlands to familiarize himself on the spot with Dutch drugs policy. The Netherlands would not exclude the possibility that if Mr. McCaffrey familiarizes himself with the results of Dutch drugs policy, he will bring his views more closely into line with the facts." Financial Times, July 16, 1998, p. 2. For More on McCaffrey's visit, see Craig Reinarman, *The Dutch example shows that liberal drug laws can be beneficial* (2000)

found at the bottom of Europe's drug death statistics, and the UN Office on Drugs and Crime solved this problem by mixing its numbers with Luxembourg—a country that, according to the EMCDDA, was the worst of 14 European countries.

This report was prepared by the UN, an apparatus whose bias is well-known[143] and whose commitment to ignorance has made it notorious among human rights defenders.[144] Being dedicated to keeping the psychosis in place, the UN has had big problems with Holland and an episode from 1982 is telling. The INCB President sent the Dutch Prime Minister a letter where he complained about the separation between soft drugs and hard drugs. He held that it was "somewhat artificial and arbitrary, and [that this] might lead to misunderstandings which in turn carries the risk of undermining the Conventions."[145] To avoid undermining the drug control treaties, he encouraged the Dutch to seize their experiment immediately and to submit to INCB's logic.

Now, in the real world it is the drug classification system that is arbitrary, irrational, and unscientific. It is to guard against the unfortunate side-effects of prohibition that Holland has created their own drug policies and it is difficult to find a better example

---

[143] Researchers Thoumi & Kamminga: "In the past UNODC and its predecessor organizations have not been transparent in handling evidence and at times they have actually manipulated and twisted the evidence to portray a mistaken vision of the drug phenomena. Furthermore, many important issues discussed and polices questioned informally by its staff, have been taboo to discuss openly." Francisco E. Thoumi & Jorrit E.M. Kamminga *The Recent Changes at UNODC and its Role in Advancing and Innovating Anti-Drug Policies: Old Wine in New Cleaner Bottles?* (2004)

[144] The Beckley Foundation is only one of many to criticize INCB for neglecting human rights implications: "The INCB has claimed, incorrectly, that it is 'unique in international relations,' and has used this position to justify working methods that are out of step with the rest of the UN system, including the similarly constituted human rights treaty bodies. All meetings are conducted in secret. None of its letters to governments nor are any minutes of its meetings are published. As noted above, the Board expressly refuses to engage with civil society and has also publicly stated that it will not discuss human rights, despite the specific mention of human rights protection in the 1988 drug convention and the prominence of human rights in the Charter of the United Nations." *Recalibrating the regime: The Need for a Human Rights-Based Approach to International Drug Policy,* Beckley Foundation (2008) 46

[145] PETER REUTER & ROBERT MCCOUN, *DRUG WAR HERESIES: LEARNING FROM OTHER VICES, TIMES, AND PLACES* (2005) 248

of INCB's commitment to ignorance. The drug warriors' irritation with Holland, after all, is the ramblings of false authority hoping not to be observed, and yet there is more. While appearing on television—and confronted with the fact that Dutch drug policy was working—the INCB President, Dr Schroeder, put it even more bluntly: "I'm not really interested if it's working or not working. What I'm interested in is what you are doing within the lines of the international treaty. That's what we have to check. We're not really interested if it works or not."[146]

The INCB here puts any doubt to rest. They are not interested in reality, and they do not care about the consequences of their policies. All they care about is persecuting drug users and having no one questioning their premises. On this ideological set-up the UN bureaucrats have continued their policies and it is a shame that no one has held them accountable for crimes against humanity. The drug war, after all, has been the cause of millions of people dying and yet they remain firm in their resolve. As seen from this perspective, INCB, CND, and UNODC is in the exact same position of authority as the Congregation for the Doctrine of the Faith, which was formed in 1542 to defend the Church from heresy. It was this office that was responsible for the Inquisition, and they are both responsible for promulgating and defending false grounds while providing totalitarian solutions.[147]

---

[146] Australian Drug Law Reform Foundation, *Drug Lore—The questioning of our current drug law* (1996) chapter 4:6

[147] In 2007, the INCB also criticized Bolivia for allowing traditional chewing of coca plants. UN bureaucrats demanded that the population stop using this beneficial plant, one that had been popularly embraced and unproblematic for 5000 years.

6.2. Halfway Regulation Remains the Problem

> *"The analysis shows that the legalization of drugs should be complete and include the production of the substances in question. Half-way legalization in Holland has caused a problem of organized crime and public order that will be hard to contain. It shows that leaving drugs production to forces in the (illegal) market leads to unacceptable consequences. Legalization should be complete and include government regulation."*[148]

—Frank Bovenkerk, professor of criminology—

Now we have seen how prohibitionists, to make hard-line policies look good, paint the Dutch experiment as a failure. Not only that, but to paint it as a failure they must (1) distort reality, and (2) maintain a level of fear which ensures that no one calls their bluff. This is the only way for bullies to run the schoolyard and this formula has served prohibitionists well.

We shall soon have more to say on this pressure from above as it materializes in international relations. Throughout the years, however, because of international relations, hardliners have controlled the playing field, and there have been times when Holland could have gone on in a different direction. As in other countries, there is no lack of politicians who cater to the whims of faction and the refusal to anchor drug policy in first principles has ensured a fluctuation between trends. Even so, by and large, Dutch debate has been more informed than in other countries and people generally have a relaxed attitude towards the drug problem. They know that things are worse elsewhere and when politicians have tried to upgrade the War on Drugs, local government, academics, and civil society have resisted such efforts.

---

[148] Frank Bovenkerk, *The dark side of Dutch drug policy or the failure of half-way legalization* (2004)

This push for sanity, however, has not resulted in a solution to the backdoor problem—that of a halfway regulation of the cannabis industry. For that the prohibitionist psychosis has been too powerful also in this country. While being a leader policy-wise, therefore, the failure to reason by first principles has slowed down the reform movement. Even so, as moral panic elsewhere is beginning to yield, there is a well-established apparatus ready to bring Holland forward and not only have academics begun to argue that human rights reasoning is the solution to the problem,[149] but, for the first time, the majority of MPs look to back a bill that would regulate cannabis cultivation.[150]

The forces of oppression, however, remain firm also in this country. And even though research undertaken by Radboud University concluded that legalizing cannabis production would have benefits for public health and human rights, the Minister of Justice could be quoted to reply that "the report's findings were no reason to change policy on cannabis cafes." According to him, "the researchers had not proved that crime would be reduced with legalized cultivation and it would also conflict with the official strategy to discourage youngsters from taking up the habit."[151]

Thus, prohibitionists keep up their act. One must be more than naïve to believe that regulating a criminal market worth an estimated €1.25bn, would not reduce crime. To survive in this business murder, extortion, torture, theft, etc., is not uncommon, and as a majority of those within prisons are incarcerated for these reasons, logic indicates that regulating the drug market would

---

[149] "The regulation of cannabis cultivation and trade for recreational use because of the interests of individual and public health, security and crime control can find its basis in positive human rights obligations that arise from international human rights conventions (Chapter 2). Under international law, states must give priority to their human rights obligations over and above any conflicting obligations under the UN Drugs Conventions (Chapter 3). This means that states have the possibility under international law to regulate cannabis despite their obligations under the UN Drugs Conventions." Piet Hein van Kempen and M.I. Fedorova, *International law and cannabis II*, Executive summary (2016) 338

[150] https://www.dutchnews.nl/news/2016/09/the-netherlands-comes-a-step-closer-to-legalised-marijuana-cultivation/

[151] Ibid.

reduce crime by more than 50 percent—to where it was before prohibition took hold.

This coming from a Minister of Justice, then, is simply ridiculous—and so is his other argument, which relies upon the deterrent effect. This has been proved many times, and an occasion worth remembering is the Cannabis tribunal, which was held in Hague, December 1-2, 2008.

6.2.1. THE CANNABIS-TRIBUNAL

Because of the refusal to deal with the evidence, in 2008, the reform movement prepared an independent, impartial, and competent tribunal where the matter could be settled once and for all. Half-way legalization had had problematic effects on society and now the Dutch had a chance to find out which direction to continue. The legalization movement had presented 18 statements which indicated that a full legalization of the cannabis industry was the solution. These statements were presented to those responsible for Dutch drug policy (as well as other politicians) and they were offered €200.000 if they could refute these points. As the organizers held:

"The reason for organizing the Tribunal is the fact that, more than thirty years after the introduction of liberal cannabis policies in the Netherlands, a drastic reform is urgently needed. During past years, many representatives of municipalities, police, justice, community organizations and involved citizens have called for a renewal of policy regarding cannabis in the Netherlands. This may be total prohibition or legalization, as long as the law is clear. In the meantime, government and parliament have repeatedly postponed a decision on the subject. The Cannabis Tribunal wants to find out the reasons for this inaction and delay."[152]

---

[152] www.cannabistribunaal.nl

In other words, prohibitionists had a chance to make a great deal of money defending what they loved the most. If they were sincere, they would rejoice at the opportunity, but Dutch politicians were not that keen on defending prohibition. Only CDA, the leading prohibitionist-party in the coalition government, accepted the challenge, but as the Chairman of the Court, Dr. Hendrik Kaptein, concluded, their arguments were "fallacies" and "absolutely worthless".[153]

The court could not find any argument against the plea for legalization of the cannabis market as proposed by Hans van Duijn, former president of the Dutch Police Association and a member of LEAP. According to Van Duijn, the CDA was responsible for 50 percent of the criminality in the Netherlands, and every year, one and a half billion euro of tax money was wasted on a useless War on Drugs.

Failing to argue against this, it was evident what had to be done, but the CDA did not reverse its position. Nor did any other politician, and so the state apparatus would continue to pursue policies that only made matters worse.

6.2.2 PRESSURE FROM BELOW

"All laws which can be violated without doing anyone any injury are laughed at."

—Baruch Spinoza—

As seen, we have a system with a vested interest in the status quo. Because of this, maintaining the gap between theory and practice has been an integral part the political process and civil servants can be expected to rise to the top based on their ability to leave integrity behind. On this backdrop, it comes as no surprise that the pressure for evidence-based drug policies has come from below.

---

[153] http://www.encod.org/info/THE-CANNABIS-TRIBUNAL-IN-THE-HAGUE.html

As truthfulness has been anathema to the evolution of policy, there always have been people at the top willing to maintain or escalate a program of prohibition based upon totalitarian inclinations and the only reason why life is not worse for the Dutch people is that drug policy has been formed at the local level.

In Holland it is not the state that has enforced a regime of drug sales on the citizenry. Instead, it is the citizenry that has forced the state to allow a system of coffee shops,[154] and it is for each municipality to decide about sales. When it comes to this, most mayors are part of the movement towards full regulation,[155] and they continue to push for a government-regulated solution to the illicit cannabis market. As international winds are becoming less repressive, this movement is gaining ground, and they finally have the attention of the Dutch Parliament.

6.2.3. What About a Legalization of All Drugs?

As we can see, there is no doubt that regulating the cannabis industry makes sense. However, even if this merchandise is likely to become legalized soon, the problem with hard drugs will remain and many are sceptical of applying the same position to these substances. When it comes to cocaine and heroin, the fear of "being hooked" is so great that a criminalization is perceived as the only viable option. Even so, there is evidence which

---

[154] "The settlement of coffee shops was a bottom-up development. Individuals took the initiative to start a commercial cannabis outlet. The official policy followed and shaped the conditions. The phenomenon of the coffee shop started in the bigger cities. The development was facilitated by the change of law in 1976, which followed a growing practice of tolerance with regard to cannabis use in the years before. In the 1980s and 1990s coffee shops were initiated all over the country. In 1995, the number of coffee shops was estimated at 1100-1200. They prospered especially in municipalities near the German and Belgian border." Marianne M. J. van Ooyen-Houben, *The Dutch Coffee shop system: Tension and Benefits*, Michigan State International Law Review Vol. 25:3 (2017) 628

[155] According to the Dutch Magazine Binnenlands Bestuur, a poll undertaken in November 2008 showed that of 88 mayors, 54 wanted a full legalization of the cannabis market, 25 preferred it as it was, and only 9 wanted the coffee shop system gone. This means that almost 90 percent of all mayors are against more repressive policies.

indicates that also a regulation of the hard drugs will be beneficial for users and society alike.

We shall have more to say on this, but in 1996 the Dutch erected a commission consisting of eight experts from a variety of disciplines that looked at the implications of a fully regulated drug market. They published their findings in *Drug Control Through Legalization—A plan for regulation of the drug problem in the Netherlands*, and their insights were noteworthy. Not only did they conclude that Holland was not legally bound by the prohibitionist interpretation of the UN drug conventions, but it was estimated that legalization would have incremental effect upon the prevalence of users; that society would save billions; and that prohibition was an ineffective, unjust, unnecessary, and destructive endeavour. Most interesting, perhaps, is the effect a legalization would have on crime:

> *"[A] general legalization of drugs in the Netherlands will result in a reduction of the criminal money circuit by about 1 billion Dutch guilders and of total crime by about 50-80%. This unprecedented decrease will reduce the crime rate back to the level of the late seventies. This illustrates that the ever-increasing rate of crime has not been merely a natural phenomenon, to be attributed to factors that are hard to influence, such as the disintegration of traditional religious and socio-political organizations, divorces, tv-violence, immigration, unemployment etc. The rise of crime appears to have a clear and rectifiable cause: The prohibition of drugs."*

It probably comes as no surprise that this report was shelved without prohibitionists second-guessing the terms of their trade. We know now, however, that prohibitionists have some explaining to do, and to put another nail in the coffin of the War on Drugs we shall look at the United States—the country that has fought this war harder than anyone else.

7

THE UNITED STATES

"The United States government has waged a war on drugs for nearly thirty-five years, since 1972 when President Richard Nixon opened the first front on the 'scourge' of psychotropic substances by declaring a 'war on drugs.' Since then, the war on drugs has cost billions and billions of dollars and many lives; fed a correctional-industrial complex that is becoming a burden to society; wreaked havoc with the Judicial System; soured relations with other countries and irked many a world leader, particularly in Latin America; and created and expanded an enormous bureaucracy. Yet, in spite of all its mostly unpleasant consequences, US anti-narcotics policy has had practically no results in stemming the flow of drugs into the United States or in curbing the Americans' thirst for mind-bending substances. Simply put, as we enter the 21st century still waging the longest war in US history, the results are abysmal."[156]

—Tony Payan, Professor of Political Science—

THE MODERN DRUG war began in 1969 with Richard Nixon's presidency. Drug prohibition had already been around for decades, but Nixon would elevate drugs to public enemy number one. Posing as advocate of law and order, he needed a problem to be dealt with—and as a "war" on poverty, loneliness, or human rights abuses were infeasible, he decided to go with the drug problem. Until then, drug warriors had concentrated on fighting opiates, and rehabilitation and prevention were primary pillars of

---

[156] TONY PAYAN, *COPS, SOLDIERS, AND DIPLOMATS: EXPLAINING AGENCY BEHAVIOR IN THE WAR ON DRUGS* (2006) ix

the drug control program. Cannabis had been a problem of no significance, but it was not to last.

7.1. Nixon's War on Drugs

The escalation began with the 1970 Comprehensive Drug Abuse Prevention and Control Act. This act would bring 50 former items of legislation under one overall system of drug control and responsibility was taken from the Department of Health and given to the Department of Justice. From now on cops and prosecutors would deal with the drug problem and Americans were in for a ride.

As in other places, because Americans could not face that the problems of society were symptoms of the extent to which they had abandoned the ideals of their founders, they came to rely upon the scapegoating mechanism to feel better about themselves. Thus, as the system was geared for an unconscious drift towards tyranny, the drug war became a tactical necessity. It was the natural way for a system low on self-esteem to vindicate its failures, as Americans could not think that crime, suicide, drug abuse, and youthful revolt were signs of structural problems. Instead, as elsewhere, drugs were blamed. And by making an enemy out of the drug habit, Nixon not only succeeded in winning an election, but his administration found a way to deal with the Anti-war movement.

Prohibitionists, of course, like to imagine it being the other way around, as if the War on Drugs began as a duty to protect youth and the morale of society. However, in 1969, only three percent of the electorate considered drugs to be a major issue[157] and privately President Nixon admitted that his reason for going to war was to profit on the enemy image.[158]

---

[157] DORIS MARIE PROVINE, *UNEQUAL UNDER LAW: RACE IN THE WAR ON DRUGS* (2007) 99

[158] Testifying before a Senate Committee, John Ehrlichman noted that the administration took on the drug problem because "Narcotics suppression is a very sexy political issue. It usually has high media visibility . . . Therefore, the White House often wants to be involved

The drug war, therefore, cannot be construed as a response to popular demand. Instead, its primary basis as a tool of social control could rapidly be observed,[159] and Edward J. Epstein would later elaborate on the Nixon administration's reasons for going to war. His book *Agency of Fear* put any disbelief to rest, showing that "the drug issue was typically used to build empires, garner political headlines in the news media, and provide the rationale for the development of a national, White House directed police force to be used for political tasks." Not only did his extensive research reveal "no real interest in either understanding or combating the drug and narcotics problem", but "high level officials involved in the War on Drugs had a prior history of using the drug problem for personal political gain."[160]

In part three, we shall have more to say on this prior history. As shall be seen, the drug laws originated as a tool to control blacks and other minorities, and science has never been much appreciated.

---

in narcotics problems even when it doesn't need to be. For example, the feds went into street enforcement partly in response to the obvious political mileage to be gained." DAN BAUM, *SMOKE AND MIRRORS; THE WAR ON DRUGS AND THE POLITICS OF FAILURE* (1996) 67. Also, Bob Haldeman, Nixon's chief of staff, wrote in his diary: "[President Nixon] emphasized that you have to face the fact that the whole problem is really the blacks. The key is to devise a system that recognizes this while appearing not to." H.R. HALDEMAN, *THE HALDEMAN DIARIES: INSIDE THE NIXON WHITE HOUSE* (1969) 53

[159] Arrests on cannabis charges rose from 18 000 in 1965 to 188 000 five years later. Moreover, during an antiwar rally in 1970, 8000 activists were detained. PROVINE, *UNEQUAL UNDER LAW* (2007) 99; BAUM, *SMOKE AND MIRRORS* (1996) 54.

[160] JOSEPH D. DOUGLASS, *RED COCAINE; THE DRUGGING OF AMERICA AND THE WEST* (1999) 94

7.1.1 SCIENCE: NEVER POPULAR

"A clearer case of misapplication of the criminal sanction would be difficult to imagine."[161]

—Herbert Packer, Professor of Criminology, 1968—

To begin his War on Drugs, Nixon focused on heroin. There were half a million opiate addicts in the United States and by tradition drug enforcement had been directed towards this group and those delivering their products. To expand the drug war, however, Nixon needed another enemy, a more widespread threat, and by focusing on cannabis the White House saw an opportunity for growth.

Until this point, authority had relied on the testimony of police and the headlines of tabloid newspapers to justify a prohibition on this product. The existing scientific reports were nothing Nixon could use to support an escalation of tensions,[162] and to have some scientific validation Congress created the National Commission on Marijuana and Drug Abuse (also known as the Shafer Commission). This was a conservative commission, consisting of scientists and experts handpicked by the president himself.

To Nixon's horror, however, the commission's research into cannabis did not result in a cart blanche for war. After a two-year study, its scientists concluded in 1972 that "the actual and potential harm of use of the drug is not great enough to justify intrusion by the criminal law into private behavior," and that decriminalization was recommended.

Nixon did not listen. Around 80 percent of all illegal drug users would swear by this substance and the president needed to

---

[161] HERBERT L. PACKER, *THE LIMITS OF THE CRIMINAL SANCTION* (1968) 333

[162] The Indian Hemp Drugs Commission Report (1894), The LaGuardia report (1944), The British' Wooton-report (1968). Also, periodic reports of the Panama Canal Zone Governor's Committee "to study the physical and moral effects of the use of marijuana" were available to legislators before the passage of the Uniform Act. None of these reports provided reasons to support a criminal campaign against drug users.

justify the persecution of this group. Consequently, he would have to continue his search for "good" scientists, and the Shafer Commission was not his only problem. Canada had just released the report of the LeDain Commission which concluded much the same and as cannabis became increasingly popular among the white middleclass, more research was being done—which did not support the president's preconvictions.

One sign of the troubles to come was *Marijuana: The New Prohibition*, written by John Kaplan in 1970. Kaplan was a professor of law which had been asked to take part in a legislative study of California's Penal Code. His assignment was the drug laws and after a two-year study he found that it was "impossible to make a rational case that marijuana should be treated more stringently than is alcohol."[163] Weighing the pros and cons of drug policy, the professor concluded "that the costs of the marijuana laws far outweigh their benefits and that a drastic change in our whole approach to this problem is necessary to avoid a national tragedy of major proportions."[164] Kaplan submitted his findings to the penal committee but was summarily fired.

Kaplan was not the first and he would not be the last to oppose prohibition at personal costs. The drug warriors had a long history of terrorizing others until they submitted to their demands,[165] and would continue their war on integrity. Nevertheless, trailblazers like Kaplan produced materials which left no doubt that the arguments used to support a prohibition were so weak as to count for naught.[166] And as the 1970s advanced, many would discover the same.

---

[163] JOHN KAPLAN, *MARIJUANA: THE NEW PROHIBITION* (1971) 316

[164] Ibid., 2

[165] FBN would arrest thousands of doctors who did not conform to the FBN's idea of decent drug policies. They were also busy attacking others who did not buy into their lies. Alfred Lindesmith, a professor of sociology, for instance, were subjected to discrediting campaigns from the narcotics police for his opposition to the drug law. See John F. Galliher, David P. Keys, Michael Elsner, *Lindesmith v. Anslinger: An Early Government Victory in the Failed War on Drugs*, The Journal of Criminal Law and Criminology, Vol. 88, No. 2 (Winter, 1998) 661–682.

[166] "Indeed, proceeding through the book one will note that the arguments minimizing the costs and enhancing the benefits of the marijuana laws are often so transparently flimsy that

A testimony to this was *Marijuana Reconsidered*, a book published in 1971 by James Bakalar and Lester Grinspoon, both academics at Harvard University. While Bakalar was a lecturer of Law, Grinspoon was a conservative psychologist, and they had intended a defence of prohibition. Even so, the plot took a different turn, and as they "reviewed the scientific, medical and lay literature", they came to understand that they "like so many other people in this country, had been brainwashed."[167]

Following the evidence, these scholars would become activists for change. The medical properties of cannabis were confirmed to Grinspoon while his son was dying from leukaemia and together with Bakalar he would go on to write *Psychedelic Drugs Reconsidered* and *Marijuana: The Forbidden Medicine*. The former was an enlightened exposure of the promising potentials of psychedelic drugs, while the latter described the medical benefits of marihuana, explained why it was forbidden, and argued for its full legalization.

All these books provided valid, non-frightening information on drugs and drug use, and another bombshell was the Consumers Union Report. In their special publication, *Licit and Illicit Drugs*, issued in 1972, an exhaustive study of the scientific, social, and legal evidence was done. Based on the evidence, the CU "recommended that marijuana should be regulated rather than prohibited, that all persons currently imprisoned for marijuana possession or for sharing marijuana with friends should be released, and that past offenses of these kinds should be erased from the legal records."[168]

Back in the 1970's, this was not as controversial as one may think. Until the 1960's, nearly all "information" on illegal substances had been propaganda from drug warriors and the

---

one can hardly believe they have been put forward seriously." KAPLAN, *MARIJUANA* (1971) 3

[167] DAN RUSSELL, *DRUG WAR: COVERT MONEY, POWER AND POLICY* (2000) 579

[168] Edward M. Brecher and the Editors of Consumer Reports, *Marijuana: The Health Questions: Is Marijuana as damaging as recent reports make it appear?* Consumer Reports (Mach 1975) 143

public perception mirrored this trend. Even so, as the 1970's moved forward, more than 20 percent had tried cannabis and most users appeared to remain in good health. Thus, it would become increasingly clear that moral panic prevailed and in the face of the newly launched War on Drugs, prohibitionists were losing the hearts and minds of the population. Despite their best efforts, no convincing data had come to the aid of the Nixon administration, and as no documentation of relevance to the prohibition quest could be deduced in looking at short-term effects, prohibitionists began to speculate in adverse long-term effects. To maintain the panic, this was the only way to go, and so drug warriors put their hopes with dire predictions.

Scientific minds, however, suggested that rather than rely upon predictions, these projections could be studied in other countries where marijuana had been a daily custom for generations. If adverse effects existed, they argued, "they would surely be visible there, observable without air encephalograms, Implanted electrodes, or other sophisticated laboratory procedures. Scientists dispatched to such countries would not have to predict the long-term consequences of marijuana use; they could readily see and measure those effects."[169]

Now, there were places nearby where smoking cannabis had been prevalent for generations. For decades, Jamaicans had smoked marijuana much stronger than that smoked in the United States and a study of its inhabitants would provide a clue if there were problems to come. To find out more, therefore, the National Institute of Mental Health commissioned the Research Institute for the Study of Man to study marijuana effects on this island.

What were the results? To prohibitionists' dismay, the report on Jamaica proved to be useless. Even though about 60 to 70 percent of the population occasionally used cannabis, researchers found no social problem and no differences between cannabis smokers and control subjects on any psychological or physiological dimension. All prohibitionists could do, was to hide

---

[169] Ibid.

the report from becoming known,[170] and so the U.S. government refused to publish. In 1975, therefore, Drs. Vera Rubin and Lambros Comitas, the director and associate director of the Research Institute commissioned for the study, published the report as a book,[171] and prohibitionists suffered another defeat.

From this point, no more time was needed to assess the evidence. Previously, also the Indian Hemp Drugs Commission had released a study which confirmed that the widespread use of cannabis was unproblematic to society, and prohibitionists were running out of places to hide. Thus, they would have to rely upon corrupt scientists to minimize the impact of the Jamaica report. This would buy the prohibitionists room to continue operations, but as time passed this report would be substantiated and by more reports, commissions, and books—one of them being *The Marijuana Conviction: The Legal History of Drugs in the United States*, written by Richard Bonner and Charles Whitebread, two professors of Law at the University of Virginia.

Professor Bonnie had been the Nixon Commission's Associate Director (Whitebread also took part) and already in 1970, they had written a deadly expose of the origins of the drug war.[172] Now, they produced a book, and it was another lethal blow. During their research they enjoyed access to the archives of the Federal Bureau of Narcotics, a precursor to the modern DEA, and their work documented the corruptness of the political process leading up to the present. They found that "neither philosophy nor science have been shapers of drug policy; instead, the central influence on government action has been the social context— political, economic, and cultural." More specifically, Bonnie and Whitebread noted that "fearmongering and sloppy journalism,

---

[170] As Edward M. Brecher, the lead investigator of the Consumers Union report noted: "Although the Jamaica report was completed nearly three years ago, it has still not been published in the United States. Indeed, the Consumers Union was unable to obtain a copy from the Government agencies concerned." Ibid., 144

[171] VERA RUBIN AND LAMBROS COMITAS, *GANJA IN JAMAICA: A MEDICAL ANTHROPOLOGICAL STUDY OF CHRONIC MARIHUANA USE* (1975)

[172] Bonner and Whitebread, *The Forbidden Fruit and the Tree of Knowledge*, Virginia Law Review, Vol. 56:5 (1970)

sham science, and shameless propaganda, racism and xenophobia—all contributed to the emergence and institutionalization of marijuana prohibition."[173] On this basis, they concluded: "we cast our lot with the reformers. In so doing, we suspect we side with the inevitable; but more important we believe that these laws are indefensible and therefore ought to be changed. We are convinced that logic, science and philosophy have had almost nothing to do with the evolution of drug policy."[174]

This was in 1974 and life was not good for Nixon. A series of wrong turns in power-politics made sure that he was replaced by Gerald Ford, another known associate of gangsters, and while he continued to build on what Nixon had begun there were trouble to come.

Due to the increased awareness on cannabis, more and more began to question if it was right to treat its users differently from alcohol users. Indeed, as more and more legal scholars denounced the drug war,[175] it became difficult for the Courts to ignore the plea for just and humane policies, and so Alaska legalized the recreational use of cannabis in 1975. Several states also decriminalized possession, and this increasing pressure for a regime of tolerance, not repression, was constantly growing. By the mid-1970s, one in three adults preferred a legalization of cannabis and professionals predicted that, in the near future, it would become a legally regulated substance.[176]

Obviously, something had to be done if the prohibitionist quest should provide cover for tyrannical tendencies—and it was. To counter the trend of increasingly problematic evidence, in 1974, all scientific research in the United States was put under the

---

[173] Raymond P. Shafer, Foreword to the 1999 Edition of BONNIE & WHITEBREAD, *THE MARIJUANA CONVICTION* (1974) xi

[174] Ibid., 298

[175] See also ARTHUR D. HELLMAN, *LAWS AGAINST MARIJUANA: THE PRICE WE PAY* (1975)

[176] In 1977 Lester Grinspoon wrote: "It is likely that within a decade marijuana will be sold in the United States as a legal intoxicant." PATRICK MATTHEWS, *CANNABIS CULTURE: A JOURNEY THROUGH DISPUTED TERRITORY* (1999) 187

responsibility of the National Institute on Drug Abuse (NIDA). Acting as SIRUS in Norway and ACMD in the UK, it would support the role of government by consistently seeking out negative perspectives on the cannabis plant and other illegal substances—only with more vigour. According to NIDA, until this day, the institute would finance 85 percent of the world's cannabis research, and we shall have a look at how they kept reason at bay.

7.1.2. DRUGS AND CRIME

"It is now widely recognized and accepted that our language both reflects and shapes our experience. This sophistication has, however, had no appreciable effect on our contemporary attitudes and policies toward social problems in which the verbal shaping of the 'problem' itself constitutes much or even all of the ensuing problem. We seem to have learned little or nothing from the fact that we had no problem with drugs until we quite literally talked ourselves into having one: we declared first this and then that drug 'bad' and 'dangerous'; gave them nasty names like 'dope' and 'narcotic'; and passed laws prohibiting their use. The result: our present 'problems of drug abuse and addiction.'"[177]

—Thomas Szasz—

When it comes to the shaping of American drug policy, Dr. Robert L. DuPont is worth noting. Not only was he the director of NIDA from 1973-78, but he contributed with research that served to justify a continuing regime of prohibition. For instance, as second in charge of Special Action Office for Drug Abuse (a precursor to ONDCP), he claimed that heroin addicts stole valuables for as much as $6.3 billion a year. As others later noted, it was difficult

---

[177] SZASZ, *CEREMONIAL CHEMISTRY* (2003) 11

to understand how he could arrive at such an estimate, considering that it was nearly five times the total value of all reported stolen property in the United States that year.[178] DuPont, however, had a vested interest in methadone-maintenance, and this exaggeration would serve him and his friends very well.[179]

Adding to this, DuPont was central to the research used to support an alleged link between drugs and crime. This is a key tenet of prohibitionist reasoning and without a link between the two, the drug war would fall on its own merits. Because of this, it has been important to establish a connection, no matter how imaginary. Robert DuPont took care of this in 1968 as an advisor to the D.C. Department of Corrections. After a study of the inmates, he put together a report which concluded that "the addict poses a very real threat to property as well as to persons in the community," and while the evidence for this was inconclusive, the report was welcomed by Nixon.[180]

---

[178] BAUM, *SMOKE AND MIRRORS* (1996) 70

[179] The War on Drugs has been a boon for war profiteers and methadone maintenance is one of the big cash cows. Building upon the theory that the opiate addict is sick and that he needs his "medicine", it has become popular among drug users who reject responsibility, as well as the therapeutic community whose salary depends upon them keeping drug addicts maintained. The irony of forcing upon these poor souls a medicine that many claim is more lethal, addictive, and damaging than that substance which they originally preferred is lost on most—as is the profit incentive. However, while methadone was developed by Nazi scientists in 1937 (the Nazis believed that the drug had too many side-effects and chose not use it), it was taken as spoils of war by American elites and patented by Ely Lily. The market was tiny, but after a group of studies performed at the Rockefeller University in New York, methadone became big business.

Was this a coincidence? In part three, we shall see that elites certainly have the power to shape policy and we know that war profiteers can be expected to push any solution that deprives the individual of autonomy. When it comes to methadone treatment, this is what they have done: These corporations now profit on drug users whether they are incarcerated or medicalized, and while the results of Methadone treatment were promising, they were exactly what one could expect when drug addicts were given a similar but legal opiate. As soon as the stress of having to get money for their next fix no longer overshadowed every aspect of their lives, it was inevitable that addicts showed enhanced mental health and quit crime. It was also inevitable that they largely stopped taking heroin and that they expressed an interest in family, friends, work, and becoming fully engaged members of society once more: As soon as they no longer saw themselves as criminals, but patients, these individuals had an increased sense of self-worth, and they resumed family responsibilities as well as employment. To give methadone the credit, however, one had to be delusional, as these results are merely what one can expect to see when drug users are left alone.

[180] BAUM, *SMOKE AND MIRRORS* (1996) 70, 18-19

After DuPont's report, no more research was done to see if an alleged relationship between drugs and crime existed, not by prohibitionists. This was confirmed by Benjamin H. Renshaw in 1989. Working in the Department of Justice, he had access to the Drug Enforcement Agency's library in Washington where he was investigating this connection. He ended up with nothing and after looking at reports and numbers, he realized that it was not because the DEA did not have the capacity but because they did not want to know more about this relationship.[181]

Renshaw was not the first and he would not be the last to condemn the failure to fact-check premises.[182] Even so, the will to ignorance aside, there are others who have looked at this connection and come to conclusions unfavourable of prohibition. To mention a few, Jeffrey A Miron, an economist at Harvard, presents evidence in his book *Drug War Crimes: The Consequences of Prohibition*, and a study done by Jonathan Shelder and Jack Block attests to the same.[183] These findings indicate that problem drug use is a symptom, not a cause, of personal and social maladjustment, and the same conclusion was drawn in a study paid for by NIDA in 1993.[184]

That drug abuse, just as alcohol abuse, is a symptom of psychological and social issues is therefore documented. It has only been ignored because, if scientists such as these are right,

---

[181] Ibid., 281

[182] That prohibition has never been exposed to meaningful scrutiny was also admitted in 2001 when the US National Academy of Sciences produced a 200-page report for the White House Office of Drug Control Policy titled *Informing America's Policy on Illegal Drugs: What We Don't Know Keeps Hurting Us*. It concluded that "It is unconscionable for this country to continue to carry out a policy of this magnitude and cost without any way of knowing whether or to what extent it is having the desired effect."

[183] Jonathan Shelder & Jack Block, *Adolescent Drug Use and Psychological Health*, American Psychologist (May 1990) 612-30

[184] As Neil Swan, the author of the NIDA report noted: "Conduct disorder is in large part the common forerunner of both drug abuse and criminality, challenging the assumption that drug use causes crime." Neil Swan, *Researchers Probe Which Comes First: Drug Abuse or Antisocial Behaviour* (1993). For more on these reports, see JACOB SULLUM, *SAYING YES; IN DEFENCE OF DRUG USE* (2004) 14-15. For a good book on drug abuse, see Gabor Maté, MD, In the Realm of Hungry Ghosts: Close Encounters with Addiction (2010)

drug prohibition—not drug use—is responsible for the generation of crime.[185]

7.1.3. THE GATEWAY THEORY

"It is a stunning indictment of our current drug regime that a black man born in the 1960s, after the civil rights era, is more than twice as likely to go to jail as one born in the Jim Crow era".[186]

—Ekow N. Yankah, Professor of Law—

A central tenet of prohibition is the Gateway hypothesis. It became popular in the 1950's when it was embraced by Harry Anslinger, the lead U.S. drug fighter. Formerly, he had denied any association between cannabis use and hard drugs, but in 1951 he reversed his position telling Congress that "Over 50 percent of those young addicts started on marihuana smoking. They started there and graduated to heroin; they took the needle when the thrill of marijuana was gone."[187]

Since that day, the gateway theory has been used to justify a criminalization of cannabis. Even so, there is no more a

---

[185]Professor Steven B. Duke affirms: "From an original budget of less than $100 million per year, Nixon's drug budget grew enormously. The federal drug war budget is now more than 130 times that, at $13 billion. Our violent crime rates nearly doubled in the same period. The simultaneous ascents in drug war budgets and crime rates are not coincidental. The drug war causes crime—far more than most people realize. It also wastes huge sums of money, contributes to the destruction of our cities, spreads disease, destroys our liberties, tears our families apart, foments racism, and imposes most of its costs on those who do not even use illegal drugs. . . . [the collection of] data suggests that about 75% of our robberies, thefts, burglaries, and related assaults are committed by drug abusers. Some of the crimes committed by drug abusers-perhaps one-third-would be committed in any event, but numerous studies show that drug users commit far fewer crimes when undergoing outpatient treatment or even when the prices of drugs go down. Half of America's property crime, robberies, and burglaries are probably the result of the high costs of drug acquisition created by the drug war." Steven B. Duke, *Drug Prohibition: An Unnatural Disaster*, 27 Connecticut L. Rev. 571 (1995) 5, 8

[186] Ekow N. Yankah, *A Paradox in Overcriminalization*, New Criminal Law Review Vol. 14:1 (2011) 21

[187] SULLUM, *SAYING YES* (2004) 128

connection between the use of cannabis and harder substances than there is between playing cards as a child and gambling at casinos as an adult. Of course, there are those who begin playing cards and go on to gamble at casinos, but they are few and blaming a deck of cards is ridiculous. Prohibitionists may just as well argue that alcohol or tobacco is a gateway to heroin—or mother's milk.[188]

This argument, then, has been used for far more than it is worth. Just as Robert DuPont tried to prove a connection between crime and drugs by checking the numbers of drug addicts in prison, so proving a link between soft and hard drugs by looking at how many heroin users who have used cannabis is nonsensical. For every heroin user who started with cannabis, there are 1000 cannabis users who did not go on to become heroin addicts, and prohibitionists might just as well have explained the connection between violence and poverty by referring to the genetic makeup of blacks.

Former US Drug Czar Bill Bennett seemed to make this mistake in 2005, when he declared that "If you wanted to reduce crime, you could—if that were your sole purpose—you could abort every black baby in this country".[189] Nevertheless, violence and drug abuse are secondary to the type of society we live in and prohibitionists have symptom and cause confused. Not only does evidence for this abound, but reason dictates that desperate and stressed individuals will act out in ways that healthy minds do not—and so the result of living in hierarchical, control-, and competition-oriented societies is seen in the disproportional statistics on violence and drug abuse attributed to poorer neighbourhoods.

---

[188] Tobacco was claimed to be a gateway drug by Benjamin Rush in 1798: "This thirst cannot be allayed by water, for no sedative or even insipid liquor will be relished after the mouth and throat have been exposed to the stimulus of the smoke, or juice of tobacco. A Desire of course is exited for strong drinks, and these when taken between meals soon lead to intemperance and drunkenness." Ibid., 127

[189] http://edition.cnn.com/2005/POLITICS/09/30/bennett.comments/

It should be self-evident that the link between crime and drug abuse—or crime and poverty—in both cases result from the pressure of having to cope with demanding relations and that it can be explained no more by referring to the inherent trait of illicit drugs than to that of race. As seen from this perspective it makes more sense to reverse the Gateway theory,[190] and there are those who conclude that the lack of cannabis leads to harder drugs.[191]

Thanks to NIDA, however, the gateway theory would become accepted as gospel. Thus, we have heard it every time prohibitionists needed a justification, and they can be relied upon to continue to promulgate this hypothesis, even though science has put any objective doubt to rest.[192]

7.1.4. BIASED SCIENTISTS

Flawed premises are bad enough. As seen, they have supported a deeply dysfunctional structure of dominance, but the will to denial indicates more than mere incompetence. If we look closer, therefore, the War on Drugs has not only been the work of power-hungry bureaucrats and policemen, but that they have been helped by predisposed scientists.

---

[190] For more on this, see Australian Drug Law Reform Foundation, *Drug Lore: The Questioning of our Current Drug Law* (1996) chapter 4:47

[191] BAUM, *SMOKE AND MIRRORS* (1996) 24

[192] As a Canadian Senate Committee concluded: "The 'stepping stone' theory holds that cannabis use inevitably leads to use of other drugs. In this theory, cannabis use would lead to neurophysiological changes, affecting in particular the dopaminergic system (also called the reward system), thus creating the need to move on to the use of other drugs. This theory has been completely dismissed by research. We share this conclusion with several international bodies doing drug research, including the British organization *DrugScope*: 'The Stepping-Stone theory has proved unsustainable and lacking any real evidence base. The 'evidence' that most heroin users started with cannabis is hardly surprising and demonstrably fails to account for the overwhelmingly vast majority of cannabis users who do not progress to drugs like crack and heroin. The Stepping-Stone theory has been dismissed by scientific inquiry. The notion that cannabis use 'causes' further harmful drug use has been, and should be, comprehensively rejected.'" Canadian Senate Special Committee on Illegal Drugs, 37th Parliament, 1st Session (January 29, 2001 - September 16, 2002)

When it comes to this, examples are found in the research of Dr. Robert Heath and Dr. Gabriel Nahas. Nahas was not only a key figure in having all drug research put under NIDA in 1974, but a seasoned advisor to the UN prohibition apparatus. All in all, he wrote more than 700 articles in scientific journals which suggested that marijuana contributed to cancers of the head and neck, leukaemia, infertility, brain damage and a weakening of the immune system. He also wrote two books on cocaine, (which he contended could cause irreversible brain damage) and frequently testified at government hearings.

Robert Heath, for his part, was an American psychiatrist, embedded with the CIA. As Chairman of the Department of Psychiatry and Neurology at Tulane University from 1949 to 1980, he performed many controversial experiments involving electrical stimulation of the brain, to find a cure for homosexuality and more. Not much is known about his connection to the MK Ultra experiments, but we do know a great deal about his research into cannabis. He implanted electrodes deep in the brains of six rhesus monkeys and recorded the monkeys' brain waves before, during, and after heavy exposure to marijuana smoke. In monkeys, as in humans, momentary changes in brain-wave patterns are observed with almost any change in the body or its environment. Persistent changes, however, are cause for concern, and after his monkeys were subjected to marijuana smoke in large doses daily for months, Dr. Heath reported that the changes could be observed as long as five days after marijuana exposure was discontinued. Furthermore, an autopsy report on two monkeys indicated "structural alteration of cells in the septal region of the brain," and "our previous experience with similar conditions," Dr. Heath stated, "would lead us to assume that this chronic smoking of marijuana has probably produced irreversible changes in brain function."

Eager to contribute to the propaganda campaign, Heath wrote *Marijuana and the Brain*, a book in which he claimed to have proved that smoking cannabis caused brain injury,[193] and his studies were among those cited by Dr. Robert DuPont when he, as the White House adviser on drug abuse, took the official position before a Senate Subcommittee that relaxing laws against marijuana would be unwise. Citing a new Federal report titled *Marijuana and Health*, DuPont told the committee of NIDA's new evidence which suggested that pot could cause lower male hormone levels, interfere with immunity mechanisms, and affect the fundamental chemistry of living cells.

Such research no longer carries any merit in the scientific community.[194] To arrive at his conclusions, Heath had pumped massive amounts of marijuana smoke through gas masks attached to monkeys—and as others noted, asphyxiation, not cannabis, had caused the death of brain cells. Even so, while Nahas and Heath became infamous for the politicization of science, this did not stop prohibitionists from relying upon their services. Nahas wrote the article that would be used to cast doubt on the previously mentioned Jamaica report, and to refute their conclusions (and any other unfavourable report that came his way) he would continue to recite "recent medical evidence", indicating "that long-term marijuana smoking in amounts currently used in the U.S. is associated with the following hazards: Hormonal imbalance, inhibition of spermatogenesis, lung damage, impairment of immunity, increased formation of chromosome deficient cells

---

[193] RUSSELL, *DRUG WAR* (2000) 585-87

[194] As Gerber noted: "Probably no drug abuse scholar in the past century since Anslinger has been subject of such scanting criticism in scientific journals. The *New England Journal of Medicine* called his research 'psychopharmacological McCarthyism' peppered with 'half-truths, innuendo and unverifiable assertions.' The *Journal of the American Medical Association* found his research littered with 'examples of biased selection and that omissions of facts abound in every chapter.' *Contemporary Drug Problems* called his research 'meretricious trash.' Nahas's papers, which often heavily quote himself, offer repeated references that have been found misleading or distorted. Nonetheless, his work remains a primary source of pseudoscientific justification for research-hungry drug warriors, especially gateway theorists, seeking medical justification for the pot prohibition." RUDOLPH J. GERBER, *LEGALIZING MARIJUANA: DRUG REFORM AND PROHIBITION POLITICS* (2004)

with possible damage to the offspring, interference with memory and speech and impairment of driving performance."[195]

Now, again, hardly any of this research has withstood the test of time. Still, prohibitionists can be relied upon to recite their favourite scientific papers to an unknowing audience also in the future. Even if Heath and Nahas are gone, there will always be successors willing to play politics and NIDA has continued to provide science for politicians to this day.

Even so, science was never easy on prohibitionists. And as academics, objectively speaking, could not find a good reason to support a regime of persecution, they began to speculate in what-ifs. This tactic of defending policy based upon hitherto unknown variables would become the ultimate weapon in the fight against civil rights—and not knowing (or ignoring) that the Constitution puts the burden of proof with them, prohibitionists have embraced it wholeheartedly.

The dedication to ignorance would serve prohibitionists well. Coupled with the government's propaganda machinery and the people's fondness for scapegoats, everything was set for a defeat of reason, and it worked. As we have seen, until the mid-1970s, wholesome values such as tolerance and understanding had gained more ground; Alaska had already legalized, and a variety of influential organizations wanted the rest of the United States to follow.[196]

This trend, however, would be offset by a regime dedicated to psychosis. And as the fog of war regained influence, the reform movement would not only suffer a retreat, but as the enemy image gained more weight, the forces of tyranny took more powers.

---

[195] Walter Sullivan, *Marijuana Study by U.S. Finds No Serious Harm,* New York Times, July 9, 1975

[196] By 1975, the Consumers Union, American Bar Association, American Public Health Association, Governing Board of the American Medical Association, National Advisory Commission on Criminal Justice Standards and Goals, National Commission on Marijuana and Drug Abuse (The Shafer Commission), National Conference of Commissioners on Uniform State Laws, National Council of Churches, and the National Education Association recommended the removal of all criminal penalties for marijuana possession and personal use.

During Nixon's first term, federal spending increased more than 1000 percent. This produced an apparatus of drug warriors keen on further expansion, and between 1973 and 1993 the enforcement budget increased a total of 12,000 percent.[197] This escalated the prohibitionist psychosis. Drug warriors measured in the millions—and even though the increased budget did nothing to reduce the drug using population or the availability of drugs, it did lead to increased death, horror, and incarceration. While there were 18,815 arrests reported in 1965, by 1971 arrests had risen to 225,828. Two years later, arrests had nearly doubled to 420,700, and this trend would continue. The alienation of drug users also had other effects and while the drug-related death rate in 1979 was 3.2 per 100,000, in 1998 mortality had risen to 7.5 per 100,000,[198] and by 2017 it was 21,7 per 100,000.[199] Hence, the War on Drugs made possible an escalation of terror and tyranny that was unprecedented in US history, and we shall now have a look at the intellectual environment behind the police state.

7.2. THE 1980S: UNCONSCIOUSNESS PREVAILS

"Between 1977 and 1992 a conservative cultural revolution occurred in America. It was called the drug war."[200]

—John Walters, US Drug Czar—

Throughout this period, prohibitionists experienced their heydays. Joined by her favourite scientist, Dr. Gabriel Nahas, the First Lady appealed to the citizenry with her *Just say No* campaign.

---

[197] Juan R. Torruella, *The "War on Drugs": One Judge's Attempt at a Rational Discussion*, Yale Journal on Regulation 14 (1997) 241

[198] Eric E. Sterling, *Drug Policy: A Challenge of Values* (2004) 52

[199] www.cdc.gov/nchs/pressroom/sosmap/drug_poisoning_mortality/drug_poisoning.htm

[200] BAUM, *SMOKE AND MIRRORS* (1996) 104

Propagandists were living large, preaching hatred and intolerance with impunity, and President Reagan together with Vice President George H.W. Bush pressed on for greater powers. In this period, the drug war became militarized. It was now ok for the United States to invade other countries in search of suspected drug smugglers; it was even ok to bomb them and to kill thousands of civilians in the process,[201] and while foreign policy suffered, the US Government enacted no less Orwellian legislation directed at stopping drug users, producers, and traffickers at home.

As in other places, moral panic reached its zenith during the 1980s, and politicians no longer cared to present a case for prohibition. Instead, unconsciousness prevailed to the point where the White House would define all drug use as abuse—and where drug abuse was a moral problem, nothing else. The only reason why people did drugs, authority claimed, was that people were bad; they were disobeying true morality, and the problem was a lack of respect.[202]

Hence, authority would not need to reason with these people.[203] All the drug warriors had to do was to find a way for the citizenry to respect authority, and we know how fake authority craves respect. Spreading fear, misinformation, and violence is the only way, and the War on Drugs was elevated to its logical conclusion when authority began to suppress or delete anything considered objectionable. Because of the ideological breakdown,

---

[201] The US invasion of Panama to arrest General Noriega on drug charges in 1989 is just one example. More shall be said on this in part three.

[202] As Bill Bennett, President Bush's Drug Czar declared, the drug problem was a "crisis of authority", and what was needed was "to reconstitute authority." That is, more prisons, more law enforcement officers and more prosecutors. *Drug Czar: Go After Casual Users, Parents*, Chicago Tribune, May 4, 1989

[203] This psychological predisposition, of course, was evident all along. Already in the 1960's, the hatred for drug users was exemplified by the state prosecution when Timothy Leary, a former teacher at Harvard, tried to defend himself on constitutional grounds: During the proceedings, the prosecutor stated that the appellant was "irresponsible" (especially with reference to the welfare of his children), his defense was a "colossal hoax," "just hogwash", and his emotional perspective was further evident when he stated to the Government counsel that "I cannot remember a case I have felt more strongly about than I have this case," and his further statement that "I don't mean to shout, for shouting's sake, but I feel so strongly about this case and his acts that I can't help myself." *Leary v. United States*, C05. 643, 383 F.2d 851 (1967)

not only could reason not be consulted but history had to be altered. To do so, 64 NIDA pamphlets and other incriminating tracts which refuted the Reagan administration's War on Drugs were removed from public libraries,[204] research was destroyed, and the war on truth would be continued by the Bush administration.

7.2.1. THE BUSH ADMINISTRATION'S WAR ON DRUGS

Forget about thinking in principled terms. During the reign of Bush Sr., even discussing drug abuse as a health-related issue was frowned upon, for as William Bennett, the White House Drug Czar, decreed: "I find no merit in the legalizers' case. The simple fact is that drug use is wrong. And the moral argument, in the end, is the most compelling argument."[205]

Until this point, prohibitionists had been troubled when asked to explain why illicit drug users were persecuted while alcohol users remained free to go. Bennett would not have it. As he said:

"A citizen in a drug-induced haze, whether on his back-yard deck or on a mattress in a ghetto crack house, is not what the founding fathers meant by the 'pursuit of happiness'. Despite the legalizers' arguments that drug use is a matter of 'personal freedom', our nation's notion of liberty is rooted in the ideal of a self-reliant citizenry. Helpless wrecks in treatment centers, men chained by their noses to cocaine—these people are slaves."[206]

Thus, Bennett denied drug users autonomy rights by decreeing that they were slaves—and he was right. By this time, not only

---

[204] BAUM, *SMOKE AND MIRRORS* (1996) 164

[205] William Bennett, *Should Drugs Be Legalized?* Reader's Digest, March 1990

[206] Id.

was it clear that the political process was corrupt;[207] it was evident that the citizenry did not care, and that other institutions of government also had failed. At the courts, for instance, drug users had sought to have their constitutional rights determined more than a hundred times, only to be denied protections inherent in the Constitution.[208] As a result, the social contract was already in shambles, and Bennet only made clear to drug users their true status. According to the U.S. government, the 100 million Americans who would have an interest in taking illicit substances were clearly defined as fiends to society; they would be terrorized by zealots even more indifferent to their fate than the slave owners of old, and Bennett advocated concentration camps for youth and that the military be used to rid the streets of drugs.

This was before he came into office. The Attorney General and others had denied his request, but now that he was in command of the drug war, he would make the most of it. Since quitting his job in disgust at Harvard in 1970, when he caught two undergraduates selling cannabis and administrators chose to forgive, he had staked out a reputation for belligerence. This was a reputation of which he was proud and having a doctorate in philosophy, he was perfect for the job. He would, prohibitionists believed, provide the intellectual alibi for US drug policy—but events did not pan out as planned.

The new Drug Czar's approach to the drug problem was one of "Consequences and Confrontation." "For those guilty of drug offenses", Bennett announced, "punishment must be inevitable"

---

[207] Already in 1938 Congressman John M. Coffee, in vain, sought to gain support for a House Joint Resolution which called for the U.S. Public Health Service to review and evaluate the drug situation. He pointed out that drug prohibition only benefitted gangsters and war-profiteers, while leading to an intolerable amount of human misery among the general populace. He therefore stated that "If we, the representatives of the people, are to continue to let our narcotics authorities conduct themselves in a manner tantamount to upholding and in effect supporting the billion-dollar drug racket, we should at least be able to explain to our constituents why we do so." (EVA BERTRAM ET AL., *DRUG WAR POLITICS: THE PRICE OF DENIAL* (1996) 83). Predictably, nothing came of his request, and while US politicians since then have failed their constitutional duties, professionals have complained about the totalitarian approach since the 1960's. See, for instance, PACKER, *THE LIMITS OF THE CRIMINAL SANCTION* (1968)

[208] MIKALSEN, *CONSTITUTIONAL CHALLENGES TO THE DRUG LAW: A CASE STUDY* (2017)

and parents must be held liable for their children's drug use.[209] To have people respect authority, society should confront them with the consequences of their actions and it was a local responsibility to ensure that every drug user was held accountable.[210] On this basis, Bennett urged prosecutors to go after casual users whose lives were manageable, because their example might send a confusing signal to their friends, neighbours, and children. He also promoted drug-testing of pregnant women, which resulted in many losing custody of their new-born babies, and to get all this done he increased the ONDCP budget with more than 50 percent.

However, as in the first place there was no logical explanation why the government had reduced illicit drug users to slaves and not alcohol users, constitutional scholars and others wondered how he, a former teacher of ethics, could justify reducing the debate to one where drug users were "bad". When pushed on this reasoning, Bennett could never quite explain. Instead, he was always forced to resort to circular logic, replying that "drug use is immoral because drugs are illegal, and drugs are illegal because they're immoral." Being himself an alcohol drinker, a heavy user of tobacco, and a compulsive gambler[211] the irony was complete, but few noticed the deception.

Bennet, therefore, could bully his way around. As the moral climate did not allow for a proper debate, ONDCP continued its strategy of spreading fear and falsehoods; Bennett would present misinformation on Alaska and other liberal regimes,[212] and when

---

[209] *Drug Czar: Go After Casual Users, Parents*, Chicago Tribune, May 4, 1989

[210] Id.

[211] In 2003 Bennett was exposed by Newsweek, The New York Times, and the Washington Monthly as a big-time compulsive gambler who holed up at Las Vegas casinos for three-day binges. Bennett had spent at least $8 million at the slot machines.

[212] This was the standard propaganda coming from Bennett: "Even limited experiments in drug legalization have shown that when drugs are more widely available, addiction skyrockets. In 1975 Italy liberalized its drug law and now has one of the highest heroin related death rates in Western Europe. In Alaska, where marijuana was decriminalized in 1975, the easy atmosphere has increased usage of the drug, particularly among children. Nor does it stop there. Some Alaskan schoolchildren now tout 'coca puffs', marijuana cigarettes laced with cocaine." William Bennett, *Should Drugs Be Legalized?* Reader's Digest, March 1990

asked by a caller on the CNN's Larry King show about the idea of executing street dealers by the Saudi Arabian method of a sword to the neck, Bennett replied, "Morally, I don't have a problem with it." King, amazed, interrupted but Bennett cut him off and said: "It's not a moral problem. I used to teach ethics."

Neither Bennett nor the masses noticed the Orwellian spectacle he had become, and so the American dream continued going from bad to worse. The dumbed-down debate on totalitarian premises made the American public forget all about the 60's and 70's trend of increased tolerance, and even though the percentage of drug users had dropped, the fear of drugs continued to despoil social relations. Thus, polls in 1987-89 confirmed that 83 percent of the U.S population would report drug using family members to the police and that 62 percent had no problem with giving up more freedoms in the War against Drugs.[213]

These were all good news to the drug warriors. The moral panic was a marvel of social engineering,[214] and they could sleep well knowing that high treason went unnoticed.

Hence, it was a glorious time to be Bennett. Not only were offenders vilified, detested, hated, persecuted, imprisoned, and murdered with enhanced intensity; the psychosis was nearly complete, and those who knew better had no say.

It only made sense, then, to focus upon the kids. It was, after all, difficult to convince those who knew a thing or two about

---

[213] BAUM, *SMOKE AND MIRRORS* (1996) 241, 277

[214] The propaganda campaign would be noted by many. Here, professor Fish: "For decades the federal government—the President, the Congress, and the courts—as well as state governments, both political parties, and a wide array of extra governmental forces have combined to stifle the expression of a simple truth: drug prohibition, and its instrument of oppression, the war on drugs, makes the drug problem worse rather than better by creating a giant black market; America has the world's worst drug problem because America has the world's worst drug policy." JEFFERSON M. FISH (ED.), *HOW TO LEGALIZE DRUGS* (1998) xvi. Professors Duke and Cross put it this way: "The government goes to great efforts to keep Americans from understanding that most deaths from drug overdoses are the products of prohibition, not the intrinsic qualities of the drugs themselves; that virtually all of the drug-related crime is the result of prohibition, not the pharmacological properties of the drugs; that the drug business as we know it is solely and entirely the consequence of prohibition. As a result, Americans attribute the evils of prohibition to illicit drugs themselves. The government calculatedly promotes such beliefs." STEVEN B. DUKE & ALBERT C. CROSS, *AMERICA'S LONGEST WAR: RETHINKING OUR TRAGIC CRUSADE AGAINST DRUGS* (1993) 159

constitutional law and life in general that prohibition had any merit, and so Bennett befriended the young. To further escalate persecution, he travelled high schools to enlist kids in the War on Drugs, and to Bennett betraying parents was not enough. He also instructed students to tell on their friends—and to those who had second thoughts, this philosopher king smugly added: "It isn't snitching or betrayal to tell an adult that a friend of yours is using drugs and needs help. It's an act of true loyalty, of true friendship."[215]

Because of this, more kids began to call the police on their parents and others involved with drugs, and the Drug Czar "was not worried that students would make false allegations."[216]

---

[215] THOMAS SZASZ, *OUR RIGHT TO DRUGS: THE CASE FOR A FREE MARKET* (1992) 79

[216] Ibid.

7.3. THE UNITED STATES AS A POLICE STATE

"This country's Founders would be disappointed with what we have done to their legacy of liberty: The War on Drugs, by its very nature, is a war on the Bill of Rights. When the Founders rebelled against British tyranny, they grounded their cause in a belief in the natural rights of the individual and the Enlightenment ideas of progress through reason. Understanding the dangers of an excessive concentration of political power, they divided and limited the reach of that power through a federal structure with the states, the separation of powers among the three branches, and the guarantees of personal freedom in the Constitution itself and in the Bill of Rights. With the War on Drugs, however, the wisdom of the Founders has been cast aside. In their shortsighted zeal to create a 'Drug-Free America' . . . our political leaders—state and federal, elected and appointed—have acted as though the end justifies the means, repudiating our heritage of limited government and individual freedoms while endowing the bureaucratic state with unprecedented powers." [217]

—Steven Wisotsky, professor of law—

The 1980s was the decade when the prohibitionist psychosis ruled supreme. Since then, the trend towards regulation of cannabis has been increasing, but authority has fought it as well as it could. In the period until today, therefore, not only has there been a widening gap between theory and practice but between the people and their government. While the former, collectively, have come to greater appreciation of their autonomy rights, the latter has become more influenced by totalitarian premises, and we shall see how this dynamic has shaped society.

---

[217] Wisotsky, *A Society of Suspects: The War on Drugs and our Civil Liberties*, Cato Institute Policy Analysis No. 180, 1992

7.3.1. TYRANNY AND INTEGRITY: AMERICAN STYLE

"When I became an agent, I thought I was out there stopping the flow of narcotics, being an aid to society, helping people out, taking it off the street and all that. I just didn't realize how crooked the bureau was and how people really don't care. I think I believed all the propaganda I read. I felt really bad that I would go to somebody and say, 'Hey, I'm somebody I'm not and I want to buy some narcotics and I'm not an agent.' I felt bad deceiving people and I felt bad busting people. It still makes me feel guilty. I shouldn't have been an agent. I don't like to lie to people and trick them and stuff. It's a hypocritical way of living and I don't like to live that way. After a while, it's all just a lie. You don't know the truth from a lie, you're so used to it. I began to figure I was just a big fraud. And I think the bureau's a fraud. They're a corrupt, unethical organization. I think they ought to be looked into and they ought to be stopped."[218]

—Pat Saunders, former Narcotics agent—

Contrary to popular lore, the United States is no longer governed by the rule of law. Instead, the U.S. government has become a tool for elite factions dedicated to the overthrow of wholesome values and part three will make this clear. The United States, then, is in big trouble. And while nobody likes waking up to trouble, not only is it plain to see that the political system with time has become more influenced by special interest groups than reason; it is also easy to deduce that the interest of factions such as Big Pharma, Wall Street, the police, the prison system, and the military industrial complex is opposed to that of the ordinary man and woman.

---

[218] David Harris, *An Inside Look at Federal Narcotics Enforcement*, Rolling Stone, December 5, 1974

Hence, we need not look at it from a perspective of conspiracy theory to understand why the U.S. government, after more than 200 years of being an arena for these groups to clash, make amends, cooperate, and prosper, has come to represent the interest of war profiteers rather than its people. Despite assurances to the contrary, the evidence is overwhelming. And it is for this reason that the War on Drugs persists, and a majority do not trust in the government.

That there is a connection is self-evident. If the United States government really represented the interests of the people, officials would have gone with principled thinking and abided by the social contract. Politicians would be virtuous and truth be their leading light, but this is not the case. Instead, the difference between what politicians say and do is apparent to the point where nine out of ten Americans have lost confidence in their trade,[219] and the War on Drugs is just one indication of how war profiteers have come to influence policy. Without an apparatus dedicated to keep the wheels of war running, people would follow their natural drive to cooperate and thrive; they would crave a government that provided actual services, and this is not what shadowy rulers want. Top positions, therefore, are filled with spineless individuals who cater to the will of power rather than reason. But even though the drug war remains embraced by authority, its destructive impact has not gone unnoticed.

Indeed, of the countries discussed, the American government has to the greatest extent left constitutional ground. No matter how hard false authority pushes, however, there will always be a shove, and it is no coincidence that the United States is the country with the most potent reform movement. Looking at the constitutionality of the drug laws, many have noted the basic

---

[219] "Just 7 percent of Americans surveyed said they have 'a great deal' or 'quite a lot' of confidence overall in Congress, down from 10 percent last year, the non-partisan polling firm said. 'This is the lowest confidence score Gallup has recorded for any institution— ever,' Gallup said in a statement. 'This is also the first time Gallup has ever measured confidence in a major U.S. institution in the single digits.'" Susan Heavey, *Poll finds confidence in U.S. Congress at historic low*, Reuters, June 19, 2014

problem with first principles,[220] and even magistrates of the court have been known to agree. As noted, Alaska legalized the recreational use of cannabis in 1975 for reasons of individual liberty, and other courts has had justices who opposed the drug law but had to settle for dissent. [221]

Despite the magistrates' traditional fear of being seen as political activists, some would write books and articles

---

[220] Some professionals who have critiqued the drug war include: Margaret P. Battin, Arthur G. Lipman, Paul M. Gahlinger, Douglas E. Rollins, Jeanette C. Roberts, Troy L. Booher (*Drugs and Justice: Seeking a Consistent, Coherent, and Comprehensive View*, 2008), Norval Morris & Gordon Hawkins (*The Honest Politician's Guide to Crime Control*, 1970), Charles H. Whitebread (*Us and Them and the Nature of Moral Regulation*, Southern California Law Review Vol. 74:361), Steven Wisotsky (*Beyond the War on Drugs: Overcoming a Failed Policy*, 1990; *A Society of Suspects: the War on Drugs and our Civil Liberties*, 1992), Steven B. Duke (*Drug Prohibition: An Unnatural Disaster*, 1995), Timothy Lynch (*After Prohibition: an Adult Approach to Drug Policies in the 21st Century*, 2000), Andrew Weil & Winnifred Rosen (*From Chocolate to Morphine: Everything You Need to Know about Mind-Altering Drugs*, 2004), Doris Marie Provine (*Unequal under Law: Race in the War on Drugs*, 2007),), Randy E. Barnett (Bad Trip: Drug Prohibition and the Weakness of Public Policy, 1994), Troy Duster (*Legislation of Morality: Law, Drugs, and Moral Judgment*), Mitch Earleywine (*Pot politics: Marijuana and the costs of prohibition*), Steven B. Duke & Albert C. Gross (*America's Longest War: Rethinking Our Tragic Crusade Against Drugs*, 1993), Rufus King (*The Drug Hang-up: America's Fifty-year Folly*), Andrew D. Leipold (*The War on Drugs and the Puzzle of Deterrence*, 2002), Graham Boyd (*Collateral Damage in the War on Drugs*, 2002), Frank Rudy Cooper (*The Unbalanced Fourth Amendment: A Cultural Study of the Drug War, Racial Profiling and Arvizu*, 2002), Elliot G. Hicks (*Shooting Ourselves in The Foot in The Drug War*, 1999), John F. Galliher, David P. Keys & Michael Elsner (*Lindesmith v. Anslinger: An Early Government Victory in the Failed War on Drugs*, 1998), Daniel D. Polsby (*Ending The War on Drugs And Children*, 1997), Erik Grant Luna (*Our Vietnam: The Prohibition Apocalypse*, 1997), Steven Jonas (*The Drug War: Myth, Reality And Politics*, 1995), Helen M. Kemp (*Presumed Guilty: When the War on Drugs Becomes a War on The Constitution*, 1994), Doug Bandow (*War on Drugs or War on America?* 1991), David Elkins (*Drug Legalization: Cost Effective and Morally Permissible*, 1991), Robinson & Scherlen (*Lies, Damn Lies, and Drug War Statistics*, 2007), Jeffrey A. Miron (*Drug War Crimes: The Consequences of Prohibition*, 2004), Lester Grinspoon (*Marijuana Reconsidered*, 1977). A book that includes many expert voices is James A. Inciardi and Karen McElrath (ed.), *The American Drug Scene* (forty-one authors from a wide range of fields), and another book that presents a broad range of experts is Jefferson Fish, *How to Legalize Drugs* (thirty authors, also from many fields).

[221] Justice Kobayashi of the Supreme Court of Hawaii (and former Attorney General) was one: "It has not been shown that consumption of marijuana is any more harmful than a comparable consumption of alcohol and it is doubtful that the presently known effects of marijuana are as adverse as those of alcohol. Until legitimate research indicates otherwise, the harm created by placing a criminal sanction on the activity of a significant percentage of our population who would otherwise be law abiding citizens far outweighs any present benefit to be derived from the effects of classifying marijuana as a narcotic. There is no logical or otherwise rational reason for our society, on the basis of a law that has little or no merit in its application, to continue to make criminals out of and consequently alienate the youth of today. *State v. Kantner*, 493 P.2d 306 (1972) at 320 (Kobayashi, J., dissenting))

denouncing drug prohibition and one is Juan R. Torruella, a United States Circuit Judge. In 1996, he wrote a public letter, reminding that "Ever since, [its discovery] the American continent has existed between dream and reality, in a divorce between the good society that we desire and the imperfect society in which we really live."[222] In this regard, he called attention to the premises of prohibition, noting that its "enforcement has had a devastating impact on the rights of the individual citizen" and that "the control costs are seriously threatening the preservation of values that are central to our form of government."[223]

There are other intellectuals who have warned against the trend of emerging tyranny,[224] and Craig Reinarman, a Professor of Sociology and Legal Studies at the University of California, observed it thus:

"Under the banner of the war on drugs, a kind of creeping totalitarianism tramples more human rights and civil liberties each year. Tens of millions of citizens—most of whom have never used drugs and all of whom are supposed to be presumed innocent—are subjected to supervised urine tests to get jobs and then to keep jobs. Hundreds of thousands more are searched in their homes or, on the basis of racist 'trafficker profiles,' on freeways and at airports. Houses, cars, and businesses are seized by the state on the slimmest of suspicions alone. And U.S. school children have

---

[222] Juan R. Torruella, *One Judge's Attempt at a Rational Discussion of the So-called War on Drugs* (1996)

[223] Id.

[224] "Are we being hysterical in categorizing present drug law as a form of servitude? No, our drug laws amount to partial slavery. We must all question the practices of roadblocks, strip-searches, urine tests, locker searches, and money laundering laws. Philosophically speaking, drug prohibition severely threatens our civil liberties and is inconsistent with the anti-slavery philosophy and the founding documents of the United States. The legalization of drugs would give a basic civil liberty back to U.S. citizens, by granting them control over their own bodies." Meaghan Cussen & Walter E. Block, *Legalize Drugs Now! An Analysis of the Benefits of Legalized Drugs*, American Journal of Economics and Sociology, Vol. 59, No. 3, July 2000.

been bombarded with more antidrug propaganda than any generation in history. "[225]

This is only the top layer of the control costs that accommodate a War on Drugs. Compared to the nuisance experienced by the drug users, producers, and salesmen, they are obviously insignificant. Even so, to those not directly affected by the persecution, these costs are reminders of its totalitarian basis and it is easy to see why the government's agenda is opposed by integrity. To the extent that a War on Drugs is encouraged, these and other control costs must increase, and as the 1980s progressed, this dynamic ensured that more and more opposed the drug war.

A notable example is Eric Sterling, the Executive Director of The Criminal Justice Policy Foundation, an organization that helps educate about criminal justice issues and failed global drug policy. I say "notable" because, before coming to this position, he was a firm believer in prohibition and a principal aide in developing the Comprehensive Crime Control Act of 1984, the Anti-Drug Abuse Acts of 1986 and 1988, as well as other legislation. As a counsel to the Subcommittee on Crime, however, he saw how policy was driven by scapegoating and reversed his position. At a presentation before the Colorado Bar Association in 1989, he had this to say:

"Essentially the legal basis for the War on Drugs depends on the assumption of total power by the Congress and the Federal government to regulate the most intimate aspects of our lives, the very dreams that we have. And the propaganda arm of the War on Drugs has been successful in persuading us to unwittingly surrender this vital power over ourselves to the Federal government. Indeed, the propaganda of the urgency of the War on Drugs has been so successful, many

---

[225] Craig Reinarman, *The Dutch example shows that liberal drug laws can be beneficial* (2000)

of our fellow citizens consciously believe we must surrender ourselves for the good of the state. Seen in this light, the War on Drugs is the corner stone of an as yet unbuilt edifice of totalitarianism. Challenging the War on Drugs is the most important issue facing civil liberties and the preservation of the Bill of Rights. "[226]

This was 1990, and the police state would only advance. After the terror attacks of 9/11, the War on Terror was added to the picture, and building upon this enemy image what was left of constitutional protections would become obliterated. Today, therefore, thanks to legislation such as the Patriot Act and the Freedom Act, authority has the legislative framework needed to deal with all perceived threats—and it should come as a concern that violent opposition is not a requirement for becoming identified as a terrorist. More than a million non-violent Americans are currently placed on such lists, and their common denominator is that they oppose the status quo.

Just as the Reagan administration's revision of history, therefore, these are ominous signs of a system that is prepared to embrace any means to maintain its grip on the populace; this brings misery and moral confusion, and we shall now have a look at the corruption that comes with the territory.

---

[226] RUSSELL, *DRUG WAR* (2000) 591

7.3.2. The Corruption of Prohibition

"I'm not proud of what I did. It was a dirty job. It was a form of amorality, and to this day I feel tremendous guilt and have unending nightmares as a result of what I did as a narcotics agent."[227]

—Jim Attie, FBN agent for 35 years—

The corruptive influence of the drugs economy is difficult to fathom. On the one hand, there is the ever-increasing budgets which serves as a financial motive for continued psychosis, and on the other there is the black-market economy measuring hundreds of billions. Because of this economy, temptation, treachery, and hypocrisy is everywhere to be found;[228] and because authority, the harder it has fought the drug war, has lost its moral compass, it is not so easy to separate good guys from bad guys. Judge James P. Gray elaborates:

"Law enforcement corruption, sparked mostly by illicit drugs, has become so chronic that the number of federal, state, and local police and law enforcement officials serving terms in federal prisons increased fivefold in four years, from 107 in 1994 to 548 in 1998. In Los Angeles, twenty-six members of the sheriff's office were convicted after a six-year investigation for skimming drug money they had seized. In Philadelphia, a judge threw out nine drug convictions

---

[227] Douglas Valentine, *The Strength of the Wolf* (2004) 292

[228] Professor Alan A. Block observed thus: "Police corruption, when it comes to drug enforcement, is legendary. About a quarter of a century ago in New York an investigation into narcotics found police eager to be assigned to Harlem drug work in order to make extra money. Some used their political patrons to help them get transferred. In fact, the New York State Commission of Investigation (1972) reported that drug corruption had become an equal opportunity issue. Black politicians tried to intercede for black cops 'certain that the black policemen were being discriminated against because they were not allowed to participate in the graft and corruption on the Narcotics Squad' that worked Harlem. Recurring scandals in the U.S. and elsewhere make it clear that policing narcotics has become the most criminogenic of occupations." Traver & Gaylord (Ed.), *Drugs, Law and the State: A Reexamination of the Physics of Motion* (1992) xx

after he found that six police officers had planted drugs on the suspects, stolen their money, and falsified police reports. In Fort Lauderdale, Florida, five years after DEA supervisor Rene de la Cova had received great notoriety for taking former Panamanian strongman Manuel Noriega into custody, de la Cova plead guilty to stealing $760 000 in laundered drug money and was sentenced to prison. In New Orleans, eleven police officers and a civilian employee were convicted and about two hundred police officers were fired after an FBI sting operation disclosed that they were involved in widespread violence and theft of cocaine from drug dealers.

. . . Not only is this drug-money corruption a problem of enormous concern in its own right, but additional lawless behaviour is derived from it as well. For example, the entire southern California area was shocked in September 1999 when a former officer of the Rampart Division of the LAPD who had been convicted of stealing eight pounds of cocaine started testifying about drug-related offenses. He confessed that he and fellow officers had been stealing drugs and drug money from drug dealers, using prostitutes to sell the drugs for them, planting evidence, and committing perjury repeatedly in court. He further testifies that he and a fellow officer had shot an unarmed black man they believed was a drug dealer, after he was in handcuffs, and then framed him by planting a sawed off .22 rifle on him and testifying falsely that the man had assaulted them with it. That young man was convicted, and had already served three years of his twenty-three-year sentence before the truth came out. Worse yet, the police bullets will keep this man in a wheel-chair for the rest of his life."[229]

---

[229] GRAY, *WHY OUR DRUG LAWS HAVE FAILED AND WHAT WE CAN DO ABOUT IT* (2001) 74-75

Subsequent investigation revealed that at least 28 more officers from the LAPD were involved in similar schemes, making it clear that more than hundred citizens had been wrongfully convicted. Similar stories have been told before, not least of the New York Police Department,[230] and this is a problem with big city police squads. The personal relationship between them and the citizenry is not only strained, but a culture has evolved which makes officers prone to justify lying and other improprieties to beat criminals at their own game. This immorality has planted deep roots, and former police officer Barry Cooper estimates that as much as 85 percent of the U.S. police force commit perjury, steal, and plant evidence to improve statistics.

Now, as we are raised to see America as a shining example, this seems like a lot. However, we already know that the police, backed by the system, murder more than 1000 citizens a year, and the US police apparatus has come to look like something out of Orwell's *1984*.

This was the reason why Barry Cooper quit the force. He had been working as a narcotics officer for eight years, convinced of the drug war's merits, but a daily routine of invading other people's homes made his stomach slowly turn. Being a family man himself, it was not easy to process a career spent on wrongful persecution, and his job description made him sink into depression. As he recalled those days:

"I was upset and crying because I've got four kids that I see every day, and we are big on family. And then I remembered the look of kids on these raids that I was involved in; kicking

---

[230] In 1986, in New York City's 77th Precinct, twelve police officers were arrested for stealing and selling drugs. Miami's problem was of no less magnitude. In June 1986, seven officers were indicted for using their jobs to run a drug operation that used murders, threats, and bribery. Norm Stamper, a policeman for 34 years, and a former Chief of Police, has more to say: "As an illicit commodity, drugs cost and generate extravagant sums of (laundered, untaxed) money, a powerful magnet for character-challenged police officers. Although small in numbers of offenders, there isn't a major police force . . . that has escaped the problem: cops, sworn to uphold the law, seizing and converting drugs to their own use, planting dope on suspects, robbing and extorting pushers, taking up dealing themselves, intimidating or murdering witnesses." Norm Stamper, *Legalize drugs—all of them*, LA Times, December 4, 2005

in doors at 3 o'clock in the morning after throwing in a flash-grenade, mom and dad screaming, and we're screwing pistols into their ears, and the kids are screaming and then we haul the kids off to the Department of Human Services. And I remember these kids crying, and you know that didn't go away just because I left that house. That person is marked forever with that terror.[231]

Around 50,000 such violent police raids are committed every year. Cooper briefly summarized this experience from the perspective of the victims and the brutality is horrific. As we can see, however, also the oppressors are traumatized by these events, for they are in the same position as soldiers fighting illegal wars. Despite authority's best efforts to the contrary, man was not built to kill and plunder—and no matter how many Medals of Honour the soldiers receive, they can sense that something is wrong. The numbers of military veterans who commit suicide and suffer from PTSD is evidence for this—and even if this has been a topic of scientific neglect, we can expect the rest of the U.S. police squad to suffer much as Barry.

The tougher these people appear on the outside, the more they suffer on the inside, and luckily for these veterans, there are medicines that have been known to improve their condition. Foremost among them are plants and substances such as ayahuasca, LSD, psilocybin, MDMA and cannabis,[232] and Barry discovered the therapeutic effects of the latter when he met his girlfriend. Not only did it provide relief from anxiety, but it helped deprogram psychosis and rearrange his value system. From this point Cooper found healing and redemption in becoming an activist for change.[233]

---

[231] Interview with Cooper at the Alex Jones Show, January 7, 2009.

[232] See *supra* note 130.

[233] "[Marijuana] helped me. It made me a more compassionate person, and I stopped and slowed down [drinking] long enough to realize the harms I was creating on this earth instead of helping". Interview with Alex Jones, January 7, 2009. For more on Barry Cooper, see: www.neverget busted.com and www.copbusters.com

We shall meet others, and another drug warrior that can attest to the endemic state of corruption is Sandalio "Sandy" Gonzalez. She was a DEA agent for 27 years, at one point running agency operations in South America. Even so, she was fired in 2005 after blowing the whistle on how agents working with immigration and customs authorities (ICE) let an informant murder and kill at least a dozen people in a house in Ciudad Juarez, Mexico. She summarizes her experience in law enforcement thus: "[I]n general I think there is a tendency throughout the government to cover up misconduct, whether it's informant-related or otherwise. At least in the law enforcement agencies . . . I think the American people would be justified in believing that their own government may be as corrupt as any of the countries our government criticizes for corruption."[234]

7.3.3. Drug Enforcement and Social Calamity

"From 1972-1981 I was primarily in Washington DC, and hated it. With nary an exception, the government employees in Washington running the drug agencies enforcement and treatment were the most naive people I ever met on the drug issue. US drug policies are deliberately ignorant, mean-spirited and socially destructive, yet unstoppable. My views and government policy were so at odds that my best years from 1974-1981 was spent on a farm."[235]

—Jerry Mandel, Professor of Sociology—

The surreal level of corruption and intellectual despondency that we have touched upon is another sign of a system gone haywire—

---

²³⁴ Radley Balko, *The House of Death: An interview with DEA whistleblower Sandy Gonzalez*, 30. September 2008. http://www.reason.com/news/show/128893.html

²³⁵ http://sociology.berkeley.edu/jerry-mandel-1960

one that is hell-bent on crushing integrity where it is found. Hence, authority instinctively rejects the implications of principled reasoning, the police are trained to see the citizenry as its enemy, and the game is rigged against the individual. When it comes to the justice system, this trend is clearly seen, and under the Bush administration the Justice Department doubled the number of state attorneys while the lawyers at the American Bar Association were being treated as deserters and not welcome at headquarters.[236]

Because of this pressure to maintain psychosis, it is difficult to find magistrates who honour the implications of first principles, and the judicial system ensures that no one stands a chance. If you cannot afford a lawyer, the system will provide one so overwhelmed with clients that all he can do is to recommend you make a deal. If you can afford a lawyer, you may have a "friend" that will fight the system until you can pay no more, but the odds are poor. The Department of Justice has a 93 percent conviction rate,[237] and so you will be advised to cooperate, plead guilty, and make a deal.

In the United States, however, it is very much the prosecutor, not the judge, that determines the outcome of proceedings and 94,6-97 percent of all Federal Court cases are plea bargains.[238] The reason why is the Mandatory Minimum legislation, enacted in 1986. The system then transferred powers to the prosecution by erecting a framework for sentencing which was for the U.S. State Attorney, not the judge, to pick and choose. To have any chance in this system, therefore, cooperation with the prosecution is a prerequisite—and for any relief in sentencing, information on criminal activity must be provided. Because of this, many lower-level criminals who knew nothing has ended up with longer sentences than drug kingpins who were willing to snitch, and

---

[236] BAUM, *SMOKE AND MIRRORS* (1996) 292

[237] *United States Attorneys' Annual Statistical Report for Fiscal Year 2012*, United States Department of Justice.

[238] PROVINE, *UNEQUAL UNDER LAW* (2007) 164

another indication of the conditions for the rule of law is the legislation surrounding asset forfeiture.

7.3.3.1. ASSET FORFEITURE

In 1978, Congress enacted a law which made it possible for the DEA to profit more directly on the War on Drugs, and with the 1984 Comprehensive Crime Control Act this was expanded upon. From this point on the troops could loot at will and Judge Gray describes their operations:

> *"The statutory scheme involving asset forfeiture is unprecedented in U.S. legal history. Not only can property be forfeited without a criminal conviction, but about 80 percent of the people whose property is taken are not even charged with a criminal offense. Further, these laws require that the people from whom the property is seized have the burden to prove that it was not used to facilitate the sale of drugs or purchased with drug money. In other words, the property owners are presumed to be guilty. Never before in the history of U.S. jurisprudence has the burden been placed on the individual citizens to prove their innocence. As every schoolchild knows—or should know—it is supposed to be the other way around."[239]*

Gray forgets that the asset forfeiture scheme was not the first time in U.S. jurisprudence that the liberty presumption was turned. As we have seen, it has been the problem with the drug laws all along, but this neglect aside he is among the magistrates capable of principled reasoning.[240] Consequently, knowing that

---

[239] GRAY, *WHY OUR DRUG LAWS HAVE FAILED AND WHAT WE CAN DO ABOUT IT* (2001) 118

[240] A case study done on constitutional challenges to the drug laws reveal that no more than ten percent of judges apply principled reasoning to drug cases. The rest remain too enthralled by psychosis to put two and two together, and so principled reasoning on the

the drug laws would make the founders turn in their graves, he has been important to the reform movement.

As pertains to asset forfeiture, a closer examination reveals that the game is rigged against the individual and everything is arranged for a theft. Only to make a claim against their own possessions the citizenry must pay a fee of $200—and as the cops get to keep what they take, there is an incentive for abuse. Today, entire departments depend upon the valuables they collect, and this has resulted in a heap of abuses. Only to mention a few, there is Paul and Ruth Derbacher of Connecticut who lost their house because their grandson, which they had raised since he was 10, had used cannabis and cocaine in his room. There is Elizabeth Young, an 80-year-old widow in poor health, who lost her house and her car because her grandson, who lived with her, had stored drugs on these premises. And there is James Burton, a 37-year-old man with Glaucoma, who, in addition to a year imprisonment, lost his house because he grew cannabis plants as medicine.

Many thousands have experienced the same, and while most get to keep their life, some do not. An example is Donald Scott, a near blind 61-year-old man who owned a two hundred acres farm in Malibu, California. On October 2, 1992, two dozen officers, plus national guard units, plus the DEA, plus the L.A. Sheriff's Department (thirty armed men in full combat gear) broke in and entered his home on a "tip" from an anonymous "informant" that Scott was growing marijuana. As they knocked down his door, Scott thought that the armed officers were robbers and grabbed a pistol. The drug warriors then killed him and took his property (which, before operations, they had estimated to be worth $5 million). No trial by jury, no search warrant, no arrest, no cause for armed robbery: there was no marijuana found anywhere on his property—drug warriors just wanted it.[241]

---

subject is always found in dissents. MIKALSEN, *CONSTITUTIONAL CHALLENGES TO THE DRUG LAW* (2017)

[241] These examples are found in BAUM, *SMOKE AND MIRRORS* (1996) 243, 319-21, and Louis S. Rulli, *Seizing Family Homes from the Innocent: Can the Eighth Amendment Protect Minorities and the Poor from Excessive Punishment in Civil Forfeiture?* (2017)

These examples are by no means unique, and this has become a lucrative deal for authority. Between 1986 and 1990 alone, the US Justice Department confiscated $1.5 billion worth of valuables and kept 95 percent of the profits.[242] Add to this that 80 percent was from civilians not accused of a crime and it should be obvious why, in the introduction, I said that the morality of prohibition is one of thugs.

We have already seen how Bennett and the ONDCP travelled high schools, encouraging students to give up their friends and loved ones. In times of tyranny, becoming a snitch is always encouraged and an environment of distrust persists. Hence, if you pay with cash at the airport or elsewhere, you can expect clerks to want an explanation, and if not satisfied they will call the police. Authority then collects—and the informant is given 10 percent. Adding to the everyday vigilante, there are informants who receive regular salaries. Perhaps as much as 100,000 citizens are engaged in these affairs and according to the television show 60-Minutes, the Justice Department spent at least $40 million in one year paying for their services.

Money is one thing. Another is the morality that comes with betrayal, and a third is its consequences—broken relations and lives ruined. An operation by the police in Arizona should suffice as an example. In 1989, the Arizona police imported 9 tons of cannabis which it sold on to the community through informants. Not only did 7 out of 9 tons disappear without no one accounting for them, but this sting made it possible to profit legally by the help of asset forfeiture laws. This netted another $3 million from detainees—and if we really want to go into details, here is the morality encouraged by prohibitionists: The DEA "paid a handsome informant $73 000 to seduce innocent women into drug deals so they could be busted. Eighteen women, most with no criminal record, were tricked into prison after the informant

---

[242] Ibid., 282, 321.

promised them love and marriage in return for 'one little favour.'"[243]

This, then, is the price we pay by letting drug warriors roam free. To fill their quotas and justify their budgets they arrest 1,5 million drug users every year, the majority being cannabis smokers. As we have seen, however, they cast a wide net, and among the prison population there are many others who should never have been there.

7.3.4. The Spectrum of Dominance and Incarceration

"It's not a stretch to conclude that our Draconian approach to drug use is the most injurious domestic policy since slavery."[244]

—Norm Stamper, former Chief of Police—

Because of escalating persecution, there has been an increase in the prison population. Looking at this, there was slight variation in statistics from the post-World War period until the late 1970's. As in Europe and Canada, the imprisonment rate was around 100 prisoners per 100,000 people, but the drug policies of the 1980s contributed to a climb. This resulted in a doubling of incarcerated and the rise continued until 2008.

Thus, while the United States in 1980 had approximately 500,000 prisoners, the figure today is 2.3 million. And while the percentage of drug convicts in federal prisons in 1970 was at 16 percent, it is now more than 60 percent. We can see from this why the United States has become known as "Incarceration Nation." America holds one fourth of the world's inmate population and not even China, with its 1.3 million prisoners, comes close.

---

[243] Ibid., 277

[244] Norm Stamper, *Legalize Drugs—All of Them*, LA Times, December 4, 2005

Despite what some may assume, these statistics do not mirror an increase in crime. According to the data, real crime in America (which included real victims) went down 25 percent in the period between 1988 and 2008,[245] and this escalation in incarceration is the result of a political process that caters to populism and corporate interests. Because there is money to be made by encouraging fear, speculators have profited on the War on Drugs to the point where entire cities rely on the prison industry for jobs.[246] This financial incentive, coupled with power political pressure, has ensured an increasing apparatus dedicated to dominance, and while Americans in 1982 spent $35 billion on their criminal justice system, by 2006 the amount had reached $214 billion. An estimated $100 billion to the police, $47 billion to the justice system, and 70 billion to prison authorities.[247] Adding to this comes another $100 billion spent on private security, not to mention the military with almost $1 trillion. This is nearly as much as the rest of the world combined, and one can safely say that Americans have lost their ways.

This obsession with dominance and control, after all, must mirror the extent to which the people have abandoned the ideals, values, and principles of their founders. Even so, because the citizenry refuses to face that they have been seduced by false authority, the masses continue to worship foreign and national campaigns of terror and the collective psyche is split between an inner allegiance to truth and loyalty to authority. Until the people wake up and question their authorities, therefore, the psychosis will only worsen as the war profiteers control the political process—and they do not mind murder to maintain a hold on power.

---

[245] Solomon Moore, *Prison Spending Outpaces All but Medicaid*, New York Times, March 2, 2009

[246] According to the American Jail Association, in 1994, more than 100,000 were working at local prisons and this market was worth $65 billion. NILS CHRISTIE, *KRIMINALITETSKONTROLL SOM INDUSTRI* (2000) 104

[247] *Sourcebook of Criminal Justice Statistics Online* at http://www.albany.edu/sourcebook/pdf/ t122006.pdf

Indeed, assassination and cover ups have been as prevalent on the American continent as any other. To the elite, staying in power depends upon maintaining an unhealthy level of fear, and without a War on Drugs, events would grind to a halt. If it were not for the psychosis it generates, people would follow their natural inclination to cooperate and thrive and the world would be a more blissful place. Prohibitionists, however, do not want this. They want a world without drug users, and they are ready to terrorize until they give up.

We have previously seen how a tight knit community of prohibitionists has kept reason at bay and they all have a stake in the status quo. Bennett, for instance, made a fat living feeding off enemy images and has continued to do so till this day. Other prohibitionists are Robert DuPont and Carlton Turner. From 1971 to 1980, Turner (while working at the University of Mississippi) was responsible for NIDA's cannabis crops and he went on to become the Reagan administration's Drug Czar. Throughout this period, he not only recommend the death penalty for drug sales but when the DEA sprayed cannabis crops with Paraquat, he would defend the decision, affirming that dying cannabis users got what they deserved.

No doubt, he meant business. Indeed, Turner would make a healthy profit selling Paraquat-test-kits which did not work, and when he in 1986 was forced to resign (because of comments that cannabis smoking would lead to homosexuality, immune deficiency, and AIDS), he continued to profit on the drug laws privately. Together with DuPont and Pete Bensinger, these guys wined and dined the right people and in return made millions selling most of the United States' (and probably the world's) urine-sample equipment.[248]

As long as the drug war is this kind of milking cow, we cannot expect them to vote for change. The War on Drugs, therefore, is continuing to ruin lives—and while a few stand to profit, society falls apart. As criminologists know, nothing is less cost-efficient

---

[248] JACK HERER, *THE EMPEROR WEARS NO CLOTHES* (1998) 114-15

than removing non-violent citizens from their community. It can only make matters worse,[249] and if the moral argument is not likely to convince so should economic considerations. It costs society as much to imprison an individual for one year ($23,000) as it takes to get ten through college, and that a greater percentage of blacks are incarcerated than enrolled in universities should be a warning.[250]

According to Project Censored, the persecution of cannabis users costs between $10-12 billion a year and not only does arrest result in unemployment; when released, they come out as second-class citizens, stripped of basic civil rights like the right to vote, the right to serve on juries, and the right to be free of legal discrimination in employment, housing, access to public benefits. In sum, there are around 400 services for with drug law violators are not eligible,[251] and this is tearing society apart.

Another example that speaks to the state of affairs is California. Between 1984 and 1999, twenty prisons were built to house the flood of inmates; in the same period, only one university was built, and there are more prisoners in this state than in France, England, Germany, Japan, and Holland combined—even though California has one tenth of the population. As in other places, Blacks and other minorities are especially targeted.

---

[249] As noted by Doris Marie Provine: "Long prison terms, as have been well documented, tend to exacerbate social inequalities, to create dysfunctional personal relationships, and to produce more imprisonment. State and federal legislatures have created additional penalties that make those convicted of crimes ineligible for public assistance, education loans, driving privileges, public housing, and food stamps. Most states restrict rights to vote, and many make it easier to terminate parental rights. Some felons are required to register with the police for the remainder of their lives, and some can be deported." PROVINE, *UNEQUAL UNDER LAW* (2007) 19

[250] ROY KRØVEL, *KOKAINKRIGEN: 20 ÅR AV EN VELSIGNET FORBANNELSE* (2004) 32

[251] ROBINSON & SCHERLEN, *LIES, DAMN LIES, AND DRUG WAR STATISTICS* (2007) 30

7.3.4.1 THE RACIAL COMPONENT

"Afro-Americans represent 12 percent of the population in the United States, 13 percent of illicit drug users, 35 percent of those arrested for drug possession, 55 percent of those convicted for drug possession and 74 percent of those sent to prison for drug possession. There is an urgent need for examination of these polices from a human rights perspective, let alone a health perspective."[252]

—Report from Australian Drug Law Reform Foundation—

Because the drug law took over after the Jim Crow laws as a mechanism for continuing the scapegoating phenomenon,[253] it comes as no surprise that drug enforcement has been inherently racist. When it comes to drug crimes, Human Rights Watch has shown that Afro-Americans are incarcerated at 13.4 times the rate of whites,[254] and consequences are noticeable. In 2003, nearly 8 percent of all adult African American males were imprisoned on any given day, and those born in 2001 or later have a 32 percent chance of being incarcerated at some point in his life, compared to a 17 percent chance for a Hispanic boy, and a 6 percent chance for a white boy.[255]

Adding to this, for every inmate there are two on parole (or otherwise under criminal justice supervision), and these disparities do not reflect a difference in drug using trends between populations. Instead, it is the same systemic trend of scapegoating

---

[252] Australian Drug Law Reform Foundation, *Drug Lore – The questioning of our current drug law*, 1996, Chapter 4:25

[253] See part one. For another document, see Eric E. Sterling, *Drug Policy: A Challenge of Values* (2004) (This paper argues that since the seventeenth century, to be black was to be deviant in the American "collective conscience", and that status has been punished through slavery, through segregation, and now through the criminal justice system, especially by means of the "war on drugs.")

[254] *Recalibrating the regime: The Need for a Human Rights-Based Approach to International Drug Policy*, Beckley Foundation (2008)

[255] PROVINE, *UNEQUAL UNDER LAW* (2007) 2

that makes Black males more likely to be sentenced to the death penalty and pregnant Black women 10 times more likely to lose custody of their children.[256]

The racial component is evident in the crack-cocaine disparity. In 1986, authority demanded that punishment for one gram of crack-cocaine should be the same as for 100 grams of cocaine. The push was a result of racist thinking, as the nonverbalised justification must be that blacks under the influence of cocaine is more dangerous than whites. Due to such stereotypical thinking, more than 80 percent of those incarcerated are Afro-Americans even though whites are more frequent users. Not only Blacks: Poor people and minorities as a whole suffer disproportionally, but the sum total is that America, as measured per capita, incarcerates at least 6 times as many black citizens as the South African Apartheid regime ever did. For those touched by the crack-cocaine legislation, the average sentencing received is almost nine years, and Judge James Gray puts it in perspective:

"For example, under the Rockefeller drug laws in New York, a man named Lawrence V. Cipolione, Jr. was serving a sentence of fifteen years to life for selling 2.34 ounces of cocaine to an undercover officer. Meanwhile, in the same prison, Amy Fisher was to be released after serving only four years and ten months for shooting a woman in the head, and Robert Chambers was serving a five-year sentence for a Central Park strangling. Under these circumstances, even the New York State Commissioner of Corrections was quoted as saying that 'The people doing the big time in the system really aren't the people you want doing the big time.'"[257]

---

[256] BAUM, *SMOKE AND MIRROR* (1996) 271

[257] GRAY, *WHY OUR DRUG LAWS HAVE FAILED AND WHAT WE CAN DO ABOUT IT* (2001) 32

7.4. The Futility of a War on Drugs

"The thought process that creates this massive social distortion in our minds and in society, the War on Drugs, acts exactly like a narcotic. The more we pursue it, the worse our problems become. The more we use prohibition the more we think we need it. As we pour more and more public funds into the war on drugs, the less we have for worthwhile social programs: low income housing, public schools, activity centers for youth and elders, clinics and counseling programs for drug users, jobs for the inner-cities and for the infrastructure on which our society runs. By these prohibitions, we are continually reinforcing the conditions that are creating crime. Instead of alleviating these conditions the War on Drugs makes them worse."[258]

—Max Hartstein—

So, what is the upside to this tyranny? Have the hundreds of billions spent had any positive impact? Have they reduced problems? Are drug users and others learning to respect authority? Are drugs less available, or can prohibitionists give us any indication that they are winning?

Hardly—but do not take my word for it. According to law enforcement personnel, professors, and researchers at Law Enforcement Against Prohibition (LEAP) and Criminal Justice Policy Foundation (CJPF) the result has been less than satisfactory:

"After spending a trillion tax dollars and making 39 million arrests for nonviolent drug offenses, drugs are now generally cheaper, more potent and easier for our children to access than they were 40 years ago at the beginning of the 'drug war'. Whenever we attempt to confront our very

---

[258] Max Hartstein, *The War on Drugs: The Worst Addiction of All* (2003) 11

real drug problems with the brute force of prohibition, we make little progress. The few who have been helped are greatly exceeded by the millions who have been hurt, all while precious resources and opportunities are squandered in the process.

According to the federal government, in the decade preceding the start of the war, 4 million people in the United States above the age of 12 had used an illegal drug in their lifetime (2 percent of the population). By 2007, the government revealed that 114 million people above the age of 12 had tried an illegal drug (46 percent of that population), an increase of 2,850 percent. Drug use became a badge of rebellion, although very widely worn. According to the World Health Organization, the United States has the highest rates of marijuana and cocaine use in the world, despite our having some of the harshest penalties. Drugs have become more concentrated and potent, a natural result of the costs involved in avoiding law enforcement. The average purity of cocaine at retail increased from 40 percent pure in 1981 to 70 percent pure in 2003, while its wholesale cost dropped by 84 percent over the same period. The purity of street-level heroin nearly tripled, while its wholesale cost has dropped by more than 86 percent. The homicide rate skyrocketed through the 1970s and 1980s, corresponding with increasing expenditures on enforcing prohibition."[259]

It is difficult to find an upside. These findings are widely shared,[260] and Judge Gray summarizes his perspective:

---

[259] LEAP & Criminal Justice Policy Foundation, *We Can Do it Again* (2008)

[260] John Curtin, a district Judge from New York: "In spite of the expenditure of billions of dollars, we have failed to reduce consumption, to reduce violent crime, to cut importation, and to lessen the huge profits gained by organized criminals. We have repeated the mistakes of prohibition with far more serious consequences. Criminal sanction has made for increased drug use rather than opposite." PROVINE, *UNEQUAL UNDER LAW* (2007) 149

"The War on Drugs has resulted in the loss of more civil liberties protections than has any other phenomenon in our history. Instead of being shielded, our children are being recruited into a lifestyle of drug selling and drug usage by the current system. And revolutionaries and insurgents abroad are using money procured from the illegal sale of drugs to undermine legitimate governments all over the world. We could not have achieved worse results if we had tried."[261]

As I have said, these perceptions are not uncommon.[262] In 1993, Federal authorities estimated that 50 out of 680 senior judges refused to hear drug cases and it speaks volumes. Ordinary judges would be fired for taking such a moral stand and this number—roughly ten percent—is compatible to that minority who knows how to read a constitution.

It is no coincidence that their insights are confirmed by a trove of reports, commissions,[263] and experts on law. For those with

---

[261] GRAY, *WHY OUR DRUG LAWS HAVE FAILED AND WHAT WE CAN DO ABOUT IT* (2001) 2

[262] Judge Gray elaborates: "There may be a few judges in this country who believe that our current drug policy is working, but they are surely a small minority. . . . I have had many private conversations on this subject with other judges, who know that the war on drugs have failed . . . But just like many politicians and law enforcement officers, judges are also concerned about undermining their effectiveness or exposing themselves to an electoral challenge by addressing this issue publicly." Ibid., 77

[263] Some official enquiries whose conclusions are irreconcilable with the current regime: The Indian Hemp Drugs Commission (1894); the Panama Canal Zone Report (1925); Departmental Committee on Morphine and Heroin Addiction (Rolleston Report) (1926); The Wickersham Commission (USA, 1931); the LaGuardia Report (USA, 1944); Joint Committee of the American Bar Association and the American Medical Association on Narcotic Drugs, Drug Addiction: Crime or Disease? (USA, 1961); Interdepartmental Committee, Drug Addiction (Brain I, 1961); Interdepartmental Committee, Drug Addiction (Brain II, 1965); the Wootton Report (UK, 1968); Canadian Government's Commission of Inquiry, Non-Medical Use of Drugs (the LeDain Report) (1970); the Baan Commission (the Netherlands, 1970); the Hulsman Commission (the Netherlands, 1971); National Commission on Marihuana and Drug Abuse, Marijuana: A Signal of Misunderstanding (USA, 1972); National Commission on Marijuana and Drug Abuse, Drug Use in America: Problem in Perspective (USA, 1973); National Research Council of the National Academy of Sciences, An Analysis of Marijuana Policy (1982); the report of the Expert Group on the Effects of Cannabis Use (UK, 1982); Legislative options for cannabis use in Australia, Monograph No. 26 (Australia, 1994); report of the New Zealand Health Committee, Inquiry into the Mental Health Effects of Cannabis (1998); the House of Lords Science and Technology Select Committee, Ninth Report, Cannabis: the Scientific and Medical evidence (UK, 1998); Swiss Federal Commission for Drug Issues, Cannabis Report (1999);

eyes to see, the drug war violates fundamental principles, and professionals would become increasingly concerned of the refusal to deal with reason.[264] As Roger Pilon, a Vice President for Legal Affairs for the Cato Institute, noted with frustration some 15 years ago:

"In the realm of ideas, there simply are no credible arguments left for continuing this endless War on Drugs. . . . From a consideration of both principle and policy, reason reveals that the war is wrong and counterproductive. It is now the visceral response that has to be confronted, the blind, irrational reaction to calls for ending the war that stop thought when thought is most needed, that ignore inconsistency and hypocrisy that is as plain as day."

Randy Barnett, a professor of law (and former prosecutor), was no less blunt. As he chided the prohibitionist psychosis:

"It seems that no facts are sufficient to shake the prohibitionists' faith in this tragic policy. As . . . suggested elsewhere, some persons act as though they are addicted to drug laws, with all the connotations of irrationality that term is meant to convey when applied to drug users. Consequently, they are unlikely to be swayed by the copious facts and arguments presented [by reform activists]. . . .

---

report of the National Commission on Ganja (Jamaica, 2001); the UK Report of the Advisory Committee on Drug Dependence (2002); The Senate Special Committee on Illegal Drugs, Cannabis: our position for a Canadian public policy (Canada, 2002); the report by the Advisory Committee on Drug Dependence, The Classification of Cannabis under the Misuse of Drugs Act 1971 (UK, 2002); Rapport de la Commission d'enquête du Sénat français sur la politique nationale de lutte contre les drogues illicites, No. 321 (France, 2003); the report by the Advisory Council on the Misuse of Drugs, Further consideration of the classification of cannabis under the Misuse of Drugs Act 1971 (UK, 2005).

[264] Susan Stuart, a professor of law, stated: "The oh-so-successful marketing tactics that Nixon started, that Reagan energized, and that the Bushes sent into the stratosphere to support a Forty-Years War are now employed with little or no self-reflection, and certainly no justification nor ethical consideration." Susan Stuart, *War as Metaphor and the Rule of Law in Crisis: The Lessons We Should Have Learned from the War on Drugs*, Valparasio University School of Law, Legal Studies Research Paper (2011) 49

[Nonetheless] the case against prohibition is overwhelming, precisely because so many different types of considerations all point to a single solution: the legalization of illicit drugs. "[265]

7.5. COUNTERMOVEMENT

"The prestige of government has undoubtedly been lowered considerably by the Prohibition law. For nothing is more destructive of respect of the government and the law of the land, than passing laws which cannot be enforced. It is an open secret that the dangerous increase of crime in this country is closely connected with this." [266]

—Albert Einstein—

Since the 1990s, there has been an increase in people who want to legalize drugs. Looking at cannabis, which is the most widely discussed and used substance, only 16 percent supported an end to cannabis prohibition in 1990, but there has been a steady increase—and it is continuing to rise. Currently, more than 60 percent of the population want to see a government regulated market and this process has already begun in several states. As neighbouring Canada has legalized cannabis, there is a pressure building to review policy, and we can expect a change at the Federal level very soon. Until this day, Federal authorities have resisted tendencies towards state-level legalization, but the game is nearly up. We have soon seen the last US Attorney General to defend a prohibition on cannabis, and in not too many years, we can expect the same for harder drugs.

---

[265] Barnett, *Bad Trip: Drug Prohibition and the Weakness of Public Policy*, 103 Yale Law Journal (1994) 2598

[266] GRAY, *WHY OUR DRUG LAWS HAVE FAILED AND WHAT WE CAN DO ABOUT IT* (2001)

One must give the population some credit. The trend towards legalization has been despite a pressure from authority to maintain psychosis, and it is a testimony to the destructiveness of prohibition that the citizenry so vehemently has opposed it. It is also testimony to the evermore hollow rang of prohibitionist lore, and now that prohibitionists no longer can peddle propaganda without becoming ridiculed, they are in a tight spot. It is no longer easy to find scientists willing to vouch for present policies, and the only result authority can achieve by continuing its campaign of oppression is increasing alienation.

Hence, we see a rise in tensions. The George Floyd protests, Black Lives Matter, and Defund the Police movement resulted in open riot during Trump's presidency. Mayors of large cities like Seattle and Portland ceded "autonomous zones" to protesters, and it all leads back to the flawed War on Drugs. If only one of the many constitutional challenges to the drug law had been handled correctly in the 1960s-70s, America would have gone down a different route. The integrity of law would have been secured and a culture of rights violations had not continued to corrupt the police force. However, America went down a different path, and reaps the consequences. "Left" and "Right" blame each other, but the only way out of this predicament is ending drug prohibition.

Not that no one saw it coming. The mayors of both Newark and San Francisco held press conferences 15 years ago stating that the War on Drugs must be stopped before their cities are destroyed.[267] In 2008, San Francisco Mayor Gavin Newsom insisted that the crime rate would go down 70 percent if the government spent money on treatment as opposed to jailing people. Cory Booker, the Mayor of Newark, went on to become a senator, and has introduced bold drug reform legislation in the Senate, including a plan to commute the sentences of about 17,000 federal prisoners. Together with Sen. Ron Wyden, of Oregon, and Senate Majority Leader Chuck Schumer, he has

---

[267] *Drugs and Crime Across America: Police Chiefs Speak Out*, Drug Strategies & Police Foundation (2004)

pushed to pass sweeping legislation in 2021 that would end the federal prohibition on marijuana, which has been legalized to some degree by many states. The bill would provide so-called restorative justice for people who have been convicted of pot-related crimes, and it will be interesting to see how it goes. A Gallup poll in November 2020 showed that 68% of Americans, a record high, favoured marijuana legalization, and it is difficult to disagree. As of 2021, 15 states and the District of Columbia have legalized marijuana for adult recreational use, and 36 states permit medical use of the drug. Oregon is the first to have decriminalized hard drugs, and these experiments have positive results. It is for this reason that every initiative that involved the decriminalization or legalization of marijuana on the ballot in 2020 passed, and in 2008 LEAP prophetically described the opposition within rank and populace:

> *"Recent polls show that 67 percent of police chiefs and 76 percent of the public agree that the 'War on Drugs' is a failure. Thirteen states have legalized medical marijuana despite dire warnings of a floodgate effect from this 'loophole' in the prohibition. And in not one of those states did youthful marijuana subsequently increase. Just last month, despite predictably dramatic opposition, voters in Massachusetts overwhelmingly approved a ballot question decriminalizing possession of up to an ounce of marijuana. The warnings of the prohibitionists are increasingly shrill, increasingly desperate, increasingly ignored."[268]*

As of today, it is difficult to find a health organization, a lawyer's guild, or even a newspaper that supports cannabis prohibition. Congressmen are quietly shifting sides, and even drug warriors see the writing on the wall.[269] When old hardliners like

---

[268] LEAP & Criminal Justice Policy Foundation, *We Can Do it Again*, December 2008

[269] As Gary Hale, a DEA Chief of intelligence noted: "At some point in the not-too-distant future, whether a year or 10 years from now, legalization is going to happen. We need to

John Boehner goes from being Speaker of the House to becoming advisors for cannabis companies,[270] we know that is no longer a matter of "if" but a matter of "when". And as Judge Gray predicted, "Within a few years of this change, we will look back in astonishment that we allowed our former policy to persist for so long, much as we look back now on slavery, or Jim Craw laws, or the days when women were prohibited from voting—and we will wish fervently that we had not waited so long to abandon these failed and destructive policies."[271]

---

prepare for that." William Martin, *The War on Drugs Has Failed: Is Legalization the Answer?* Conference Report, James A. Baker institute (March 2012) 20

[270] In 2018, John A. Boehner, the speaker of the House from 2011 to 2015, reversed a long-held stance against legalization, when he tweeted that "my thinking on cannabis has evolved," and that he had joined the board of advisors of Acreage Holdings.

[271] GRAY, *WHY OUR DRUG LAWS HAVE FAILED AND WHAT WE CAN DO ABOUT IT* (2001) 5

7.6. Resisting the Inevitable

"The messiah of drug legalization has not yet arrived, but the prohibitionists can hear the heavens rumbling with skepticism and with concomitant expectations of a different future. Increasingly large cohorts of the public and even the enforcement personnel are sensing the futile and Sisyphian nature of using the penal law and prisons as a response to drug use and sale. The citizenry is coming to realize how costly the penal drug war is in terms of dollar expenditures and the sacrifice of civil liberties, and that the drug war, rather than the drugs themselves, is the gratuitous and avoidable cause of many societal distortions. Drug prohibition is wearily shuffling in tattered robe and floppy slippers towards its deathbed, and the only truly undecided questions are how expensive the funeral is going to be, and what the post-prohibitionist generation of drug policy will look like."[272]

—Stanley Neustadter, New York lawyer—

As we have seen, the case against prohibition is overwhelming. And yet, despite reason and a powerful movement for change, the prohibitionist psychosis persists. As in other countries, there is agreement among most officials that prohibition remains a decent venture, one without which the world would be much worse off, and it is difficult to find inroads to a closed mindset. Indeed, the dedication to ignorance has been profound, and professionals have noted the insincerity with which the drug war has been pursued. Judge Gray provides an example:

"Talk to someone who has attempted to organize a public discussion, as opposed to a speech about our drug policy,

---

[272] Stanley Neustadter, *Legalization Legislation: Confronting the Details and Policy Choices,* in Jefferson M. Fish (ed.), *How to Legalize Drugs* (1998) 388

and you will find that public officials favoring the continuation of our drug policies will almost never attend. This has happened to me on many occasions. For example, at the meeting of the World Affairs Council in Orange County, General McCaffrey was invited to participate in a debate on drug policy. He responded that he did not have time to be involved in a debate—but he did have time to give a speech. The same thing happened when Dr. Lee Brown, the Drug Czar under President Bush, spoke at a drug policy forum at the Harvard Law School. Without taking any questions, he left the hall and went downstairs to talk to the press. Since I was scheduled to speak directly after Dr. Brown, I offered half of my time to him if he would only stay and answer questions from the audience present. He refused."[273]

Another investigator, James Ostrowski, served as a vice chairman of the New York County Lawyers Association Committee on Law Reform (1986-88). In this period, he wrote two widely quoted reports critical of the law enforcement approach. He summarized his experience thus:

"In 1988, I wrote to Vice President George Bush, then head of the South Florida Drug Task Force; to Education Secretary William Bennett; to Assistant Secretary of State for Drug Policy Ann Wrobleski; to White House drug policy adviser Dr. Donald I. McDonald; and to the public information directors of the Federal Bureau of Investigation, Drug Enforcement Administration, General Accounting Office, National Institute of Justice, and National Institute on Drug Abuse. None of these officials was able to cite any study that demonstrated the beneficial effects of drug prohibition when weighed against its costs. The leaders of the War on Drugs are apparently unable to

---

[273] GRAY, *WHY OUR DRUG LAWS HAVE FAILED AND WHAT WE CAN DO ABOUT IT* (2001) 146

defend on rational cost-benefit grounds their 70-year-old policy, which costs nearly $10 billion per year (out of pocket), imprisons 750,000 Americans, and fills our cities with violent crime. "[274]

As we can see, prohibitionists have won the debate by refusing to participate. In following this strategy, they have successfully held back the momentum for change—and even if prohibitionists are keen to assure us that they have had the best of intentions, there is little to suggest that they are truthful. Truthfulness, after all, has been missing from their campaign since day one, and their actions over the past hundred years speak louder than words.

7.6.1. BUREAUCRATS' VESTED INTEREST

"When a private enterprise fails, it is closed down; when a government enterprise fails, it is expanded. Isn't that exactly what's been happening with drugs?"

—Milton Friedman, American economist—

We have seen how corporations' profit from the War on Drugs. However, the drug war has provided many a bureaucrat with powers and budgets, and to quote Peter Moskos, a professor of sociology, it is easy to see that "the War on Drugs is not about saving lives or stopping crime. It's about yesteryear's ideologues and future profits from prison jobs, asset forfeiture, court overtime pay, and federal largess."[275]

---

[274] James Ostrowski, *Thinking about Drug Legalization*, Cato institute Policy analysis nr. 121 (1989)

[275] Peter Moskos, *Two Takes: Drugs Are Too Dangerous Not to Regulate—We Should Legalize Them*, July 25, 2008

As Moskos implies, a bureaucratic machinery has nourished on the War on Drugs for more than 50 years and many have come to depend on this for survival. Because of this, criticizing the drug war has been repugnant. And even if the days are gone when prohibitionists could inspire moral awe by their position alone, there remains plenty of drug warriors willing to pursue a strategy on these terms. A report that attests to the backward approach is Rationalizing Drug Policy:

> *"In a representative democracy there is a tendency to expect that public opinion drives drug policy. This is not the case, as 'every detailed study of the emergence of legal norms has consistently shown the immense importance of interest-group activity, not the 'public interest,' as the critical variable.' Drug war, the excessive application of enforcement that aggravates rather than mitigates the social consequences of drug use, is waged because it is in the interests of particular politically influential groups, including law enforcement bureaucracies and public officials."[276]*

We have already discussed how corporations and elites with a vested interest in dominance has kept the drug war going, and we shall now focus on the ONDCP.

---

[276] David W. Rasmussen & Bruce L. Benson, *Rationalizing Drug Policy*, Florida State University Law Review,Vol. 30 (2003) 679. This perspective is shared by Professor Douglas Husak: "If the 'War on Drugs' is unjustifiable, why does it continue to be waged? No single answer can be given. An important factor, however, is the financial gain to law-enforcement agencies that assign a high priority to the apprehension of drug offenders." Douglas Husak, *Liberal Neutrality, Autonomy, and Drug Prohibitions*, Philosophy and Public Affairs, Vol. 29, No. 1 (2000) 80. For more on the bureaucratic thrust of the drug war, see Eric Blumenson and Eva Nilsen, *Policing for Profit: The Drug War's Hidden Economic Agenda*, University of Chicago Law Review 65 (1998) 35; BERTRAM, ET AL., *DRUG WAR POLITICS: THE PRICE OF DENIAL* (1996) 102-62; WISOTSKY, *BEYOND THE WAR ON DRUGS: OVERCOMING A FAILED PUBLIC POLICY* (1990) 173-97; BARNETT, *THE STRUCTURE OF LIBERTY: JUSTICE AND THE RULE OF LAW* (2014) 135-337; MILLER, *THE CASE FOR LEGALIZING DRUGS* (1991) 85-107; MILLER, *DRUG WARRIORS AND THEIR PREY: FROM POLICE POWER TO POLICE STATE* (1996) 164-69

7.6.1.1. ONDCP

The Office of National Drug Control Policy (ONDCP) is the lead agency in America's War on Drugs. When it was created in 1988, it was to make the drug war more effective by coordinating the drug control activities and related funding of 16 federal departments and agencies under its authority. This centralized system of control should have made the United States drug-free by 1995 and so the ONDCP was mandated to last for only 5 years. Things, however, did not pan out that way, and so the ONDCP's mandate was renewed in 1994, 1998, 2003, 2008, 2013, and 2018. Every year its officials testify before Congress to present their idea of progress—and every year politicians are encouraged by warmongering and deceitful statistics to continue the drug war.[277]

An example is found in Barry McCaffrey, Bill Clinton's Drug Czar. When he testified before the Government reform and oversight Committee, June 16th, 1999, he characterized the ONDCP strategy as a success and promised that this war effort, over the next ten years, would reduce drug abuse by 50 percent. He assured Congress that a War on Drugs was the only way, and used the Dutch as an example:

---

[277] ONDCP's John Walters, for instance, defended policy like this in 2008: "Whatever challenges await him, President-elect Barack Obama will not have to reinvent the wheel when it comes to keeping a lid on the use of illegal drugs. Our policy has been a success—although that success is one of Washington's best kept secrets. Reported drug use among eighth, 10th and 12th graders has declined for six straight years. Teen use of cocaine, marijuana and inhalants is down significantly, while consumption of methamphetamine and hallucinogens like LSD and Ecstasy has all but collapsed. The number of workplace tests that are positive for cocaine is down sharply, to the lowest levels on record. Even the sudden spike of meth use—remember the headlines from just a few years ago?—has yielded to a combination of state and federal regulations controlling meth ingredients. And abroad, crackdowns in Colombia and Mexico have caused the price of cocaine to roughly double in the past two years." (John Walters, *Our Drug Policy Is a Success; Workplace tests for cocaine show the lowest use on record,* Wall street journal, December 5, 2008.) Despite his enthusiasm, books like *Lies, Damn Lies, And Drug War Statistics*, shows how Walters and the ONDCP abuse statistics. As its authors summarize the ONDCP role: "We find that ONDCP generally claims success in reducing drug use, both when it is warranted and when it is not. Among other things, ONDCP, focuses almost exclusively on the good news with regard to drug trends, downplays or totally ignores the bad news about drug use trends, and 'spins the data' by selectively presenting certain statistics while ignoring others to show positive results." ROBINSON & SCHERLEN, *LIES, DAMN LIES, AND DRUG WAR STATISTICS* (2007) xv

"If the Dutch experience with drugs is an appropriate model at all, it is because it illustrates the harms that result from increased tolerance of illegal drugs. This conclusion was brought home to all of us from the Office of National Drug Control Policy who travelled to the Netherlands in July of 1998 to gain a better understanding of the Dutch approach. . . . Proponents of legalization argue that the Dutch experience provides a model for a 'softer approach' to fighting drug use. Upon close examination the pitfalls of the Dutch experience offer more than ample evidence to dissuade the United States from adopting the drug policies of the Netherlands. Instead the Dutch example clearly argues in favor of continuing the balanced U.S. approach, which is producing results."

Now, we have seen the insincerity with which McCaffrey and the ONDCP evaluated the Dutch experiment. We have also seen that the United States comparatively comes up short,[278] and so it is difficult to resist the conclusion that Barry is committing perjury.

Nevertheless, in this manner, the ONDCP has not only ensured a continuation of its mandate but an increase in spending. The ONDCP's budget started out at one billion. By 1998 it had reached $17 billion, and the 2020 budget was $34.6 billion. Considering that the ONDCP never has been able to show that its efforts are worthwhile, nor within the limits of constitutional law, this is a rather astonishing increase of funds. To those not caught in the grips of psychosis, bureaucratic cowardice and self-interest is the only explanation, and the same applies to any other agency involved with the drug war. Theodore Dalrymple, a medical

---

[278] This is uncontroversial. In 2008, for instance, the World Health Organization produced a document that countered all the conclusions made by McCaffrey (*Toward a Global View of Alcohol, Tobacco, Cannabis, and Cocaine Use: Findings from the WHO World Mental Health Surveys*). According to this report, out of 17 nations, the United States had the highest prevalence of drug use and liberal nations suffered less problems.

doctor who has seen the phenomenon evolve, summarized the situation for NIDA, ONDCP's partner in crime:

> *"[W]here bureaucracies are concerned, nothing succeeds like failure. For example, the budget for the National Institute of Drug Abuse increased by 16.2 percent from 2001 to 2002 alone, which would be quite a creditable performance if it had been a purely commercial enterprise. $126,390,000 was added to its budget in the period, but it would be a brave or foolhardy man who asserted that a single drug addict stopped, or ever will stop, taking drugs because of this extra funding. Nor would you have to be Nostradamus to predict that the budget will keep growing, however many or few drug addicts there are, unless of course there is a general economic collapse necessitating drastic budgetary retrenchment. What one can say with a fair degree of certainty is that the funding of the NIDA will remain sturdily independent of the importance or usefulness of its findings, and of the social importance or otherwise of the problem it addresses. The bureaucratic solution to waste is always more waste."*[279]

---

[279] THEODORE DALRYMPLE, *ROMANCING OPIATES: PHARMACOLOGICAL LIES AND THE ADDICTION BUREAUCRACY* (2008) 11

8

ETERNAL WAR FOR ETERNAL PEACE

"Should humanity accept paedophilia, human trafficking, or arms smuggling out of a naïve sense of market inevitability or intractability?"[280]

—Antonio Maria Costa, Executive Director, UNODC—

IN THIS PART, we have followed the evolution of drug policy in Western countries. We have seen the dynamic generated by a prohibition on drugs and that more and more people, for this reason, have begun to think in terms of a regulation of drugs. This only makes sense, considering that the attempt to rid the world of drugs is proved a fool's errand. That the ideal of a drug-free world is unconscientious is evidenced by its effects and consequences, and that it is unrealistic is seen on how drug warriors come up short as to their stated intentions.[281]

We have already seen that the prohibitionists in 1961, when the Single Convention was enacted, promised a drug-free world within 25 years. This did not happen, but when the UN had its first

---

[280] Statement by Antonio Maria Costa to the Opening of the high-level segment of the Commission on Narcotic Drugs at its fifty-second session.

[281] Professor Steven Wisotsky drives home this point: "It is difficult to find in modern American history an obviously defective and destructive policy so rigidly locked in place. A partial explanation for this unique rigidity lies in the fact that the ordinary corrective mechanisms that operate for some other failed governmental policies do not function here. First, the lack of even a minimal standard of performance by which to measure results precludes responsible dialog within the government. Without real goals there can be no accountability. Not once in the history of the War on Drugs . . . has the Government ever stated a realistic objective. . . . Second, the Government has effectively immunized itself from outside criticism, managing to preempt any serious public debate calling into question the premises of drug enforcement policy," WISOTSKY, *BEYOND THE WAR ON DRUGS* (1990) 173-74

UN General Assembly Special Session (UNGASS) on drugs in 1991, the prohibitionists were no less encouraged. By this time world leaders had too much vested in this quest to rethink fundamental premises and the General Assembly expanded the mandate of the Commission on Narcotic Drugs (CND) to enable it to function as the governing body of the UN Office of Drugs and Crime (UNODC). Since then, drug fighting has been the primus motor behind united police efforts and in 1998, at the second UNGASS meeting to discuss the drug problem, the slogan for the event was: "A drug-free world—we can do it!"

At this meeting, world leaders reaffirmed their commitment to the eradication of drugs, this time by 2008. By this time, however, the folly of this operation was plain. Experts on drug policy not only referred to the UN drug fighting apparatus as "Ivory Towers developing a stone-age ideology;" they noted that prohibition had "become a real material force" and feared that it would become "a vehicle of fascism."[282] Thus, editors of Ottawa Citizen, a Canadian newspaper, spoke for many when they decreed:

"Today in New York City, an act of almost indescribable stupidity will be committed. Eighteen years after Ronald Reagan announced he would stamp out drugs, the 'War on Drugs' will be declared once again. This time the United Nations will play the fool, with an announcement of the most ambitious international anti-drug program ever. . . . The

---

[282] Peter Cohen said this while running Amsterdam's Drug Research Project: "I cannot stress enough the importance of the behavior of large international bodies. Up till now they acted as the divine global executioners of—mostly American instigated—debilitating international treaties. Only when state representatives in the working committees of these bodies are no longer selected from the blind and faithful, can some of the real world enter these bureaucratic fortresses. We do need some fresh air in these international bodies, otherwise nations that simply ask questions and request data will have no chance. This means that researchers intent on change in the drug control system will have to do the work, to expose these bodies as Ivory Towers developing a stone-age ideology, 'Prohibitionism,' that has become a real material force. It not only kills thousands of people each year, it has given birth to the largest criminal network the world has ever seen. But far more serious is the possibility that Prohibitionism becomes a vehicle for fascism, as many drug workers in the U.S. have pointed out to me." Peter Cohen, *Building upon the successes of Dutch drug policy.*

*stated goal of the UN plan: To eradicate the world's entire
production of heroin, cocaine, and marijuana in 10 years.
. . . What about Canada? As always, the federal government
is clambering onto the bandwagon and cheering on the war.
Since the Trudeau years, it has seldom given serious thought
to drug policy, preferring instead to follow whatever
variation on failure is being proposed. That, sadly, is true
of most of the world's nations. Sense and experience are
ignored, folly is repeated, and the War on Drugs becomes a
war on reason itself."*[283]

In other words, a continued expansion of the prohibition
strategy was unadvisable. Still, leaders pledged their alliance, and
when time came to review policy in 2008 they renewed their
intent. Even though the world had more drugs and drug users than
ever, UN bureaucrats reasoned that all was well and decided to
give us more of the same policies until 2019, when they planned
the next Special Session on drugs.

By this time, however, the UN drug control apparatus had
become infamous for its bias.[284] No impartial or competent
researcher would vouch for their policies[285] and the War on Drugs
was beginning to destroy nations. For this reason, Mexico,
Guatemala, and Colombia called for an emergency meeting,
scheduling the next general assembly special session for April
2016. These countries, then, asked for a more "humane solution"
to the drugs problem, one that went beyond a focus on
enforcement and criminalization. It was a show of integrity, one
that was called for. Nevertheless, the push towards a government

---

[283] GRAY, *WHY OUR DRUG LAWS HAVE FAILED AND WHAT WE CAN DO ABOUT IT* (2001) 83

[284] For more on this, see: Martin Jelsma, *Drugs in the UN system: The Unwritten History of
the 1998 United Nations General Assembly Special Session on Drugs,* International Journal
of Drug Policy 14 (2003) 181-195.

[285] While UNODC concluded that the strategy was working, an independent report
published by the European Union came to the opposite conclusion (the Reuter-Trautmann
report). Also, in *Rewriting history; A response to the 2008 World Drug Report* (TNI Drug
Policy Briefing nr 26, June 2008) the Transnational Institute confirms the failure of the
status quo.

regulated marked in drugs was met by prohibitionists dedicated to the status quo. And while the world, because of this, was doomed to suffer another round of suffering, it was easy to see that the system was crumbling.

8.1. UNGASS 2016

At this meeting, the rift between countries interested in drug policy reform and those with repressive drug control attitudes was evident. On the one hand, there were regimes dedicated to murdering drug users, and on the other there were regimes who had begun to think about protecting liberty and autonomy rights. The United States, the country that traditionally had forced upon all others their idea of proper policies, supported the current framework but not with the same fanfare as before. By this time states like Colorado, Washington, and Oregon had legalized the recreational use of cannabis and now US delegates, being criticized by the INCB for violating the UN drug control conventions, were unsure what to do.

The empire was on its last legs. And as delegates for Indonesia was booed when they defended the country's use of the death penalty as "an important component" of the country's drug control policy, it was clear that a change was in the air. Up to this point, the UN drug apparatus had praised hard-line countries such as Saudi Arabia, Iran, and Indonesia for their commitment to rid society of drugs and drug users, but not anymore. The moral climate did no longer make such penalties pass as a proper expression of law, and the Norwegian delegation—full of hypocrisy—called for an approach to drug control centred on human rights.

I say hypocrisy, as with "human rights" the Norwegian mission did not think principles of equality, proportionality, and autonomy: it did not even speak of drug users and the folly of persecuting this group. Not at all. As we have seen, nearly 10 years after drug users had been denied basic protections by

Norwegian and international courts, Norway remained committed to the persecution of drug users. Thinking of human rights in meaningful terms, therefore, was impossible—and so with human rights, the delegation simply meant "opium replacement therapy" and "an end to drug crime executions."

The nefarious plot to reduce human rights to what is acceptable to power aside, the Norwegian delegate held that "Norway intends to be a clear voice for a more progressive approach," and its position was celebrated by the audience of international delegates and activists.

It was difficult to disagree: Even agents of power had to concede that human rights had to be the basis of drug policy, and so, for the first time in history, it was decided "that all aspects of demand reduction and related measures, supply reduction and related measures, and international cooperation are addressed in full conformity with the purposes and principles of the Charter of the United Nations, international law and the Universal Declaration of Human Rights."[286]

However, as no one wanted to check if the prohibitionist quest was compatible with human rights principles, these words would count for naught. Before the meeting, UN bodies and public officials had declared their allegiance to an open and inclusive debate where all stakeholders and perspectives were heard. They talked of "the importance of a comprehensive, multi-dimensional and collaborative approach to finding practical and sustainable solutions to the drug issues facing communities throughout the world";[287] of "addressing all the consequences of the world drug problem, including in the health, social, human rights, economic, justice and security fields,"[288] and they seemed concerned about "the importance of a broad, transparent, inclusive and scientific

---

[286] UNODC, *Outcome Document of the 2016 United Nations General Assembly Special Session on the World Drug Problem*, New York, April 19-21, 2016, 2

[287] *High-level General Assembly Thematic Debate in support of the process towards the 2016 Special Session of the General Assembly on the World Drug Problem*, New York, May 7, 2015.

[288] Id.

evidence-based discussion . . . on the most effective ways to counter the world drug problem, consistent with the three international drug control conventions and other relevant international instruments."[289]

World leaders even declared that at its special session in 2016, the General Assembly should "address substantive issues on the basis of the principle of common and shared responsibility and in full conformity with the purposes and principles of the Charter of the United Nations, international law and the Universal Declaration of Human Rights,"[290] and that "special attention should be given to all human rights-related matters."[291]

Still, such words proved to be little more than window dressing, conceivably put in place to cover up a more sinister reality. At its website, for instance, the United Nations boasted the participance of civil society, claiming to ensure that drug users were represented at UNGASS. Hundreds of NGOs jumped on the opportunity to have a voice in these Ivory Towers and every bit of information passed on to the UN were available at its site. Officially that is, for when civil society pushed on for a rights-oriented debate, one where first principles were brought into the equation, the UN would censor these papers from their website.[292]

---

[289] *Special Segment: Preparations for, the Possible Outcomes of and Organizational Matters Relating to the Special Session of the General Assembly on the World Drug Problem to Be Held in 2016*, Report of the Secretariat, E/CN.7/2014/17, 4.

[290] Id.

[291] Ibid., 5

[292] These were letters from the Alliance for Rights-Oriented Drug Policies (AROD). For a more detailed look at the censored letters, see www.arodpolicies.org/ungass-2016. The same episode repeated itself in 2020 when the US State Department's Unalienable Rights Commission did its work. Communication with civil society was put on its website, except for ARODs letters which exposed a distance between theory and practice that did not fit the official narrative. The State Department promised to correct this situation, but never did. Thus, both the UN and American bureaucracy has shown that the façade is more important than a principled foundation for policy.

For those who looked more closely, therefore, it was evident that it was all a sham. As so many suspected and tried to avoid, the UNGASS 2016 became another occasion for world leaders to hide behind fine words; to assure citizens that their rights were a priority and that the rule of law mattered, when there were forces at play that would ensure that any discussion on drug policy remained established within the parameters of the law-and-order paradigm.

As evident from the proceedings, these forces had sufficient control of the UN apparatus to deny first principles. Even so, the push from the rest of civil society was notable, and while INCB and CND struggled to ignore these voices, they were warned about the implication of continuing the status quo. Mr. J. Calzada, Secretary General of the National Drugs Bureau of Uruguay, for example, pointed out to the UN drug warriors that the assumption that criminal sanctions are an effective way to eliminate drug use was not borne out by the evidence and that it would be senseless to continue pursuing current policies in the hope of achieving results.[293] In addition, UNDP and NGOs such as the Global Commission on Drug Policy, ENCOD, Transform Drug Policy Foundation, Health Poverty Action, Open Society foundations, the West Africa Commission on Drugs, IDCP and INPUD impressed upon UN officials the fact that the degree of criminalization had had little to no impact on the prevalence of drug use;[294] that many of the harms and costs associated with drug use were substantially driven by prohibition; and that it was absurd to justify the status quo, claiming that drug use is harmful,

---

[293] Inter-Parliamentary Union, *Panel Discussion on the Legalization of Drugs: Can it Help Curb Organized Crime?* 2

[294] UNDP, *Perspectives on the Development Dimensions of Drug Control Policy*, March 2015; Jean-Paul Grund & Joost Breeksema, *Coffee Shops and Compromise: Separated Illicit Drug Markets in the Netherlands*, Open Society Foundations, 2013; Transform Drug Policy Foundation, *Drug Decriminalisation in Portugal: Setting the Record Straight*, 2014; Artur Domosławski, *Drug Policy in Portugal: The Benefits of Decriminalizing Drug Use*, Open Society Foundations 2011.

"when the perverse irony is that prohibition itself creates, drives, and perpetuates drug-related harms."[295]

Together with the Organization of American States, these actors presented information that some form of legalization was the only sensible solution to the drug problem,[296] and they noted the importance that UN agencies act on the available evidence and review the pros and cons of prohibition versus alternatives.

While this was plenty, they were not the only actors to note the importance of an honest, inclusive, and open debate at UNGASS 2016. In the run-up to this meeting the United Nations University had pointed out a host of little recognized, detrimental side-effects of prohibition,[297] as well as the importance of seizing the special session as an opportunity to ensure that the drug policy reflect the original concern of the drug control conventions—that is "the health and welfare of mankind."[298] The Secretary General, Ban Ki-moon, had called for a "wide-ranging and open debate that considers all options";[299] the Assistant Secretary-General of the UN Development Program, Jessica Faieta, had underscored that rather than engaging in limited reforms of existing policies, it was "crucial to undertake a paradigm shift";[300] the General Assembly had reaffirmed "that countering the world drug problem must be

---

[295] INPUD, *Drug User Peace Initiative: A War on the Health of People who Use Drugs*, 2014,1

[296] Organization of American States, *The Drug Problem in the Americas*, 2013; Transform Drug Policy Foundation, *How to Regulate Cannabis: A Practical Guide*, 2014; Transform Drug Policy Foundation, *After the War on Drugs: Blueprint for Regulation*, 2009; IDPC, *The Road to UNGASS 2016: Process and Policy Asks from the IDPC*, November 2014; Global Commission on Drug Policy, *Taking Control: Pathways to Drug Policies that Work*, 2014; Catherine Martin, *Casualties of War: How the Drug War is Harming the World's Poorest*, Health Poverty Action, 2015; WACD, *Not Just in Transit: Drugs, the State and Society in West Africa*, An Independent Report of the West Africa Commission on Drugs, June 2014.

[297] United Nations University, *Improving the Development Impact of Drugs Policy: Meeting Note from a Luncheon Roundtable*, July 2014

[298] United Nations University, *The Road to UNGASS 2016 on the World Drug Problem: Meeting Note from a Roundtable Discussion*, November 2014, 1

[299] Remarks of the Secretary-General at the special event on the International Day against Drug Abuse and Illicit Trafficking, New York, June 26, 2013

[300] United Nations University, *The Road to UNGASS 2016 on the World Drug Problem: Meeting Note from a Roundtable Discussion*, November 2014, 2

done in full conformity with the purposes and principles of the Charter of the United Nations and other provisions of international law, including the Universal Declaration of Human Rights";[301] and the head of United Nations University's UN Office, James Cockayne, had warned that if the CND does not broaden its horizons in its preparations for UNGASS 2016, this special session will be seen by the media and the global public as disconnected from current realities on the ground, and as avoiding a "wide-ranging debate" in favour of the status quo.

As an example, Mr. Cockayne mentioned the permissibility and practicality of regulating the supply of certain scheduled substances (notably cannabis) as among the important issues excluded from the UNGASS agenda.[302] While the question of regulating drugs had been a taboo among world leaders, by now the War on Drugs was killing 150,000 people a year in the Americas alone and several presidents were personally invested in the legalization proposal. Adding to this, the Organization of American States (OAS) and the European Union delivered reports where they underlined the importance of considering new approaches based on knowledge and scientific evidence,[303] one that was based on respect for the principles of equality, proportionality, human rights, and the rule of law—and also they noted that this could only be achieved if issues that had been ignored got the attention that they deserved.[304]

---

[301] General Assembly resolution 68/197 of 18 December 2013

[302] Ibid., 2

[303] AG/RES. 1 (XLVI-E/14): Reflections and Guidelines to Formulate and Follow up on Comprehensive Policies to Address the World Drug Problem, September 19, 2014

[304] As the UNDP reminded the treaty bodies: "Ultimately, the UN's involvement in drug control should be a means to achieve its core objectives as embodied in the UN Charter and the Universal Declaration of Human Rights, and enshrined in numerous treaties: peace, development, and human rights. Therefore, a clearer consideration and evaluation of the impact of drug policies impacts on these key objectives would greatly enhance the debate. UNGASS 2016, and preparations thereto, provide important opportunities for a comprehensive discussion of successes and challenges around drug control policy . . . and ultimately, to promote system-wide coherence with respect to global drug control strategies." UNDP, *Perspectives on the Development Dimensions of Drug Control Policy*, March 3, 2015

All this considered, prohibitionists could not keep the possibility of a regulation of drugs off the table without weakening the authority of the status quo. From the documentation received, an honest, unbiased review included the discussion of alternatives to prohibition—and yet public officials, while giving lip service to the principles of human rights and the importance of evidence-based policies, continued under the prejudiced opinion that policies had to be firmly set within the current law-and-order paradigm.

As drug policy from the beginning was a political, not an evidence-based construct, it was hardly surprising that drug warriors at the UN ignored their obligations to the UN Charter and citizens worldwide. Nevertheless, the drug control system, being openly in contempt of the rule of law, was in shambles. The regime of psychosis and doublespeak ensured that individual countries like Uruguay, Mexico, Colombia, Ecuador, Costa Rica, Guatemala, the Czech Republic, and the Canadian government gave up on the outdated and indefensible system, promising to go their own way. And while the most progressive-oriented states had to return home with not much accomplished, this theatre of absurdity would be noticed by newspapers and civil society all over the world.

Hence, even though the prohibitionist psychosis was to remain intact the UNGASS 2016 meeting was not for naught. It revealed that the system itself was crumbling, that there was no justification to the status quo, and that most leaders still lacked the integrity to oppose the mindless ramblings of prohibitionist lore.

As we have already discussed the psychological reasons behind this betrayal, we know that projection and denial was the only coping mechanism. Nevertheless, there were more sinister forces at work, and we shall now introduce another part of the equation—power politics.

Part Three:
Power Politics

9

CREATION OF THE DRUG CONTROL COMPLEX

"[The legislative] process involves the selection of certain sets of circumstances and the treatment of them as problematic, while other sets of circumstances are ignored. A large body of research explores the dimensions of this 'picking out' process.' The people who do the 'picking out' are moral entrepreneurs—activists who claim to represent public values as they push a specific policy agenda. Sometimes, as in the case of the War on Drugs, they help to create a 'moral panic' that speeds up, and may overwhelm, democratic deliberation. Punitive policies like the contemporary War on Drugs are the typical result of moral panics."[305]

—Doris Marie Provine, Professor of Law—

PROHIBITIONISTS HAVE EXPLAINED our drug policies as a response to the 19th Century's rise in drug abuse. The marked, unregulated at this time, was bursting with products that promised to alleviate a variety of common problems and it was usually some tincture of cocaine, opiates, or cannabis. These drugs were hailed as the solution to most ailments; not only "female irritations" but infants were targeted as appropriate candidates for opium products, and the uncritical embrace of this trade made addiction a problem.

---

[305] PROVINE, *UNEQUAL UNDER LAW* (2007) 8

Drug historian David Musto estimates that by 1870 the United States had 250 000 opiate addicts,[306] and to address this concern the Pure Food and Drug Act (1906) provided relief. From now on, producers could no longer tempt consumers with promises of reprieve without naming their secret ingrediencies, and from 1910 and onward this legislation was backed up by stronger regulatory measures at the state, federal, and international level.

At this time, however, few wanted a prohibition. Even though countries like the United States and China pressed on for greater controls (and even though, in most countries, there were high-pitched temperance communities), there were strong liberal and economic reasons to respect the free market. As to the liberal reasons, the British Empire had approved the appointment of a Royal Commission on Opium in 1893. The Commission was to report on whether India's opium exports to the Far East should be ended and whether poppy growing and consumption of opium in India itself should be prohibited, except for medical purposes.

After an extended inquiry the Royal Commission released its report in 1895, running to around two thousand pages. The report firmly rejected the claims made by prohibitionists regarding the harm wrought to India by this traffic. Instead, it claimed that opium use in Asia was analogous to alcohol use in Europe, that opium was not harmful to Asians, and that Chinese complaints were based on commercial concerns, not medical evidence. This proved to be an unexpected and devastating blow to the hopes of the anti-opium reformers in Britain, a country who had fought two wars against China so that its merchants could sell opium to the citizenry. And while this display of power (and the influence of opium magnates on world politics) were a reminder that issues of morality and power-politics go hand in hand, reason still had enough sway for governments to let people choose for themselves in this matter.

---

[306] DAVID MUSTO, *THE AMERICAN DISEASE: ORIGINS OF ORIGINS OF NARCOTIC CONTROL* (1973). Bonnie and Whitebread estimate "between one-quarter and one-half million Americans addicted to narcotics around the turn of the century, comprising at least one percent of the population." Bonnie & Whitebread, *The Forbidden Fruit and the Tree of Knowledge* (1970) 981-82

The first international treaty system, therefore, was a regulatory measure. The International Opium Convention (1912) and the Geneva Convention (1925) left no agreement on a prioritized law-and-order approach and many countries were so uncooperative that the American delegation went home in protest. It was not until the Agreement for the Control of Opium Smoking in the Far East (also known as the Agreement concerning the Suppression of Opium Smoking), which became effective in 1937, that eight nations would agree upon a prohibition regime—and then for minors under the age of 21.

9.1. Racist Origins

Still, these developments are not the entire story. While the temperance movement in the 19th century focused on alcohol, there were legislation which sought to regulate other substances, and a common denominator was a lack of principled thinking.

The people back then could be forgiven, considering that the failures of prohibition were not yet obvious. On the U.S. state level, the first round of legislation came in the 1850's when 13 states criminalized the manufacture and sale of intoxicating beverages. The constitutionality of such laws was determined on the basis of the License Cases in 1847, where in six separate opinions the Supreme Court upheld Massachusetts, New Hampshire, and Rhode Island laws regulating wholesale and retail sales of liquor. In one of these opinions, Chief Justice Taney had stated that: "if any State deems the retail and internal traffic in ardent spirits injurious to its citizens, and calculated to produce idleness, vice, or debauchery, I see nothing in the constitution of the United States to prevent it from regulating and restraining the traffic, or from prohibiting it altogether, if it thinks proper."[307]

Inspired by this statement, the courts of eight states gave little attention to objections. They simply defined the police power in

---

[307] Ibid., 991

broad terms (meaning that they blindly accepted the opinion of politicians' that alcohol was a dangerous threat to the welfare of society and that prohibition was a proper way of dealing with this threat) and rejected the constitutional challenges under their state constitutions. There were, however, exceptions, and while alcohol had strong defenders which made sure that Congress had to pass another constitutional Amendment (the Eighteenth) before its constitutionality was accepted, few spoke for cannabis, cocaine, and opiates.

When it came to these substances, they were commonly associated with minorities,[308] and the first legislation of these products were open attempts to control and beleaguer certain population groups. Hence, while the government's response to the alcohol problem was a topic of some debate, there were no serious discussion associated with narcotics legislation.[309] Instead, the scapegoating mechanism was easy to distinguish, and this has been noted by many scholars.[310]

When the first drug laws came into being, therefore, it was not because of the dangers associated with the drugs per se, but it was because the users were considered a problem and needed to be

---

[308] In the 1800s, "this rather large addict population included more females than males, more whites than blacks, and was confined neither to particular geographical regions nor to areas of high population concentration. Its most significant characteristic was its predominantly middle-class composition." (Ibid., 981-82) Addiction then was a medical side-effect, not the result of thrill-seeking adventure, but at the end of the century this pattern was changing and these substances would become associated with minorities.

[309] Bonnie and Whitebread refer to the early legislation as "promulgated largely in a vacuum. Public and even professional ignorance of the effects of narcotic drugs contributed both to the dimensions of the problem and the nature of the legislated cure. The initial legislation was attended by no operation of the public opinion process, and instead generated a new public image of narcotics use. Only after this creation of a public perception occurred did the legislative approach comport with what we shall call latent public opinion." Id.

[310] As David Musto noted: "The most passionate support for legal prohibition of narcotics has been associated with fear of a given drug's effect on a specific minority. Certain drugs were dreaded, because they seemed to undermine essential social restrictions, which kept these groups under control: cocaine was supposed to enable blacks to withstand bullets which would kill normal persons and to stimulate sexual assault. Fear that smoking opium facilitated sexual contact between Chinese and white Americans was also a factor in its total prohibition. Chicanos [Mexicans] in the South West were believed to be incited to violence by smoking marijuana.   . . . In each instance, use of a particular drug was attributed to an identifiable and threatening minority group." MUSTO, *THE AMERICAN DISEASE* (1973) 245

dealt with. As Bonnie and Whitebread documented, it was ignorance and racism that brought these laws into being, and Musto and others have noted the "coincidence" that these drugs were criminalized at a time when there was an intense crisis between the drug-linked group and the rest of society.

The racist origin of the drug laws being established, this mentality led to the establishment of a prohibitionist machinery; as a matter of fact, drugs were not even seen as a problem before prohibitionists created a drug problem,[311] and after the Second World War, the American drug warriors took their lies and their bigotry to the international scene where they used their political clout to make way for the UN Single Convention.

From this point on, prohibitionism was to become the ruling ideology, the market was in the hands of organized crime, and drug warriors and profit margins were running wild. Since that day, they have all had a mutual interest in keeping the status quo, and we shall see how they positioned themselves.

---

[311] After researching the beginning of the drug war, its first 50 years from 1860 to 1910, Professor Mandel concludes that the War on Drugs preceded the drug use problem; that the war is rooted in racism; that the war shaped and worsened drug use; that the War on Drugs effectively created the drug problem; that people enjoy the melodrama of fighting this war; that the war on drugs has caused a collective memory loss of how drugs were unproblematic in a free market; and that this memory loss handicaps the imagination of those making policy today. Jerry Mandel, *The Opening Shots of the War on Drugs*, in JEFFERSON M. FISH (ED.), *HOW TO LEGALIZE DRUGS* (1998) 248-49. For similar conclusions, see MILLER, *THE CASE FOR LEGALIZING DRUGS* (1991) 109

9.2. THE FOUNDING DRUG WARRIORS

"Racism was the prime reason for the initial half-century of the War on Drugs. The War on Drugs provided a venue for gratuitously punishing selected types of people while providing a rationale that one was really doing good. It enabled sadism without guilt or embarrassment, without legal or public censure. The titillating melodrama of the War on Drugs—agent versus smuggler, good versus evil—served as cover for the cultural oppression of the War on Drugs."[312]

—Jerry Mandel, Professor of Sociology—

The murky history of drug prohibition has been elucidated upon by few and neglected by many. Even so, we know that the refusal to deal with first principles was not only due to the scapegoating phenomenon; this refusal may have been evidence of the extent to which integrity was left behind, but it was also a testimony to the power of special interests and their will to increase in power and scope. Hence, if we look at this from a perspective of power-politics, the U.S. Congress by the late 1800's had become infamous for pandering to special interest groups. Independent newspapers at this time would openly paint Congress as being under the influence of opium smugglers[313] and their power was vast.

By the 1830's, opium had become the largest business in the world and with the establishment of the Skull and Bones society,

---

[312] Mandel, *The Opening Shots of the War on Drugs*, in JEFFERSON M. FISH (ED.), *HOW TO LEGALIZE DRUGS* (1998) 213

[313] According to The New York Herald's special correspondent: "The leaders of the opium ring . . . induced the Billion Dollar Congress to impose a duty of $12 a pound upon opium, knowing that this would enhance the value of the drug, keep out legal importations and swell the profits on the smuggled opium. They persuaded the same Congress to enact legislation which places such a high license and heavy internal revenue tax upon manufacturers of opium in the United States as to effectually and absolutely keep out all manufacturers of the drug and leave the market entirely [to them]." Ibid., 222

the smugglers accumulated great political power.[314] Founded in 1832, this secret society group (with headquarters at Yale and a fondness for death) would manipulate events according to their own incentives and were highly successful.

As we shall see, this group would connect with others who had an interest in population control and together they arranged so that politics favoured their product. In this regard, a legalization of drugs was off the table.[315] In the early days of the drug war, therefore, as documented by Mandel, drug barons would profit by making Congress pass increasingly outrageous tolls on imports, while in later years they would push on for greater international regulations. As Musto noted, it was the Philippines that gave the United States leadership of the international control of narcotics,[316] (in addition to providing an experiment in American Imperialism and population eradication) and the Skull and Bones society had key members on board. William Howard Taft, the Governor of the Philippines, was himself a Bonesman, and not only did he supervise the murdering of more than a million civilians, but he appointed a three-man "Opium Committee" to investigate the opium situation.

This committee, in turn, produced a report that could be used to spur the prohibitionist-movement. Based on its findings,

---

[314] The Russell, Whitney, Delano, Cabot, Cleve, Lowell, Taft, Roosevelt, Coolidge, Perkins, Sturgis, Forbes, and later, the Harriman, Prescott, and Bush family seem to have been key players in this plot.

[315] "One of the largest opium importers of the day were Jardine-Matheson, a company still in existence today. A memo from their company directors revealed sinister motives for opposing legalization, 'If the trade is ever legalized, it will cease to be profitable from that time. The more difficulties that attend it, the better for you and us.' They were right, the price soared after opium was made illegal through an international ban in 1914." ASA, Nevada County, *The History of Prohibition*, (Part 4) January 19, 2013

[316] David F. Musto, *The History of Legislative Control Over Opium, Cocaine, and Their Derivatives* (1987). At the national level, before this, Henry Cabot Lodge, another insider and a collaborator with Root, had pushed a resolution through the Senate in 1901 forbidding the sale of alcohol and opium "to aboriginal tribes and uncivilized races." The provisions of the Native Races Act were later expanded, banning the sale of stimulants to "uncivilized elements in America itself and in its territories, such as Indians, Alaskans, the inhabitants of Hawaii, railroad workers, and immigrants at ports of entry."

Secretary of State Elihu Root (who was nearly a Bonesman[317]) in 1905 submitted a draft bill to Congress that would ban the import of opium prepared for smoking and punish possession with up to five years in prison. Congress jumped on the opportunity, and at the federal level a law was passed in February 1909, now offering prison sentences to all U.S. citizens. Not only did it limit supply and drive prices up,[318] but American imperialists could put Filipinos and others behind bars for indulging in habits of ancient tradition.

In this quest, fascist imperialists and moral zealots never had much consideration for first principles. "As to Opium in China and liquors among thi savage races," Root declared, "they are a disgrace to civilization," and as Secretary of State he formulated a plan for controlling the oriental commerce in opium—the Shanghai Commission of 1909. This was ostensibly an effort to help the Chinese deal with their opium problem, but this commission more likely was an attempt to eradicate competition. After all, being in control of the Navy, courts, politicians, and local police, the American opium barons had nothing to fear and everything to gain by international controls, and they would pursue this strategy with a cunning that left competitors dazzled.[319]

---

[317] Elihu Root was an attorney and close associate off William Whitney (a key Bonesman). As Anthony Sutton, an early investigator of the Skull and Bones noted: "Although not a member of The Order, Root has been called 'Whitney's artful attorney'. Root, one of the sharpest legal minds in American history and a power in his own right, worked along with the purposes of The Order." ANTHONY C. SUTTON, *AMERICA'S SECRET ESTABLISHMENT: AN INTRODUCTION TO THE ORDER OF SKULL & BONES* (2002)

[318] According to one New York City addict interviewed for a study quoted in Acker's book the price of "a can of hop" jumped from $4 to $50. This pushed addicts toward more potent opiates, especially morphine and heroin. CAROLINE JEAN ACKER, *CREATING THE AMERICAN JUNKIE: ADDICTION RESEARCH IN THE CLASSIC ERA OF NARCOTIC CONTROL* (2002)

[319] Anthony Sutton speaks to it: "Not only did Skull and Bones become a major force in drug smuggling (the Bush and Prescott families in the 1860s), but in true Hegelian fashion, generated the antithesis, the so-called 'war on drugs.' This hypocritical policy maintains the price of drugs, controls supply, and puts millions in jail while the gainers, in great part, are none other than the same 'Bonesmen' who pass the laws to prohibit." SUTTON, *AMERICA'S SECRET ESTABLISHMENT* (2002) xiii

9.2.1. The Harrison Act

First, however, a federal legislation had to be enacted at home. This was accomplished with the Harrison Narcotics Tax Act of 1914. Being a mere tax act, the Harrison Act did not criminalize drug use, but it did make it difficult to get a dose of opiates without spending more money. While a gram of morphine cost 60 cents before the Act, it would cost $35 dollars after,[320]—but more importantly, Bonesmen were key plotters. The act was proposed by Representative Francis Burton Harrison of New York. He was a Bonesman—and the president at this time, was Taft himself (1909-13). As Chief of State, Taft was not only key to the establishment of the First International Opium Conference in Hague, 1912, but in ensuring that Congress followed up on their work.[321]

To get legislation through Congress, the Harrison Act had been presented as a Tax Act. Even so, this group wanted so much more and Taft later, as Chief Justice of the United States, (1921–1930) would ensure that the Harrison Act was interpreted as a means for repressing drug users.[322] To be sure, there were many

---

[320] BARBARA HODGSON, *IN THE ARMS OF MORPHEUS* (2001) 128

[321] In his message on foreign relations communicated to the two Houses of Congress December 7, 1911, President Taft called "especial attention to the assembling of the Opium Conference at The Hague, to the fact that that conference was to review all pertinent municipal laws relating to the opium and allied evils, and certainly all international rules regarding these evils, and to the fact that it seemed to me most essential that the Congress should take immediate action on the antinarcotic legislation before the Congress, to which I had previously called attention by a special message." He noted that "It was most unfortunate that this Government, having taken the initiative in the international action which eventuated in the important international opium convention, failed to do its share in the great work by neglecting to pass the necessary legislation to correct the deplorable narcotic evils in the United States as well as to redeem international pledges upon which it entered by virtue of the abovementioned convention. The Congress at its present session should enact into law those bills now before it which have been so carefully drawn up in collaboration between the Department of State and the other executive departments, and which have behind them not only the moral sentiment of the country, but the practical support of all the legitimate trade interests likely to be affected." William Howard Taft, *Fourth Annual Message*, December 3, 1912

[322]As Charles Merrill Hough, a longtime federal judge in New York City, noted in 1917: "The one thing common to all this regulation of behavior, production and business, is that the Congress, not being able directly to prohibit men from doing what they have hitherto done, nor directly compel them to do what the majority desires, has created by statute a new standard of conduct or method of business procedure, put upon it the seal of congressional

others involved, but with players like these the project move ahead.

9.2.2. Early Crusaders

"It is more than a coincidence that . . . sensational publicity . . . preceded this type of legislation . . . followed by underworld and spread of addiction of non-therapeutic origin among the youthful and curious." [323]

—Lester Volk, a doctor who became Congressman, 1923—

In 1908, President Theodore Roosevelt named Hamilton Wright as the United States first Opium Commissioner. Being a good old-fashioned racist,[324] he was perfect for the job, and he would promote a regime of prohibition with great enthusiasm. As Wright was a political opportunist who dreamed about becoming Minister to China,[325] he did not need a Skull and Bones membership to advance the interests of secret drug lords, and in February 1909 he served as U.S. delegate to the International Opium Commission in Shanghai.[326] He also served at the follow-on conference at the

approval, and by taxation, or exclusion from the post or interstate commerce, made life miserable for those who refuse to square their lives in accordance with the legislative preference." Charles Merrill Hough, *Covert Legislation and the Constitution*, Harvard Law Review Vol. 30, No. 8 (1917) 808

[323] Mandel, *The Opening Shots of the War on Drugs*, in JEFFERSON M. FISH (ED.), *HOW TO LEGALIZE DRUGS* (1998) 249

[324] Dr. Hamilton Wright elucidated thus on the threat of the opiates: "One of the most unfortunate phases of the habit of opium smoking in this country is the large number of women who have become involved and were living as common-law wives of or cohabiting with Chinese in the Chinatowns of our various cities." (PROVINE, *UNEQUAL UNDER LAW*, 74) He had this to say on cocaine: "It has been stated on very high authority that the use of cocaine by the negroes of the South is one of the most elusive and troublesome questions which confront the enforcement of the law in most of the Southern States." Ibid., 75

[325] David F. Musto, *The History of Legislative Control Over Opium, Cocaine, and Their Derivatives* (1987)

[326] Wright was accompanied by Bishop Charles Henry Brent, the Protestant Episcopal bishop of the Philippines, who had come with President Taft to help in Americanization of

Hague in 1911, and while he died in an automobile accident in 1917, friends in high places made sure that his wife Elizabeth Wright, as an assistant to the League of Nations Opium Advisory Committee in the 1920's, could continue to spoil international relations.[327]

Bullying, however, was an obvious part of the plan. By this time, US drug warriors had already shown their true colours at home, where the Treasury Department had turned the Harrison Act into an appropriate tool of oppression. To ensure that it was, agents of state interpreted it as carte blanche to eradicate "non-medical" opiate and cocaine use. Its section II provided that it was "illegal for any physician or druggist to prescribe narcotics to an addict", and this effectively turned 250,000 patients and their doctors into criminals. During the first 14 years of the Harrison Act, therefore, the Treasury Department prosecuted more than 77,000 violations, most of them medical professionals. In the period between 1914 and 1938 some 25,000 doctors were arrested for assisting addicts with products: the average sentence was 21 months, and these people lost their careers and so much more.

For the nation's drug addicts, this not only meant that the last clinic closed down in 1925; it meant that they from now on would have to get their dope from criminals, while being hounded by agents of the Treasury. Thus, the world's most lucrative market in illegal drugs was created.[328]

---

this new possession. During his seventeen years as missionary bishop, Brent was major force for a prohibition of opium smoking in the Philippines. He was a part of the three-man commission to study the problem and would continue this work as the lead delegate to the 1909 International Opium Commission in Shanghai. After this, he also went to the Hague in 1912 as the chairman of the American delegation.

[327] The British Foreign Office called her "incompetent, prejudiced, ignorant, and so constituted temperamentally as to afford a ready means of mischief-making." Minute by B.C. Newton, 5 March 1925, FO 371/10966, National Archives, Kew, UK.

[328] In 1926, after 11 years of narcotics prohibition, an editorial in the Illinois Medical Journal stated: "The Harrison Narcotic law should never have been placed upon the statute books of the United States. It is to be granted that the well-meaning blunderers who put it there had in mind only the idea of making it impossible for addicts to secure their supply of 'dope' and to prevent unprincipled people from making fortunes, and fattening themselves upon the infirmities of their fellow men. As is the case with most prohibitive laws, however, this one fell far short of the mark. So far, in fact, that instead of stopping the traffic, those who deal in dope now make double their money from the poor unfortunates upon whom they prey. . . .The doctor who needs narcotics, used in reason to cure and allay human misery,

It was the perfect scheme. Their power ensured that they could have legislation enacted, even though drugs were hardly a problem to begin with.[329] As soon as some legal precedent was found, however, prohibitionists would build on this to hype up the enemy image of drugs and to escalate persecution.[330] The more they could obscure the facts, the more power they would wield, the more they could terrorize and control others, and the more money they would make. After the prohibition of alcohol ended in 1929, the drug warriors at the Treasury Department lost much that had been gained, but they would continue the persecution of drug users with a vengeance, seeking out new enemies.

9.2.3. ANSLINGER'S CRUSADE

The leading crusader was Harry Anslinger. He had been Assistant Prohibition Commissioner during alcohol prohibition, and in 1932 he took over the narcotics division. A natural born bureaucrat, he would over the next three decades take the Federal Bureau of Narcotics (FBN) from its position as a minor club and turn it into

---

finds himself in a pit of trouble. The lawbreaker is in fact in clover. . . . It is costing the United States more to support bootleggers of both narcotics and alcoholics than there is good coming from the farcical laws now on the statute books. *As to the Harrison Narcotic law . . . people are beginning to ask, 'Who did that, anyway?'*" Edward M. Brecher et al., *Licit and Illicit Drugs* (1972) 52 (my emphasis)

[329] After checking U.S. newspapers from 1894 to 1908 Professor Mandel found that newspapers were "drugfree" and that drugs were largely irrelevant to the populace and media. As he noted: "There wasn't a gambler in the Wild West in early 1908 who would have bet that a year later the U.S. would launch a full-scale war on drugs that would escalate time and again until the twenty-first century." Mandel, *The Opening Shots of the War on Drugs*, in JEFFERSON M. FISH (ED.), *HOW TO LEGALIZE DRUGS* (1998) 230

[330] Bonnie and Whitebread noted this trend thus: "As noted above, the Harrison Act engendered a shift in public perception of the narcotics addict. With ever-increasing frequency and venom, he was portrayed in the public media as the criminal 'dope fiend.' This hysteria, coupled with the actual increases in drug-related criminal conduct due to the closing of the clinics, was the basis for a good many of the post-Harrison Act narcotic statutes. Other forces such as lurid accounts in the media, publications of private narcotics associations, and the effective separation of the addict and his problems from the medical profession, all pressed legislatures into action to deal more effectively with what was perceived as a growing narcotics problem." Bonnie & Whitebread, *The Forbidden Fruit and the Tree of Knowledge* (1970) 1011

a state agency of great influence. In this period, he was a key player in getting the UN Single Convention in place, not to mention the Marijuana Tax Act—both major achievements in prohibitionists' book. This, however, was all in the future, and as the new head of FBN, Anslinger started a campaign to have cannabis outlawed. As the editors of the Consumers Union Report wrote:

"Commissioner Anslinger had no legal jurisdiction over marijuana, but his interest in it was intense. The Bureau's first Annual Report under his aegis warned that marijuana, dismissed as a minor problem by the Treasury one year earlier, had now 'come into wide and increasing abuse in many states, and the Bureau of Narcotics has therefore been endeavouring to impress on the various States the urgent need for vigorous enforcement of the local cannabis laws.'"[331]

While a federal prohibition was years ahead, several states already had criminalized cannabis, the first being Utah in 1915. Utah because it was a Mormon State, but cannabis prohibitions also flourished in the South where it kept Mexicans in their place. Because at this time, during the Great Depression, there were great tensions between whites and other minorities, drug researchers have drawn parallels to the opium prohibitions of the 1870's which were used to control Chinese immigrants. Also at this time the middleclass was struggling and those who provided cheap labour got the blame. Hence, not only were 400,000 Mexican immigrants deported, but Anslinger and the FBN would profit on this national crisis.

To get a national campaign against cannabis going, Anslinger and the FBN would spread falsehoods and propaganda directed at hyping up the enemy image while they attacked those who

---

[331] Ibid., Chapter 56

departed from the heard.[332] In this way, backed by powerful elites, Anslinger and the FBN succeeded in erasing much of American history, making cannabis, a well-known medicine for millennia, become "marijuana", the killer weed.[333]

The Press, after all, did not let Anslinger down. Supported by friends in high places (he was the son-in-law of Andrew Mellon) he got the coverage to spike up persecution,[334] as everything was prepared for the Marijuana Tax Act.

9.2.4. THE MARIJUANA TAX ACT

When the Marijuana Tax Act came up before Congress in 1937, it was after a massive and well-coordinated misinformation campaign. The plot and the players were so suspicious that conspiracy theories are accepted as a legitimate endeavour, and the idea is that business interests united to quench competition.[335]

---

[332] This FBN information pamphlet from the 1930s was instructive: "Prolonged use of Marihuana frequently develops a delirious rage which sometimes leads to high crimes, such as assault and murder. Hence Marihuana has been called the 'killer drug.' The habitual use of this narcotic poison always causes a marked deterioration and sometimes produces insanity. . . . While the Marihuana habit leads to physical wreckage and mental decay, its effects upon character and morality are even more devastating. The victim frequently undergoes such moral degeneracy that he will lie and steal without scruple." ROBINSON & SCHERLEN, *LIES, DAMN LIES, AND DRUG WAR STATISTICS* (2007) 11

[333] As Doris Marie Provine noted: "The rapidity with which marijuana became a dangerous drug provides a useful object lesson in the power of a few skillful tacticians, aided by an uncritical mass media, to shape public policy. In less than a decade, marijuana rose from its lowly status as an ingredient in patent medicines to cure migraines, rheumatism, and insomnia to a source of insanity, suicide and major crime." PROVINE, *UNEQUAL UNDER LAW* (2007) 82

[334] In *Marijuana: A Sociological Overview*, Professor Harry Becker shows how the media assisted the FBN campaign. Between 1925 and 1935 he found no articles on marijuana, but between 1935-39 there were 21, nearly all promulgating FBN propaganda.

[335] "A closer look at the behind-the-scenes intrigue involving certain influential Americans in the 1930s reveals how the sudden federal campaign against marijuana was more likely related to economic factors and to commercial interests more than to any legitimate fears over the drug itself. In the 1920s the Du Pont Company had developed and patented numerous petroleum-based products, including fuel additives, chemical processes for the manufacture of paper from wood pulp and numerous synthetic products such as nylon, cellophane and other plastics. At the same time other firms were developing synthetic products from renewable biomass resources, especially from hemp (cannabis). By 1935 raw cellulose from hemp had become a viable option for fuel, fabric and plastics and paper—a cheaper, cleaner and renewable raw material compared to petroleum. Faced with this

Even so, the moral panic that prohibitionists wanted to inspire was obstructed by the fact that few had heard about the drug. The congressmen voting on the bill hardly knew a thing about "marijuana," nor that it was Mexican slang for cannabis, a plant embraced in pharmacopeia around the world.[336]

During the proceedings, Anslinger would be the main witness and his credentials were relied upon to present a summary of facts. Thus, he was perfectly positioned and could tell the committee that: "Here you have a drug that is not like opium. Opium has all of the good of Dr. Jekyll and all of the evil of Mr. Hyde. This drug is entirely the monster Hyde, the harmful effect of which cannot be measured."[337] Marijuana, Anslinger claimed, led to insanity and violent crime—and to prove his case, he relied upon the testimony of police, the frontpages of the yellow press, as well as the FBNs statistics. As seen from this exchange, congressmen were easy to impress:

Senator Brown: *"There is the impression that it is stimulating to a certain extent? It is used by criminals when they want to go out and perform some deed that they would not commit in their ordinary frame of mind?"*

---

competition, Lammont DuPont lobbied the U.S. Treasury Department to seek the prohibition of hemp. Business interests of William Randolph Hearst, the newspaper magnate, were also threatened by hemp, as his timber holdings and his joint enterprises with DuPont for wood-based pulp papermaking would have been rendered uncompetitive. Hearst used his chain of newspapers to aggravate racial tensions, portraying Mexicans in particular as lazy, degenerate and violent and as job stealers and smokers of 'marihuana'—a word brought into the common parlance due in part to frequent mentions in Hearst's publications. The aggressive efforts to demonize cannabis were effective, as the sheer number of newspapers, tabloids, magazines and film reels under Hearst's control enabled him to inundate American media with propaganda." Report of the Legal Frameworks Group to the King County Bar Association, *Drugs and the Drug Laws: Historical and Cultural Contexts*, January 19, 2005

[336] Two episodes are instructive. Under the hearings, Anslinger presented pictures of murders allegedly committed under the influence of marijuana, and a Senator asked Anslinger whether the person bludgeoned to death had a skin disease connected to the substance ("Was there in this case a blood or skin disease caused by marihuana?"). Another episode was revealed in this conversation between two Congressmen: "I do not know anything about the bill," said a representative who complained about the timing of the legislation. Another responded: "It has something to do with something that is called marihuana, I believe it is a narcotic of some kind." SULLUM, *SAYING YES* (2004) 204

[337] HERER, *THE EMPEROR WEARS NO CLOTHES* (1998) 190

Anslinger: *"That is demonstrated by these seven boys, who said they did not know what they were doing after they smoked marihuana. They conceived the series of crimes in while in a state of marihuana intoxication."*

Senator Davis: *"How many cigarettes would you have to smoke before you got this vicious mental attitude toward your neighbor?"*

Anslinger: *"I believe in some cases one cigarette might develop a homicidal mania, probably to kill his brother. It depends on the physical characteristics of the individual. Every individual reacts differently to the drug. It stimulates some and others it depresses. It is impossible to say just what the action of the drug will be on a given individual, or the amount. Probably some people could smoke five before it would take effect, but all the experts agree that the continued use leads to insanity."*[338]

With good reason, the Marijuana Tax Act proceedings have become a Rosetta stone for understanding the legislative environment of the day. The bill was presented as a largely symbolic gesture, one which would require no additional enforcement expenditures, and as the editors of the Consumers Union report noted:

> *"No medical testimony in favor of the proposed federal anti-marijuana law was presented at the 1937 Congressional hearings. Indeed, the only physician to testify was a representative of the American Medical Association—and he opposed the bill. Marijuana, he pointed out, was a recognized medicine in good standing, distributed by leading pharmaceutical firms, and on sale at many*

---

[338] Ibid., 190-91

pharmacies. At least twenty-eight medicinal products containing marijuana were on the market in 1937."[339]

The representative of the American Medical Association (AMA) was Dr. William Woodward, who was also a lawyer. According to him, there was no need for this legislation as there was no indication that the use of cannabis had spread, nor that it was a problem or any magnitude.[340] The Congressmen, however, did not appreciate his concern. They had their mission, and Professor Whitebread elaborates on the response:

> *"What's amazing is what the Congressmen then said to him. Immediately upon his saying, 'The American Medical Association knows of no evidence that marihuana is a dangerous drug,' one of the Congressmen said, 'Doctor, if you can't say something good about what we are trying to do, why don't you go home?' That's an exact quote. The next Congressman said, 'Doctor, if you haven't got something better to say than that, we are sick of hearing you.'"[341]*

Thus, it should be clear what kind of environment that made the Marijuana Tax Act pass. It took this bill no more than three days to get through Congress, and as Judge Gray summarized these proceedings, "the congressional record show that public health and safety issues were not even considered by Congress in making this substance illegal. Instead, the motives appear to have been racism, fear, empire building, and ignorance."[342]

---

[339] Edward M. Brecher et al, *The Consumers Union Report—Licit and Illicit Drugs* (1972) Chapter 56

[340] As he said: "Since the medical use of cannabis has not caused and is not causing addiction, the prevention of the use of the drug for medical purposes can accomplish no good end whatsoever. How far it may serve to deprive the public of the benefits of a drug that on further research may prove to be of substantial value, it is impossible to foresee." HERER, *THE EMPEROR WEARS NO CLOTHES* (1998) 195

[341] Charles Whitebread, speech to the California Judges Association 1995 annual conference.

[342] GRAY, *WHY OUR DRUG LAWS HAVE FAILED AND WHAT WE CAN DO ABOUT IT* (2001) 11

Nevertheless, as Dr Woodward noted, the Marijuana Tax Act had been secretly prepared for two years, and it was another ingenious feat by the war profiteers. While pretending to be a tax act, this legislation (like the Harrison Act) would be used by prohibitionists as a carte blanche to escalate persecution of drug users—and with it, the enemy image of marijuana was elevated to new highs.

9.3. FRAMING DRUG USERS AND COMMUNISTS

"There are limits set by big-city vice squads . . . kickbacks are funneled to the top through them. In big cities like New York, Chicago, and Los Angeles, in the days before the Kennedys, certain neighborhoods were controlled by political machines working with the vice squad and the Mafia. There wasn't a drug deal on the South Side of Chicago that didn't pass through the police to the politicians."[343]

—Martin Pera, former FBN agent—

It was under these circumstances that the Boggs Act, which set mandatory sentences for drug-related offenses, was pushed through Congress.[344] Building upon the Marijuana Tax Act, drug

---

[343] VALENTINE, *STRENGTH OF THE WOLF* (2004) 60

[344] Bonnie and Whitebread summarizes the proceedings: "The crime, pauperism and insanity rationale was accepted unquestioningly as late as 1951. Under this rationale, harsher penalties were certainly as imperative for marijuana offenders as they were for opiate offenders. However, in a paper filed as an exhibit to the hearings on the Boggs Act, Dr. Harris Isbell, Director of Research at the Public Health Service hospital in Lexington, Kentucky, exploded the traditional rationale. He stated that marijuana was not physically addictive and that Marijuana smokers generally bother no one and have a good time. He stated that it has not been proved that smoking marijuana leads to crimes of violence or to crimes of a sexual nature, that no dependence is developed on the drug, and that the practice can easily be stopped at any time. His statements that marijuana does not cause a physical dependence were supported by other doctors, prison officials, and perhaps most significantly by the statement of a number of narcotics addicts. Despite this testimony the legislators approved greatly increased penalties for marijuana users. They would rather listen to Anslinger who told them that 'The danger is this: Over 50 percent of those young

warriors had been busy terrorizing mostly black populations and now a first-offense conviction for marijuana possession carried a minimum sentence of 2 to 10 years (with a fine of up to $20,000).

With this legislation, the drug warriors' persecution of drug users escalated; there was no lack of politically motivated harassment,[345] and it should be noted that Representative Boggs, like Anslinger, was a politician with connections to the intelligence community. Not only did he serve on the Warren Commission, which was an obvious cover-up of the assassination of John F. Kennedy, but he later disappeared in a plane that was never found. By this time, his loyalty to powerbrokers must have diminished, but his immorality was otherwise plain in his leadership in the movement to break the political machine of U.S. Senator Huey Pierce Long, Jr. Long was not only, according to Chief Justice William Howard Taft, "the most brilliant lawyer who ever practiced before the United States Supreme Court", but a politician who fought the Rockefeller Empire with some success. For his efforts, he would be assassinated in 1935,[346] but

---

addicts started on marijuana smoking. They started there and graduated to heroin; they took the needle when the thrill of marijuana was gone.'" Bonnie & Whitebread, *The Forbidden Fruit and the Tree of Knowledge* (1970) 1072-73

[345] Mr. Ravitz, the lawyer of John A. Sinclair, a political activist who was sentenced to ten years imprisonment for possession of two marijuana cigarettes, stated in court: "In America, which has never known anything but the history of racism, and in America which practices those imperialistic and those brutalistic and inhumane wars in Asia and elsewhere around the globe, and in America which sends a man to the moon while millions of its citizens starve, John Sinclair is brought before this Court and he is said to be a criminal. He isn't a criminal. He isn't a criminal at all. The criminals with respect to this law, are the doctors, the legislators, the attorneys who know, who know, because they have knowledge that these laws are unconstitutional. That these laws defy all knowledge of science. That this sumptuary legislation, like its predecessors and like other forms of sumptuary legislation, are on the books to go after and to impress politically unpopular people and groups and minorities. That's the only reason they are on the books. This very day, 25% of the future doctors of America who are studying medicine at Wayne State University Medical School, have possessed marijuana. Twenty-five percent of the future lawyers, indeed future judges who will be sitting on that bench some day, have possessed and have smoked marijuana." *People v. Sinclair*, 387 Mich. 91, 194 N.W.2d 878 (1972) 137 (Justice Brennan, Separate Opinion)

[346] By the summer of 1935, Long's Share Our Wealth clubs had 7.5 million members nationwide; he regularly garnered 25 million radio listeners and was receiving 60,000 letters a week from supporters (more than the president) In his final year, Long was preoccupied

at the very least we know that Boggs and the people who opposed Long were at the wrong side of history.

In the 1950's paranoid cold-war environment, however, the drug warriors could spin drug political trends according to the myths of prohibitionist lore. While Anslinger formerly had refuted the gateway theory, FBN and politicians would now draw upon this to justify increased persecution and in staged press briefings presenting confiscated heroin the FBN accused communist-China of destroying America's young.[347] As we shall see later, this heroin stemmed from the Kuomintang, a fascist organization in league with the CIA, but the Bureau sought to hide this and needed a scapegoat. Communists became the perfect solution, and a key propagandist was George White, Anslinger's right-hand man and a sadistic alcoholic with ties to the OSS. From the late 1940's, he was part of the MKULTRA experiments, and from 1953 to 1965 White and FBN provided the CIA with apartments, where prostitutes would dose unsuspecting diplomats and officials with cannabis and LSD while videotaping the affair.[348] This would be used for blackmail purposes, and quite a few was compromised in this manner.

---

with presidential ambitions and attempted to limit the influence of his Louisiana opponents. After his assassination, his political machine broke up into factions, although it would remain a force in state politics into the 21st century. (Wikipedia)

[347] Many authors have documented how officials have exploited public ignorance, ensuring that the growing fear of drugs rode the tide of other national fears. During the First World War, U.S. officials claimed that Germans corrupted America by smuggling drugs into the country; during the Second World War, they claimed that Japanese fascists were doing it; and during the cold war, they claimed that Chinese, Soviet, and Cuban communists were responsible for undermining society in this fashion. See BERTRAM, ET AL., *DRUG WAR POLITICS* (1996) 70, 84; WISOTSKY, *BEYOND THE WAR ON DRUGS* (1990) 181-84; MILLER, *THE CASE FOR LEGALIZING DRUGS* (1991) 89-115; SCOTT, *AMERICAN WAR MACHINE* (2014)

[348] VALENTINE, *THE STRENGTH OF THE WOLF* (2004) 128

9.3.1. THE DANIEL ACT

"I believe authoritarians are manufacturing and manipulating public fears about drug use in order to create a police state where a much broader agenda of social control can be implemented . . . I believe the war on drug users masks a war on democracy."[349]

—Richard Lawrence Miller—

Adding to this, in 1956 the Daniel Act (named after Senator Price Daniel, an insider with the Freemasonry) increased penalties by a factor of eight over those specified in the Boggs Act. Drug users now faced a mandatory minimum sentence of twenty years, no part of which they were eligible for parole or probation, or a suspended sentence.

By now, however, the American Medical Association had joined forces with the American Bar Association in questioning America's drug policies. They called for a re-examination of the drug laws, and in response Senator Price Daniel (D-TX) called for a study of the U.S. approach to the drug problem. Even so, it was another whitewash and to push America further towards tyranny, the Daniel Subcommittee published a report which concluded that no health approach "to the problem could be undertaken because it would be unreasonable to expect employers to give jobs to addicts."[350] Building on Anslinger's deranged reasoning, Senator Price held that drug users would become sexually impotent and that the fate of America was sealed if legislators did not act fast.

Even experimenting with drug therapy for addicts would, as the Subcommittee had learned from Anslinger, "oblige the United States to withdraw from all its treaty commitments, require major changes in the federal statutes, and conflict with the laws of all the states. The 1920's experience proved—according to the report—

---

[349] MILLER, *DRUG WARRIORS AND THEIR PREY* (1996) 191

[350] RUFUS KING, *THE DRUG HANG UP: AMERICA'S FIFTY-YEAR FOLLY* (1972) Chapter 16

that drug clinics were crime breeders and total failures; and finally, any such notion would be unthinkable because it would give a stamp of respectability to 'the heinous habit' and because in the opinion of the Subcommittee 'it would be absolutely immoral to give in to drug addiction and help perpetuate such pitiful conditions for the individual human being.'"[351]

The Senate, therefore, "was urged to adopt resolutions pushing Commissioner Anslinger's pending international projects: urging recalcitrant nations to ratify the U.S.-sponsored protocol of 1953 limiting cultivation of the poppy plant; pressing the U.N. to move faster on the proposed Single Convention; pushing countries like Belgium, France, and Great Britain, whose medical professions still esteemed heroin, to follow the U.S. lead and outlaw it; and even urging that the U.N. Division of Narcotic Drugs, which had recently been moved to Geneva, be returned to the U.N. headquarters in New York, 'where the full force of wide public opinion can be brought to bear in the fight against illicit narcotics traffic.' On the domestic scene, the Subcommittee called for sharp increases in maximum and minimum penalties for drug offenses, with capital punishment for smuggling and sales involving heroin, 'the most deadly of all.'"[352]

The Daniel Subcommittee, furthermore, held that "Heroin smugglers and peddlers are selling murder, robbery, and rape, and should be dealt with accordingly. Their offense is human destruction as surely as that of the murderer. In truth and in fact, it is 'murder on the instalment plan,' leading not only to the final loss of one life but to others who acquire this contagious infection through association with the original victim. The Subcommittee proposed that ordinary limitations on the right of federal drug agents to search and seize be abrogated, and that Anslinger's men be authorized to tap telephones, carry firearms, and arrest without warrants. Persons accused of drug offenses should be held on higher bail than other defendants and convicted more swiftly by

---

[351] Id.

[352] Id.

the courts lest they commit new offenses while awaiting trial. The Bureau's reporting system to list all addicts coming to the attention of any public authority should of course be made a mandatory requirement for all affected agencies. And the Bureau itself should be enlarged and given bigger appropriations. The Subcommittee's final recommendation in the illicit-traffic report was that addicts and marijuana users, and anyone who had been convicted of any drug violation should be forbidden to travel outside the continental limits of the United States except under special procedures approved by the Secretary of State and the Bureau of Narcotics."

Totalitarianism, then, was well advanced in the 1950's, and to escalate pressure on Congress, Rep. Boggs again came in handy. He turned up as Chairman of the Ways and Means Subcommittee on Narcotics, repeating FBN's propaganda, and as Rufus King summarized these events:

"Out of all this came the Narcotic Control Act of 1956, signed by President Eisenhower on July 18, 1956. In one package, rushed through Congress with virtually no questions or dissent,[353] this Act brought into the law exaggerated new presumptions as to possession of marijuana; increased the minimum and maximum penalties for all drug offenses to two-to-ten years, five-to-twenty years, and ten-to-forty years for succeeding convictions. [It also] imposed five-to-twenty years upon first conviction for any smuggling or sale violation, and ten-to-forty years thereafter, with a separate penalty of ten-to-forty years or any sale or distribution by a person over eighteen to a minor, and from ten years to life, or death when a jury so recommended, if the drug was heroin. All discretion to suspend sentences or grant probation, and all parole

---

[353] Bonnie and Whitebread speak to it thus: "In some ways, this legislation represents the high-water mark of uninformed public policy regarding marijuana. In almost every respect, the provisions of the Act and the legislative motivation bear absolutely no rational relation to marijuana's pharmacology and to the drug's actual use and traffic patterns." Bonnie & Whitebread, *The Forbidden Fruit and the Tree of Knowledge* (1970) 1077

eligibility—generally available to anyone convicted under any other federal criminal law—were prohibited except for first offenders convicted of possession only. Narcotic agents and, for good measure, customs officers were given authority to carry guns, to serve warrants, and to arrest without warrant. A new compounding offense was added to allow an extra charge and added sentence in prosecuting federal drug cases-making use of any interstate communication facility in connection with a drug violation, carrying a separate two-to--five-year term and $5,000 fine."[354]

9.3.2. BEHIND THE SCENES COLLUSION

"It has long been blackletter law . . . that the power to punish . . . is grounded in the police power. This doctrinal fact, however, is treated as though it were of no consequence whatsoever, if it is noted at all. It is odd, to say the least, that the foundation of criminal law, the basis for the right to punish, has attracted so little attention. Despite an ever-expanding literature on the 'theory of punishment,' the nature of the legal or political authority underlying the state's criminal process has been left unexplored. How can this be?"[355]

—Markus D. Dubber, professor of law—

With this grid in place, population control was ensured, and drug warriors would make America incarceration nation number one. Abroad and at home, driven by the enemy image of drugs, the

---

[354] KING, *THE DRUG HANG UP* (1972) Chapter 16

[355] Dubber, *The New Police Science and the Police Power Model of the Criminal Process* (2004) 2

drug warriors would continue to fight this menace and those associated with it, while elite networks, with their help, raked in profits and centralized markets.

Sure, there were principled drug warriors who believed in this crusade and who would not have taken a dime of drug money nor compromised an investigation. We shall meet some of them in the following chapters, but they all discovered that the world that they had been raised to believe in did not exist. Instead, in all the major cities, the police provided a link between elites and the criminal element, and the system treated those who did not turn a blind eye towards corruption as the enemy. As Mike Ruppert found out when he reported on CIA narcotics trafficking to superiors in the LAPD, his life was suddenly in danger, and it was not uncommon that agents would be shot by fellow officers.[356] Alfred W. McCoy had this to say on the corruption at the BNDDs New York Department:

> *"In New York during the 1960s, the regional office of the Bureau of Narcotics and Dangerous Drugs achieved a . . . symbiosis with a Mafia drug syndicate, accepting regular bribes to arrest only those dealers nominated by the syndicate. The system gave federal agents an impressive record of arrests and allowed them rapid promotions while simultaneously eliminating any competition for the mafia."[357]*

These connections between crime and politics would not go away. As we shall see, the FBN, BNDD, and DEA had deep ties to the intelligence community,[358] and the police had orders to stay

---

[356] VALENTINE, *THE STRENGTH OF THE WOLF* (2004)

[357] McCOY, *THE POLITICS OF HEROIN* (1991) 15

[358] Professor Alan Block noted the connection thus: "The FBN's history (and those of its successors) reveals that its enforcement tasks have been secondary, the result of a subordinate relationship with the intelligence establishment. Drug enforcement abroad has been compromised because intelligence agencies care nothing about drug enforcement, although they often care quite a lot about narcotics. They have used it as a common coin for the purposes of espionage, paramilitary operations, covert trade and counterintelligence. The Federal Bureau of Narcotics provided cover for the Central Intelligence Agency since

away from those targets deemed worthy of "National Security" status.[359] As author Douglas Valentine, the most prominent researcher of the FBN's history, summarized the period:

> *"As the Kennedys burst upon the scene, the CIA had turned the FBN completely upside down. CIA agents were blackmailing spies, diplomats, and politicians at three bureau safehouses. With the support of complicit FBN agents, the CIA was hiring Corsican drug smugglers as assassins and using Mafiosi to smuggle MKULTRA poisons into Cuba to assassinate Fidel Castro. On behalf of the Agency, FBN headquarters focused public attention on the phantom Chinese Communist-Cuban connection—even going so far . . . as to allow top members of a Kuomintang drug smuggling ring in San Francisco to escape punishment, while George White covered up for them by telling the press that their heroin had come from Communist China. Meanwhile the CIA's anti-Castro terrorists were smuggling spies and assassins into Cuba and returning with shiploads of narcotics for sale in America."[360]*

---

just about the day it was formed. That has meant profound drug abuse at home in the name of counterintelligence experimentation, and support for anti-communist drug dealers abroad. It is simply impossible to take pronouncements about federal drug policy at face value given the history of compromise and prevarication." PETER DALE SCOTT & JONATHAN MARSHALL, *COCAINE POLITICS: DRUGS, ARMIES AND THE CIA IN CENTRAL AMERICA* (1998) 171

[359] Mike Ruppert, a police officer with the LAPD in the late 1970's, describes this system: "At the time all police agencies belonged to an organization known as the Narcotics Intelligence Network (NIN). Any law enforcement agency conducting an investigation of a drug trafficker must first run the suspect's name through a computer search to find out if anyone else has an ongoing investigation of that suspect. Such an arrangement is necessary to prevent one agency from arresting another agency's undercover operatives. What the CIA does is to use its contract agents or deep covers within local police departments to constantly monitor NIN, which has to be notified of pending raids. The CIA also uses its deep covers within police departments to monitor investigations and warn CIA assets in time to avoid arrest." http://www.fromthe wilderness.com/free/pandora/blacks-targeted.html

[360] VALENTINE, *THE STRENGTH OF THE WOLF* (2004) 235

Under these conditions, there was not much those dedicated to the eradication of drug markets could do.[361] While they arrested plenty of small fish and some bigger players, corrupt police officers and bureaucrats in collusion with gangsters would ensure that the real kingpins went on unharmed to consolidate drug markets. As a matter of fact, the game was rigged so that integrity among drug warriors would be rooted out.[362] In a 1974 Rolling Stone article, former narcotics officers Sergio Borquez, Jerry Laveroni, and Pat Saunders all agree that the Inspection unit's "real function was as an arm in the political wrestle for control in the local office and the bureau at large."[363] To the elite on top, these units were invaluable as they provided an opportunity for controlling law enforcement; Sergio Borquez would compare it to the Gestapo, and according to these three officers, the local centres, like L.A.'s Office of Inspection, was just one more vantage point to strike from.

While these centres, then, were created to ensure that law enforcement walked the straight and narrow, they evolved to become political arenas of intense infighting. As there were plenty

---

[361] Michael Levine, a DEA agent for 25 years, attested to this: "We could not avoid witnessing the CIA protecting major drug dealers. Not a single important source in Southeast Asia was ever indicted by US law enforcement. This was no accident. Case after case was killed by CIA and State Department intervention and there wasn't a damned thing we could do about it. . . . [They] were protecting more and more politically powerful drug traffickers around the world: the Mujahedeen in Afghanistan, the Bolivian cocaine cartels, the top levels of Mexican government, Nicaraguan Contras, Colombian drug dealers and politicians, and others. Media's duties, as I experienced firsthand, were twofold: first, to keep quiet about the gush of drugs that was allowed to flow unimpeded into the US; second, to divert the public's attention by shilling them into believing the drug war was legitimate by falsely presenting the few trickles we were permitted to indict as though they were major 'victories,' when in fact we were doing nothing more than getting rid of the inefficient competitors of CIA assets." Michael Levine, *America's "War on Drugs": CIA- Recruited Mercenaries and Drug-Traffickers*, Global Research, January 13, 2011

[362] "Between 1973 and 1978 I led the New York office in arrests, undercover buys, and drug seizures, and had never lost a case in court, yet I was never considered for promotion. To inflame my impetuous and egotistical young heart even further, the agents being promoted had little or no enforcement accomplishments and no street expertise; in some cases, they were even considered office jokes. What they did have were good political connections. I was not the only DEA street agent hurt and deceived by this policy; it was agency wide." MICHAEL LEVINE, *THE BIG WHITE LIE* (1994) 51

[363] David Harris, *An Inside Look at Federal Narcotics Enforcement*, Rolling Stone, December 5, 1974

of violations taking place, everyone was susceptible to punishment,[364] and blackmailing became the best defence. Not only from the top down, but also the bottom up, and this "amounted to a balance of terror". Narcotics agents in the Los Angeles office, for instance, were busy tapping each other's phones, breaking into each other's desks, and working hard to feed their weaker members into the jaws of Inspection. They were "so busy fighting each other," Borquez told the Rolling Stone, that "they didn't have time for the real criminals."[365]

According to him and the other law-enforcement officers, "the struggle for control at the organization's base, like the split and the rip-offs, took place behind closed doors. The winners went public as 'Mr. Clean' and the losers were cast as 'corruption.' And it wasn't just a question of Los Angeles."[366] Indeed, it was not. The internal corruption among law-enforcement was systemwide, and we shall now see how this helped a cabal of elites to take control of the world's drug supply.

---

[364] Michael Levine wrote *the Big White Lie* and *Deep Cover* about his work for the DEA. As he described the office climate: "DEA street agents are administratively vulnerable to being fired at almost any time. Their lives are governed by three manuals, each the size of the Manhattan telephone directory, that include some of the most ridiculous, unrealistic, and oppressive regulations the suits have invented—regulations that are clearly intended to cover the bureaucrats' asses and to keep the street agents silenced, fearful of their jobs, and under absolute control."364 LEVINE, *THE BIG WHITE LIE* (1994) 107

[365] David Harris, *An Inside Look at Federal Narcotics Enforcement*, Rolling Stone, December 5, 1974

[366] Id.

10

DRUGS AND POWER

"Federal drug law enforcement is essentially a function of national security, as that term is applied in its broadest sense: that is, not just defending America from its foreign enemies, but preserving its traditional values of class, race, and gender at home, while expanding its economic and military influence abroad."[367]

—Douglas Valentine—

IN FOLLOWING THE factions that have contributed to the increased monopolization of the drugs economy, our quest begins with the not-so-easy realization that this world is not what it seems. The group and the individuals named here most certainly exist and they could not have achieved what they did without controlling the agencies that were established to hunt them down. This may seem too farfetched to consider. Yet the evidence is there. And hiding behind official positions of authority, this cabal has successfully positioned at top of politics, while effectively derailing healthy progress and state relations.

In the world of cloak-and-dagger operations, then, this is the bad-boys crew, the one that has been dreaded by U.S. presidents since the days of Andrew Jackson (1829-37).[368] This coincides with the rising

---

[367] VALENTINE, *THE STRENGTH OF THE WOLF* (2004) 3

[368] Franklin Roosevelt, the 32nd President, said this "element in the large centers has owned the government ever since the days of Andrew Jackson," Letter to Col. Edward Mandell House (21 November 1933); as quoted in ELLIOTT ROOSEVELT (ED.), *F.D.R.: HIS PERSONAL LETTERS*, 1928-1945 (1950) 373

influence of the opium magnates, which established the Skull and Bones/322 Society at Yale in 1832. We shall now delve into its world of operations, and while there are other factions and interests involved, this group—the society of Death—would bend the U.S. government to its will.[369]

Indeed, drugs have always been part of a bigger picture. Their illegal status not only ensures a vast network of intrigue; it connects the dots between the biggest players in power-politics, and to understand drug policy we must recognize that politics is not what it appears. In reality, bankers with an agenda of their own have been in control, and so, as Senator Dan Inouye observed, "with the passing of time, a shadow government structure has evolved, one that "has its own Air Force, its own Navy, its own fundraising mechanisms, and the ability to pursue its own ideas of the national interest, free from all checks and balances, and free from the law itself."[370]

This cabal of elites, which includes the Rothschilds and other banking families, would use terror, deceit, blackmail, and murder as political currency. One insider, Samuel Todd Churchill, at his deathbed, revealed the Skull and Bones society to be "nothing more than a political assassination hit team against those United States politicians who do not fall in line with the House of Rothschild's plans for a blood elitist domination and control over the world's economy". And while this may be hard to believe, the quote is from one of the

---

[369] Anthony Sutton, a professor of economics, was delivered an anonymous package containing inside information on the Skull and Bones society. Among other information, it included lists of initiates, and Sutton described this elite faction's influence: "The Order has set up or penetrated just about every significant research, policy, opinion-making organization in the United States, in addition to the church, business, law, government and politics. Not all at the same time, but persistently and consistently enough to dominate the direction of American society. The evolution of American society is not, and has not been for a century, a voluntary development reflecting individual opinion, ideas, and decisions at the grass roots. On the contrary, the broad direction has been created artificially and simulated by the Order." SUTTON, *AMERICA'S SECRET ESTABLISHMENT* (203) 25

[370] Upon discovering its tentacles, Daniel Inouye, Chairman of the Senate Select Committee on Secret Military Assistance to Iran and the Nicaraguan Opposition, said this during the Iran Contra hearings.

most noteworthy deathbed-confessions in history.[371] As a high-level member of the secret New Orleans Mardi Gras Society called *The Mystick Crewe of Comus*, Todd was intimately involved with 19th century power-politics. His daughter recorded his deathbed confession and according to this insider, the Skull and Bones had killed seven U.S. presidents by the Second World War.

President Kennedy experienced this cabal's ruthlessness when he was assassinated—and his family and others experienced its power in the Warren Commission's cover-up. This commission, of which every member was an insider (most were Freemasons, but the Skull and Bones was also represented) would whitewash the lone gunman theory, providing shelter to the real plotters.

It is only fitting, then, when we are to introduce this underworld of operatives, to begin with President Kennedy's most trusted General, Fletcher S. Prouty. As first Chief of Special Operations with the U.S. Joint Chiefs of Staff, his duty was structured to provide the military support of the world-wide clandestine activities of the CIA. In other words, he had daily interactions with the world of covert operations, and after retiring wrote a book that explained some hidden history. He described the operations of a "secret team", one that we are now to become familiar with, and according to General Prouty this "network was ancient and worldwide." It was the "functional element of the dominant power," and would "operate everywhere with the best of all supporting facilities from special weaponry and advanced communications, with the assurance that its members would never be prosecuted." This network would "topple government, create governments, and influence governments almost anywhere in the world;" it was lawless, and would "get the job done whether it had political authorization or not."[372]

---

[371] Mimi L. Eustis, the daughter of Samuel Todd, recorded his deathbed confession. Her article *the Mardi Gras Secrets* relates her father's confession: http://www.whale.to/c/mardi_gras.html

[372] FLETCHER L. PROUTY, *THE SECRET TEAM: THE CIA AND ITS ALLIES IN CONTROL OF THE UNITED STATES AND THE WORLD* (2008) xxxvi

It certainly boggles the mind. Yet, there are others, familiar with this group, who have lived to tell their tale. Another operator is Al Martin, a retired U.S. Navy lieutenant commander attached to the Office of Naval Intelligence, who described its operations thus:

"It's a Government within the Government, comprising some thirty to forty thousand people the American Government turns to, when it wishes certain illegal covert operations to be extant pursuant to a political objective. . . . Imagine a 'system' in which insiders use government agencies and programs as their own private piggy bank, like a criminal privatized public sector, and you can begin to understand the highest levels of corruption and criminality in the USA."[373]

The intelligence services are an integral part of this set up, and it comes as no surprise that the rise of prohibition was followed by an expansion of their trade. To intelligence services much interesting is happening in the area where crime and politics meet; this is where they usually operate, and as the drugs economy became an important area of control, the difference between drug dealers and government agents would be difficult to distinguish.

Indeed, the tale that is to be told will make this **an understatement**. As more perceptive academics and politicians have noted, there has been a coup in the United States,[374] and we shall now see how "the CIA within the CIA" fed off the drugs economy in its quest to undermine the fabric of governments around the world.

---

[373] AL MARTIN, *THE CONSPIRATORS: SECRETS OF AN IRAN-CONTRA INSIDER* (2002) vii-viii

[374] In 2010, Congressman Ron Paul spoke to it: "There's been a coup, have you heard? It's the CIA coup. The CIA runs everything, they run the military. They're the ones who are over there, lobbing missiles and bombs on countries. . . . Think of the harm they have done since they were established [after] World War II. They are a government unto themselves. They're in businesses, in drug businesses, they take out dictators . . . We need to take out the CIA!" http://rawstory.com/2010/01/ron-paul-cia/

10.1. CONNECTING DRUGS AND THE CIA

"In my 30-year history in the Drug Enforcement Administration and related agencies, the major targets of my investigations almost invariably turned out to be working for the CIA."[375]

—Dennis Dayle, DEA Agent—

When it comes to the control of global drug markets, the CIA's Directorate of Intelligence (DI) has been a crucial component. In 2004, the name was changed to the National Clandestine Service (NCS) and it is the directorate's Deputy Director of Operations which seems to have been the most busy covering up drug operations.[376] Tracing the agency back to its origins, we find the Office of Policy Coordination (OPC), which was incorporated into the Office of Special Operations (OSO) in 1952.[377] This shady operations unit was established in 1948 without Congressional authorization. Beginning with the Korean war, its budgets and personnel would increase rapidly, and key players in this scheme was Frank Wisner,[378] William

---

[375] SCOTT & MARSHALL, *COCAINE POLITICS* (1998) xvii

[376] MARTIN, *THE CONSPIRATORS* (2002) 162

[377] For more on OPC, see McCOY, *THE POLITICS OF HEROIN* (1991) 166-178

[378] Frank G. Wisner was head of intelligence operations in south-eastern Europe at the end of World War II. He became head of the Office of Policy Coordination (OPC) at its creation in 1947 and oversaw the CIA's Directorate of Plans (DDP) from 1951-58. In this capacity, Wisner oversaw the creation of all the stay-behind (Gladio) networks in East and West Europe.

Colby,[379] James Jesus Angleton,[380] Allen Dulles,[381] Richard Helms, William Donovan,[382] General Richard Stilwell (the American commander in Asia), and Col. Paul Helliwell.

---

[379] Bill Colby was an OSS officer during World War II. After the war he joined the newly created CIA where he spent 12 years setting up the stay-behind network known as *Operation Gladio*. He then went to Vietnam where he served as chief of station in Saigon and chief of the CIA's Far East Division. After Vietnam, Colby became CIA director under Nixon and Ford and during his tenure adopted a policy of relative openness about U.S. intelligence activities to the Senate Church Committee and House Pike Committee. He would depart from the group we are to discuss and was murdered in 1996.

[380] In May 1949, Angleton was made head of Staff of the CIA's Office of Special Operations, where he was responsible for the collection of foreign intelligence and liaison with the CIA's counterpart organizations (he got the job after agreeing not to polygraph Dulles and 50 of his cronies). Beginning in 1951, Angleton was responsible for liaison with Israel's Mossad and Shin Bet agencies ("the Israeli desk"), and he would continue this role after CIA Chief Allen Dulles in 1954 named Angleton head of the Counterintelligence Staff. Angleton had a close relationship with the founders of US intelligence and was forced to retire in 1975. He remained loyal to Dulles for many more years, but at the end of his life passed his private papers on to Joseph Trento—a treasure trove for history. As he noted on his deathbed, "Fundamentally, the founding fathers of U.S. intelligence were liars. The better you lied and the more you betrayed, the more likely you would be promoted. . . . Outside of their duplicity, the only thing they had in common was a desire for absolute power." Speaking of men like Dulles, Helms, and Wisner, he noted that these men were "the grand masters. If you were in a room with them, you were in a room full of people that you had to believe would deservedly end up in hell. . . . I guess I will see them there soon." See TRENTO, *THE SECRET HISTORY OF THE CIA* (2005)

[381] Allen Dulles was an American diplomat and lawyer connected with the Rockefellers who became the Council on Foreign Relations (CFR) first director in 1927. He was the Council's secretary from 1933 to 1944 and became the first Director of Central Intelligence (DCI). He would serve in this position from 1953 to 1961 and was its longest-serving director to date. As head of CIA, Dulles oversaw the 1953 coup d'état against democratically elected Mossadegh (along with Frank Wisner) and his replacement with the Shah of Iran. He then oversaw the 1954 Guatemalan coup, where he paved the way for American corporations, but was fired by John F. Kennedy after the failed Bay of Pigs invasion. Kennedy swore that he would break the CIA into a thousand pieces, but his assassination put an end to this quest. Dulles then, as a show of how utterly corrupt the U.S. government was, would become a member of the Warren Commission, orchestrating the cover-up. Between his stints of government service, Dulles was a corporate lawyer and partner at Sullivan &

These agents were connected with the inner echelons of the elite's old boy network, people like the Rockefellers, Bushes, Mellons, Rothschilds, etc. They were all former OSS agents, and while there were many others involved—beginning with this group—the modern alliance between drug traffickers and governments would evolve to become the international web of intrigue, deceit, violence, and mayhem that we know today.[383]

Cromwell. His older brother, John Foster Dulles, was the Secretary of State during the Eisenhower Administration. For more on this man, see TALBOT, *THE DEVIL'S CHESSBOARD: ALLEN DULLES, THE CIA, AND THE RISE OF AMERICA'S SECRET GOVERNMENT* (2015).

[382] William "Wild Bill" Donovan was an American lawyer, intelligence officer, and diplomat interlinked with the Rockefeller and J.P. Morgan banking empire. Donovan was head of OSS during World War II and would become known as the "Father of American Intelligence".

[383] A most interesting FBI document in this regard was addressed to Senator Edward Kennedy in 1989. In this letter, the FBI presented the connections between a sinister cast of characters, and this top-secret document illuminates much of what will be documented. As it went on to explain: "During the tenure of Richard Helms as Director of the Central Intelligence Agency, decisions were made by the director, with implied approval of the Oval Office, to draft a blue-print and put into motion a plan by which the CIA could have as much funds as, and when, needed, without knowledge of Congress. This would accomplish the dual purpose of carrying out clandestine and covert operations without the "clearance" of the Congress, as well as avoid the necessity of having to request any extra funds, and thus, divulging the workings of any covert operations in progress or planned. . . . Director Helms put together a team of five top people. The five experts picked were, General Edward Landsdale, who ran the CIA activities in Vietnam; William Colby, who was to be put in total command of the blue-print operation when enacted; George Bush, who asked and received approval to have his top aid, Richard Armitage be brought aboard, and Lt.Col. Robert Ferrera, a top CIA asset. . . . The master plan called for the CIA to enter into the drug smuggling business, in a total and complete fashion." https://cloverchronicle.com/2018/12/08/   george-h-w-bushs-top-secret-cia-drug-running-empire/

10.1.1. THE GOLDEN TRIANGLE

"We were never dealing opium in Laos. And if we were it was policy."[384]

—Richard Secord, US Air Force General—

Before the Second World War, Western drug markets were declining and opiate production was mostly confined to other regions of the world, like Turkey, Iran, and Southeast Asia. Delivering the product to Chinese users was Chiang Kai-shek, a right-wing general who used opium as a source of profits to fight the Communist forces. This was the 1940's, and Col. Paul E Helliwell served in China as a Chief of Special Intelligence for the OSS. His mission was to provide covert assistance to the Kuomintang (KMT) forces, the General's army, and knowing that it was difficult for Chiang to get the opium from producers to consumers, Helliwell saw a way in.

He therefore spoke with "Wild Bill" Donovan about flying opium for the KMT forces. His boss agreed and together with E. Howard Hunt (of Watergate fame), Lucein Conein (a French ex-soldier with ties to the Corsican mafia who would later become Nixon's chief of DEA covert operations), Lt. General Claire L Chennault, (the military advisor to Chiang Kai-shek), and Tommy "the Cork" Corcoran (an ultimate insider from the Roosevelt to the Reagan Administration), Helliwell and the CIA created the Civil Air Transport (CAT) from surplus aircraft in 1946.

Thus, the process of turning Southeast Asia into the world's biggest producer of opium had begun. President Franklin D. Roosevelt believed that the best way of stopping Japanese imperialism in this region was to arm the Chinese general, but Congress was opposed to this idea as this might cause a war with Japan. Hence, Roosevelt tasked Corcoran to establish a private corporation to aid the nationalist government, not knowing that this would trigger an expanding illicit economy in drugs. This, at the very

---

[384] VALENTINE, *THE STRENGTH OF THE WOLF* (2004) 511

least, is the official explanation. However, it is uncontroversial that secret services had connections to organized crime before this period.[385] It is also uncontroversial that secret societies are a breeding ground for corrupt politics,[386] and Roosevelt was not only a 33-degree mason, but a grandson of Warren Delano Jr., an intimate accomplice with William Russell, founder of the Skull and Bones. Thus, the plot thickens, and the actors involved fed off a pre-existing network of shady connections.

Helliwell himself was a member of the inner circle of the OSS, along with wealthy American dignitaries, including Henry Sturgis Morgan (Son of J.P. Morgan Jr.) Nicholas Roosevelt, Paul Mellon (son of Andrew Mellon) David K.E. Bruce (Andrew Mellon's son in law), and members of the Vanderbilt, Carnegie, DuPont, and Ryan families. Several of these families had profited from prohibitions in the 1800's, and the opium magnates of old had an interest in getting the drugs economy going.

Before the War, the American market was in ruins with opiate addicts being few and far between. The addict population was supplied by Jewish and Italian gangsters like Arnold Rothstein, Lucky Luciano, and Meyer Lansky and there was a tremendous potential for growth. The newly established international drug control regime had disrupted old markets—and even if it is hard to imagine that powerful players already at this point sought to use the American drug-fighting machinery as a means of eradicating competition and maximizing profits (while building a police state), this is what appears to have taken place.

---

[385] Professor Peter Dale Scott: "The U.S. government's narcotics Mafia connection goes back, as is well known, to World War II. Two controversial joint operations between OSS (Office of Strategic Services) and ONI (Office of Naval Intelligence) established contacts (via Lucky Luciano) with the Sicilian Mafia; and (via Tai Li) with the dope-dealing Green Gang of Tu Yueh Sheng in Shanghai. Both connections were extended into the post-war period as the Luciano and KMT networks slowly resumed their pre-war contacts." HENRIK KRUGER, *THE GREAT HEROIN COUP: DRUGS, INTELLIGENCE, AND INTERNATIONAL FASCISM* (2015) 13

[386] See Mimi L. Eustis, *New Orleans Mardi Gras Mystick Krewe of Comus Secrets Revealed* 2010. Found at http://www.whale.to/c/mardi_gras.html

Indeed, Professor Anthony Sutton has noted how Skull and Bones not only became a major force in drug smuggling, but "in true Hegelian fashion, generated the antithesis, the so-called war on drugs."[387] FBI-documents have also been released, showing that "during the tenure of Richard Helms as Director of the Central Intelligence Agency, decisions were made to draft a blue-print and put into motion a plan by which the CIA could have as much funds as, and when, needed, without knowledge of Congress." The result was the Five Star Trust, and people like General Edward Landsdale, William Colby, and George Bush Sr, were three of five players in a "master plan to enter into the drug smuggling business, in a total and complete fashion."[388]

Thus, a larger conspiracy seems to have been afoot. The FBI found connections between these guys and Baron Phillipe duDaphne, an agent of the Rothschilds banking empire. We shall later link them to money laundering activities, and the connection between politics and crime is deep. President Nixon himself started his career as a lawyer for Meyer Lansky. He was recommended to the CIA-connected mob boss by his long-time lawyer, Moses Polakoff,[389] and it is no coincidence that the world of crime and politics is connected through lawyers such as Nixon. As others have noted, the bigger the crime boss, the more prominent is his counsel's relationship with the CIA,[390] and Richard Ben-Veniste, the lawyer of Barry Seal, (who we

---

[387] SUTTON, *AMERICA'S SECRET ESTABLISHMENT* (2002) xiii

[388] https://cloverchronicle.com/2018/12/08/george-h-w-bushs-top-secret-cia-drug-running-empire/

[389] ESCOHOTADO, *A BRIEF HISTORY OF DRUGS* (1999) 102

[390] "There is an interesting common theme that runs through all CIA connected narcotics traffickers of this period. These included men who were prosecuted—from Jack DeVoe to Barry Seal, Tony Fernandez, Bill Blakemore, Roberto Ruiz, Donald Raulerson and his son, Don Jr., who virtually controlled CIA narcotics trafficking in Georgia. There are about fifty-four names in all, but the common thread that runs through all these supposed defendants is the connection of their defense counsels to the government. Every defense counsel that was involved in defending these gentlemen was a former employee of the CIA. . . . The more prominent the narcotics

shall meet later) performed this function. His presence on the Whitewater and the 9/11 Commissions speaks volumes—and another lawyer that has specialized in this area is Bob Bennett, the brother of Bill Bennett.

While the former Drug Czar still enjoys his position as a moral entrepreneur, both Bennetts have been accused by Cathy O'Brien, a former sex slave, of committing highly immoral acts of violence.[391] Her story checks out on many points but as they never have had to face these charges, this must be a story for another day. What we know for sure is that criminals crave these lawyers for their ability to pull weight behind the scenes. And as Victor Marchetti, a former executive assistant to the Deputy Director of the CIA, said, "the CIA's involvement in the trafficking of heroin goes all the way back to the predecessor organization OSS and its involvement with the Italian mafia, the Cosa Nostra in Sicily and Southern Italy."[392] This was during the Second World War, and from this point of departure the unholy alliance between corrupt government agents and the criminal element would only strengthen.[393]

It is also clear that the drug enforcement agencies erected to combat the threat of narcotics were no match for this group and were taken over by double agents. Thus, the FBN, BNDD, and later the DEA would eliminate competition, while the network with the best connections were free to control an ever-greater percentage of the world drug market. This is what happened, and the Vietnam War seems to have been a side show created to take attention away from the real operation.

---

trafficker defendant in question, the more prominent was his counsel's relationship with the Agency." MARTIN, *THE CONSPIRATORS* (2002) 163

[391] CATHY O'BRIEN, *TRANCE FORMATION OF AMERICA* (1995)

[392] PAUL L. WILLIAMS, *OPERATION GLADIO: THE UNHOLY ALLIANCE BETWEEN THE VATICAN, THE CIA, AND THE MAFIA* (2015) 53

[393] "My CIA, OSS, and DEA informants described their roles in the intelligence agency drug trafficking starting in the late 1940's and early 1950's." RODNEY STICH, *DEFRAUDING AMERICA* (1994) 294

10.1.2. THE INDOCHINA OPIUM WAR

To oversee development in the Golden Triangle, CIA operatives Theodore Shackley and Thomas G. Clines came to Laos in 1966.[394] The OSS/CIA, however, had been active in the region since French intelligence left, and as opium had been their primary source of income, this business must have been a part of the deal. At the very least, when Major General Edward Lansdale, an OSS/CIA agent, came to Vietnam in 1953 he discovered opium smuggling by French intelligence but was told not to interfere by his superiors.[395] Instead, drawing upon his connections, he would spin a web of intrigue that set the region aflame, a job he had spent many years preparing for in the Philippines.

Reading between the lines, after the Spanish-American War, we have seen that the Philippines was controlled by the Skull and Bones. With three consecutive governors, the secret society plundered and terrorized the colony, and from a power-political perspective, the modern War on Drugs appears to have its origin in the need to justify a regime of arbitrary violence upon the civil population. The same operation was now repeated in Indochina. According to several authors, Lansdale was part of a team of covert operatives who had looted the Asians for more than trillions of dollars' worth of gold,[396] and the same cast of characters arrived in Vietnam.

---

[394] The story of Shackley, Clines, Dulles, Prescott Bush, George H.W. Bush (and others discussed here) connected with the mob, organized the drugs economy, and created a rouge CIA is excellently told by JOSEPH TRENTO IN *PRELUDE TO TERROR* (2005)

[395] McCoy, *THE POLITICS OF HEROIN* (1991) 102, 242

[396] The Philippines was an important hub in the US Imperialist Empire and Lansdale was appointed Chief of the Intelligence Division at the CIA station in Manila. There he took part in torturous interrogations aimed at silencing political dissent, rooting out political enemies, and locating secret chambers of bullion. As Seagrave explains "In 1945, US Intelligence officers in Manila discovered that the Japanese had hidden large quantities of gold bullion and other looted treasure in the Philippines. President Truman decided to recover the gold but to keep its riches secret. These would be combined with treasure recovered inside Japan during the US occupation, and with

The scene was already set by Chiang Kai-shek's army of 12,000 mercenaries who were stationed in the opium rich hills of Burma and Thailand. To finance the secret war against the Chinese government, they had taken control of opium production in this area, and together with 30,000 Hmong tribesmen the Americans relied on this network to substantiate their presence. Portable heroin processing facilities, a creation of the CIA's technical division,[397] was brought in and they trained the locals to run them. Profits soon became enormous, but the Communist government in China did not go away. Hence, assisted by the CIA, in 1950, this band of warlords appropriated Formosa, renamed it Taiwan, declared martial law, killed those who protested, and ran the country as despots until 1987.

As fascists know how to make a profit, it is no coincidence that Taiwan would provide a blueprint for the merging trend of turning traditional cultures into export-production-zones for international corporations. Nor was it a coincidence that, before this, the Philippines was the only Asian country to allow Chiang's army to function openly as a political party. The "secret team" was in control of its government and under the guise of a War on Communism, they would wreak havoc on the region, installing their own puppet regimes.

10.1.2.1 The Vietnam War

To observant readers, it should come as no surprise that the War on Communism was another front for meddling in the internal affairs of

---

Nazi loot recovered in Europe, to create a worldwide American political action fund to fight communism. Overseen by General MacArthur, President Truman, and John Foster Dulles, this 'Black Gold' gave Washington virtually limitless, unaccountable funds, providing an asset base to reinforce the treasuries of America's allies, to bribe political and military leaders, and to manipulate elections in foreign countries for more than fifty years." STERLING SEAGRAVE & PEGGY SEAGRAVE, *GOLD WARRIORS: AMERICA'S SECRET RECOVERY OF YAMASHITA'S GOLD* (2005); SEE ALSO DAVID WILCOCK, *FINANCIAL TYRANNY: DEFEATING THE GREATEST COVER-UP OF ALL TIME* (2012) for more on how the elite robbed the Asians of their gold in the 1920-40s.

[397] TRENTO, *PRELUDE TO TERROR* (2005) 26

sovereign people, and the Vietnam War is a prime example. While 80 percent of the people supported Ho Chi Minh and the Viet Minh independence movement, the CIA prepped up a regime of their own in Saigon and made sure that war was the only option.[398] In 1968, Nixon even had had Anna Chennault, the wife of Claire Chennault, use her connections with the Saigon regime to delay peace talks for another two years;[399] this would serve the war profiteers well, while providing CIA with room to finish operations in the Golden Triangle.

Opium was the name of the game,[400] and Shackley was well-connected with drug runners. Before coming to Laos, he had been Chief at the JM/WAVE CIA Station in Miami (1962-1965). There, together with Clines, he had prepped Cuban exiles for Anti-Castro operations, and this plot included political assassinations as well as lots of drug running.[401] It also included the Bay of Pigs invasion, an attempt of 1500 soldiers of fortune to oust Castro. The Skull and

---

[398] See RUSSELL, *DRUG WAR* (2000); MCCOY, *THE POLITICS OF HEROIN* (1991); BLUM, *KILLING HOPE* (2003)

[399] ANTHONY SUMMERS, *THE ARROGANCE OF POWER: THE SECRET WORLD OF RICHARD NIXON* (2003) 298-306, 322

[400] As General Tuan Shi-wen, a veteran from the CIA's warfare in Burma, said: "To fight you must have an army; an army must have guns, and to buy guns you must have money. In these mountains, the only money is opium." MCCOY, *THE POLITICS OF HEROIN* (1991) 129

[401] When Castro ousted Fulgencio Batista, the U.S. installed dictator, he not only obstructed the American elite's business investments; he also threw out the Mob who ran Havana's Casinos and underworld, and the CIA would ally with these forces. Hence, in 1960 Paul Helliwell had been sent to the Bahamas where he set up offshore banks for CIA use. After that he went to Florida, where he cemented the CIA's relationship with organized crime (Lansky and Trafficante), and (accompanied by Mitch WerBell and Lucien Conein) nourished relations with the Cuban mercenaries as they were prepped for the Bay of Pigs Invasion. The connection to drugs has been discussed by authors such as Peter Dale Scott, Joseph Trento, Henrik Kruger, and Joel Binerman, and it could also be seen in 1973 when Newsday reported that "at least eight percent of the 1500-man Bay of Pigs invasion force has subsequently been investigated or arrested for drug dealing." KRUGER, *THE GREAT HEROIN COUP* (2015) 16

Bones could be seen lurking behind the scenes,[402] and while it failed to open Cuba for exploitation it did provide alliances that would reach across the globe.

As shall be seen, these Cuban extremists would take part in terror operations in Latin America, as well as Europe and the Middle East. In 1966, Ted Shackley brought some of them to Laos (this included Carl E. Jenkins, David Morales, Rafael Quintero, Felix Rodriguez and Edwin Wilson).[403] There the CIA backed General Vang Pao, who was a major figure in the opium business, and helped him establish a monopoly over the heroin trade by setting him up with the Corsican and Italian Mafia.[404] Assisted by "Wild Bill" Donovan, who arrived in Thailand as Ambassador in 1953, at the same time as Lansdale arrived in Vietnam, the CIA also conspired with the Thai military police who helped the KMT thrive in the opium rich mountains. And while Donovan returned to the United States the next year to continue his work for the Rockefeller and Morgan interests (and registered as a

---

[402] The Bay of Pigs Operation was overseen by the Skull and Bones society through William P. Bundy, McGeorge Bundy, Richard Drain, and George H.W. Bush—all Bonesmen. Shackley, E. Howard Hunt, and Clines, their subsidiaries, ran the Cubans. The Bundy brothers were close advisors to JFK, advising him on Cuba and Vietnam, and according to Colonel Fletcher Prouty (Chief of Special Operations under the Joint Chiefs of Staff under JFK) McGeorge Bundy not only sabotaged the Bay of Pigs invasion in an attempt to force Kennedy into overt American involvement, but had prior knowledge of the President's assassination. See PROUTY, *JFK: THE CIA, VIETNAM, AND THE PLOT TO ASSASSINATE JOHN F. KENNEDY* (2011) x

[403] For more on this period, see TRENTO, *PRELUDE TO TERROR* (2005) and BAINERMAN, *CRIMES OF A PRESIDENT: NEW REVELATIONS ON THE CONSPIRACY AND COVER UP IN THE BUSH AND REAGAN ADMINISTRATION* (1992)

[404] In 1968 Shackley (known as the Blond Ghost) arranged for Santos Trafficante Jr. to visit Saigon and meet with drug lord Vang Pao in the Continental Palace Hotel. The meeting concerned Vang's ability to provide the supply for the ever-increasing demand. During his stay, Trafficante also met with prominent Corsican gangsters to assure them of increased shipments to their laboratories in Marseilles." WILLIAMS, *OPERATION GLADIO* (2015) 88

lobbyist for the Thai government), these forces would ensure that the Golden Triangle became the world's greatest producer of opium.[405]

From this point, KMT heroin would be produced deep in the jungles of Burma, Thailand, and Laos, and then shipped to Western markets. To launder the drug money, Shackley had Richard L. Armitage (who later became Deputy Secretary of State under George W. Bush) set up a secret conduit to Australian and American banks,[406] and after the Vietnam War the same cast of characters would move their operations to Latin America, doing the same to the drug market of this region—and finally to Afghanistan where they now control 90 percent of the world opium supply.[407]

While operations in Afghanistan will be a story for another day, we shall see how this group set up shop in Latin America. For now, however, we focus on the Golden Triangle, which by 1989 would produce 70 percent (3000 tons) of the world's opium—and while this was going on the FBN, BNDD, and the DEA were always two steps behind. The FBN would ignore the Golden Triangle and focus upon other regions of the world, places like Turkey, Marseille, and the Middle East. Until the 1970's they would claim that 80 percent of the heroin shipped to America came from Turkey and that only 5 percent came from Southeast Asia—but as the FBNs head, John Warner,

---

[405] As William Blum, a former employee of the U.S. State Department, noted: "The operation was not a paragon of discretion. Heroin was refined in a laboratory located on the site of CIA headquarters in northern Laos. After a decade of American military intervention, Southeast Asia had become the source of 70 percent of the world's illicit opium and the major supplier of raw materials for Americas booming heroin market." BLUM, *KILLING HOPE* (2003) 142

[406] TRENTO, *PRELUDE TO TERROR* (2005)

[407] As author Paul L. Williams noted the situation "Heroin had become a $400 billion business, with two hundred million users throughout the world. The CIA's share of this business was used to finance the mujahideen in Afghanistan, the guerrilla forces in Angola, the Contras in Nicaragua, the puppet regimes in South America, and the death squads in El Salvador. Paul E. Helliwell's brainstorm had produced an intelligence agency with seemingly limitless funds for seemingly endless operations." WILLIAMS, *OPERATION GLADIO* (2015) 220

admitted in a 1971 interview, this assumption was pure guesswork.[408] More likely, it was the result of a deal with the CIA, as FBN agents in the region were sent home by Anslinger in 1949 when they reported that opium was the primary source of income for the French. Ten years would pass before FBN again put boots on the ground, and by then production had increased more than 500 percent since the end of World War II, when production hit a rock bottom of 80 tons.[409]

Doing his part was President Richard Nixon, who in 1971 provided $100 million in aid to end opium production in Turkey, a country that produced 5 percent of the world opium supply. By this time, the CIA had set up shop elsewhere and the Golden Triangle was preparing to become the world's primary source of opium. Thus, to the CIA, this move seems to have been about eliminating competition so that a more centralized system under its control could emerge. And while this interpretation is open for questioning—and the CIA will have us believe that this was not their intention—the story of Khun Sa suggests otherwise.

10.1.2.2. KHUN-SA: THE IDEALISTIC DRUG LORD

Khun Sa was a Burmese opium lord who received military equipment and training from the Kuomintang and Burmese Army before establishing his own independent territory. In the period between 1976-1996, he was the dominant player in the region, but there is more to this man than meets the eye. He is interesting not only because his biggest customer was the CIA but because his ambitions made him a nuisance, and his fate reveals the true ambitions of the CIA in the Indochina theatre. It was for this reason that the Reagan administration would pronounce him enemy number one in the Golden Triangle, but his problems with the CIA started in the early 1960's.

---

[408] McCoy, *The Politics of Heroin* (1991) 281

[409] Ibid., 162

In this period, Khun Sa became one of Burma's most notorious drug traffickers and would increasingly challenge the local dominance of the KMT. In 1967, however, in a battle involving the KMT and the Laotian army on the Thai-Burma-Laos border, Khun Sa was ambushed while leading a convoy of 500 men and 300 opium-filled mules. The Laotian Air Force showed up, bombed the battleground, and stole the opium. At that time, General Ouane Rattikone, the commander-in-chief of the Royal Lao Army, ran several heroin refineries in the nearby Ban Houey Sai area. He was backed by the CIA, and as the Laotian military continued to ambush Khun Sa's drug shipments, his military strength declined. Thus, a period of trouble ensued until 1974, when he was free from Burmese prison in a release secretly brokered by Thai General Kriangsak Chomanan.

Over the next two decades (1974-1994), Khun Sa became the dominant opium warlord in the Golden Triangle. In 1981, however, his luck ran out when the Thai army, pressured by the Americans, decided to turn against him. The Thai government announced a bounty on his head and in October 1981, a 39-man unit of Thai Rangers and local rebel guerrillas attempted to assassinate Khun Sa at the insistence of the DEA. The attempt failed, and the American ambassador to Thailand, William Brown, denounced him as "the worst enemy the world has."[410]

Curiously, this coincided with him being a nuisance to the secret team: In 1977 he had offered to take his territory's entire opium crop off the black market by selling it to the American government, but his offer was rejected. Undeterred, he continued his attempt to get the U.S. government (and others) to recognize the sovereignty of the Shan State by offering to destroy the illicit market in drugs, but his offers were turned down. Why? The official explanation of the Australian government, which also rejected his plan, was that the "Government is simply not in the business of paying criminals to refrain from criminal activity." The U.S. government, for its part, simply rejected Khun Sa's proposal as blackmail and placed a $2 million-dollar bounty on him.

---

[410] Bertil Lintner, *Death of a Drug Lord*, Asia Times Online. November 1, 2007

Into this fray arrived James "Bo" Gritz. He was one of the most decorated soldiers of the Vietnam era and after retirement at the rank of lieutenant colonel in 1979, he continued his work in black ops. In his book *A Nation Betrayed* Gritz documents why, most likely, the American and other governments rejected Khun Sa's offer of stopping the flow of heroin,[411] and the story begins with missing American prisoners of war. There was a reason to believe that at least 135 U.S. soldiers had been left behind when the United States withdrew from Indochina and Gritz's mission was to contact Khun Sa to see what he knew.

The CIA, for its part, claimed that Khun Sa was dead and made travel arrangements difficult. Even so, Gritz prevailed and in 1986 met with the drug lord at his stronghold, where they conversed for two days. At this meeting Khun Sa claimed that he did not know about American POWs, but he would provide Gritz with 2500 soldiers if he would pass on a message to President Reagan. Again, the offer of eradicating opium production came up, and as proof of his good will Khun Sa offered to surrender one ton of pure heroin. Not only that, but the opium lord offered to give up the names of his best customers. As he expected the Reagan administration to jump on this opportunity, Gritz was delighted and promised to return a few months later.

Coming back to the United States, however, Gritz was surprised at the White House's disinterest in Khun Sa's proposal. He could sense powerful forces conspiring against him and his team members were imprisoned on trumped-up charges. Nevertheless, Gritz and two compatriots, Barry Flynn and Lance Trimmer, a private detective from San Francisco, managed to return as promised. At this meeting Khun Sa showed his accounting records and they discovered that his biggest clients the past 25 years had been the CIA.

Khun Sa specifically mentioned Theodore Shackley, the Deputy Director of CIA's Covert Operations, and Daniel Arnold, the CIA Station Chief in Thailand, as key operators, and Richard Armitage as

---

[411] James Gritz, *A Nation Betrayed* (1989)

the one that laundered the money. Armitage, who was Assistant Secretary of Defence for International Security Affairs, held several positions with the State Department which suggested Khun Sa was right. These charges, furthermore, were supported by Ronald Rewald, a Honolulu businessman who ran Bishop, Baldwin, Rewald, Dillingham and Wong, a CIA connected bank we shall learn more about, and Khun Sa also charged that, after leaving the State Department, Armitage organized the Far East Trading Company as a front to continue opium trafficking.

These clues were easy to pursue. When Armitage predictably denied the allegation, the House Judiciary Committee's subcommittee on crime was tasked to assess the charges, but Congress dared not follow through. Instead, Congress parroted CIA's position that these men were beyond reproach and joined President Bush and the Justice Department in the lynching of scapegoats.

Upon his return to the United States, Gritz had been told by the White House to erase and forget what he had learned.[412] Gritz, however, did not obey, and the Congress and the media was informed.[413] He was also in touch with the Christic Institute, which prepared a case for the US justice system, but the secret team ensured that these efforts were made an example of.[414]

---

[412] "Instead of receiving an 'Atta Boy' for bringing back video tape showing Khun Sa's offer to stop 900 tons of illegal narcotics and expose dirty USG officials, Scott was jailed and I was threatened. I was told that if I didn't 'erase and forget' all that we had discovered, I would, 'hurt the government'. Further, I was promised a prison sentence of 15 years." James Bo Gritz, Letter to Vice President George H.W. Bush, February 1, 1988

[413] In June 1987, Gritz delivered copies of a videotape with Khun Sa's confession to the Chairman of the Select Committee on Intelligence; the Chairman of the House on Foreign Affairs Task Force on Narcotics Control; the Co-Chairman of the Senate Narcotics Committee; Senator Harry Reid, NV; Representative James Bilbray, NV; and other Congressional members. Senator Ross Perot would investigate these charges and deliver evidence to George H.W. Bush, but the Vice President angrily denied the charges and set up a team of military men to neutralize the Senator. These men included Chip Tatum, which we shall meet later.

[414] In 1986, attorney Daniel Sheehan named Shackley, Armitage, Clines and 27 other conspirators in a $24 million civil lawsuit filed by the Christic Institute. In 1988, the

The cover-up made Gritz realize the extent to which the U.S. government had become corrupted, and he left Washington to join the militia movement along with other "conspiracy theorists". When George H.W. Bush became president, he wrote a letter that exposed his connections to the secret team, but Bush did not respond. By then Bush was busy having to deal with the fallout of Iran-Contra and silencing more immediate threats, like Ross Perot, a fellow Texas Republican who threatened to expose his dirty laundry. Another threat was General Noriega, who also knew too much about the President's past. To silence him, Bush sent the U.S. Army to invade Panama and to bring the general to America in chains. Then there were Khun Sa who threatened to expose the secret team's activities in Indochina; the $2 million offer on his head had not provided a solution, and the White House intensified the DEA's efforts to arrest him.

He had been indicted in absentia on drug trafficking charges by a federal grand jury in Brooklyn, New York, in January 1990, and Bush would use the hunt for Khun Sa to pose as a defender of law and order. No doubt, he really wanted this man who threatened to bring light to a dark chapter of CIA history. Bush himself was thick as thieves with the conspirators, but Khun Sa had good friends. He was a hero to the Shan people, and while the DEA was chasing him, he continued to live comfortably at his headquarters at Hmong near the Thai border. In January 1996, he eventually surrendered to the Burmese military. Even so he continued to live prosperously the remainder of his life (he died in 2007, at the age of 73 in Yangon), and the fact that he "spent the last years of his life incommunicado inside a compound protected by Myanmar's secret intelligence service gives some indication as to how important the country's ruling junta considered it to keep him isolated and quiet."[415]

United States District Court for the Southern District of Florida dismissed the Christic suit after finding it to be frivolous and ordered the Institute to pay $955,000 in attorney fees and $79,500 in court costs. The ruling was subsequently upheld by the United States Court of Appeals for the Eleventh Circuit and the Supreme Court of the United States.

[415] Bertil Lintner, *Death of a Drug Lord*, Asia Times Online, November 1, 2007. For more on Kuhn Sa, see McCoy, *The Politics of Heroin* (1991) 348, 419-35.

10.1.3. The Vietnam Theatre

"Look, if you think any American official is going to tell you the truth then you're stupid. Did you hear that? Stupid."[416]

—Arthur Sylvester, Assistant Secretary of Defense for Public Affairs, speaking to U.S. correspondents in Saigon, 1965—

The story of Khun Sa suggests that there may be some truth to these tales of government complicity in the drug trade. It is also notable that George Bush and Richard Armitage were named by the FBI as two of five individuals involved in the Five Star Trust, the CIA's master plan to control the drugs economy. As the FBIs division of Intelligence put it:

"Each of the five planners would have his own field to handle. Bush would be the secret head of ONA and handle all the shipping of the drugs under forged waybills. Armitage would be the "gopher" for the group and the intermediary with any "undesirables". General Landsdale would handle all the distribution network and collection services within the military in Vietnam. William Colby was to handle the setting up of all the man-power—from runners, peddlers, pushers, collectors, and so forth, as well as the elimination of any who might prove to be uncontrollable, be they American or Vietnamese. Lt.Col. Ferrera was to use his contacts in Latin America and in the middle east, to obtain 'from various governments the needed drugs–heroin, cocaine, marijuana, LSD, etc, as ordered by Colby, Bush was to handle the opium from China."[417]

---

[416] MIKE LOFGREN, *THE DEEP STATE: THE FALL OF THE CONSTITUTION AND THE RISE OF THE SHADOW GOVERNMENT* (2016) 48

[417] https://cloverchronicle.com/2018/12/08/george-h-w-bushs-top-secret-cia-drug-running-empire/

This information was addressed to Senator Ed Kennedy in 1989. Thus, if not for the corruption of government, this plot could have been exposed. Kennedy, however, had met with a conspiracy too big; one where those who pursued the truth were murdered or threatened into submission, and so the story of Khun Sa and government-sponsored drug smuggling never made the headlines.

Nevertheless, what we have seen is a microcosm of a much greater picture, and behind the Indochina War there was a trend of increased opium production; an ever more professionalized heroin industry; and a streamlining of markets according to the wisdom of a few. Working for these chosen few were the henchmen of the secret team, and when Shackley and Clines had coordinated a working opium-program in Laos, they left for Vietnam. Bringing his elite force of assassins, Shackley took over the CIA Station in Saigon, where he and Bill Colby oversaw the Phoenix Program.

Under this program, within a two-year period, some 30,000 civilians were murdered with extreme prejudice as the CIA helped eradicate political opposition and set up new kings in the drug business. Lansdale had already arranged so that President Ngo Dinh Diem's advisor (and brother), Ngo Dinh Nhu, controlled the South Vietnamese opiate trade, while Diem ran the country. In 1963, however, the Diem brothers would be killed in a CIA sanctioned coup instigated by Henry Cabot Lodge, the newly arrived U.S. Ambassador. After this, two generals of the Air Force, Ngyen Cao Ky and Ngyen Ngoc Loan, would be the CIAs greatest allies in Vietnam's illegal drug business.[418]

As history went on to show, the arrival of Ambassador Lodge signalled a turn for the worse. Connecting the Lodges and the Cabots, he belonged to a long lineage of initiates, and together with W.

---

[418] McCoy, *The Politics of Heroin* (1991). See also Trento, *The Secret History of the CIA* (2005) 343-49: "The nasty secret of the early phase of the Vietnam War was that Conein's clients, Ngo Dinh Diem and Ngo Dinh Nhu, were at the Vietnamese end of the Corsican heroin trail. What the CIA had taken over from the French colonial administration in Vietnam was the Southeast Asian drug business." (p. 345)

Averell Harriman and McGeorge Bundy, both of the Skull and Bones society, he would ensure that the death cult proved victorious.

10.1.3.1. ENTER HARRIMAN

"It is a Princeton tradition that whenever a Yale man who is a member of the widely advertised "Skull and Bones" hears the sacred name mentioned, he must leave the room. It is also a tradition that the members are invariably successful in later life, amassing fortunes or votes or coupons or whatever they choose to amass."

—F. Scott Fitzgerald, This Side of Paradise, 1920—

A look at history reveals that few have been more eager to profit on war than the Skull and Bones. At any given time, some 600 Bonesmen are active on this planet, continuing the age-old plot to control populations, and W. Averell Harriman was a true king. Together with the Bush family, he would finance Russian revolutionaries and the rise of Hitler[419]—and not only did he get away with it, but he was rewarded by President Roosevelt as a special envoy to Europe during the War. Being a Skull and Bones member, then, comes with certain

---

[419] The connections between the Bush family, Harriman, and the rise of Hitler can be found in STONE & HUNT, *THE BUSH CRIME FAMILY* (2016) 84-89. These industrialists would profit from slave labour in Auschwitz and other concentration camps (where IBM serviced the machinery), and it is possible that Hitler invaded Poland to keep this scheme going. At the very least, the Polish government accused the Americans and Germans of gross mismanagement, excessive borrowing, fictitious bookkeeping, and gambling in securities, and when Hitler invaded Poland, any fears that Prescott Bush or Averell Harriman may have had about losing their Polish steel and coal operations vanished. See also BLACK, *NAZI NEXUS: AMERICA'S CORPORATE CONNECTIONS TO HITLER'S HOLOCAUST* (2009).

privileges.[420] In 1943, Harriman became Ambassador to the Soviet Union and after the War served as ambassador to Britain before he moved on to become United States Secretary of Commerce. In 1948, he was put in charge of the Marshall Plan and throughout the 1950's, he would orchestrate the Cold War. Hence, it is difficult to overrate his impact on world affairs and the Indochina situation was no exception.

In January 1961, Averell Harriman was appointed Ambassador at Large by President Kennedy, a position he held until November, when he became Assistant Secretary of State for Far Eastern Affairs. During this period, he advocated U.S. support of a "neutral" government in Laos, while providing cover for the real events. He remained in this position until April 1963, when he became Under Secretary of State for Political Affairs. He retained that position during the transition to the Johnson administration until March 1965, when he again became Ambassador at Large. He held that position for the remainder of Johnson's presidency and headed the U.S. delegation to the preliminary peace talks in Paris between the United States and North Vietnam (1968–69). In short, he was on top of things, and while controlling drug markets was fine, a bigger game was being played— one that occasioned murder and mayhem.

By this time, 500,000 American troops had mustered in Indochina. War on a more massive scale was being prepared, and in the 1964 *Gulf of Tonkin* incident politicians found a pretence for going to war. Never mind that the alleged North Vietnamese attack did not take place; never mind that President Kennedy tried to stop the

---

[420] Roosevelt, in a letter to Senator Sherman in 1906, had described Harriman's father as a man of "deep seated corruption," an "undesirable citizen" and "an enemy of the Republic." (Harriman, in a fit of anger, had boasted "that whenever he wants legislation from a state legislature he could buy it; that he could buy Congress, and that if necessary he could buy the judiciary.") KENNAN, E. H. *HARRIMAN: RAILROAD CZAR* (2011) 209. At the CIA, also James Angleton was worried about Harriman and began a secret counterintelligence investigation code named DINOSAUR. The investigation never went anywhere, but as Angleton said: "There was a strong circumstantial case that Harriman was at least an agent of Soviet influence and maybe much worse." TRENTO, *THE SECRET HISTORY OF THE CIA* (2005) 355

escalating crisis; thanks to Harriman and his accomplices,[421] the American military would bomb the country asunder, leaving some five million dead, while ensuring vast profits for U.S. corporations.

The Skull and Bones was clearly on top of events. One key player was William H. Sullivan. Having served as Harriman's deputy at the Geneva negotiations on the future of Laos in 1961, he was a reliable protegee, and Harriman appointed him ambassador to this country from 1964–1969. When the war escalated, he served briefly as deputy chief of mission to the U.S. Embassy in Saigon, and would be followed by G. McMurtrie Godley, who served as ambassador to Laos from 1969-1973.

Godley was as corrupt as they come. Before taking this position, he had been the United States ambassador to the Democratic Republic of the Congo, when Mobutu Sese Seko staged coup and seized control of the country. Now, he would ensure that the FBN and others kept away while the CIA did its dirty work.[422] After this, Godley would continue to Lebanon for more mischief, and he would be succeeded by another high-level insider, Charles S. Whitehouse—who was also a member of the Skull and Bones. Mr. Whitehouse oversaw the downsizing of the U.S. involvement in Laos and then left Vientiane to become ambassador to Thailand in 1975. There, the CIA was in deep with the fascist military police, and only a year later, with the bloody suppression of student demonstrations on October 6, 1976, a coup followed.

---

[421]Author Joseph Trento has done an amazing job piecing together this puzzle. In his great work *The Secret History of the CIA* (2005), relying on insider testimony, he shows that Harriman, by 1963, was running Vietnam without consulting the president or the attorney general, and that the violent coup that Harriman set in motion against the Diem brothers seemed "designed to throw American policy in that country into chaos." (p. 334-35)

[422] In December 1970, Godley used the FBN's rigged statistics to marginalize attention to the real events and he would also oppose the BNDD (FBN's successor) establishing a foothold in Laos. See McCoy, *THE POLITICS OF HEROIN* (1991) 304, 381

It was this shady cast of characters that dominated U.S. policy and covered up for the events. Harriman was a top dog,[423] but he had plenty of help and we shall look at one important ally.

10.1.4. Fascists of the World: Unite!

A front organization was the World Anti Communist League (WACL). It was officially established in in 1966 by the KMT but had chapters at least a decade before. Hunt and Conein personally established its Latin American forerunners in 1954, and while it currently goes by the name World League for Freedom and Democracy (WLFD), WACL would unite "Latin American death squads, Croatian and Cuban terrorists, Japanese gangsters, the Moonies' bizarre and dictatorial sex cult, scientific racists, Waffen SS veterans, high-ranking Nazis, Saudi princes, supporters of apartheid in South Africa and Rhodesia, supporters of America's Jim Crow

---

[423] Joseph Trento summarizes the big picture: "President-elect Kennedy appointed Harriman as ambassador-at-large, to operate 'with the full confidence of the president and an intimate knowledge of all aspects of United States policy.' But by 1963, Kennedy had come to suspect the loyalty of certain members on his national security team. According to Colonel William Corson, USMC, by 1963 Harriman was running 'Vietnam without consulting the president or the attorney general.' Corson said Kenny O'Donnell, JFK's appointments secretary, was convinced that the National Security Advisor, McGeorge Bundy, followed the orders of Harriman rather than the president. Corson also claimed that O'Donnell was particularly concerned about Michael Forrestal, a young White House staffer who handled liaison on Vietnam with Harriman. Harriman certainly supported the coup against the South Vietnam president Ngo Dinh Diem in 1963. However, it is alleged that the orders that ended in the deaths of Diem and his brother actually originated with Harriman and were carried out by Henry Cabot Lodge's military assistant. The fundamental question about the murders was the sudden and unusual recall of Saigon Station Chief John 'Jocko' Richardson by an unknown authority. Special Operations Army officer, John Michael Dunn, was sent to Vietnam in his stead. He followed the orders of Harriman and Forrestal rather than the CIA. According to Corson, Dunn's role in the incident has never been made public but he was assigned to Ambassador Lodge for 'special operations' with the authority to act without hindrance; and he was known to have access to the coup plotters." Wikipedia summary of JOSEPH TRENTO, *THE SECRET HISTORY OF THE CIA* (2005) 334–335

apartheid (well into the 1980's), Corsican gangsters, KMT drug dealers, right-wing Asian, Latin American, European, Middle Eastern and African Dictators, Italian and Mexican secret societies, bishops, priests, ministers, generals, special forces vets, military men, spies, secret police, mainstream western politicians, academics, and journalists."[424]

This network would use the drugs economy, murder, and propaganda to get their way—and "Freedom" or "Democracy" was not on the agenda.[425] To the contrary, at least three European chapters were controlled by former SS officers from Nazi Germany, and as Hugo Turner noted, this is only the tip of the iceberg:

> *"WACL is undoubtedly one of the most important organizations that most people have never heard of. WACL played a far greater role in history than anyone ever realized. It was closely connected to the Korean and Vietnam Wars, the death of JFK, the string of coups that swept Latin America for decades and has, after a brief interruption begun, to sweep Latin America again. It was involved in the wars in Angola and Mozambique. WACL members founded and led the Latin*

---

[424] Hugo Turner, *Beyond the Iran-Contra Affair Part 3: The World Anti-Communist League*, July 19, 2016. For more on WACL, see SCOTT AND JON LEE ANDERSON, *INSIDE THE LEAGUE: THE SHOCKING EXPOSÉ OF HOW TERRORISTS, NAZIS, AND LATIN AMERICAN DEATH SQUADS HAVE INFILTRATED THE WORLD ANTI-COMMUNIST LEAGUE* (1986); SCOTT & MARSHALL, *COCAINE POLITICS* (1998)

[425] As Professor Peter Dale Scott noted: "Before World War II the KMT regime in China was perhaps the best example of political manipulation of the narcotics traffic., under the guise of an 'opium suppression campaign', to finance both a political and an intelligence apparatus (under General Tai Li). This practice spread after World War 2 to a number of other WACL World Anti-Communist League) member countries and groups. Today there is cause to fear that Nixon's superagency, the Drug Enforcement Administration, has, like other narcotics enforcement agencies before it, come to use corrupt personnel who are actually a part of the traffic, as part of a covert war against revolution. This is easiest to argue in the case of corrupt police forces overseas, such as the DEA-supported Thai Border Patrol police who, by a massacre of unarmed Thai students, contributed to the overthrow of Thai democracy in October 1976." KRUGER, *THE GREAT HEROIN COUP* (2015) 12

American death squads that claimed hundreds of thousands of victims. WACL was instrumental in both the start of the 'cold war' and its end with the destruction of the Soviet Union and the Warsaw Pact. WACL helped get Nixon, Reagan, and Bush into office. WACL was tied to terror attacks, hijackings, bombings, and assassinations. It was deeply involved in the global drug trade. It served to keep fascism alive after its defeat in World War 2.[426]

For those interested, History Channel's *Hunting Hitler* series documents how the Nazi elite, aided by the Vatican and the OSS/CIA, relocated to South America after the war. They were given large territories in Argentina under Peron, and also flourished in neighbouring Paraguay and Chile. Unrestrained by local authorities, they would draw upon the drugs economy to renew their strength and they had ties to the intelligence services and police in the region. Like the American elite, these forces had mutual interest in keeping authoritarian governments in place, and aided by the CIA they conspired to keep positions of power.

The secret team was instrumental in this plot and a key WACL player in Indochina was General John Singlaub who became chief of MACV-SOG in 1964. This was an unconventional warfare task force which oversaw political assassination and paramilitary operations all over Southeast Asia and Ted Shackley, the CIA chief in Laos, had monthly meetings with the general. His boss throughout this period was Richard Stillwell, another key member of the secret team, and after the Vietnam War Singlaub would serve as Chief of staff of the United Nations Command in South Korea. He was forced to resign in May 1978, after criticizing President Jimmy Carter and his plans to reduce the number of troops in South Korea. After this, he would join in attacking Carter and preparing for the inauguration of Reagan— and he would play a sinister role in Latin America doing so.

This, however, is a story for later, and we shall now see how this group centralized the Latin American drug market.

---

[426] Id.

10.1.5. THE WAR ON COMMUNISM

*"When I give food to the poor, they call me a saint. When I ask
why the poor have no food, they call me a communist."*

—Dom Helder Câmara, Archbishop of Brazil—

When it comes to the CIA's dealings in Latin America, its operations
leave no doubt about the preferred ideology. It invariably has allied
with fascists and right-wing dictators, rulers that have prioritized the
interests of U.S. corporations rather than the people. Thus, the citizens
of Guatemala (1954, 1962-80's), Chile (1964-73), Costa Rica (1955,
1970), Haiti (1959-63, 1986-94), Ecuador (1960-63), Brazil (1961-
64), Peru (1960-65), the Dominican Republic (1960-66), Cuba (1959-
2012), Uruguay (1964-70), Bolivia (1964-75), Jamaica (1976-80),
Grenada (1979-84), Panama (1969-91), and El Salvador (1980-94) all
got a taste of CIA's "medicine" when they began dreaming of a better
world.[427] As soon as they did, they would be overrun by a military-
political machine which ensured that the wheels of oppression
continued, and this pattern has historical roots.

It goes back at least 500 years to the arrival of Columbus, and the
American elite took over the region as Spain and other European
powers withdrew. The United States Marines was a creation of these
elites and together with other corrupt institutions of power they would
be used as tools to ensure that the hemisphere remained safe for
investments.[428] The result was strongly oppressive regimes, and after
the Second World War events proceeded much as before.

---

[427] BLUM, *KILLING HOPE* (2003)

[428] As Major General Smedley Butler said in a 1933 speech: "I spent thirty-three years
and four months in active military service as a member of this country's most agile
military force, the Marine Corps. I served in all commissioned ranks from Second
Lieutenant to Major-General. And during that period, I spent most of my time being
a high-class muscleman for Big Business, for Wall Street and for the Bankers. In
short, I was a racketeer, a gangster for capitalism. I helped make Mexico and
especially Tampico safe for American oil interests in 1914. I helped make Haiti and
Cuba a decent place for the National City Bank boys to collect revenues in. I helped

The elite, however, could no longer justify imperial ambitions by alluding to "the white man's burden". Instead, they had to invent a more plausible scenario, and the War on Communism was born. To the elite, it would serve as an excuse to intervene wherever integrity and solidarity threatened to overthrow regimes of unjust rule. This scheme worked great until 1991, when the Soviet Union was dissolved. The end of the cold war made the elite seek out new enemy images to justify their policies, and with the War on Terrorism and the War on Drugs they could continue the status quo.

These campaigns are identical in that their practical application is the control of populations—and to anyone based in the region it was a front for fascism, which surely was alive and kicking. As Celerino Castillo, a DEA agent in El Salvador and Guatemala testified to Congress in 1996:

"The CIA and the Guatemalan army . . . label as communist sympathizers anyone who opposes the traditional oppressive role of the Guatemalan military. Therefore, they label as communists or communist sympathizers, priests and nuns who work to elevate the position of the poor in the society, union organizers . . . indigenous leaders (the Indians are kept down so they can be used as cheap laborers by the rich, who are supporters of the military) and student activists. . . . The CIA supports the intimidation, kidnapping and torture, surveillance and murder of these people."

As Celerino discovered, the Guatemalan military used the War on Drugs to subject the citizenry to a reign of terror. They would do this by keeping control of drug markets, ensuring that profits went to the

---

in the raping of half a dozen Central American republics for the benefit of Wall Street. I helped purify Nicaragua for the International Banking House of Brown Brothers in 1902-1912. I brought light to the Dominican Republic for the American sugar interests in 1916. I helped make Honduras right for the American fruit companies in 1903. In China in 1927 I helped see to it that Standard Oil went on its way unmolested. Looking back on it, I might have given Al Capone a few hints. The best he could do was to operate his racket in three districts. I operated on three continents." SMEDLEY BUTLER, *WAR IS A RACKET* (1935)

right people and subjecting the citizenry to an arbitrary regime of violence. When the spoils of war were not shared between public officials and drug warriors, it would be presented as evidence that the drug war was working, then burned or used to frame political opponents.[429] The feared Guatemalan G2 police was frank about these procedures; they would even take Castillo to areas where they tortured and killed people off for politics, but the DEA insisted that he should work with local authorities.

This was the mid-1980's and there was nothing new about this situation. In 1954, President Jacobo Árbenz had been overthrown in a CIA instigated coup after a series of reforms which included an expanded right to vote, the ability of workers to organize, legitimizing political parties, and allowing public debate. The "worst" part was a program for agrarian reform under which uncultivated portions of large landholdings were expropriated in return for compensation and redistributed to poverty-stricken agricultural laborers. Approximately 500,000 people benefited from the program, the majority being indigenous people, but the United Fruit Company which owned half of Guatemala's lands and much infrastructure was not impressed. The Dulles brothers were heavily invested in this Rockefeller-controlled company. The CEOs wanted a fascist dictatorship because it was the most stable environment for their investments, and so the U.S. installed their own puppet regime.

For this reason, between 1954 and 1985, more than 60,000 people were murdered to preserve a healthy business environment. WACL was a player in this,[430] and the Guatemalan coup was part of a bigger pattern—one where the drug market provided funding as well as motivation for regime change.

---

[429] CELERINO CASTILLO, *POWDERBURNS: COCAINE, CONTRAS AND THE DRUG WAR* (1994)

[430] In the Guatemalan military, an important figure was Mario Sandoval Alarcon, architect of the Guatemalan death squads, and a Vice President from 1974 to 1978. He was a key WACL member, and the Latin American death squads were all linked through an umbrella group of Central and South American rightists called the Latin American Anti-Communist Confederation (CAL). CAL, in turn, was affiliated with the World Anti-Communist League, which was led by retired U.S. Major General John Singlaub. See ANDERSON, *INSIDE THE LEAGUE* (1986)

10.1.5.1. OPERATION CONDOR

We already know that the death squads of this period were connected to Nazi networks in the region; they, in turn, were protected and assisted by the CIA and the political result was that General Stroessner took control of Paraguay in 1954; the Brazilian military overthrew the president in 1964; General Hugo Banzer took power in Bolivia in 1971; a civic-military dictatorship seized power in Uruguay on 27 June 1973; forces loyal to General Pinochet bombed the presidential palace in Chile on 11 September 1973, overthrowing the democratically elected president; and a military junta headed by General Jorge Rafael Videla seized power in Argentina on 24 March 1976.

Assisted by the CIA in 1974 (in what would become known as *Operation Condor*), security officials from these countries met in Buenos Aires to prepare coordinated actions against subversive targets. That these governments were in league with the network of exiled SS Nazis was seen in the following Bolivia coup, where Hugo Banzer (trained by the Americans at the SOA)[431] allied with Klaus Barbie, an SS officer formerly known as the Butcher of Lyon. French Intelligence wanted him arrested for war crimes; he was suspected of being directly involved with the deaths of 14,000 people, but he had protection. Thus, together with Roberto Suarez, the biggest coca producer in the world, Barbie helped Banzer overthrow the Bolivian regime in 1980.

This was the second time that Banzer grabbed power. It was such an obvious display of collusion between criminal elements and government agents that it would go down in history as the "Cocaine Coup", but his collaboration with drug barons and Nazi war criminals was evident from before. As Paul Williams noted, during his first

---

[431] The School of the Americas, which in Latin Amerika is known as "escuela de golpes," (school of Coups) has trained most military juntas in the region, teaching them interrogation techniques, combat skills, and setting them up with a network intended to promote U.S. corporate interests.

period, land in coca production tripled,[432] and Banzer was part of an elite network of military officers which had been collaborating with Nazis and coca producers for decades. The Vatican itself was in bed with this group, as was the Propaganda Due (P2) Masonic Lodge of Italy, who had a powerful influence in the Argentinian military and political circles. President Peron's ties to this organization made sure that Licio Gelli, the P2s Worshipful Master, could arrange for Argentina as a safe-haven for Nazis after the War—and Gelli had close ties to the Vatican and the CIA. So close, that by 1970 the P2 received an estimated $10 million a month from CIA black funds to commit terror attacks in Europe and South America.[433]

10.1.6. OPERATION GLADIO AND THE VATICAN CONNECTION

The terrorist campaign on the European continent would be known as *Operation Gladio*. In the period from 1956-1990, to make Europe align with American interests, the CIA would draw upon the international network of fascists to carry out more than 2000 terrorist attacks on European soil, leaving hundreds dead and thousands wounded.[434] Drug dealing was part of the operation, as was bank

---

[432] "To fund the army, Banzer ordered coca trees to be planted throughout the country's ailing cotton fields. Between 1974 and 1980, land in coca production tripled. The coca was exported to Colombian cartel laboratories, including Barbie's Transmaritania. A Multibillion-dollar industry was born. The tremendous upsurge in coca supply from Bolivia sharply drove down the price of Cocaine, fuelling a huge new market and the rise of the Colombian cartels. The street price of cocaine in 1975 was fifteen hundred dollars a gram. Within a decade, the price fell to two hundred dollars per gram. The CIA became an active participant in this new drug network by creating a pipeline between the Colombian cartels and the black neighbourhoods of Compton and Los Angeles." WILLIAMS, *OPERATION GLADIO* (2015) 118-19

[433] Ibid., 70, 76, 95

[434] As Giovanni Pellegrino, president of Italy's parliamentary commission investigating Gladio, noted the situation: "The official figures say that alone in the period between January 1, 1969, and December 31, 1987, there have been in Italy 14,591 acts of violence with a political motivation. It is maybe worth remembering

fraud, but South America would experience the worst atrocities. Under *Operation Condor*, not only were union leaders, students, parents, journalists, generals, and politicians—anyone with integrity—attacked with extreme prejudice; as we have seen, death squads ensured that those who opposed this group would disappear,[435] and in 1975 the Bolivian Interior Ministry drew up a master plan with the help of Vatican officials for the elimination of liberation theology. This scheme, called the Banzer Plan, was adopted by ten Latin American governments; they would kill even priests and nuns, and the Vatican joined this quest while laundering drug money.[436]

For those who have any doubt, the story of how the Vatican, the CIA, and the Italian Mafia connected with Nazis and right-wing dictators to profit on the drugs economy is excellently told by Paul Williams in *Operation Gladio: The Unholy alliance between the Vatican, the CIA, and the Mafia.* The connection went back to World War II, when the Vatican and the OSS helped thousands of Nazis flee Europe. Traditionally, the Church of Peter aligned with the elite, and the Pope had no love for liberation theology as it sided with the oppressed. The Vatican, therefore, were intimately connected with the

---

that these acts have left behind 491 dead and 1,181 injured and maimed—figure of a war without parallel in any other European country." Ibid., 95

[435] DEA agent Michael Levine was intimately familiar with this situation. Here is how he summarized life in Argentine under the military dictatorship: "In 1980, death was very much a way of life in Argentina. The military government believed itself to be in a life-and-death struggle against communism. It was called la Guerra sucia—'the dirty war.' If you were an idealistic Argentine with sympathies that could in any way be construed as leftist, you kept your mouth shut, or got your butt out of Argentina. Otherwise, you stood a good chance of hearing a knock on the door at any time and greeting cold-eyed men in civilian clothes carrying official government identification cards. They would take you to a secret subbasement of a military or government building, where they would methodically savage your body and brain with the latest 'advances' in torture methods, designed to inflict the maximum pain a human can tolerate without losing consciousness or dying, until you named other 'leftists' you knew. You would then disappear from the face of the earth, and these men would pay a visit to everyone you had named. From 1976 to 1982, it was estimated that some 25 000 Argentines had been turned into desaparecidos—'disappeared ones.'" LEVINE, *THE BIG WHITE LIE* (1994) 29

[436] Id.

networks that came to control the drug market, and a key figure in this scheme was Michele Sidona, a mob lawyer who controlled the cash flow from American streets to the Vatican Bank.[437]

Sidona was a member of P2. His mafia connections extended back to 1957, when he managed profits for the Gambino family, and ten years later he became the Pope's banker. Sidona was not only an unlikely friend of Sir Jocelyn Hambro, the heir to one of England's most prestigious banking families,[438] but he developed a friendship with Chiang Kai-shek and members of the general's family. On several occasions, he travelled to Formosa to provide funds to Chiang and the remnants of the KMT who continued to cultivate the poppy fields of Laos and Thailand. He would set up shell corporations and buy banks to hide the wrongdoing, but it all went sour in 1981 with the *Banco Ambrosiano* scandal. Sidona then received a life sentence for the murder of a lawyer, and it should come as no surprise that he was poisoned in prison. By 1986, he was dead and would be replaced by others, equally eager to make a living in this market.

10.1.7. PROPAGANDA DUE

In this manner, the Vatican continued its money laundering practices. And while all this is very hush-hush, there is evidence that the Vatican Bank (IOR) has been a loyal servant of Nazis, dictators, and drug dealers since at least the 1950's. Intricately involved with this plot was the Propaganda Due (P2) Masonic Lodge of Italy, who's list of membership was discovered by the police investigating the *Banco*

---

[437] WILLIAMS, *OPERATION GLADIO* (2015) 80

[438] After World War II, Hambros became known as the "diamond bank" with its thriving activity in financing the diamond industry and its trade. Traditionally, this is a way of laundering money, and Hambros was one of the top three banks in the Euromarket by the mid-1960s. As Williams noted, "The sole explanation for the bizarre partnership resides in the longstanding ties of Hambro to the intelligence community. He was one of the founders of the OSS, and his presence on the board of the World Commerce Company (WCC) smacks of complicity in the heroin trade." Ibid., 82

Ambrosiano scandal. It contained 962 names, among which were important state officials, politicians, and military officers, including the heads of the three Italian secret services. This was the shadow government of Italy. It was fascist to its bone, and P2 was also active in Uruguay, Brazil, and Argentina. Among its Argentine members were Raúl Alberto Lastiri, interim president in 1973 during the height of the Dirty War; Emilio Massera, who was part of the military junta led by Jorge Rafael Videla from 1976 to 1978 (he was also a member of WACL); José López Rega, a Minister of Social Welfare from 1973–1975 and founder of the Argentine Anticommunist Alliance; and General Guillermo Suárez Mason.

These were the CIA's allies. It is no coincidence that George H.W. Bush, after becoming Director of CIA in 1976, became an honorary member of P2. Nor was it accidental that Cuban mercenaries would work for Argentinean, Chilean, and other intelligence services, assisting with population control. These connections were the result of the secret team's cloak-and-dagger operations, and it was the same band of thugs that would assist Nixon in the Watergate break-in, as well with other problems. Nixon had wanted a team of assassins under White House control to be used for extra-legal activities and so he set up Lucien Conein with such a department in the DEA. Hunt was integral to this plot and when the Watergate case broke, he had recruited 120 Cuban exiles to murder at Nixon's command.[439]

It was Latin America, however, that would bear the brunt of these assaults, and CORU and other terrorist organizations ensured that the hemisphere experienced a wave of terror attacks.[440] In 1974-75, this wave reached Florida, and from 1974 to 1976 Miami was rocked by over 700 bombings. Even airplanes would drop from the sky, and the CIA made sure that hunting down these terrorists was extremely hard.

---

[439] KRUGER, *THE GREAT HEROIN COUP* (2015) 19

[440] For more on this, see Ibid., and SCOTT & MARSHAL, *COCAINE POLITICS* (1991)

10.1.8. The Ultimate Cocaine Coup

We now have a backdrop to view the evolution of Latin American drug markets. With the military coup of Banzer in Bolivia, coca production became effectively legalized and the Suarez organization would control much of these lands. By 1977, cartels had formed which would buy coca paste in Bolivia, turn it into cocaine in Colombian laboratories, and smugglers would use different routes to the United States, usually going through Mexico.[441] While the market, at this point, was becoming professionalized, there was room for improvement, and the CIA took care of it.

When it comes to the details, the CIA has had several operations which were intended to control and centralize the Latin American drug market. According to Rodney Stich, CIA agents Trenton Parker and Gunther Russbacher went to Colombia in 1981-1982 (there were two meetings) to have the cartels organize their own death squads, comparable to those of other governments in the region.[442] To arrange for their cooperation, the CIA ensured the kidnapping of Martha Nieves Ochoa, the sister of Jorge Luis Ochoa, by M-19, a left-wing group. Based on this, the Colombian drug barons got together and created *Muerte a Sequestradores* (MAS), an army of 2000 men.[443]

---

[441] To Mexicans, the drugs economy is worth up to $40 bn and the state is intimately involved. As Roberto Alcaino, a Medellin drug dealer, noted the situation in 1987: "It has the okay of the federal government there. If there's no police or army involved in the contract, you cannot come through. And they tell you point blank, it costs you so much to come in and so much to get out. . . . When the plane comes in, there's one general in Mexico who has to say okay—so you pay the money so the plane can take off. And that's the way it goes, in an airfield owned by the army. If you deal with somebody else, who's not with the government, they kill the people. They confiscate the plane; they kill the people as if they'd resisted arrest. And then they sell the merchandise. . . . There's not an honest Mexican. They don't make them. They're born rotten." ROBERT MAZUR, *THE INFILTRATOr* (2009) 65

[442] RODNEY STICH, *DEFRAUDING AMERICA* (1998) 367

[443] "Such de facto collaboration between drug traffickers and government security forces, common in countries such as Mexico, Peru, Brazil, Chile, and Argentina, had been characteristic of Colombia through the 1970s, when high-level corruption pervaded the security police. The drug cartel's death squads and the military were

MAS—Death to Kidnappers—would function as a rogue element, a paramilitary group that did what the Colombian Army could not do.[444] They had thirty pilots and an assortment of helicopters and fixed-wing aircraft. U.S., Israeli, British, and Australian military instructors would teach at paramilitary training centres, and the CIA's involvement provided for increased cooperation. From now on Escobar's organization focused on production, the murderous Rodriguez Gacha and the Ochoa brothers concentrated on transport, and the Lehder-organization dealt with distribution.[445]

This cooperation would make the cartels more effective. They would provide insurance that commodities lost would be repaid in full, and in 1984 another meeting took place in Zurich, Switzerland. Kenneth Bucci, a captain of the US Air Force, was tasked to get the drug lords together,[446] and this was the offer:

---

consolidated in 1981, when Colombian drug traffickers, in collaboration with the Colombian army, convened a 'general assembly' to create their own counterterrorist network, Muerte a Sequestradores (Death to Kidnappers), or MAS." SCOTT & MARSHAL, *COCAINE POLITICS* (1998) 89

[444] "Collaboration between Colombian security forces and the drug traffickers' death squads has significantly escalated since 1985, according to Amnesty International. In an October 1989 press release, Amnesty charged that in Colombia 'sectors of the armed forces—often operating in alliance with alleged drug traffickers—and paramilitary groups acting on their orders had killed unarmed civilians on an unprecedented scale in the past months. . . . The victims have included trade union leaders, human rights workers, teachers, priests, peasants, and more recently, members of the judiciary trying to investigate human rights abuses.'" Ibid., 90

[445] MCCOY, *THE POLITICS OF HEROIN* (1991) 479. For more on MAS, see ATTWOOD, *AMERICAN MADE* (2016) 182-86

[446] As he described this operation: "We were to intercept Colombian cocaine coming into America by posing as the Coast Guard. Once we secured the vessel, we were to send the crew back to its port of origin with a message for the drug lord to send a representative to Zurich, Switzerland, to meet with other cocaleros and discuss an operation of mutual benefit to themselves and the U.S. government. This coterie of drug lords would be given the means to destroy the numerically superior but smaller drug traffickers in Latin America and the Caribbean; specifically, they would receive U.S. intelligence on the exact locations of competitors' cocaine laboratories and be given weapons to destroy the labs and any collateral resistance. This was designed to centralize Colombian drug trafficking operations and to give the CIA more control

"The Peruvians and the Bolivians would be partners with the Colombians in the drug trade. They would remain the primary growers of the coca and would process the raw material into coca paste, which they would supply to the Columbians, but they would essentially be excluded from the distribution network into North America. The deal would also exclude affiliates of Shining Path or other revolutionary movements."[447]

"Accepting this deal made the drug traffickers keep 50 percent of their product [while the Secret Team collected the rest]. Louis Porto's and Roberto Suarez organizations from Bolivia were elated with the final agreement. They would produce most of the coca paste in South America and would do so predominantly with their own crops. The climate, rainfall, and altitude of Peru and Bolivia produce the richest plant in the world, and for this reason, the Colombians were pleased to receive the paste from there. The fact that the Peruvians and Bolivians would no longer pose as a competitive threat to their business also pleased the Columbians. For their part, the Porto and Suarez camps were happy not to have to fly drugs into America and face the possibility of arrest or extradition for drug trafficking"[448]

At this meeting much was accomplished, and these forces conspired to get rid of competition. As indicated, this meant revolutionary forces and leftist organizations that fed off the drugs economy, and so, after the Colombian cartels were gone, right-wing paramilitary groups would take control of Colombian drug markets.[449]

---

over them." KENNETH C. BUCCHI, *OPERATION PSEUDO MIRANDA: A VETERAN OF THE CIA DRUG WARS TELLS ALL* (2000) 59

[447] Ibid., (2000) 59

[448] Ibid., 93

[449] Professor Scott elaborates: "A recent Colombian government investigation collected compelling evidence that through the years 1997 to 1999 'Army officers

The same pattern evolved elsewhere, and we shall look at one episode
that threatened to expose the Reagan administration.

10.2. PRELUDE TO IRAN-CONTRA

*"Someday, perhaps, if it's decided that the stories can be told,
you'll see that the state has been involved in acts which are a
thousand times more dirty than anything going on in Colombia.
As long as the government decides to do something, something
that the national interest demanded, then it's legitimate."*[450]

—Rafael Eitan, former Chief of Staff of the Israeli army—

President Carter, next to Kennedy, was the worst president that the
CIA ever had. While Johnson, Nixon, and Ford posed few problems
to the secret team, it comes as no surprise that the activities of this

---

worked intimately with paramilitaries under the command of Carlos Castaño,'
Colombia's chief paramilitary leader, who is from a family of drug traffickers. In a
rare television interview, Castaño stated that 70 percent of the income for his group .
. . came from drugs." (SCOTT, DRUGS, OIL, AND WAR (2003) 74). In the 1980's,
Castaño had been involved with the Medellin- and Cali cartels, but as paramilitary
groups took over the drug trade, he became leader of AUC. AUC is again connected
to Mossad, who in 2001 provided them with 3000 Kalashnikov rifles (Ibid., 91), and
Scott and Marshall explain why: "The fact is that connections to powerful drug
traffickers with local killers and political influence are assets to any international
intelligence agency. Or, to turn the argument around, it is those who enjoy the best
connections with the international intelligence milieu who gain the protection and
power to emerge as the most powerful drug kingpins." (SCOTT & MARSHALL, *COCAINE
POLITICS* (1998) 88) As seen in this light, the strong position of paramilitary groups
in Columbia is explained. Explained is also why, in the period between 1990 and
1997, there were only seven confrontations between these groups and the army
(compared to 5000 between FARC and the army), even though the former is
responsible for 70-80 percent of the killings in this country. See KRØVEL,
KOKAINKRIGEN (2004) 114

[450] SCOTT & MARSHALL, *COCAINE POLITICS* (1998) 78

group made more sane individuals fear for the nation's security—and Carter was such a person. By this time, George H.W. Bush was Director of the CIA and Shackley was his Deputy of Operations. The secret team was running rampant and the network behind Carter had had enough. Thus, Carter fired Bush and replaced him with Stansfield Turner, an Admiral of the Navy. With Turner as the new director a battle raged within the CIA. Turner appointed eight high-ranking naval officers (called the "Navy mafia") to leadership positions—and not only did he eliminate over 800 operational positions, most of them in the clandestine service, but he secured the release of 20,000 documents relating to Project MKULTRA.

This revelation led to a Senate inquiry in 1977, but the Bush-faction pushed back. Hence, another wave of right-wing terrorism would hit the Southern hemisphere, and although Carter would right many wrongs, such as cutting aid to the fascist network of dictatorships, the American and local elites fought back.[451] Not only did they ensure that there was no solution to the Iranian hostage crisis; Shackley, the Skull and Bones, and the Israelis would undermine his every effort at changing the course of policy, and with the inauguration of President Reagan the rogue elements returned to power.

10.2.1. THE CONTRAS AND THE SANDINISTAS

From 1853 to 1933, the U.S. Marines invaded Nicaragua twelve times to secure conditions more suitable for the elite. When they left the country in 1933, they set up Anastasio Somoza as the local dictator,

---

[451] As Fred Sherwood, a CIA pilot during the overthrow of the Arbenz who settled in Guatemala in 1954 and became president of the American Chamber of Commerce said: "Why should we be worried about the death squads? They're bumping off the commies, our enemies. I'd give them more power. Hell, I'd get some cartridges if I could, and everyone else would too . . . Why should we criticize them? The death squad—I'm for it . . . Shit! There's no question, we can't wait 'til Reagan gets in. We hope Carter falls in the ocean real quick . . . We all feel that he [Reagan] is our saviour." BLUM, *KILLING HOPE* (2003) 236. For more on the intrigues at the CIA and the activities of the rogue CIA faction, see TRENTO, *PRELUDE TO TERROR* (2005)

and his family would rule Nicaragua with iron fist over the next 43 years. As William Blum summarized this reign:

> *"While the Guardsmen, consistently maintained by the United States, passed their time on martial law, rape, torture, murder of the opposition, and massacres of the peasants, as well as violent pursuits such as robbery, extortion, contraband, running brothels and other government functions, the Somoza clan laid claim to the lion's share of Nicaragua's land and business."*[452]

It is with this backdrop in mind that we must see the Sandinistas' rise to power. When they took control of Nicaragua in 1979, Somoza left behind a country broken by debt ($1,6 billion) and where two-thirds of the population earned less than $300 a year. The Sandinistas sought to change this—and while Somoza settled in Miami with an account worth $900 million, they began a program of social reform. By prioritizing healthcare, education, gender equality, and agrarian reform, the new government improved rural and urban working conditions. They provided free unionization for all workers, improved public services, housing conditions, and schools, while they abolished torture, political assassination, and the death penalty.

Within six months, half a million had been taught rudimentary reading, bringing the national illiteracy rate down from 50 percent to 12 percent. The success of the campaign was recognized by UNESCO and life was better for the Nicaraguan people. With President Carter in the White House, the poor nation had been allowed some room to operate and the wounds of war were beginning to heal.

In 1980, however, President Reagan came into office. The secret team was back, and his administration denounced the Sandinistas as terrorists, increased funding to the opposition, and stopped all aid and investments programs that the Carter administration had allowed. The U.S. not only imposed their own embargo, but pressured the IMF, World bank, Inter-American Development Bank (IDB), and EU to

---

[452] Ibid., 290

hold back loans. To make these policies look good, Reagan recalled the U.S. Ambassador after admitting that the Sandinistas had done some good in terms of education. To counter such nonsense, the Reagan administration produced evidence that the Nicaraguan regime was in league with narco-terrorists and Alexander Haig, Reagan's Secretary of State, showed the world a picture of a burning body as an example of what the Sandinistas were capable of. The photo was later revealed to be a fraud, as it was taken in 1978 and depicted atrocities of the Somoza regime.[453] Even so, the damage was done, and Reagan had an excuse for preparing for war.

To oust the Sandinistas, however, the elite needed a viable opposition and so the CIA created the contras. These were mostly the remnants of Somoza's National Guard. To Reagan, they were "freedom fighters" and "the moral equal of our founding fathers," but in truth they were a ragtag group of fascists, murderers, rapists, torturers, and drug runners that would pillage at will. As author William Blum noted their modus operandi:

"The contras' brutality earned them a wide notoriety. They regularly destroyed health centres, schools, agricultural cooperatives, and community centres—symbols of the Sandinistas' social programs in rural areas. People caught in these assaults were often tortured and killed in the most gruesome ways. One example, reported by The Guardian of London, suffices. In the words of a survivor of a raid in Jinotega province, which borders on Honduras: 'Rosa had her breasts cut off. Then they cut into her chest and took out her heart. The men had their arms broken, their testicles cut off, and their eyes poked out. They were killed by slitting their throats and pulling their tongue out through the slit.'"[454]

Such instances were so common with the contras that Americas Watch concluded that "the contras systematically engage in violent

---

[453] Ibid., 301

[454] Ibid., 293

abuses . . . so prevalent that these may be said to be their principal means of waging war."[455] Even so, the Reagan administration provided these groups with training, equipment, as well as funding, and there is no reason to presume that these behaviours were not encouraged. To the contrary, using terror to overwhelm populations has been a key component of U.S. policy since the Monroe Doctrine in 1823,[456] and the U.S. government did what it could to aggravate the situation by mining Nicaraguan waters. This operation would be denounced by the International Court of Justice in 1984 as an act of state terrorism. Nevertheless, while the Court held that the United States had been in violation of international law when it supported the contras, this warfare successfully undermined the Nicaraguan government.

Because of the Reagan administration, the Sandinistas more positive ventures were obstructed. The contras carried out a systematic campaign to disrupt the program of social reform. This ensured that people were increasingly distraught, and so the US government finally got its regime change.

Throughout this campaign, the contras received military and financial support from the CIA and the White House. They were based in CIA-protected camps in neighbouring Honduras and Costa Rica and would operate across the border, spreading murder, rape, and mayhem. Congress, however, became increasingly opposed, and in 1983 prohibited federal funding of the contras through the Boland Amendment. The Reagan administration then continued to back the contras by raising money from foreign allies and covertly selling arms to Iran.

---

[455] Id.

[456] This Doctrine of a policy directed at U.S. hegemony in Latin America was used as a defense by such Iran-Contra conspirators as Robert Gates, another insider, and a key operator for the secret team. In 1984, as deputy director of CIA under Reagan, he advocated that the U.S. initiate a bombing campaign against Nicaragua and that the U.S. do everything to stop the Sandinista regime. Mossad agent Ari Ben Menashe has implicated him in drug operations (see his book *Profits of War*), and as President Bush's Director of the CIA, he would later assist in covering up operations.

Officially, this was the essence of the Iran–Contra affair. Even so, it is only the top layer, and for those who dig deeper the truth is more sinister.

10.3. IRAN-CONTRA

"[I]f people ever knew what we had done, we'd be chased down the streets and lynched."[457]

—George H.W. Bush—

Between 1982 and 1984, 1984, the U.S. Congress passed three amendments to prohibit support for the Contras. Instead of conforming to these constitutional limitations, however, the Reagan administration decided to continue its funding and the drugs economy became the solution. A variety of programs, commissions, and personnel therefore were put in place to cover for the real events, but we know that between 1982 and 1986 the White House fought a secret war against Nicaragua assisted by an airbridge which flew guns to bases in Central America and drugs back.[458] Cocaine imports doubled

---

[457] Bush discussing Iran-Contra with journalist Sarah McClendon, June 1992. MARTIN, *THE CONSPIRATORS* (2002) 20

[458] According to Barry Seal, one of the conspirators, then-CIA Director William Casey met with Adolfo Colero, the leader of the Contras, and it was decided that the Contras would get money and weapons in exchange for cocaine. Casey put Oliver North to oversee the project and North, prompted by the CIA, recruited Seal to oversee delivery of the products. A man named Ramon Navarro from the Medellin Cartel then began to train the Contras in the manufacturing process. Colero was the 'point man' for the Contras, the one who dealt with Washington and others as needed and Contra leader Enrique Bermudez was tasked with getting the cocaine kitchens built and protected. According to Barry, "Bermudez had solicited three other Contra commanders to assist in this project. Their names are Commander Fernando, Commander Franklin, and Commander Marlan. Ramon Navarro supplied the cocaine paste and raw coca leaves to the Contras. The U.S. provided the equipment. It was delivered to the camps by Chinook helicopters (CH-47) out of Ft. Campbell, Kentucky (159th Aviation Battalion) It was Barry's job to deliver the finished product and monies to destinations as dictated by Mr. North." Barry himself told this

as a result of government orchestrated drug smuggling, and Palmer National Bank of Washington D.C.[459] and other banks would launder immense profits.

It all went well until a plane crash and other events compromised the operation and exposed the network behind it. A cover-up immediately begun and the government's first official response—the press conference held by Ed Meese, Reagan's Attorney General on November 25, 1986—was an attempt at damage control. So was the investigative committee proposed by the president the same day, and if we want to know more about this operation, we must accept testimony of the individuals who were involved.

As this story broke there were many who came forward to expose the dirty dealings of the White House. Even so, they faced a powerful apparatus of oppression and agents of the state ensured that the authority of the U.S. government did not suffer a too serious blow. Like the Warren Commission and the 9/11 Commission, therefore, the investigative efforts of government were set up to fail. Nonetheless, investigative reporters and whistleblowers have revealed enough of the Iran-Contra affair to have senior conspirators (and those who keep covering their tracks) put away for a long time. We are talking of a shady network who have fed on corruption to this day—and as this network still wreaks havoc, another look at this episode can do some good. After all, if the U.S. government is ever to claim credibility, it will have to confront these serious charges; it must also confront this

---

to Chip Tatum, a CIA agent working for Bush, at a meeting in San Lorenzo, Honduras, April 10, 1985. See GENE CHIP TATUM, *THE CHIP TATUM CHRONICLES* (1985)

[459] Stefan Halper, an insider who has served the secret cabal well until today, dealt with much of the money laundering. From 1984 to 1990 he was chairman and majority shareholder of the Palmer National Bank of Washington, D.C., the National Bank of Northern Virginia and the George Washington National Bank. Palmer National Bank was used to transfer money to Swiss Bank Accounts controlled by White House aid Oliver North. See PIZZO; STEPHEN; FRICKER; MARY; MUOLO; PAUL, *INSIDE JOB: THE LOOTING OF AMERICA'S SAVINGS AND LOANS* (2015).; PATRICIA GOLDSTONE, *INTERLOCK: ART, CONSPIRACY, AND THE SHADOW WORLDS OF MARK LOMBARDI* (2015) p 120.

network which remains above the law, and so let us begin with the main characters.

10.3.1. THE USUAL SUSPECTS

"I have put thousands of Americans away for tens of thousands of years for less evidence than is available against Ollie North and CIA people. . . . I personally was involved in a deep-cover case that went to the top of the drug world in three countries. The CIA killed it."[460]

—Michael Levine, Former DEA Agent—

For those investigating Iran-Contra, Al Martin, a lieutenant commander with the Office of Naval Intelligence (ONI), is essential reading. In 1984, he ran a financial scheme involving Florida-based corporations laundering of money to the contras, and he later wrote *The Conspirators* on his connections with the secret team.

This man was directly involved. He personally knew the Bush family and had frequent meetings with Jeb Bush, Oliver North, and Richard Secord.[461] In his book, he implicates George H.W. Bush and his son Jeb in several hundred financial crimes,[462] and according to him what became known as the Iran-Contra affair was a conspiracy

---

[460] Michael Levine interview CNBC-TV, October 8, 1996

[461] Major General Richard Secord came to Vietnam in 1961 and was responsible for coordinating the airbridge in the Golden Triangle. He would later provide much the same services for the Reagan administration in Latin America, and in Afghanistan after 9/11. After his retirement from the USAF, Secord went into business, and in the Iran–Contra affair Secord made $2 million on illegal arms transactions. He was later convicted of lying to Congress about it and was sentenced on January 24, 1990, to two years' probation.

[462] "George Bush, Sr. would invariably be given a piece of everything, of every fraud that was done, because he was at the very top of the pyramid, and much of this fraud could not have been committed without either his protection or his influence." MARTIN, *THE CONSPIRATORS* (2002) 255

by Vice President George H.W. Bush, CIA director Bill Casey, and the National Security Council's (NSC) Lieutenant Colonel Oliver North to support the contra movement. This would be done by large-scale drugs and guns running, including a variety of financial schemes. The idea was to raise $35 million, and they intended to use no more than 500 personnel. Events, however, did not go according to plan. Agents and elites were running rampant and by 1986 the operation had become a monstrosity, involving some 5000 individuals and raking in more than $350 billion in profits.[463]

Al Martin explains that Oliver North's importance to the operation was his position as chairman of the National Programs Office (NPO). This organization was a crucial component of the government's plans for martial law and North had access to logistics and facilities that was key to the venture. His organization also possessed the authority to keep secrets, and so everything was arranged.

North's superiors were Casey and Bush. The CIA Director established three Restricted Access Groups (RAGs) and the Vice President was put in charge of RAG 1—that dealing with weapons, drugs smuggling, and transfer of funds to the contras. His underlings were working on a need-to-know basis; most were used to this kind of work, and so it was that this operation could succeed over a period of years even though the conspirators were operating in plain sight.[464]

In this operation, Bonesman George H.W. Bush was on top. President Reagan was a puppet in the early stages of Alzheimer's—and if he ever thought differently, he learned better three months into his presidency. Reagan, then, was shot by John Hinckley, a

---

[463] Ibid., viii

[464] Also included in these RAGs, Al Martin names Reagan's National Security Advisor Col. Donald Gregg, Secretary of State Lawrence Eagleburger, Assistant Secretary of State Elliot Abrahams, and Richard Armitage, the Assistant Secretary of Defense for International Security Policy. From the Department of Defense, they included Frank Carlucci (National Security Advisor and later Assistant Secretary of Defense) and Richard Stillwell (Assistant Secretary of Defense), Robert Gates (Deputy Director of CIA), and Caspar Weinberger (Secretary of Defense). From the CIA, they included Bill Casey, Clair George (Deputy Director of Operations) and Alan Fiers (Assistant Deputy Director of Operations). Ibid., 14

psychiatric patient who happened to know Neil Bush, one of the Vice President's sons. Even so, it took no more than four hours before the FBI and Secret Service concluded that no conspiracy was involved, and after this Bush ran the country officially for 44 days—and unofficially for the rest of Reagan's eight-years. When he returned from the hospital, Reagan let Bush handle all matters relating to National security, and so the Vice President was perfectly positioned. After Reagan's second term, Bush became president, and he would use his position to continue the cover-up and to pardon his accomplices, those convicted of lying to Congress and for crimes against the state.

It is for good reason, therefore, that Bush has been called the world's biggest drug lord. Indeed, he was one of the greatest villains of the 20th century, and this is saying a lot.

10.3.2. DRUGS AND GUNS RUNNING: THE BIG PICTURE

The contras were positioned in bases near the borders of Nicaragua. In the South they invaded from Costa Rica and from the north they came from Honduras. The contra camps were protected by the NSC and CIA, and while they did not forget to rape and plunder, cocaine became an important business. Chip Tatum, a CIA agent who worked directly for the Vice President, has told of helicopters ostensibly supplying medicines and other aid that would return loaded with cocaine. He also claims to have visited contra camps in Honduras with Oliver North for the purpose of inspecting cocaine production. This took place on March 30, 1985,[465] and in Costa Rica the ranch of John Hull, a local CIA agent, was used as an airstrip for all kinds of transport.

John Hull was not only friends with George Bush and Joe Fernandez, the CIA Station Chief in Costa Rica; he was, according to Bucchi, present at the meeting between drug lords at Hotel Zurich in

---

[465] See *Presidential Secrets*, an interview by Ted Gunderson, a former FBI special agent, with Chip Tatum.

1984, when the drug market was being organized to the dictates of the CIA. The story of Hull and his ranch is told by author Leslie Cockburn in her book *Out of Control*, and while the governments of Costa Rica and Honduras officially remained neutral, Hull conspired with corrupt officials.

The only problem was the DEA station in Honduras. Established in 1981, Thomas Zepeda, its chief agent, soon discovered that drugs were shipped by the Honduran military and other agents of state.[466] Because they were supporting the contras, CIA told him to keep away, but Zepeda did not obey and begun to investigate SETCO in May 1983. This was a CIA contractor who flew drugs and weapons to the contras—and one month later, the DEA station in Honduras was closed.[467]

As this took place, the CIA tripled its personnel in the region and while Honduras now was open for business, Celerino Castillo, the local DEA agent in El Salvador and Guatemala, would become another problem.

10.3.2.1. THE AIR BRIDGE

According to Oliver North's testimony, he tasked General Richard Secord to arrange an air bridge to the Contras in July 1984. As US Air Force Liaison to the CIA, Secord had assisted in the air bridge of the Golden Triangle, and he was perfect for the job. Being an integral part of the secret team, he could be relied upon to keep the operation going,

---

[466] As Zepeda testified to Senator John Kerry's investigative committee: "It was difficult to conduct an investigation and expect the Honduran authorities to assist in arrests when it was them we were trying to investigate." McCOY, *THE POLITICS OF HEROIN* (1991) 484

[467] ALEXANDER COCKBURN & JEFFREY ST. CLAIR, *WHITEOUT: THE CIA, DRUGS AND THE PRESS* (1999) 283

and the DEA estimates that cocaine imports more than doubled in this period (1981-1985).[468]

The Senate Foreign Relations Committee's Subcommittee on Terrorism, Narcotics, and International Operations was tasked to investigate. Unfortunately, the subcommittee was led by John Kerry, another Bonesman, and it was cover-up. Nevertheless, while the investigation failed to find evidence of direct CIA/contras' involvement in the drug trade, the Kerry Committee's report revealed that contracts for supplying medical aid and other goods were given to four companies which were run by drug smugglers. These contractors were paid $806 000 to fly for the contras—and they were registered as big-time drug smugglers by the FBI, DEA, and Customs before this.[469]

---

[468] According to the DEA U.S. cocaine consumption were at 34 to 45 metric tons in 1981, 45 to 54 metric tons in 1982 and 50 to 61 metric tons in 1983. In 1984 it was about 85 metric tons, and in 1985 it exceeded 100 tons. This brought the price of cocaine down from $30 grand a kilo to $12 grand. MARTIN, *THE CONSPIRATORS* (2002) 196-197

[469] SETCO was run by Juan Matta Ballesteros, who had been arrested at Dulles Airport, Washington D.C., in 1970 with 26 kilos of cocaine. As punishment he was deported to Honduras where he became a serious player in the drug trade. He was an ally of General Paz Garcia in his 1978 military coup (and the Cali Cartel) and SETCO made $ 186 000 working for the U.S. government—plus whatever they could make selling drugs. Another contractor was Frigorificos de Puntarenas, a company ostensibly in the business of freezing and exporting seafoods, but known drug smugglers since 1983. A third contractor was DIACSA, a company from Miami which had a fleet of airplanes and was run Alfredo Caballero, a Bay of Pigs veteran who was being investigated by the DEA. The fourth company was Vortex, another Miami-based company involved with aircraft. It was run by Michael Palmer, a drug pilot whose drug operations went at least a decade back. Palmer was under investigation by the FBI when Vortex was hired by the CIA—which, according to themselves, did rigorous background checks. For more on this, see SCOTT & MARSHALL, *COCAINE POLITICS* (1998) 10-17; COCKBURN & ST. CLAIR, *WHITEOUT* (1999) 281

"What I have found is a snake pit without a bottom. They will do anything to keep this covered up."

—Ross Perot, 1992 Presidential candidate—

These "humanitarians" flew guns to the contras and brought cocaine back.[470] Most likely, there were many other routes of transport,[471] but facilities such as Palmerola Air Base in Honduras and General Noriega's military bases in Panama were frequently deployed. It is, however, the U.S. airbase at Ilopango, El Salvador, that has received the most attention. This airstrip deep in the jungle was central to North's operation. It would be used by the contras for refuelling planes and storage, and in his book *Powderburns* Celerino Castillo, a DEAs agent in El Salvador, has much to say on these operations.

On arrival in 1985, he had been told by his boss Robert Stia and Jack McCavett, the CIA's Station Chief, to stay away from this base and the contras but Celerino did not listen. He was a believer in the War on Drugs and documented more than a hundred cases of contra drug running. Somehow, the Kerry Committee, failed to mention this

---

[470] According to the DEA, 4,400 kilograms of cocaine was seized nationally in 1982, 7,300 kilograms in 1983 and 11,742 kilograms in 1984. In the first six months of 1985, in south Florida alone, over 13,000 kilograms of cocaine was seized, more than in the entire country in 1984. The real amount of drugs entering the U.S. can be extrapolated if we believe an analysis by the House Subcommittee on Operations which concluded that drug warriors were intercepting only 0.5 percent of the drugs coming by air and about 5 percent of the sea shipments. See George Volsky, *U.S. Says Smugglers Bring in Record Cocaine Flow*, New York Times, August 8, 1985

[471] According to Mossad's Ari Ben Menashe, the government of Guatemala was also involved: "In 1985 Guatemala started to be used heavily as a drug transit point to the United States from South America. Meija, The Chief of the Nation, was, in fact, a much bigger drug boss than Noriega. Massive amounts of drugs were shipped into the United States . . . This would all have been impossible without the wink and the nod that the CIA gave." MENASHE, *PROFITS OF WAR* (1998) 139

man in its report. He would be questioned by Lawrence Walsh, Kerry's lead investigator, but his testimony would be buried.

Luckily for the Vice President, Senator Kerry pulled sufficient weight to hide that the CIA agent in charge of drugs and guns running at Ilopango was Felix Rodriguez—a friend of Bush. A former police chief to Battista, he had fled Cuba after Castro came to power. After that, at the Miami CIA Station, Rodriguez had joined Shackley and Clines to become part of a team of assassins that would kill for the CIA. He was part of the squad that murdered Che Guevara in Bolivia in 1967, and over the next decades he was deeply involved with shady operations in many Latin American nations. He was an ardent anti-communist, and during Iran-Contra Rodriguez had weekly meetings/communications with Donald Gregg, Bush's closest advisor. Gregg, himself, would admit to these meetings. And while he claimed that they never discussed Iran-Contra operations, this is difficult to believe, considering that Rodriguez was the man who oversaw Contra operations in El Salvador from 1982-86. His assistant was "Ramon Medina," another Cuban exile whose real name was Luis Posada Carriles—the very same terrorist who in 1976 blew up a Cuban airplane, killing 73 passengers.

Rodriguez helped Carriles out of Venezuelan prison after serving 9 years for this atrocity. Now, he ran Ilopango, while Rodriguez took care of business in the region as a whole.

10.3.2.3. PANAMA

General Noriega of Panama was another conspirator. He had been on the CIA's payroll since 1955, when he at the age of 19 joined the Socialist Party and began to spy for the Americans. The BNDD suspected him to be a bigtime drug dealer already in 1971. By the time Bush became CIA Director in 1976, he was registered in over 40 DEA databases, but the CIA still paid $110 000 for his services. Carter put an end to these transactions, but the CIA would continue its funding under Reagan, this time doubling his salary.

Under General Noriega's rule, Panama was a haven for the CIA and other drugs traffickers. The Cali and Medellin cartel had access to airstrips for a fee and Panamanian banks relied upon the drugs economy to prosper.[472] Under Iran-Contra, Noriega would let North and his network operate freely,[473] often assisted by Mike Harari, an Israeli Mossad agent. Harari had overseen a unit which dealt with political assassinations, but after a job gone wrong in Lillehammer, Norway, in 1973, he had come to Central America to enlarge Israel's involvement with the shady side of politics. He was a serious player, no doubt, and integral to another power-political faction that we shall get to know.[474] There is even reason to suspect that he was part of the 9/11 terror operation,[475] and as Noriega's security advisor, he would

---

[472] See MAZUR, *THE INFILTRATOR* (2009) 115, 216.

[473] MARTIN, *THE CONSPIRATORS* (2002) 266

[474] Ari Ben Menashe describes his connections: "[B]etween 1975 and 1977, Sharon was a private citizen who was trying to build a fortune dealing arms in Central America. He had a network of people working with him there, one being the disgraced Mossad agent Mike Harari, who had just left Israel because of his failure in the 'Moroccan Waiter Affair,' where the wrong man was shot dead in Lillehammer, Norway. . . . Sharon's network had been able to provide military equipment from Israel to various Central American countries, including, El Salvador, Guatemala, Panama, Costa Rica, and even Mexico. This was never official Israeli government policy, and it was frowned upon by the cabinet itself, but Sharon was too wild a goose for anybody to handle. . . . Gates [the CIA Deputy Director] had developed a professional interest in the arms network that Sharon and his former intelligence cowboys were operating in Central America. By 1981, Sharon and Harari were running what Harari described as more of a CIA network than an Israeli operation— and were filling their private bank accounts at the same time. It was in 1981 that they started supplying a secret army in Central America, the contras, who were trying to destabilize and eventually bring about the downfall of the Sandinista government of Nicaragua, which had come to power in 1979. . . . Sharon, with all his power, could not force the prime minister or the leaders of the Israeli intelligence community to pay for weapons from the slush fund that had grown out of the Iran arms sales. So, with the backing of Gates and the CIA, some members of the group created their own fund. They did this, according to Harari, by transporting cocaine from South America to the United States via Central America." MENASHE, *PROFITS OF WAR* (1998) 105

[475] In 2001, Dimitri Khalezov, a former officer of the Soviet nuclear intelligence, was working with Harari in Bangkok. Harari, at this point, was setting up Al-Qaeda cells

be implicated in the murder of U.S. military personnel who sought to stop the illegal operation.

We shall have more to say on that after following the drug shipments.

10.3.3. ARKANSAS: THE UNITED STATES' BANANA REPUBLIC

"If George Bush is prosecuted, and goes to jail for the crimes he committed when he was the Drug Kingpin of the 1980s, this will be the single most important historical event in decades. It will define a realm of possible action that many people right now feel is impossible, or unfathomable—that it would ever happen. It can happen, it must happen. This is the responsibility of the American people."

—Jeffrey Steinberg, EIR 1996—

Arkansas was a hub of Iran-Contra operations. As it was inside the United States homeland, federal authorities and drug fighting agencies were less present; struggling economically, its officials and elite were easily corrupted; and as Governor Bill Clinton was eager to trade principles for power, everything was arranged for the CIA.

Several contra-operations were involved. In addition to large-scale drug smuggling and money laundering,[476] the state served as a

---

in South-East Asia, and on the morning of 9/11, Harari was in excellent mood, ordering fine wine, and telling Khalezov that it was Mossad's finest hour. Khalezov have told this story in several interviews, also presenting copies of Harari's fake passport.

[476] Terry Reed, a former Air Force Intelligence operative who became a Little Rock businessman, estimated that CIA, between 1984 and 1986, laundered $250 million in drug profits in Arkansas. Governor Clinton and his conspirators received 10 percent, but as more than 100 million from cocaine sales went missing from the CIA's ledgers, it was possibly even more. This, at the very least, was believed to be true by the CIA, who by late-1985 had taken their business elsewhere. Before this, however, Dan Lasater would launder money through the Arkansas Development and Finance

training ground for the contras, and there were also an illegal weapons industry. Most of the intrigue would center around Mena, a small town with 5000 inhabitants. The arrival of strangers, drugs, drug money, and mysterious events made the local population catch on, but pressure from above ensured that the façade were kept.[477]

It was not until Clinton's bid for presidency that Mena again would become a nuisance. The event sparked renewed interest in his past and the media once more began to speculate. The Republicans,

---

Authority (ADFA). Terry Reed expands: "Arkansas offered the CIA something money launderers are rarely able to achieve, a secure business environment containing a banking industry where vast amounts of money move around unnoticed as part of the normal course of business. Through its substantial bond underwriting activities, the state had a huge cash flow that could allow dirty money to co-mingle without detection. All they were lacking was the 'dirty banker' to cooperate with them by ignoring the federal banking laws. And that they found within the Clinton administration. This 'banker' was none other than the Arkansas Development and Finance Authority, or ADFA, which was a creation of, and directly under the control of, the governor's office. Its official mandate was to loan money to businesses either already in or coming to Arkansas in order to develop an industrial base for new jobs that Clinton had made the centerpiece of his administration. ADFA, was in effect, a bank making preferred loans." REED & CUMMINGS, *COMPROMISED: CLINTON, BUSH AND THE CIA* (1994) 232. For more, see Ibid., 231-33, 244-50, 518-21, and *Presidential Secrets*, former FBI agent Ted Gunderson's interview with Chip Tatum.

[477] As federal investigation into Mena was obstructed, the Arkansas Committee sought to persuade state authorities to pursue a criminal investigation (1990-1992). The Governor, along with most politicians, however, were opposed and the media sided with authority, attacking members of the Arkansas Committee. This unfortunate legacy aside, there were journalists willing to pursue the matter, On May 21, 1992, the Arkansas Times headlined an article which delved into the connections between Barry Seal and George H.W. Bush, and also the Arkansas Gazette published a series of articles which put local and federal authorities to shame. See Michael Haddigan, *The Kingpin and his many connections*, June 27, 1988; Jack Anderson and Dale Van Atta, *Drug Runner's Legacy*, February 28, 1989; Jack Anderson and Dale Van Atta, *Small Town for Smuggling*, March 1, 1989; Michael Arbanas, *Hutchinson knew in 83 of Seal probe, ex-IRS agent says*, September 19, 1990, Michael Arbanas, *Truth on Mena, Seal shrouded in shady allegations: Drug smuggling rumors just won't die*, December 22, 1990.

however, must have known that digging into this would hurt both parties,[478] and so the matter was dropped.

Nevertheless, we know that Bill Clinton, as Governor of Arkansas, was heavily involved with criminal activities. From the available evidence, we see that the Iran-Contra operation, at the federal level, was run by Vice President George H.W. Bush, CIA Director Bill Casey, National Security Adviser Robert McFarlane, Admiral John Pointdexter (who took over after McFarlane resigned on December 4, 1985), and Oliver North, and that it was protected by officials like Bill Clinton and Robert Nash, his advisor, on the state-side.

These officials, no doubt, profited on the operation; economically in obvious ways, but politically in that their usefulness to the secret team assured future promotion. As we shall see, FBI and DEA officials, together with the Department of Justice and members of Congress, colluded to cover it up, whereas people with integrity would be threatened, fired, or in other ways forces into submission. So it was that the lie could live, and Clinton become president. Despite this, several have testified to the affairs that took place during his governorship, and—unlike the official version—they paint a coherent and overlapping picture.

---

[478] In his book Al Martin exposes political duplicity across the board: "As I've always said, Arkansas is where political liability vis-à-vis Iran-Contra crosses party lines. And I intend to show that bridge, both in context of narcotics, weapons, and money transactions. Next, I am going to build that bridge into Republican/Democratic political liability crossovers in Arkansas, vis-à-vis Arkansas-related Iran-Contra weapons, narcotics, and monies operations. I will talk about my knowledge of Governor Bill Clinton, Betsey Wright, Bruce Lindsey, Buddy Young, Patsy Thomasson, Dan Lasater, Web Hubbell, Hillary and Rose and Hubbell Law Firm, and Stephens investment group. I did a lot of business with Stephens. I did business with Lasater. I was familiar with what was going on at the time. I have extensive 1985 tape recordings of gubernatorial aides, Bruce Lindsey and Betsy Wright discussing Oliver North's operations in Arkansas. They can't say they didn't know about them— and their efforts to manipulate the Arkansas State Police on behalf of the Republicans." MARTIN, *THE CONSPIRATORS* (2002) 115.

"I can arrest an old hillbilly out here with a pound of marijuana and a local judge and jury would send him away to the penitentiary, but a guy like Seal flies in and out with hundreds of pounds of cocaine, and he stays free. . . . I resigned and retired primarily because of the injustice in the federal system, and I have spent the last several years forgetting that this ever occurred."[479]

—Polk County Sheriff A.L. Hadaway—

While drug smuggling had been a problem at Mena before 1982, it reached endemic proportions with the arrival of Barry Seal. Barry had been connected to the CIA and the anti-Castro Cubans since the early 1960's. He had done more than a 1000 parachute jumps, was one of the world's best pilots, and by the 1980's he was working with the Medellin cartel flying cocaine to the United States.[480] By this time, however, Barry also had acquired legal troubles in Louisiana and Florida—and when the Louisiana police wanted him to turn informer and the Florida police wanted him to go to jail for 10 years, Seal called old friends in the intelligence community. Having attained much information that was damaging to the U.S. government, he had

---

[479] Mara Leveritt, *Bad company: Arkansas's most notorious drug smuggler testified about his links to Colombia. His ties to Washington have yet to be explained*, Arkansas Times, May 21, 1992

[480] The FBI file given to Senator Kennedy in 1989 contains the following information on Seal: "Adler Berriman Seal was the most important organizer, facilitator, and impresario of the partnership between the CIA and organized crime. Seal earned over thirty million as his share of the drug smuggling, but what he loved more than money was the fact that he knew that we could not touch him, nor could any other agency of the United States. He loved to play the role of the back-slapping good "old boy" from Baton Rouge, and he loved flying. . . . The CIA had full knowledge of Seals total actions. He ran guns to the contras for Casey, and he always was found innocent of any accusations in the courts." https://cloverchronicle.com/2018/12/08/george-h-w-bushs-top-secret-cia-drug-running-empire/

established a reputation for "handling the handlers",[481] and after contacting George H.W. Bush, he began to work for his Drug Task Force.

He was free on condition that he would provide information linking the Sandinistas and the Medellin Cartel to drug trafficking. There is, however, more to this than meets the eye and assisted by the CIA, Seal continued to fly drugs and evading prison until he was killed in 1986.[482]

Several authors have connected the Vice President to his murder,[483] and detectives at the scene found Bush's phone number

---

[481] As he told a Louisiana newspaper reporter in November of 1984: "If they indict me, it means that I go to court. It means that then I get to tell my side of the story. All of this and much, much more than you're now hearing from me will be put out in the public eye. The Justice Department is not going to tolerate this. There's no way they can indict me." Mara Leveritt, *Bad company: Arkansas's most notorious drug smuggler testified about his links to Colombia. His ties to Washington have yet to be explained*, Arkansas Times, May 21, 1992

[482] Because of this, Louisiana Attorney General William J. Guste Jr. wrote a letter to Attorney General Ed Meese demanding to know why Seal could have been allowed to operate as he did. He estimated that Seal had brought between $3 and $5 billion worth of drugs into the US, but there was no response to his query.

[483] According to Al Martin, CIA Director Bill Casey decided that Barry had to be killed. It was supposed to look like a hit from the Colombians and Martin claims to have records showing that the alleged assassins, Raoul Herrera and Bernardo Tamayo, were CIA contractors. Martin alleges that he also, at a meeting in September 1985, heard Jeb Bush, Oliver North, Richard Secord, and Dewey Clarridge discuss the assassination of Seal. This is not the only murder in which Jeb Bush is implicated. According to Martin, Jeb Bush were also involved with the death of three other CIA connected drug dealers. (MARTIN, THE CONSPIRATORS (2002) 11, 194-97). Chip Tatum also contends that CIA were involved with the death of Barry Seal. On March 30, 1985, he heard Oliver North say that "[Vice President Bush] is very concerned about those missing monies. I think he's going to have Jeb arrange something out of Columbia." (*THE CHIP TATUM CHRONICLES*) Terry Reed is another witness to these events who can testify to the same. REED & CUMMINGS, *COMPROMISED: CLINTON, BUSH AND THE CIA* (1994) 244-49. For the whole story on the death of Barry Seal, see ATTWOOD, *AMERICAN MADE* (2016). Also STONE & HUNT, *THE BUSH CRIME FAMILY* (2016) covers the Bushes, their involvement in the drug trade, and the death of Barry Seal.

among Seal's possessions.[484] We do not know what else was found in his car, as Seal's belongings was never revealed.[485] His connections were not to be looked at, and so the White House in 1988 ordered the CIA, the Defence Intelligence Agency, and the National Security Agency to refuse to turn over information sought by the General Accounting Office for its investigation into Mena. This was not the only case pending. The IRS and the local police at Mena also had a case against the conspirators but were consistently rebuffed.[486]

There is reason, then, to suspect foul play. According to his attorney and his secretary, Seal was worried about the Medellin

---

[484] RUSSELL, *DRUG WAR* (2000) 415

[485] According to author Shaun Attwood, in Seal's car was "three boxes of precious documents, including the encrypted numbers of Swiss bank accounts, where senior politicians stashed money. One account under the encrypted code KPFBMMMBODB with over $ ten million belonged to the Secretary of Defense Caspar Weinberger, who allegedly received kickbacks on drugs and arms sales." ATTWOOD, *AMERICAN MADE* (2016) 329

[486] Joe Hardegree, the prosecuting attorney for Polk County, Arkansas, explains why there was no action taken in the Mena investigations: "I have good reason to believe that all federal law-enforcement agencies from the Justice Department down through the FBI to the DEA all received encouragement to downplay and de-emphasize any investigation or prosecution that might expose Seal's activities and the national-security involvement in them. It was in this framework that the federal grand juries and law-enforcement authorities in Arkansas apparently stopped in their serious deliberations or investigations concerning Barry Seal's activities and all of the surrounding circumstances. The really unfortunate aspect of this whole matter is the apparent fact that the federal investigation of drug trafficking in connection with the Mena airport came to be intricately involved with the internal politics and more particularly with the private wars conducted by the Reagan White House and so sensitive that no information concerning Seal's activities could be released to the public. The ultimate result is that not only Seal but all his confederates and all those who worked with or assisted him in illicit drug trafficking were protected by the government." Mara Leveritt, *Bad company: Arkansas's most notorious drug smuggler testified about his links to Colombia. His ties to Washington have yet to be explained*, Arkansas Times, May 21, 1992

Cartel, but he was more troubled by Bush, a man on which he had compromising information.[487]

Seal allegedly had a videotape of a 1985 DEA cocaine sting which had netted George Bush's two sons, George and Jeb, involved with drugs and prostitution. According to Darlene Novinger, an FBI agent who spoke with investigative journalist Rodney Stich, this was called *Operation Nimbus* and she claimed that Bush Sr. was pressured by the Medellin because they had evidence of his sons' involvement in the drug business. This was reported to senior FBI officials, who began to make life difficult for Novinger. The Bush family's involvement in the narcotics business was extremely sensitive material and not only was she threatened, but family members died suspiciously.[488]

This affair was covered up by the DEA and Customs, while the Democrats saw an opportunity to use it as leverage. Bush, however, ensured that democrats would not talk too loud when Seal helped frame Clinton's brother, Roger, for possession of cocaine. Following investigations also implicated Dan Lasater, Clinton's good friend.[489] Among other legal issues, an US Customs investigative report noted that a ski resort which he had acquired in New Mexico (and, with permission, used Clinton's name to promote) was being used for drug trafficking and money laundering, but his connections ensured that the investigation was limited to small stuff. In 1986, therefore, Lasater was sentenced to 30 months in prison for the distribution of cocaine—a sentence President Clinton would forgive after six months.

As a side note, his lawyer Gandy Baugh jumped to his death in 1994, and his law partner committed suicide one month later. These are just two of the more than 50 suspicious deaths that surround the career of Bill Clinton and a sure indication that the secret team was

---

[487] As he told Terry Reed: "Ever hear the old expression, it's not what ya know, it's who ya know? Well, whoever said that just hadn't caught the Vice President's kids in the dope business, 'cause I can tell ya for sure what ya know can definitely be more important than who you know." REED & CUMMINGS, *COMPROMISED* (1994) 212. See also ATTWOOD, *AMERICAN MADE* (2016) 149-51

[488] STICH, *DEFRAUDING AMERICA* (1998) 469, 693-96

[489] REED & CUMMINGS, *COMPROMISED* (1994) 212, 230, 235.

busy eliminating problems. Indeed, Bush had a task force dedicated to such missions—and Chip Tatum was one of his henchmen. Between 1986 and 1992 Chip was in the Terrorist Incidence Working Group, working directly for the Vice President. Tatum claims that he, on orders from Bush, was tasked to neutralize several people, one of them being Senator Ross Perot who was asking too many questions about Richard Armitage.

There is plenty, therefore, to suggest that Bush was involved with this plot—and Tatum also implicates Bill Clinton. Not in the assassination of Barry Seal, but in large-scale criminal activities.

10.3.3.2. CHIP TATUM AND MENA

Chip Tatum's contra involvement was extensive. Working for Oliver North and Felix Rodriguez, he would fly secret missions to contra camps in Honduras and pick up cocaine. Every time a hundred kilos of cocaine disguised as medical equipment were loaded onboard and when Tatum asked his superiors, North and Gregg would tell him that it was confiscated from the Sandinistas and would be taken to the World Court as evidence against Nicaragua. His story is significant because Tatum was flying missions into Mena in 1983-84 where he met Clinton's chief of Security, Raymond Young, and Dan Lasater. It was these people who received the cocaine shipments and Tatum also met Clinton.

He would continue to work with this group which included Mike Harari, the Mossad-agent connected with Noriega. After refusing to neutralize Senator Perot in 1992, however, Tatum knew that his life was in danger and he began to gather evidence that could keep him alive. By then Harari figured as a suspect in the murder of several U.S. military officers and two years later, when he was contacted by Colby, North, and Rodriguez, who warned him to give up his documents "or else", he put together *the Chip Tatum Chronicles*. While piloting the helicopter, he would listen to the intercom, sometimes recording conversations, and this dialogue between Mike Harari and Raymond "Buddy" Young is revealing:

Buddy: *"Arkansas has the capability to manufacture anything in the area of weapons—and if we don't have it, we'll get it!"*

Mike: *"How about government controls?"*

Buddy: *"The Governor's on top of it, and if the feds get nosey we hear about it and make a call. Then they're called off."* He was looking around the countryside and continued, *"Why the hell would anyone want to fight for a shit-hole like this?"*

Mike: Shaking his head in awe, answered, *"What we do has nothing to do with preserving a country's integrity—it's just business, and third world countries see their destiny as defeating borders and expanding. The more of this mentality we can produce, the greater our wealth. We train and we arm—that's our job. And, in return, we get a product far more valuable than the money for a gun. We're paid with product [cocaine]. And we credit top dollar for product."*

Buddy: (Still looked confused).

Mike: *"Look: one gun and 3,000 rounds of ammo is $1,200. A kilo of product is about $1,000. We credit the Contras $1,500 for every kilo. That's top dollar for a kilo of cocaine. It's equivalent to the American K-Mart special—buy four, get one free. On our side, we spend $1,200 for a kilo and sell it for $12,000 to $15,000. Now, that's a profit center. And the market is much greater for the product than for weapons. It's just good business sense, understand?*

Buddy: *"Damn! So you guys promote wars and revolutions to provide weapons for drugs—we provide the non-numbered parts to change out and we all win. Damn that's good!"*

Mike: *"It's good when it works—but someone is, how do you say, has his hand in the coffer."*

Buddy: Responding on the defensive, *"Well, we get our ten percent right off the top and that's plenty. GOFUS can make it go a long way."*

Mike: *"Who is GOFUS?"*

Buddy: *"Governor Clinton! That's our pet word for him. You know they call the President 'POTUS' for 'President of the United States'. Well, we call Clinton 'GOFUS' for 'Governor of the United States'. He thinks he is anyhow."*

Mike: *"That's your problem in America. You have no respect for your elected officials. They are more powerful than you think and have ears everywhere. You should heed my words and be loyal to your leaders. Especially when speaking to persons like me. Your remarks indicate a weakness—something our intelligence analysts look for."*

Buddy: *"Aw hell, Mike. Everybody knows the Clinton's want the White House and will do anything to get it. That's why I'm here instead of someone else. We know about the cocaine—hell! I've picked it up before with Lasater when he was worried about going on Little Rock Air Base to get it."*

A new line of conversation ensued. Harari questioned Young about his knowledge of who the "players" were. He went down a list. He started with "The Boss—Clinton." Here's a synopsis of the players according to Young.

Buddy: *"Clinton thinks he's in charge, but he will only go as far as Casey allows. Me and my staff, we keep the lid on things you know—complaints about night flying. Arkansas people are private folks, they don't like a lot of commotion and Mena just isn't the right place for the operation. It keeps us busy at the shredder, if you know what I mean. Dan the Man (Lasater)—He does magic with the money—between him and Jack Stevens we don't have to worry a bit. Then we got Parks—if there's a problem, he's the man. We call him the Archer, that's the codename that Casey and Colby told us to assign to that position. Finnis oversees our drop zone. Nash—he's just the boss' 'yes' man. Personally I think he's a mistake! Seal and his guys—I like his attitude 'and leave the driving to us!"* he said, quoting one of Seal's good ole boy sayings."*

Mike: *"You like Seal?"*

Buddy: *"Hell! He's the only one I trust—respect is the word."*

Mike: *"Do you see much of him?"*

Buddy: *"Hell, yea. We test drive Clinton's rides before we send 'em on, ya know? (He laughed, grinding his hips.) Say—how much coke do you recon you can make in a week?"*

Mike: *"One camp can produce 400 keys a week. The others are about half that. But that's just our operation here. We have other sources in various parts of the world. Why do you ask?"*

Buddy: *"What? Oh, the Governor wanted to know our capacity."*

This is a portion of the material Chip Tatum collected. After being threatened by Colby, North, and Rodrigues, Tatum knew that to turn over his documents would be lethal and so he began searching for the original flight plans which were in the possession of a ranking Honduran official. In 1985, the official, aware of the implications of the documents, had secured these flight plans and other briefing sheets for safe keeping, and in 1995 Tatum met with this official in San Pedro Sula, Honduras, where he was supplied certified copies. It was at this point "agreed that he would maintain possession of original documents until they were needed by authorities to seek prosecution of Messrs. Bush, Clinton, North, Rodriguez and others directly involved in the manufacturing and trafficking of cocaine."

Hence, as there are many others who have also come forward, putting these conspirators out of business should be a slam dunk case. And we shall now have a look at Mena.

10.3.3.3. Mena Operations

"I have seen the rug of 'national security' grow larger by the year, and it concerns me that so many aspects of this war on drugs are piously being swept under it. Too often 'national security' means 'don't tell the American people.'"[490]

—Mara Leveritt, Arkansas Journalist—

Barry Seal, as we have seen, was no nobody and that is why he came to Mena, Arkansas. Here everything was prepared for his arrival and Barry was free to operate due to corrupt individuals in powerful positions. According to Roger Reaves, Barry's associate and friend, Seal not only ate dinner with the Governor, but he had a deal where he paid Clinton $50.000 every time his plane hit the ground.[491] Thus, while local drug fighters such as IRS-detective Bill Duncan and Russell Welch with the Arkansas State police were pursuing investigations, higher-ups such as Asa Hutchinson, the newly arrived U.S. Attorney, and Mike Fitzhugh, his successor, ensured that such efforts went nowhere.[492]

---

[490] Mara Leveritt, *Asa and Me*, Arkansas Times, May 25, 2001

[491] Koncrete Podcast S1, E98: *The Highest Paid Drug Pilot in History, Roger Reaves.*

[492] As Mara Leveritt, a local journalist wrote: "Soon after Seal's move to Mena, U.S. Attorney Hutchinson called a meeting at his Fort Smith office to coordinate local surveillance. Among those attending were an Arkansas DEA agent, a U.S. Customs official, and U.S. Treasury agent William C. Duncan. Duncan's job was to investigate money laundering by the Seal organization. By the end of 1982, he had gathered what he believed to be substantial evidence of the crime. Duncan and an Arkansas State Police investigator, who was also monitoring Seal's enterprise, took their evidence to Hutchinson. They asked that the U.S. attorney subpoena 20 witnesses they'd identified to testify before a federal grand jury. To Duncan's surprise, however, Hutchinson seemed reluctant. Ultimately, Hutchinson called only three of the 20 witnesses the investigators had requested. The three appeared before the grand jury, but afterwards, two of them also expressed surprise at how their questioning was handled. One, a secretary at Rich Mountain Aviation, had given Duncan sworn statements about money laundering at the company, transcripts of which Duncan had provided to Hutchinson. But when the woman left the jury room, she complained that

The reason why Seal was protected was two intelligence operations called *Jade Bridge* and *Centaur Rose*.[493] The former included training of contras as well as drug smuggling operations, and the latter had to do with the production of weapons and transports to the contras in Honduras and Costa Rica. Terry Reed was intimately involved with both and met with Seal several times. Among other activities, he helped Barry smuggle money into Arkansas, dropping off $40 million on a monthly basis at a ranch owned by Seth Ward, one of Arkansas' wealthiest businessmen. The Ranch's name was triple-S, and it was used by Ward's son-in-law, Finis Shellnut, who worked for Dan Lasater.[494]

Reed also flew with Seal to Panama, via Ilopango. He learned how Barry could fly all his missions, as Seal would evade radar- and other protective measures due to advanced electronics that made it possible to disappear in thin air. This device was so effective that the military's radar did not pick up on Seal's plane and it was connected to another operation that begun in 1976, *Operation Watchtower*.

This operation consisted of a series of high-frequency radio towers dispersed throughout Central America,[495] and it was to wrest

---

Hutchinson had asked her nothing about the crime or the sworn statements she'd given to Duncan. As Duncan later testified, 'She basically said that she was allowed to give her name, address, position, and not much else.'" Mara Leveritt, *What does Hutchinson know about Arkansas's biggest drug smuggler? And when did he know it?* Arkansas Times, May 25, 2001. For more on this, see ORAL DEPOSITION OF RUSSELL FRANKLIN WELCH, a witness produced at the request of the Attorney General's Office, June 21, 1991.

[493] "Seal would later confide to Reed that there were going to be two separate, compart-mentalized operations based out of the Mena area. The one Terry was becoming sucked into, involving flight training and aerial delivery techniques, was code-named 'Jade Bridge'. . . . The second was the ferrying of large quantities of arms and munitions from Arkansas to staging areas in Central America. This tributary to the Agency cut-out was code named 'Centaur Rose.'" REED & CUMMINGS, *COMPROMISED: CLINTON, BUSH AND THE CIA* (1994) 64

[494] Ibid., 138-39, 143-44, 163

[495] "Watchtower was a series of very powerful radio transmitters on towers with beacons on the end of them, built from Andros Island off the coast of Colombia all the way up into US air space, essentially traversing all of Central America. These

control of this operation from the Defense Intelligence Agency (DIA), that the Vice President created his Drug Task Force in 1983. According to Martin, the purpose of this task force was the opposite of its stated mission and its real purpose was (1) to control the airspace between Mexico and the Unites States, and (2) to keep U.S. Customs from interfering.[496]

Edward P. Cutulo, a Colonel in U.S. Army and a key participant in the original Watchtower operation, tried to have this exposed. In a lengthy affidavit dated March 11, 1980, (which was confirmed by retired Colonel William Wilson) he exposed the illegal operations of the secret team, naming Frank Terpil, Ed Wilson, Thomas Clines, Robert Gates, Bill Casey, and Mike Harari as the main conspirators. In this affidavit, Col. Cutulo also mentions another operation (*Operation Orwell*), where the CIA, to cover its tracks, infiltrated and surveyed 8400 police departments, 1370 churches, and 17 900 American citizens. He goes on to describe how Elaine Tyree, a military officer who knew about this plot, was murdered because of a diary she kept, and how her husband, William Tyree, was set up and convicted for killing her.[497] Cutulo himself, together with a number of other military men, would be killed to keep this a secret and Mike Harari would be implicated in at least three murders.[498]

The connection to drugs becomes obvious when we consider the testimony to the Kerry Committee of Jose Blandon, a former intelligence aid to Noriega. According to Blandon, Harari was

---

beacons would emit a frequency which was changed from time to time for security reasons. Aircraft could triangulate a position from them. The beacons in essence created a corridor. It was a so-called 'safe corridor.' In other words, all aircraft flying in that corridor would not be intercepted. . . . The corridor was created originally for the same purpose it got used later on in Iran-Contra—to provide a safe corridor for the shipping north of narcotics and the shipping south of weapons pursuant to authorized narcotics and weapons transactions." MARTIN, *THE CONSPIRATORS* (2002) 264-65

[496] Ibid., 162, 221

[497] William Tyree was also involved with the Watchtower operation. For more on his unfortunate fate, see MIKE RUPPERT, *CROSSING THE RUBICON* (2004) 150-84

[498] STICH, *DEFRAUDING AMERICA* (1998) 351-62

connected to a network of Central American airstrips used by traffickers, and he agreed with Senator Kerry that, through this network, "guns would go in one shipment and drugs would come out in another."[499]

This testimony was not only substantiated by the FBI in the file to Senator Kennedy, but by the testimony of Richard Brenneke to the Kerry Committee. Since 1967, he had been running drugs with this group in the Golden Triangle and in December 1986 Brenneke was listed by the Philadelphia Inquirer as one of a cast of characters involved in the Iran-Contra affair. Because of this, he was called to testify before the Kerry Committee, and Brenneke claimed to have run drugs from Colombia through Panama to the United States as part of a contra-supply operation. Backing up the story of Blandon, he testified to having purchased arms in Czechoslovakia for the Nicaraguan rebels, but the Vice President called his testimony "slanderous." Like so many others he was in for a fight, and as the CIA denied that Brenneke had ever worked for the agency, a 1989 Senate committee concluded that he was a fraud.

Even so, others were not that easily intimidated, and on June 21, 1991, Brenneke testified before members of Congress and Arkansas State Attorney General's Office. Brenneke, at this meeting, claimed to have flown cocaine to Mena a dozen times and that the drugs, from there, were sent to Kennedy International Airport, New York, where it was distributed by John Gotti. The Congressmen were shocked to hear this, but even more bewildered when Brenneke replied that CIA had a longstanding relationship with the mob. He had himself laundered most of their money in Panama City, transferring some $50 million to European banks through an account belonging to Brown Brothers Harriman—a bank with deep Skull and Bones affiliation.[500] Brenneke, having second thoughts, had complained about the illegal activities to Don Gregg, George Bush's National Security Advisor, but Gregg had told him "To shut up and do your job".

---

[499] SCOTT & MARSHALL, *COCAINE POLITICS* (1998) 74

[500] DONALD G. LETT, *PHOENIX RISING: THE RISE AND FALL OF THE AMERICAN REPUBLIC* (2008) 273

Brenneke could provide proof of his accusations, but pressure from the top made sure that nothing come of it. By now George H.W Bush was president. He would continue to stall inquisitive minds, and when Brenneke brought supporting testimony in another case, one fingering Bush and Gregg at several meetings they did not want to be associated with, Brenneke was charged with five counts of making false declarations to a federal judge—a charge slightly stronger than perjury. He was indicted on May 12, 1989, accused of lying about his CIA connections and the meetings. Coincidentally, this was the same day that Gregg was scheduled for confirmation hearings for his appointment as Ambassador to South Korea. Adding to the political overtones, Brenneke was offered a deal that would keep him out of prison if he plead guilty. Brenneke, however, refused. He took his chances in court and was found "not guilty" on all five counts.

His testimony, then, remains a troublesome issue—and more people can confirm these tales. If we want more evidence, Michael Riconosciuto is another CIA contractor who claims to have visited Mena with drugs between 1980-89.[501] His story confirms that of Terry Reed, Chip Tatum, and Kenneth Bucci,[502] and other witnesses are

---

[501] COCKBURN & ST. CLAIR, *WHITEOUT* (1999) 335-37

[502] "The complex at Nella airstrip outside Mena, Arkansas, as I came to learn, was the hub of CIA operations in Central and South America . . . [This] included the state-of-the-art communications system that I had just stumbled on; the clandestine airstrip itself; facilities there and at the Inter-Mountain Regional Airport in Mena for refurbishing and retrofitting aircraft, especially with IFF transponders and other communication and navigational gear; a barracks and training program for Contra pilots during the Nicaraguan civil war; air transport of weapons to the Contras; and shipments of cocaine and money into the U.S. through Operation Lighthouse and similar programs. In short, it comprised a vast array of activities taking form as what Oliver North later referred to as Casey's dream of an 'off-the-shelf, totally self-sustaining, stand-alone entity that could perform certain activities on behalf of the United States." BUCCI, *OPERATION PSEUDO MIRANDA* (2000) 116

Larry Nichols,[503] Sharlene Wilson,[504] and Larry Douglass Brown, a policeman working for Clinton in Arkansas. In 1984, Clinton encouraged Brown to join the CIA, and in 1995 he testified to an investigative committee that the CIA arranged for him to meet Barry Seal. Brown would join Seal in picking up cocaine at contra camps— and when he later told Clinton about this, the governor was not surprised.[505]

All told, then, it is no wonder that Bill Clinton, as president, would continue to cover-up what Reagan began. He had been groomed for office by Pamela Harriman. She was not only an insider with the Democratic party but the widow of W. Averell Harriman, and being aligned with these sinister forces, the Clintons would continue their career on the wrong side of history. Today, therefore, the Clinton Foundation is under investigation for all sorts of wrongdoing, not only trafficking in drugs but in children—and knowing their past, if this investigation is not botched, Bill and his wife, Hillary, will be going away for a long time.

10.3.4. THE IRAN-PART OF THE CONTRA AFFAIR

After President Carter put human rights first and fired many covert operatives, this cabal would cooperate with another power-political faction to oust Carter from the White House. This was the Israelis, and together they found common cause in undermining the president's policy on Iran. If not for the infighting that followed, the scandal

---

[503] Nichols worked for Clinton in Arkansas, with a front-row seat to the money laundering that took place. He is behind *The Clinton Chronicles* (1994), a documentary exposing many shenanigans, including Mena. See also his website www.nicholslive.com.

[504] Sharlene was a friend of Roger Clinton who reported to Jean Duffy, a deputy prosecuting attorney and head of a drug task force, that she had worked "for three- or four-months unloading bags of cocaine at Mena Airport." see ATTWOOD, *AMERICAN MADE* (2016) 100

505 See L,D BROWN, *CROSSFIRE: WITNESS IN THE CLINTON INVESTIGATION* (1999) detailing his experiences with the Clintons.

would not have got much attention and so, to understand the Iran-Contra enigma, we need to look at this.

10.3.4.1. *"The October Surprise"*

On November 4, 1979, a group of Iranian students stormed the U.S. Embassy in Tehran, taking more than 60 American hostages. They were angry at Americans for supporting the Shah, a puppet of the CIA, who for nearly 30 years had ruled Iranians with an iron fist. Not surprisingly, a counterforce arose, and as religious fundamentalists had taken power, relations were tense. Both Carter and the Iranian regime had much at stake; as their populations thrived on enemy images, leaders did not want to look weak, and as the hostages remained within the embassy, the U.S. President froze Iranian assets and prohibited the sale of arms to Iran.

This was a problem for the Iranian regime because Saddam Hussein, the Iraqi dictator, was preparing for war and the Iranians needed to upgrade their armoury. The Israelis, for their part, considered Saddam to be their greatest threat, and while they did not think highly of the new Iranian leadership, they wanted to sell weapons to fight off a common enemy. They also wanted to make a profit. Thus, they were lobbying for opportunities, and George H.W. Bush and his cabal[506] was not difficult to persuade.

Through unofficial channels, therefore, meetings were arranged. These would take place in Paris and Madrid between March and October 1980, and a deal was struck where the Iranian regime, as soon as Reagan came into office, would receive arms. This was on the

---

[506] Some of the conspirators tied to these illegal negotiations were Miles Copeland, a veteran of the CIA who helped install the Shah in 1953, Robert McFarlane, Robert Gates, Bill Casey, Don Gregg, and senator John Tower, who at the time was Chairman of the Armed Services Committee. MENASHE, *PROFITS OF WAR* (1998) 52-76

condition that they did not free any hostages before the election,[507] and in the meantime the Israelis was to provide weapons.

To sweeten the deal, the Iranian priests were offered $52 million in cash. According to the Mossad agent Ari Ben Menashe, who was intimately familiar with this plot on the Israeli side, this money stemmed from "a band of former Israeli Intelligence officers who were running a drug-and arms-smuggling operation in Central America, backed by the CIA",[508] and Menashe took it from Guatemala to the United States, where he met Robert Gates at the airport to avoid customs.[509]

Gates' career took off after this, but the conspirators were not limited to Republicans. According to Menashe, Don Gregg was a key-conspirator and would fly with Bush to meetings in Europe while serving as a member of Carter's National Security Council (NSC). Gregg, then, is another insider with a lot to answer for. And while he disputes these allegations, he failed a polygraph on this matter as well as Iran-Contra, while the credibility of Menashe remains uncontested. In fact, the CIA tried to pay him $2 million not to write his book, and his accusations align with others, such as the testimony of Richard Brenneke and Gunther Russbacher.[510]

10.3.4.2. INTERNAL STRIFE

The deal with the Iranian regime turned out to be a lucrative endeavour. Between 1981 and 1987 Israel, backed by the Reagan administration, would rake in $89 billion selling arms to Iran,[511] and

---

[507] Id.

[508] Ibid., 80

[509] Ibid., 85

[510] Brenneke and Russbacher claim to have been pilot and co-pilot on the plane ride to Paris. See STICH, *DEFRAUDING AMERICA* (1998) 134-42, 152-60, 172-201

[511] Ari Ben Menashe noted the situation thus: "[I]f a question had been put to a computer about what needed to be done to: 1) get the Arabs off Israel's back; 2) part

it was internal intrigue between two Israeli factions which ensured that the scandal broke. Menashe was in the thick of it, and his book *Profits of War* documents how the power struggle evolved.

According to him, the origin of the twist was a coalition government between the Likud- and the Labour party (1984-90). From 1984 to 1986 Yitzhak Shamir (Likud) was Israeli Prime Minister while Shimon Peres (Labour) would be Foreign Minister, and then positions were switched. The Likud party had the best connections in the intelligence community and the Mossad-network mentioned was loyal to President Shamir and Rafi Eitan, his Security Advisor. Before taking office, Shamir (who was a Foreign Minister from 1980-83 and Prime Minister from 1983-84) and his faction had been key to the secret deal with Iran. They made good money on these sales,[512] but when Labour took power Amiram Nir, Peres' Anti-Terror Advisor, discovered the conspiracy and the new government wanted in. Even so, neither Likud, Mossad, nor the Bush-faction wanted to cooperate, and so Nir and Peres established their own operation.

To get in on the action, Nir travelled to Washington where he met with Robert McFarlane and told him that the CIA, from now on, should cooperate with the Labour-faction in its Iran dealings, not the Likud. After this, McFarlane put Nir in touch with Oliver North and John Pointdexter who welcomed the idea. They talked to CIA Director Bill Casey, and, with Casey onboard, Nir and North partnered up.[513]

---

the Arabs from their money; 3) keep the Iranians contained—and part them of their money; 4) keep the oil flowing; 5) make sure the world recycled its old military equipment; 6) keep the Soviets happy; and 7) make lots of arms dealers and defense contractors rich, it could not have come up with a better solution than the Iraq-Iran war." MENASHE, *PROFITS OF WAR* (1998) 126

[512] Menashe estimates that between 1984 and 1989 $90 million went to the Likud party, while Shamir and his faction made $160 million. Ibid., 120

[513] The operations of Nir and North also involved Terry Reed. As the CIA left Arkansas, they were setting up an illegal arms factory in Mexico, headed by Reed, and he met with Nir in Panama in December 1985, and a year later in Mexico. The operation was called Screw Worm, but these plans fell apart due to Oliver North's problems with Congress—and because Reed discovered that the place was used by Felix Rodriguez for storing cocaine shipments. REED & CUMMINGS, *COMPROMISED: CLINTON, BUSH AND THE CIA* (1994) 207-210, 307-317

From this point on, events would become troublesome. They both wanted to be top dogs and a fight broke out. First, the Labour faction made the FBI aware of a Likud-network of spies. This would become known as the Pollard case[514], and in return the Likud faction sabotaged North and Nir's efforts to establish a parallel weapons operation. North repaid these services by having Bar Am, an Israeli general, and several others arrested on illegal arms charges in April 1986—and this made the Likud faction expose North's activities. Thus, in May 1986 they presented the story to Raji Samghabadi, a Time Magazine journalist in the Middle East. Times editor Henry Grunwald, however, refused to publish this article[515] and the story was given to Newsday, which also were not interested. The first to expose this plot, therefore, was Al Shiraa, a Lebanese newspaper on November 3, 1986.

By then problems were brewing on several fronts. CBS News' Leslie Cockburn had followed the trail of contra drugs- and gun smuggling since 1984, and on December 20, 1985, AP reporters Brian Barger and Robert Parry had a Spanish article published. June 27, 1986, another article came out in the San Francisco Examiner; and when an American C- 123 (Barry Seal's old plane) flying equipment to the contras, on October 5, 1986, was shot down in the Nicaraguan jungle, the operation finally got the world's attention. Consequently, phase two began, the cover up.

---

[514] Ibid. 174

[515] Ibid. 183

10.3.5. Iran-Contra: The Cover Up

"We'd go down and lie to them consistently. . . . In my 25 years, I have never seen the agency tell the truth to a congressional committee."[516]

—Ralph McGehee, CIA officer for 25 years—

By late 1986, something had to give. Being a White House spokesperson was becoming ever more torturous, and so Attorney General Ed Meese held a press conference November 25, 1986, to ease tensions. He stated that illegal arms sales to Iran had been used to support the contra movement but claimed that this was limited to a few instances where North, in a fit of patriotism, had not thought legalities through.

This was the story that the White House wanted to peddle, and Congress obliged. They accepted Reagan's plea for an investigative committee, one headed by Senator John Tower—but the Senator had been compromised by the secret team.[517] Tower, therefore, did as he was told, and Mossad agent Menashe commented on his proceedings:

"The commission of inquiry was to investigate only the years 1984 to 1986. The conclusions Tower reached were nothing but a cover up. He declared that some people in the National Security Council, interested in the release of hostages in Lebanon, had tried to make a deal with the Iranians, selling them 97 TOW missiles and some Hawk missiles—and that was it. Granted, the second channel [The North-Nir channel] had not succeeded, so there wasn't much to discover about it. But Tower knew perfectly well that there was an ongoing original arms channel. Yet the Tower Commission made no mention of

---

[516] COCKBURN & ST. CLAIR, *WHITEOUT* (1999) 110. See also RALPH MCGEHEE, *DEADLY DECEITS: MY 25 YEARS IN THE CIA* (1983)

[517] According to Menashe, he was one of Bush's travel companions to the meeting in Paris with the Iranian regime in 1980. MENASHE, *PROFITS OF WAR* (1998) 52-76.

it. George Bush later rewarded Tower for his loyalty by nominating him for defense secretary, but he was never confirmed by Congress."[518]

Instead, President Bush appointed Tower as chairman of the President's Foreign Intelligence Advisory Board, but somehow his mixing with the wrong crowd must have got him into trouble. The day after his long-time friend John Heinz, a Bonesman who was him on the plane to Paris, fell from the skies, Tower's plane would also fall apart and he died in New Brunswick, Georgia, on April 5th, 1991.

The Democrats, for their part, were not entirely happy with the Tower Commission and pressed on for more investigations. On December 19, 1986, therefore, Lawrence E. Walsh was appointed Independent Counsel to investigate the Iran-Contra affair, and while his efforts led to indictments and convictions of key players,[519] President Bush, in December 1992, pardoned his co-conspirators. That was it for the Iran-Contra affair, and Walsh would go on to write a book about its cover up.[520]

Even so, parallel investigations could have reopened Pandora's box. In 1988, at the request of Congress, the GAO's National Security and International Affairs Division examined General Noriega's drug-related activities and the U.S. government's knowledge of it. The GAO had assembled a team of professional investigators and was hot on the Vice President's trail. CIA, however, refused to cooperate, as did the White House and other agencies—and the Justice Department

---

[518] Ibid., 191

[519] His investigation led to the convictions of both former Assistant to the President for National Security Affairs, Vice Admiral John Poindexter and former NSC staffer, Lieutenant Colonel Oliver North. Walsh also brought an indictment on two counts of perjury and one count of obstruction of justice against former Secretary of Defense Caspar Weinberger in June 1992. On the eve of the 1992 presidential election, on October 30, Mr. Walsh obtained a grand jury re-indictment of Weinberger on one count of false statements, but Bush intervened, ending his efforts at further indictments.

[520] LAWRENCE E. WALSH, *FIREWALL: THE IRAN-CONTRA CONSPIRACY AND COVER-UP* (1997)

put an end to this effort by deciding that the matter was "beyond GAO's statutory authority."

Another botched investigation was the House October Surprise Task Force which was to examine the allegations that a deal had been made with Iran to obstruct a solution to the hostage crisis before the 1980 presidential election. By 1991, media investigations had led to increased speculations about the role of Bush and others, and Congress answered by creating a Task Force in 1992 which was to put the record straight. However, it smelled of cover up. It was chaired by Rep Lee H. Hamilton, who had chaired the failed House Select Committee to Investigate Covert Arms Transactions with Iran. This was in 1987, and Hamilton chose not to investigate the President or the Vice President Bush, stating that he did not think it would be "good for the country" to put the public through another impeachment trial. This time, he was in league with Vice Chairman Henry Hyde, who as a member of the congressional panel investigating the Iran-Contra affair had enthusiastically defended the Reagan administration. He would compare Oliver North to Thomas Jefferson, arguing that although he and others had lied before Congress, such actions were excusable in pursuit of a greater good.

These guys, then, were to decide upon the matter, and as the Task Force's Chief Counsel, Lawrence Barcella, in 1985, had given the go-ahead in a legal opinion to an unnamed government official to an Iran-Contra-related private weapons shipment,[521] the final report, published on 13 January 1993, concluded that "there is no credible evidence supporting any attempt by the Reagan presidential campaign—or persons associated with the campaign—to delay the release of the American hostages in Iran." To put any doubt to rest, Hamilton added that the vast majority of the sources and material reviewed by the committee were "wholesale fabricators or were impeached by documentary evidence."[522]

---

[521] Lyn Bixby, *Head of Iran Hostage Probe Linked to Arms Deal*, May 29, 1992

[522] One of the congressmen, Representative Mervyn M. Dymally, refused to sign the final report. Even so, he withdrew his dissent after Hamilton threatened to fire the entire staff of another subcommittee Dymally were connected with. Hoping to save

To those who looked beyond appearances, however, a pattern of cover-ups was easy to see.[523] Hamilton would, as Vice Chairman of the 911 Commission, continue his career of cover ups, and Congress' zeal to exonerate the White House was motivated by more than the nation's good. As Menashe goes on to tell:

"Contributions were . . . made . . . to U.S. politicians, including Democrats on the Iran-contra panel. This may be one reason that the full story behind the Iran-contra scandal never materialized. Even though Israel leaked details of some of Oliver North's activities, the Democrats, many of whom were well aware of what was going on, kept quiet about the huge flood of arms that had been running to Iran from Israel. Tel Aviv, not wanting its own arms deals with Teheran to be exposed, had paid them off through various, often convoluted, contributions to the American Israeli Public Affairs Committee (AIPAC)."[524]

These were moneys coming from Iranian arms sales and such contributions must have helped soothe congressional conscience. Even so, it was a cover-up instigated from the top, and we shall now have a look at how the US Justice Department helped the White House and the CIA to hide their tracks.

---

his former staffers' jobs, Dymally agreed to withdraw his dissent. Hamilton, for his part, continued to work for the deep state, serving as Vice Chairman to the 911 Commission.

[523] Menashe quotes Spencer Oliver, the chief counsel for the House Foreign Relations Committee: "[W]e knew it was a coverup. But at the time the Democratic congressmen and senators were very weak, and also 'for the good of the nation' we did not want to start a scandal that would bring down the president." MENASHE, *PROFITS OF WAR* (1998) 193-94

[524] Ibid., 118

10.3.5.1. A Conspiracy of Repression

"From 1987 to 1991, I cooperated with every Democrat investigating committee in Washington investigating Iran-Contra and later investigating Iraqgate, BCCI, BNL, etc. from the early stages of the Kerry Commission hearings in 1987 to the Tower Commission, the Hughes Commission and the Alexander Commission. This finally ended in 1991. Despite the 1.6 million pages of testimonies, depositions, affidavits, and interrogatories accumulated by these committees, not one shred of the truth was ever revealed to the American public."[525]

—Al Martin, Naval Intelligence Officer—

Before testifying on his involvement with the Iran-Contra affair, Reagan's Attorney General, Ed Meese, told Martin to refuse to answer all questions for national security reasons.[526] Independent Counsel Lawrence Walsh also puts Meese at the centre of the cover up,[527] but there were others. We already know that the CIA has infiltrated the government's infrastructure, making it possible for a shadow government to function, and while Senator John Kerry did his bit, Martin names the Kerry Committee's lead investigator, Jack Blum, (and Jack Terrell and Ralph Maestre, members of his team) as puppets of the CIA.[528]

With such people in charge, those who knew about corruption would be excluded from the proceedings.[529] Even so, there were civil

---

[525] Martin, *The Conspirators* (2002) 8

[526] Ibid., 7

[527] Walsh, *Firewall* (1997)

[528] Martin, *The Conspirators* (2002) 8

[529] Rodney Stich was one. Throughout the years, he had been in contact with a dozen CIA operatives who had first-hand knowledge of these matters and as he said: "I mailed certified letters and transcripts to Independent Prosecutor Lawrence Walsh, who had the duty to investigate all aspects of the Iran-Contra affair . . . I reminded Walsh of his responsibilities under federal criminal statutes to receive my testimony

servants who noticed the deception and refused to play along. Senator Alan Cranston was one and addressing Don Gregg, he spoke in a committee hearing on June 15, 1989:

"In sum, you have told us a tale of an elaborate plan in which your professional colleagues and life-long friends conspired to keep you ignorant of crucial facts through days of meetings, monthly phone calls and nearly two years' worth of cables and memos. Incredibly, when senators confront you with the documentary evidence which undermines your story, you accuse us of concocting 'conspiracy theories' and you do so with a straight face . . . I think it is clear by now that many important questions may never be answered satisfactorily, especially because we have been stonewalled by the administration. The National Security Agency has rejected our legitimate enquiries out of hand. The Central Intelligence Agency provided a response with access restrictions so severe . . . as to be laughable. The Department of Defense has given an unsatisfactory response two days late. The State Department's response was utterly unresponsive. They answered our letter after their self-imposed deadline and failed to produce specific documents we requested and which we know exist."[530]

As we can see, NSA, CIA, FBI, Justice Department, State Department, and Department of Defence officials all contributed to the Iran-Contra cover-up. This cover up could never have overcome

---

and evidence and that of the CIA whistleblowers. Despite hundreds of certified mailings, each one containing over fifty pages of data, no one responded. The non-response was one of the most amazing examples of mass coverup that I ever witnessed. But it happened time and again. My letters raised very serious charges that, if only a small fraction of them were true, would inflict enormous harm upon the United States. This refusal to perform a duty made possible the continuation of the government corruption that continues to inflict great harm upon America." STICH, *DEFRAUDING AMERICA* (1998) 163. For more on the alleged Walsh cover-up, ibid., 207-18.

[530] LETT, *PHOENIX RISING* (2008) 269

the obstacles that it endured without being enormous in scope, nor without the shadow government being more powerful than the official government.[531] The fall-out of the Iran-Contra scandal, therefore, is the heart-breaking realization that U.S. institutions of government are thoroughly corrupted by an unruly power-political faction who thrives on the drugs economy, and that the proper way to undermine its presence is the regulation of drugs.

This is the only way to solve the gordian knot prohibition has made of law and order. Twisting the law of supply and demand into one of victim and oppressor has been the driving engine behind drug policy, and the drug fighting machinery has fought tooth and nail to continue the incarceration of drug law violators. Even so, liberty is on the rise, and the U.S. Justice Department will be hard pressed to justify a continuing effort to enforce a prohibition on drugs when it so many times has shown that its loyalties lie with agents of power, not justice. Until it accepts a system of principled rule, it simply will have no real authority. Instead, it will have to rely upon offensive "safety mechanisms" to obstruct those that agitate for truth and wholesome values, and there will be a continuous dynamic which feeds the darkness.

In this regard, Iran-Contra should serve as a lesson. If the American people had acted against the unsound doctrines of

---

[531] As Chip Tatum, who was refused an opportunity to testify, summarized the proceedings: "At a cost of over $40 million the investigation yielded only a few prosecutions for minor infractions. It is curious that neither the Select Committee on Secret Military Assistance to Iran and the Nicaraguan Opposition subcommittee tasked with the congressional investigation of the Iran-Contra, nor the office of the Special Prosecutor assigned to investigate criminal wrongdoings which occurred during the Iran-Contra Affair, subpoenaed any active-duty military personnel assigned to the border area of Nicaragua/Honduras. Had the service members been called to testify concerning the daily training/resupply, and support of the Contras, it would have been determined that the Boland Act, which prohibited any efforts of the United States or its military to support the Contra effort, was being violated. Testimony by military personnel would have also revealed that military aircraft and supplies were used to support the shipment of cocaine from manufacturing facilities co-located with CIA supported Contra camps. Why weren't we called to testify?" GENE 'CHIP' TATUM, *THE CHIP TATUM CHRONICLES* (1996)

government in the 1980's, they would have cleaned house and avoided the catastrophic events of September 11, 2001. At the very least, they would have had a Justice Department which was competent of handling criminal conspiracies of this magnitude,[532] and we shall now have a look at the campaign of repression that took place to preserve the authority of government.

10.3.5.2. The Suppression Unit

"Though there are no doubt other branches of the government where corruption flourishes, there is no question in my mind that the stench of evil which emanates from Washington, originates in the so-called Department of Justice, particularly in its permanent bureaucracy. . . . In case after notorious case . . . Justice Department personnel appear as liars, perverts, frame-up artists, and even assassins."[533]

—John DeCamp, former U.S. Senator—

As we have seen, the distance between what the U.S. government says and does is huge, and to cover up the distance between theory and practice a mechanism must be in place. It only makes sense that this is found in the Department of Justice, and Al Martin has some knowledge of this unit. Under Iran-Contra it was run by Deputy Attorney General George W. Terwilliger (who also covered up BCCI) and his successor William P. Barr—who later became Trump's

---

[532] Essential reading on 9/11 includes RUPPERT, *CROSSING THE RUBICON* (2004); DAVID RAY GRIFFIN, *THE 9/11 COMMISSION REPORT: OMISSIONS AND DISTORTIONS* (2004); DAVID RAY GRIFFIN, *NEW PEARL HARBOUR REVISITED: 9/11, THE COVER-UP AND THE EXPOSÉ* (2008). After reading only one of these books, it is difficult to dispute that there was a cover-up.

[533] JOHN DECAMP, *THE FRANKLIN COVER-UP* (1992) 293

Attorney General.[534] Martin goes on to say that "the function of these people was to prosecute those who had talked too much—or who might talk too much in the future. . . . The Suppression Unit in the Department of Justice is so powerful it reaches into all agencies."[535]

It is this unit that has preserved the face of authority when all else fails. To take care of affairs in Arkansas, it ensured that the position of U.S. State Attorney was filled with suits of a similar nature,[536] and so the suspicions of local IRS detective Bill Duncan that Seal's bribes reached Ed Meese was never pursued.[537] Also buried was the anthrax attack on Russel Welch, a criminal investigator in the Arkansas State Police who probed the money trail and the murders of Kevin Ives and Don Henry. These teenagers were brutally killed in Alexander, Arkansas, when they accidentally came across the police picking up cocaine. The cover-up was so obvious that it remains a deeply

---

[534] William Barr was a counsel to Bush while he served as CIA director. Terry Reed claims to have met him in a highly sensitive meeting discussing the cover-up of Arkansas operations. See REED & CUMMINGS, *COMPROMISED* (1994)

[535] MARTIN, *THE CONSPIRATORS* (2002) 19. For more on this unit, see 345-350.

[536] We have seen how U.S. Attorneys J. Michael Fitzhugh and Asa Hutchinson covered up for Governor Clinton and the White House, and part of this team was Eric Holder, the Assistant U.S. Attorney in Little Rock, Arkansas. As Asa Hutchinson went on to become Director of DEA, logic dictates that this was the same Holder who later became President Obama's Attorney General, but I am not sure. Anyway, local detectives and prosecutors tried in vain to pursue Seal and his activities, but were constantly stonewalled. In 1994, detective Bill Duncan summarized the perspective of law-enforcement officers in testimony to Congress: "By the end of 1987 . . . thousands of law enforcement man-hours and an enormous amount of evidence of drug smuggling, aiding and abetting drug smugglers, conspiracy, perjury, money laundering . . . had gone to waste. Not only were no indictments ever returned on any of the individuals under investigation for their role in the Mena Operation, there was a complete breakdown in the judicial system. The United States Attorney, Western Judicial District of Arkansas, . . . refused to issue subpoenas for critical witnesses, interfered with the investigations, misled grand juries about evidence and availability of witnesses, refused to allow investigators to present evidence to the grand jury, and in general made a mockery of the entire investigative and judicial process" STICH, *DEFRAUDING AMERICA* (1998) 413

[537] This most likely was the case. SEE REED & CUMMINGS, *COMPROMISED* (1994) 240

contested issue.[538] And while another whistleblower, William Albert Haynes, recently has gone public, disclosing that he was with the police that on the tracks that night when the boys were murdered and that he is willing to expose the politically connected drug dealers affiliated with this plot, he better speak fast before this unit gets to him.

Coming forward with such evidence surely can surely be hazardous to health as Paul Wilcher, an attorney who probed into drug smuggling at Mena discovered. Just after Clinton had become president, Wilcher went to the Department of Justice and delivered a 100-page letter which claimed that, unbeknownst to Attorney General Janet Reno and President Clinton, holdover Justice Department employees from the Reagan-Bush era were responsible for a number of cover-ups. On or about June 11, 1993, Wilcher was interviewed regarding the contents of the letter, but a few days later he was found dead.

As we shall see, there were also others, and after 9/11 this unit is probably more active than ever. Spreading fear, terror, and disinformation is the modus operandi, and as this suppression unit (and agencies of similar nature) will be inhabited by players loyal to power, its personnel have few moral qualms. These individuals have been indoctrinated to trust that the ends justify the means, and quite a few believe that they are acting for the good of the nation.

Even so, maintaining the status quo comes at a terrible cost. The machine of which these people are a part is the same machine that has denied Americans inherent liberties for centuries. It is a machine whose primary fuel is force, not reason. It uses blackmail to survive, feeds on fear, and thrives on trauma. Considering that there is an alternative to the status quo, therefore—one that public officials and bureaucrats oppose—they should not sleep so well. Truth being the

---

[538] Fahmi Malik, Clinton's corrupt state medical examiner lied and said that the boys had smoked an equivalent of 20 cannabis cigarettes, rendering them unconscious as the train arrived. Pressure from parents resulted in another autopsy which proved the lie, but further investigation was stalled. For more on this story, see MARA LEVERITT, *THE BOYS ON THE TRACKS: DEATH, DENIAL, AND A MOTHER'S CRUSADE TO BRING HER SON'S KILLERS TO JUSTICE* (1999)

enemy, only a machinery of oppression can withstand the tides of change, and what it took to sustain the façade during the Iran-Contra years was not pretty.

10.3.5.3. THE MACHINERY OF OPPRESSION

*"I feel like I live in Russia, waiting for the secret police to pounce down. The government has gotten out of control.   .
. . Men of no account find themselves in positions of power and suddenly crimes become legal. . . . Should a cop cross over the line and dare to investigate the rich and powerful, he might well prepare himself to become the victim of his own government, the government of the United States of America. The cops are all afraid to tell what they know for fear that they will lose their jobs or go to jail themselves."[539]*

—Diary of Russell Welch, An Arkansas state police detective who was attacked with anthrax for his efforts to get to the truth—

To keep Americans ignorant of truth, Al Martin claims that the U.S. government murdered 400 witnesses and through staged court cases, imprisoned 1200. [540] These people were drug dealers but also public

---

[539] TRAVER & GAYLORD (ED.), *DRUGS, LAW AND THE STATE: A REEXAMINATION OF THE PHYSICS OF MOTION* (1992) xxiv

[540] Al Martin claims that "of the 1,300 witnesses, subpoenaed, deposed, interrogated before these committees, 413 have since died under clouded circumstances." (Martin, *The Conspirators* (2002) 8). He further elaborates on his reasons for believing so: "[I]f you see the subpoenas issued (or subpoenas that were intended to be issued) by the Kerry Committee, the Hughes Commission, the Alexander Commission and so on, and even Independent Counsel Lawrence Walsh, and then you see how closely they relate to people who were murdered at the time, and just how many people were murdered on the eve of being subpoenaed by a congressional investigating committee, it becomes quite a revelation. Bill Alexander tried to make this public in 1992. He had a wonderful list prepared. He had the support of both Congressman Jack Brooks of Texas and Congressman Charlie Rose of North Carolina. The

officials such as Amiram Nir, the Israeli Anti-Terror Advisor.[541] Martin describes the procedure:

"In the aftermath of any illegal covert operation which collapsed and became public, Iran-Contra is the most egregious and notorious. When an operation collapses, people like me get put through a three-tiered strainer. We'll call it the 'A,' 'B,' and 'C' strainer.

The 'A' strainer is for people who were two rungs of the ladder above me—guys like Major General Richard Secord and Major General John K. Singlaub. These are people are on the right side of the door of liability when it slams shut. They are the ones who get their 'Briefcases' and they will always live in great financial comfort and security, just going along—endlessly committing fraud and endlessly being protected from the consequences of it . . .

The bulk of people involved in such an operation are put through the 'B' strainer. The 'B' strainer is where people are pressured, harassed, intimidated, discredited, bankrupted and sometimes imprisoned on false charges, forced into exile in an effort to maintain the deniability of their superiors and to legally discredit them before any potential congressional committee, or any court proceeding in which they might testify, or give any deposition on someone else's behalf.

Washington Post and the New York Times would not touch it with a ten-foot pole" Ibid., 168

[541] Amiram Nir was murdered on November 29, 1988. "Who was behind it? Israeli intelligence has always believed it was a well-executed CIA operation. Nir's death ensured there would be no embarrassment for Peres, Reagan, or Bush at the North trial. In fact, while in London, Nir was getting bored and unhappy. He had started talking about writing a book. He even sounded out a journalist and told him some of his conversations with U.S. officials." (MENASHE, *PROFITS OF WAR* (1998) 290). Robert Hunt, a CIA agent that Rodney Stich was in contact with, told him that Nir was killed because he had recorded a meeting with George H.W. Bush in Israel in 1986 that Nir threatened to expose. (STICH, *DEFRAUDING AMERICA* (1998) 628). Chip Tatum, for his part, claims to have executed the murder on orders from Bush. Ibid., 457

The 'C' strainer, which is the minority—in which usually one in ten people are put through—is death. Those are the people who were simply down the ladder. They were not trained intelligence people. They found out a few little kernels of something that nobody wants revealed. And these people are considered unreliable, so they are simply done away with.

As we mentioned, more than 400 people out of the 5000 involved would be in that category."[542]

Rodney Stich was not involved with Iran-Contra. Even so, he became familiar with these procedures when he was imprisoned on trumped-up financial charges for trying to expose corrupt agents. Throughout the years, Stich documented people who had suffered a similar fate, and summarizes his perspective:

"Whatever the reason, CIA and Justice Department officials acted in unison with federal judges, eliminating people who constituted a threat of exposure. The standard tactic is to charge the targeted individual with a federal offense for some act they were ordered to perform by their CIA handlers, deny them adequate legal counsel, deny them the right to have CIA witnesses testify on their behalf, and deny them the right to present CIA documents. A standard and sham excuse for denying these defences is that they are not relevant to the immediate charge, when the matter of who gave the person his or her orders is absolutely relevant.

From 200 to 300 former CIA operatives or contract agents had been sentenced to prison by Justice Department prosecutors during the 1980s on charges arising out of covert activities they were ordered to perform by their CIA bosses."[543]

---

[542] MARTIN, *THE CONSPIRATORS* (2002) 22-23

[543] STICH, *DEFRAUDING AMERICA* (1998) 144

Such trials are presided over by judges who obstruct constitutional protections and who show no conscience in their sentencing.[544] Al Martin describes how this was the case at the Miami US Attorney's office:

"All politically sensitive, Iran-Contra politically sensitive cases, would be heard by one of two judges—either the chief federal district judge, Lawrence King, now retired, or the cases would be held by the newly ensconced Republican judge Fred Merano. In some cases, when there was an overload, the cases would be bumped up to the retired judge, Claude Atkins, a solid Republican. The defendants were convicted in every single Iran-Contra sensitive case heard by these three federal district judges."[545]

These court cases, in other words, were no better than those provided to defendants in totalitarian regimes. They are a symptom of a deeply troubled society, and we can expect the same situation to surround the cover-up of 9/11, as well as modern-day CIA drug operations. As Barry Jennings,[546] a deputy director of an emergency

---

[544] Sidney Powell, former Assistant United States Attorney in three judicial districts under 9 United States Attorneys, estimates that 10 percent of the U.S. prison population is behind bars due to fabricated cases and large-scale corruption. See POWELL, *LICENSED TO LIE: EXPOSING CORRUPTION IN THE DEPARTMENT OF JUSTICE* (2014)

[545] MARTIN, *THE CONSPIRATORS* (2002) 47

[546] "On August 19, 2008, 53-year-old Barry Jennings died, two days before the release of the NIST Final Report on the collapse of WTC7. Jennings was Deputy Director of Emergency Services Department for the New York City Housing Authority. On September 11th, 2001, he saw and heard explosions BEFORE the Twin Towers fell, while attempting to evacuate the WTC 7 Command Center with NYC Corporation Counsel Michael Hess. Jennings publicly shared his experiences with a reporter on the day of 9/11/01, as well as in a lengthy 2007 video interview with Dylan Avery, a small clip of which was then released; subsequently his job was threatened and he asked that the taped interview not be included in Loose Change Final Cut. However, after an interview with Jennings was broadcast by the BBC in their program The Third Tower ostensibly refuting what he had previously stated to Avery, Avery felt

service in New York, discovered, it would be immature to believe otherwise, and there were many who worked for the Iran-Contra committees who could feel an aura of tyranny creeping upon them. Professor Peter Dale Scott, who has authored several books on drug policy and power-politics, was one:

"I had a chance to observe the viciousness of this corrupt system in 1987, when I spent six months in Washington at a think tank, supplying documentation to the Kerry congressional subcommittee. . . . Less alarming to me than the facts were their consequences for those who knew of or reported them. One conscientious witness, a Republican businessman and Reagan supporter, suffered credible death threats that appear to have been partly acted on. Another for his pains was similarly menaced and directly targeted by Oliver North in the White House as a 'terrorist threat.' Even members of our think tank were interrogated by the FBI, which was perhaps the least bothersome inconvenience suffered by those promoting the truth. Others were placed under twenty-four-hour surveillance by forces the Washington police could not identify, or deprived of their professional jobs. In an arrangement that was probably illegal, a CIA-type propaganda campaign was funded through the State Department against the American people, targeting for defeat those who had opposed the contras in Congress."[547]

---

compelled to release the full original video interview to show the distortions made by the BBC. The cause of Jennings' death has not been made public, and a private investigator hired by Avery to discover the cause and circumstances surrounding his death refused to proceed with the investigation. Despite the significance of Jennings' position with NYC on 9/11 and his controversial eyewitness testimony regarding the collapse of WTC7, the media has not investigated or reported on his death, nor reported on his statements." Quote from http://jenningsmystery.com/

[547] SCOTT, *DRUGS, OIL, AND WAR* (2003) xviii

10.3.5.4. DAMAGE CONTROL NE PLUS ULTRA

No doubt the situation was bad. But no matter how totalitarian the atmosphere, events could have gone far worse. Indeed, there is evidence that George H.W. Bush and Oliver North perceived another option, which was an open dictatorship led by the Vice President, and that they had plans to start a World War to arrange for the legal necessities. This sure sounds like the plot of a bad movie. However, people who witnessed the preparation for these events have spoken out and while the Continuation of Government (COG) planning remains shrouded in secrecy, we know that it was the responsibility of the Federal Emergency Management Agency (FEMA).

When the topic was touched upon during the Iran-Contra hearings, Congress closed its doors. Even so, authors like Peter Dale Scott have researched these plans and people like Dick Cheney and Donald Rumsfeld were key architects.[548] This, most certainly, does not bode well. Rumsfeld, at this point, did not even work for the government, and there is reason to believe that these plans have been operational since 9/11.

What remains clear is that President Reagan left all matters of state security to George H.W. Bush and that, at this time, without congressional oversight, an operational framework was created to prepare for martial law.[549] Not much can be known through official channels, but Al Martin has more to say. Until 1987, he was one of the conspirators, and he was informed about this plan in late-1984.

------

[548] Upon becoming Ford's Secretary of Defense in 1975, his immediate staff had bought Rumsfeld flowers to congratulate him on his new job. Rumsfeld, however, "instantly threw the gift in the trash can in front of the staff in order to humiliate them and show them who was boss." LOFGREN, *THE DEEP STATE* (2016) 201

[549] This was the Special Situations Group and its offspring the Standing Crisis Pre-Planning Group, created May 14, 1982; The Crisis Management Center (February 1983); The Terrorist Incident Working Group (April 3, 1984); The Task Force on Combatting Terrorism (July 1985); and The Operations Sub-Group (January 20, 1986). WEBSTER TARPLEY & ANTON CHAITKIN, *GEORGE BUSH: THE UNAUTHORIZED BIOGRAPHY* (2004) 386

At this time, with the pretence of improving business relations in Latin America, there were meetings for insiders being held at the Dade County Latin American Chamber of Commerce. The most prominent figure was Jeb Bush and every other week the conspirators would discuss Iran-Contra related events.[550] One meeting, however, stood out. At this gathering both Oliver North and Don Gregg were present, and Martin learned of *Operation Orpheus* and *Sledgehammer*:[551]

> *"Orpheus was the idea that, if what later became known as 'Iran-Contra' fell apart early and everything spilled out publicly, it would have been potentially necessary to institute a silent coup against the Government of the United States.*
>
> *Obviously it would be done with the tacit support of said government, in which case Oliver North would have been a prominent member of the new post-silent coup administration. He would then control political fallout, which would have been tremendous, if all of Iran-Contra fell apart and became revealed to the public.*
>
> *But it went beyond that. Orpheus actually went to the point, where if liability could not be controlled, it would be necessary for Casey, North, and George Bush to secretly formulate and potentially launch an outright coup d'état against the*

---

[550] MARTIN, *THE CONSPIRATORS* (2002) 194

[551] "Sledgehammer" was an alias of North. Martin describes this operation: "Operation Sledgehammer was essentially a contingency operation to institute a putsch against the United States Government (with the tacit support of said Government) should knowledge of Iran-Contra operations become publicly disseminated. The feeling was that if people were to know the quantities of narcotics and weapons being dealt and the enormity of State-sanctioned fraud against US banks (and other financial institutions which taxpayers ultimately guarantee), there would be such a reaction among the people that in order to divert public attention, it might become necessary to institute a putsch having the tacit agreement of the Reagan Administration. I know this sounds draconian, but that was the level of concern in those years)." Ibid., 15

Government of the United States. These were the three principals involved.

. . .[T]his would have been an outright coup. It was envisioned that George Bush would become acting President of the new Provisional Military Government of the United States. In order to do this, the pretext was going to be a limited nuclear exchange with the Soviet Union, wherein we would create a situation, a catalyst as it were, a military confrontation that would lead to a limited nuclear exchange. This would be in cooperation by the way with certain hardline elements within the Soviet military. That was the whole idea of the Orpheus Project.

. . . It was quite frightening what North and Casey and Bush were actually prepared to do to cover up what they were doing. They understood the egregiousness of what they were doing. They also understood that if Iran-Contra fell apart, then everything else fell apart that came before it.

All of the preceding conspiracies and coverups including the post-war conspiracies and cover-ups might also fall apart. That's what they were actually afraid of. And the temerity of this was such that it would require a new government with an iron fist. It would also require the cooperation of the Soviet Union because there were many hardliners who were also very interested in getting rid of the new and tender Gorbachev. The hardliners in the Russian military saw him as a tremendous threat. So there became commonality between hardline interests in both the United States and the Soviet Union to maintain the status quo.

The status quo of the Cold War was very good for business, and it was very good for maintenance of old power structures and cabals. Those who had benefitted from it on both sides didn't want to give it up."[552]

---

[552] Ibid., 38-39

According to Martin, Oliver North estimated that between 50 and 70 million people would die if this plan came to fruition. He also implicated the British and the German government:

"This was not simply the United States and the Soviet Union. Some of our allies, as North had mentioned, had also been consulted about this. The Thatcher government and the Kohl government—they were going to become part of this because they had exactly the same concerns. From what I heard, it was obvious that this involved the long-term post-war cooperation between deep right-wing elements within our allied governments and their concerns that conspiracies of the past would potentially come back to haunt them.

This is a really big story. . . . that there is, in fact, literally a global deep-right wing conspiracy with connections that make certain things happen, so that certain policy objectives are met and certain geo-political, economic and military spheres interact."[553]

While this may come as a shock, we have seen every indication that this is so. The story of how the elite organized the illicit drugs market and profited on maintaining controls is just one of several secrets that, if known, the elite fear will make us revolt. Even so, as these conspiracies are becoming public knowledge, we should keep in mind that these people have acted no differently than most would have done if we were in their shoes. Our leaders have been born into a network and a culture that presents them with every incentive to continue the dysfunctional behaviours of the past, and their impact on world affairs mirrors our collective refusal to abide by the very same values, ideal, and principles that we ourselves so proudly boast.

Hence, the balance of the world can either be changed for better or worse, depending upon our ability to process this information. To the extent that humanity continues the timeless tradition of looking for scapegoats, the elite rightfully fear that they will be blamed for all

---

[553] Ibid. 341

our troubles, and we will have people like Bush and North willing to take extreme protective measures. If there is ever to be a solution, therefore, playing the blame game is not what we should do, and instead we should focus on how we all, collectively, can move past the current state of affairs.

As we can see, it is neither worthy of government nor civil community and the solutions are fair and simple. Before we go on to discuss human rights and common resolve, however, we shall discuss the laundering of drug money.

10.4. THE DRUGS ECONOMY

"There is something wrong in this country; the judicial nets are so adjusted as to catch the minnows and let the whales slip through."

—Eugene V. Debbs, 1895—

Our banking system is a loan-based fiat economy. What keeps a bank afloat is assets; every loan count as an asset, and depending on how much assets they got, they can lend around ten times to customers. This is how the banks operate, like a Ponzi scheme. Thus, the most important source of growth is cheap capital—and nothing is cheaper than dirty money. Throughout the years, therefore, banks have become dependent upon the drugs economy and this was confirmed in 2009 by Antonio Maria Costa, the Executive Director of the United Nations Office on Drugs and Crime. In a rare fit of honesty, the UN Drug Czar told reporters that western banks, to survive the crash of 2008, had relied upon the drugs economy to recover and that some $352 billion were laundered in this period. Costa, however, refused to identify the countries or the banks involved, as that would be "inappropriate because his office is supposed to address the problem, not apportion blame."[554]

Even so, as Costa one year earlier condemned Amy Winehouse for being a "coke-snorting fashionista" and a "poster girl for drug abuse," this is not entirely true. What Costa means, therefore, is that blame is reserved for drug users and drug dealers, while those who sit on top of the profit chain deserves privacy. Upon this notion the drug war proceeds, but we shall now have a look at the banking activities of the CIA. While there are many others involved, we shall concentrate on three banks whose businesses and personnel overlapped with CIA operations in Indochina and Latin America.

10.4.1. THE NUGAN HAND BANK

Nugan Hand was an Australian bank linked to the laundering of drug money. It was established by Francis Nugan, Michael Hand, and Maurice Bernard Houghton in 1973, went international in 1976 (based on the Cayman Islands), and reached its zenith in 1979 with a reported turnover rising from $30m to $1bn as the bank opened offices in Hong Kong, Singapore, the Cayman Islands and Saudi Arabia.

Nugan, an Australian lawyer, managed legalities, while Hand and Houghton were intelligence operatives with a history from the Indochina theatre. Its board of employees was a who's who of shady operatives,[555] including Paul Helliwell, William Colby, Theodore Shackley, Ed Wilson, Richard Armitage, and Thomas Clines. As we

---

[554] Rajeev Sval, *Drug money saved banks in global crisis, claims UN advisor*, the Observer, December 13, 2009.

[555] In addition to the above, the president of the company was Rear-Admiral Earl P. Yates, the former Chief of Staff for Policy and Plans of the U.S. Pacific Command and a counter-insurgency specialist. Other appointments included General Leroy J. Manor, the former chief of staff of the U.S. Pacific Command and deputy director for counterinsurgency and special activities; General Edwin F. Black, former commander of U.S. forces in Thailand; Walter J. McDonald, retired CIA deputy director for economic research; Dale C. Holmgren, former chairman of the CIA's Civil Air Transport and Guy J. Pauker, senior Republican foreign policy adviser.

have seen, it was this disreputable bunch of characters who oversaw opium exploits in the Golden Triangle, and laundering drug money was central to the bank's operations.[556]

Looking at the bigger picture, Nugan Hand became the CIA's go-to bank when Castle Bank & Trust collapsed in 1977. This bank was established in 1962 by Paul Helliwell and it quickly became a "conduit for millions of dollars earmarked by the CIA for the funding of clandestine operations directed at countries in Latin America and the Far East."[557] The IRS, however, discovered that the bank was in league with underworld figures connected to the drug trade and while the CIA ensured that the matter was dropped for reasons of national security, Castle Bank and Trust was beyond salvation.

As author Paul Williams reminds us, the CIA does not take control of a bank merely to finance covert operations and launder drug money, but to "chalk up losses in a bewildering array of bogus ventures."[558] Castle was no different, and Nugan Hand would suffer the same fate three years later.

Intrigues took off on January 27, 1980, when Frank Nugan was found shot dead in his car. With his body was a bible that included a piece of paper with the name "Bob Wilson" and "Bill Colby." The former was a longstanding member of the House Armed Services Committee, while the latter not only was a Director of the CIA but the bank's legal advisor. Not long after, witnesses saw Thomas G. Clines at Wilson's office removing papers that referred to him and General Richard Secord, and Michael Hand convened a meeting of Bank directors. The cover-up was on, and Hand warned that unless managers did as they were told they would "finish up with concrete shoes" and be "liable to find their wives being delivered to them in pieces".

---

[556] For more on Nugan Hand, see: JONATHAN KWITNY, *THE CRIMES OF PATRIOTS: A TRUE TALE OF DOPE, DIRTY MONEY, AND THE CIA* (1987); STICH, *DEFRAUDING AMERICA* (1998) 241-46; MCCOY, *THE POLITICS OF HEROIN* (1991) 461-78.

[557] WILLIAMS, *OPERATION GLADIO* (2015) 85

[558] Id.

Shortly thereafter, Hand left the country accompanied by James Oswald Spencer, a man who had served with Ted Shackley in Laos. He would disappear from official records to become unavailable to angry clients and inquisitive law-enforcement officers. Even so, witnesses claim to have seen him in South America running drugs for Casey and Bush,[559] before secretly returning to the United States.[560]

While the U.S authorities covered up this mess,[561] Australian authorities took a more serious look. Three investigative committees were established to examine the bank's affairs and evidence was found that the Nugan Hand Bank was implicated in money-laundering, illegal tax avoidance schemes, and widespread violations of banking laws. Even so, the Royal Commission of inquiry was largely a cover-up.[562] Australian intelligence services (ASIO) intervened to offset further investigation into the bank's drug connections, and so the most far-reaching report would be that of the Commonwealth New South Wales Task Force on Drug Trafficking, which concluded that there was a connection between the bank,

---

[559] Trenton Parker, a CIA agent, told this to Rodney Stich. STICH, *DEFRAUDING AMERICA* (1998) 242.

[560] Investigative journalists appear to have found him: "In March 1991, the Australian magazine The Eye reported that Michael Hand was living in the United States, giving an address and other details, but Australian authorities declined to pursue an extradition. In November 2015, the Sydney Morning Herald reported that Peter Butt had located Hand living under the name Michael Jon Fuller in Idaho Falls, Idaho. Peter Butt queried the failure of the FBI to find him, given that Fuller's social security numbers are identical to Hand's." (Wikipedia June 1, 2018)

[561] US intelligence services were not forthcoming and when Australian authorities contacted the FBI they were denied access for reasons of "national security". SCOTT, *DRUGS, OIL, AND WAR* (2003) 53

[562] Clive Small, a New South Wales Task Force Task Force investigator, concluded that the Stewart Royal Commission was a whitewash: "The royal commission was so dismissive of an American connection that many people who read it simply felt that it was a cover up, because it was in effect so superficial and so dismissive. It never attempted to put into context its findings with the findings of the Joint Task Force, which have not been found to be in any way, shape or form inaccurate or unreliable." PETER BUTT, *MERCHANTS OF MENACE* (2015) 236

Indochina drug cartels, and Pentagon and CIA officials. In this regard, the report named Theodore Shackley and Thomas Clines.[563]

10.4.2. BISHOP, BALDWIN, REWALD, DILLINGHAM AND WONG

When Nugan Hand failed, the CIA needed another bank to launder drug money and fund covert operations. The answer was Bishop, Baldwin, Rewald, Dillingham and Wong (BBRDW).[564] Based in Hawaii, its operations began in 1979, and the bank's function and personnel were largely the same as that of Nugan Hand: Shady characters like General Edwin Black, General Leroy Manor, Admiral Lloyd Vassey, and Admiral Earl Yates were involved—and again, making a profit on the worldwide web of drugs- and arms dealing became a preferred livelihood.

By 1984, however, this bank had suffered unrepairable damage. The CIA set-up Ronald Rewald, its chief executive, as a fall guy and he was sentenced to 80 years. Before this, someone had cut him up, making him fear further attempts on his life, and he was probably right. On September 19-20, 1984, Scott Barnes, a CIA agent, was interviewed on ABC News Tonight where he revealed that he had been tasked to kill Rewald. The CIA not only contested the charge, but Director Bill Colby asked the Federal Communications Commission to revoke all of ABC's TV and radio licenses. In February 1985, the CIA went on to ask FCC to apply Fairness Doctrine penalties to the network—and the following month ABC was bought by Capital Cities Corporation, a media conglomerate full of spooks, with Casey on the board of directors.

From this point on, the U.S. press posed no real problem. While the big media corporations continued to act as if they watched Republicans and Democrats closely, they all sang to the Piper's tune and could be relied upon to rally behind authority when called upon.

---

[563] COCKBURN, *OUT OF CONTROL* (1987) 103

[564] For More on BBRDW, see STICH, *EXPLOSIVE SECRETS OF COVERT CIA COMPANIES* (2006); STICH, *DEFRAUDING AMERICA* (1998) 247-80

Even so, the CIA needed another bank to continue financial transactions and the Bank of Credit and Commerce International (BCCI) shouldered the load.

10.4.3. BANK OF CREDIT AND COMMERCE INTERNATIONAL

The BCCI was founded in 1972 by Agha Hasan Abedi, a Pakistani financier and an associate of Saudi Intelligence Minister Kamal Adham. The Bank was registered in Luxembourg with head offices in Karachi and London, but it was so much more. As investigative journalist Joseph Trento noted, "with the official blessing of George H. W. Bush as the head of the CIA, Adham transformed a small Pakistani merchant bank, the Bank of Credit and Commerce International (BCCI), into a worldwide money-laundering machine, buying banks around the world to create the biggest clandestine money network in history."[565]

Indeed, when French customs raided the Paris BCCI branch, they discovered that George H.W. Bush had established an account at the BCCI while he was director of the CIA, and author Trento has shown that the bank was a shell for a group of anti-communist intelligence services whose cooperation had become more difficult with Carter as president. At this time, the intelligence community was tied down by Congress, and Bush, Adham, and other heads of intelligence would work with Abedi to contrive a plan whereby the BCCI would solicit the business of every major terrorist, rebel, and underground organization in the world. The information gained would be shared with 'friends', and CIA operative Raymond Close worked with Adham on this.

The operation, at first, was hugely successful and a decade later the BCCI had over 400 branches in 78 countries, 19,000 employees, and assets in excess of $20 billion, making it the seventh largest private bank in the world. As the 1980's moved on, however, it became obvious that the bank was involved with largescale criminal

---

[565] TRENTO, *PRELUDE TO TERROR* (2005) 104

activities and as Time Magazine would explain in 1991, BCCI was not just a bank: It was probably the biggest intelligence operation in the world, and at its centre was the "black network," a secretive group consisting of some 1,500-employees who used sophisticated spy equipment and techniques, along with bribery, extortion, kidnapping, and murder to further the bank's aims.[566]

To enter the American financial market, this dubious entity needed a cover. Beginning in 1978, therefore, a group of foreign investors, fronted by Kamal Adham, attempted to buy First American Bankshares, the biggest bank in the Washington, D.C., area. First American represented old money. It was intimately connected with the CIA, and if the BCCI controlled this company, they could bank on U.S. soil. To get this done the BCCI relied upon Clark Clifford, a Washington insider and advisor to five presidents, who provided sufficient respectability to convince the Federal Reserve that everything was okay.

The Fed had every reason to be suspicious. In 1981, the Federal Reserve asked the CIA for information about investors, but the CIA withheld everything they knew including the fact that Adham was intelligence minister. As a result, the sale went through in 1982—the same year that the Bank of England, in an internal memo, called BCCI "the financial equivalent of the SS. Titanic."[567] Even so, throughout the 1980's, the British and the American central bank failed to police the BCCI, arguing that it was the responsibility of Luxembourg authorities, where the bank was registered. Thus, no one intervened and when the bank went bust in 1991 the BCCI owed more than $18 billion to its creditors.

As investigative journalists dug into this quagmire of corruption, it became clear that the BCCI was connected to Iran-Contra and hordes of other criminal enterprises. In New York, District Attorney Robert Morgenthau seized upon this information to launch his own

---

[566] Jonathan Beaty and S.C. Gwynne, *BCCI: The Dirtiest Bank of All*, Time Magazine, July 29, 1991

[567] *BCCI scandal: Long legal wrangling over collapsed bank*, The Guardian, May 17, 2012

investigation. He gathered that more than $5 billion had been stolen, and through testimony in Congress learned of the connection between the BCCI and First American Bank. He also learned of how the bank laundered Noriega's drug money.

As 99,5 percent of all U.S. financial transactions go through Manhattan, Morgenthau claimed jurisdiction. And while the Fed's New York department (which is the most intimately connected with the secretive powers of the world) joined the Justice Department in stonewalling, he had help from another Fed department and established that the BCCI, indeed, controlled First American. Moreover, it was established that Clifford and Altman had lied about this and that Agha Hasan Abedi, the BCCI's Pakistani founder, and three associates had been running the bank as a criminal conspiracy, bribing bankers, officials, and others around the world.

Except for a few convictions of politically expendable BCCI officials, however, not much came of Morgenthau's efforts. The Justice Department surely opposed his work, and in 1990 it struck a deal to protect the BCCI against RICO and money laundering charges, provided that the bank paid $14 million. This was $12 million less than BCCI over the next couple of years would spend on lawyer fees, and a good deal as it prevented other agencies from building a case.

After the scandal broke, the Justice Department would come under heavy fire for this. Senator Kerry appeared to fight for the rule of law and by mid-1991 the Senate Subcommittee on Terrorism, Narcotics and International Operations had hearings. While the subcommittee received no help from the Justice Department, the Senator was not deterred, and as he connected with Morgenthau's office—and the press started to demand answers—corrupt officials at the Department of Justice began to act like they were all about the rule of law. Thus, Assistant Attorney General Robert Mueller made a show of effort. In 1992 he assigned nearly three dozen attorneys to BCCI's case and brought several indictments. Nevertheless, it was no more than what was needed to preserve a minimum of credibility—and looking back, the chief orchestrators of this cover-up was George

Terwilliger, William Barr, and Robert Mueller.[568] Thirty years later, Barr and Mueller were involved in another game of intrigue during the Trump Presidency, this time relating to elite paedophilia, child murder, and the Clinton Foundation.[569] We shall soon learn more

---

[568] Until late 1991, DOJ stonewalled Congress, Morgenthau, and any other investigative measure which threatened to expose the bank's dirty laundry. One threat was Customs. By March 1988, high level Customs officials connected to Operation C-Chase were reporting to Commissioner Von Raab that several BCCI officials were indictable under RICO. Justice officials, however, rebutted the proposal and ensured the worst possible conditions for the agents and prosecutors who worked on the case ensuring that Mazur, the chief undercover agent, quit Customs. Also in March of 1988, the chief investigator for the Foreign Relations Committee, Jack Blum, contacted the Justice Department with astonishing information about the BCCI. In the course of his investigation into narcotics trafficking in Panama, Blum had come into contact with "a very senior BCCI officer who was in the process of disengaging from the bank." According to Blum, the BCCI banker provided him with a substantial amount of information about the bank's criminality. Blum proceeded to seek authorization from the Foreign Relations Committee to issue subpoenas to the bank, which were granted. Before issuing the subpoenas, however, Blum contacted the US attorney's office in Miami and Tampa, which asked him not to proceed. Yet another investigation was obstructed, one that had been launched in the Southern District of Florida under the direction of US Attorney Dexter Lehtinen in 1989. By mid-1989, the US Attorney's office in Tampa had information on much of the BCCI's criminal activities, as well as alleged ownership of First American from two separate sources. By September 1988, also Customs had gathered evidence that the BCCI was a major operator for drug cartels and that First American was really owned by BCCI. Even so, the Justice Department followed up on none of this and stonewalled progress. In fact, even after regulators in England, Luxembourg, and the Cayman Islands on July 5, 1991, closed down the BCCI's international operations, alleging the fraud was so massive that the bank could not be reformed, the U.S. Justice Department continued to protect the BCCI and those behind it.

[569] Sidney Powell, the lawyer of Michael Flynn, an Army Lt. General who was attacked by these corrupt forces, have several times confirmed the story of the Weiner laptop. So far, the media have largely ignored the story on how the N.Y.P.D. seized the computer of Anthony Weiner, husband of Huma Abedin, Hillary Clinton's closest confidante. On his computer was a file marked "life-insurance", containing not only 650.000 emails that Hillary had sought to hide but images of such extreme nature that experienced police officers had to throw up. FBI Director Comey made sure that this material was never looked at. Together with the testimony of Patrick Byrne, former CEO of Overstock, (note 233), this explains why Hillary Clinton and the democrats

about it, but the 2017-19 Mueller investigation was another example of biased inquiry and institutionalized corruption at the FBI, while Barr's Department of Justice continued the tradition of cover ups, holding back John Durham's investigation into the origins of the Trump-Russia probe.

Now, knowing that BCCI's involvement with Iran-Contra was only the tip of the iceberg, it comes as no surprise that the suppression unit at Justice worked hard to keep the façade. No investigative efforts into the major hotspots of conspiracy, such as the European branches, would be allowed and considering that BCCI provided services that elite networks relied upon but could not officially deliver, there is reason to believe that BCCI served as a front for more "respectable" banks like the Bank of America, Morgan Stanley, and Citigroup. Indeed, private investigative measures into the Swiss branch seems to confirm these suspicions. As Engdahl and Steinberg found:

> *"In 1976, BCCI established a Swiss base of operations by purchasing 85% of Banque de Commerce et Placements (BCP) of Geneva. The remaining 15% was retained by the original owner, Thesarus Continental Securities Corp., a wholly owned subsidiary of Union Bank of Switzerland (UBS). Under BCCI control, BCP was managed by Alfred Hartmann, a former senior official of UBS. Hartmann eventually became chief financial officer for BCC Holding, and was the person most accountable for the 'lost' $23 billion. While serving as BCCI's 'man in Switzerland,' Hartmann was always operating on behalf of the Rothschild family. Hartmann was president of Rothschild Bank AG of Zurich, was vice-chairman of NY-Intermaritime Bank of Geneva (run by Mossad operative Bruce Rappaport), and was a member of the board of directors of the elite N.M. Rothschild and Sons in London."[570]*

---

started a campaign to derail President Trump, and why Mueller and Barr were called to keep the façade.

[570] Bill Engdahl and Jeffrey Steinberg, *The real story of the BCCI*, Executive Intelligence Review, October 13, 1995

This is as high-up as we come. The Rothchild's and other banks are not only too big to fail, but too big to be probed—and so, in 1991, investigative agencies agreed with the assessment of Price Waterhouse, the BCCI's accountant, that it would be "difficult, if not impossible, to reconstruct BCCI's financial history."

Nevertheless, it is incontestable that the BCCI owed much of its success to its involvement with intelligence operations and a willingness to do the dirty work for bigger players. And while executives at CIA and Bank of America predictably would distance themselves from its operations, those who investigated the BCCI discovered an institution fully dedicated to debasing humanity.[571] As Rodney Stich described its operations:

> *"BCCI was custom-made for the covert and corrupt activities of the CIA, the Mossad, drug dealers, and terrorists. My CIA contacts, including Russbacher, told how CIA operatives used the bank to launder money from CIA enterprises. These included drug trafficking proceeds, the looting of savings and loans, funding unlawful arms shipments, financing terrorist operations, undermining foreign governments, and other covert activities."[572]*

Despite these forces' ability to control the outcome of official investigations, the BCCI's association with drug barons would be documented not only by independent researchers[573] but Congress. In

---

[571] "A class action lawsuit filed in San Francisco courts by a class of defrauded BCCI depositors charged that Bank of America officials had considerable control over BCCI and had more knowledge of its illegal operations than previously disclosed. . . . The suit charged that the wrongful acts of BCCI could not have been accomplished without the active and knowing assistance of Bank of America." STICH, *DEFRAUDING AMERICA* (1998) 311. For more on this subject, Ibid., 309-332.

[572] Ibid., 310

[573] "Numerous sources confirm that the CIA (and Arab states) used BCCI to move funds into the afghan pipeline, and that the bank was used in turn by corrupt Pakistani

the aftermath, congressional hearings discovered an abundance of evidence and one witness was Robert Mazur, the lead investigator of Operation C-Chase. This Customs operation began in 1986 and Mazur went undercover for two years as a banker for the Medellin cartel to deal with BCCI executives and drug dealers from around the world. Based upon his experience, he found that "the bank's mission was to gain power in the financial community by gathering deposits from every corner of the underworld. [The BCCI] laundered money, bribed regulators, corrupted politicians, financed arms dealers, and even provided prostitutes for favoured customers."[574]

More specifically, Mazur spent most of his time investigating the BCCI in Panama. He was meeting with its top officials, and they summarized BCCI's Latin American affairs like this:

"In Latin America . . . evidence is indisputable that the bank moved aggressively to boost its share of that region's total drug money. BCCI officers met with and opened accounts for such major Colombian cartel leaders as Pablo Escobar, Jorge Luis Ochoa and Jose Gonzalo Rodriguez Gacha. The bank established branches in such notorious drug centers as Medellín, Cali and even Pablo Escobar's hometown, Envigado. In Peru, it opened an office in the Huallaga Valley, the center of that country's coca production. In Florida, it handled accounts for some 200 drug traffickers and tax evaders. In all, according to estimates by some U.S. sources, the bank laundered nearly $1 billion in Colombian drug profits."[575]

The BCCI could only get away with these kinds of banking practices because it had political protection. As we have seen, people like Robert Altmann and Clark Clifford were key to this plot—and willingly or not Senator John Kerry came in handy. In December

---

officials to launder drug profits from the burgeoning heroin trade." SCOTT & MARSHALL, *COCAINE POLITICS* (1998) xvi)

[574] MAZUR, *THE INFILTRATOR* (2009) 331-32

[575] Ibid., xvi

1992, he provided Congress with the official account of the BCCI when he submitted his report to the Committee on Foreign Relations in 1992.[576] Even though it was one of the most scathing reports on CIA and DOJ activities ever released, Kerry ensured that the façade remained intact and that the BCCI affair ended up looking like another Arabian misadventure, largely disconnected from the bigger picture.[577]

10.5. MODERN MONEY LAUNDERING

Nevertheless, while the BCCI went down in flames, BCCI officials claimed that they were engaging in the same kind of practices that everyone else was—and they probably were right. As Robert Mazur, the lead agent on Operation C-Chase noted in 2009:

"BCCI got caught. Only that detail separates them from the rest of the international banking community. They've been out of the game for twenty years. The drug trade has produced

---

[576] Senator John Kerry and Senator Hank Brown, *The BCCI Affair: A Report to the Committee on Foreign Relations*, United States Senate, December 1992

[577] However, as his committee received no assistance from other agencies, he can hardly take credit for the cover-up. In its report, the committee confessed ignorance on many subjects and recommended investigative measures to determine (1) the use of the BCCI by key figures in arms sales to Iran during the 1980's; (2) the BCCI's involvement with foreign intelligence agencies; (3) the alleged relationship between the late CIA director William Casey and BCCI; and (4) money laundering by other major international banks. As Kerry noted: "Numerous BCCI officials told the Subcommittee that BCCI's money laundering was no different from activities they observed at other international banks and provided the names of a number of prominent U.S. and European banks which they alleged engaged in money laundering. There is no question that BCCI's laundering of drug money, while pervading the institution, constituted a small component of the total money laundering taking place in international banking. Further investigation to determine which international banks are soliciting and handling drug money should be undertaken." Ibid.

about $500 billion per year since then, but no one has been prosecuted for laundering those $10 trillion. "[578]

Since this date, several more trillions have been laundered. And while no one has been prosecuted, Wachovia, Wells Fargo, and the HSBC has admitted to laundering hundreds of billions for Mexico's drug cartels. Between 2004 and 2007, $378 billion went onto the Wachovia/Wells Fargo currency exchange system and yet none of its employees was arrested. Speaking of the HSBC, this bank admitted to breaches of anti-money-laundering norms in 2012 as it had moved hundreds of millions through the US on behalf of Mexican and Colombian drug cartels. As US Assistant Attorney General Lanny Breuer noted: "From 2006 to 2010, the Sinaloa cartel in Mexico, the Norte del Valle cartel in Colombia, and other drug traffickers laundered at least $881 million in illegal narcotics trafficking proceeds through HSBC Bank USA. These traffickers didn't have to try very hard."[579]

In all, the HSBC stood accused of failing to monitor over $670 billion in wire transfers from HSBC Mexico between 2006 and 2009. Not only that, but the bank failed to monitor the purchase of an incredible $9 billion in physical U.S. dollars from Mexico. Thus, the HSBC played a key role in the so-called Black-Market Peso Exchange, which allowed Colombian and Mexican drug cartels to convert U.S. dollars from drug sales into pesos to be used back home. The plot was so popular that drug dealers in Mexico built special cash boxes to fit the precise dimensions of HSBC teller windows,[580] but the HSBC did not stop there. It was, after all, a global operation and an astonishing $200 trillion in wire transfers went through without monitoring. This made the HSBC a banker for Russian gangsters as well as terrorist organizations linked to Al Qaeda, ISIS, and

---

[578] MAZUR, THE INFILTRATOR (2009) 340

[579] Nikhil Kumar & Jamie Dunkley, *HSBC: The Drug World's Local Bank*, The Independent, December 12, 2012

[580] Matt Taibbi, *Gangster Bankers: Too Big to Fail*, Rolling Stone, February 28, 2013

Hezbollah, and the bank also helped countries like Iran, Sudan, and North Korea evade sanctions.[581]

Serious stuff, in other words, but what the HSBC did was not indictable. Instead, the U.S. Assistant Attorney General held that criminal persecution, even withdrawal of its U.S. banking license, would be catastrophic for the stock market and that a fine of $2 billion would do. This was less than five weeks profits for the HSBC but, more importantly, the big banks now had assurance that they could continue to violate the law without suffering real consequences.

No doubt the HSBC was happy to plead guilty. Paul Thurston, the man in charge of HSBC's Mexico operation for some of the relevant period, was promoted to become head of global retail on a multi-million-dollar salary, whereas Stephen Green, the chief executive of the bank throughout its service to Chapo Guzman's cartel, was appointed to the British government. Indeed, the only persons to lose their job in this scandal were Everett Stern, Martin Woods, and Carolyn Wind, the compliance officers with the HSBC, Wachovia, and the U.S. government.

For reporting on these crimes (or systemic obstacles), they were punished so that others would get the message. And to those who did not care about integrity or the rule of law, this message was simple: They learned to ignore the distance between theory and practice; to accept a world where values have no meaning and where principles and ideals carry no weight; and to abide by the dictates of fake authority. If they could do that, they would be fine: they would be promoted and have a career at society's expense.

For those who thought wisely, however, the message would be different. And for those who cared about the truth, integrity, and the nature of government, the lesson would be that the system had become utterly corrupted and that a regulation of drugs was the only solution. When banks are not only too big to fail, but too big to do time or suffer real consequences for financing terrorism, illegal covert operations,

---

[581] Senate Permanent Subcommittee on Investigations, *U.S. Vulnerabilities to Money Laundering, Drugs, and Terrorist Financing: HSBC Case History*, September 6, 2012

wars, and drug running, there is no way that a healthy society can survive. The obvious fact remains that satanism is the open (or hidden) reversal of values, and to the extent that we accept the status quo a dark grid will be ever tightening its grip on world populations.

Indeed, when whistleblowers are punished and not corrupt agents, everything is set for the acceleration of this dynamic and these institutions are not merely banks. They are connected to a host of other profitable endeavours where human suffering is the main outcome, and as one of the largest banks in the world, Wells Fargo serves as an example. Not only did it make money laundering the profits of the world's most deeply troubled souls, people who in the last decade have murdered tens of thousands of innocent civilians in their battle for territory; it is heavily invested in the GEO Group, the second largest private prison company in the United States. Hence, it also profited (and continues to profit) on the millions that are arrested in the War on Drugs.

Along with its friends, Wells Fargo now can continue to consolidate markets, while knowing that they can get away with its criminal activities for a relatively small fine. And again, it would be extremely naïve to believe that the problem remains limited to this group of banks. As we have seen, they were only discovered because of whistleblowers, but the system was rigged, and this means that there are other banks waiting to be discovered.

Indeed, federal and state authorities have been investigating a handful of other major American banks for failing to monitor cash transactions. JPMorgan Chase, Bank of America, and Citigroup are among the institutions suspected of being involved in the drug trade— and while no one has been prosecuted, we need only consider Citigroup's history in Mexico, a hotspot of drugs- and money laundering activities. We already know that the connection between drug barons and government agents goes back to the beginning of the drug war; this also applies to Mexico—and yet, from 1940 until the late 1980's, Citibank was the only American bank to do business in this country. It would be extremely naïve to suppose that the Rockefeller-connected bank has not been a major money launderer for the Cartels. After all, we know that it helped the powerful Salinas family stash away billions in drug profits,[582] and on May 17, 2001, Citibank bought Banamex, Mexico's second-biggest bank.

The owner of Banamex, Roberto Hernandez, was overtly connected to drugs, and yet he joined Citibank's Board of Directors. As former police officer Mike Ruppert commented on the purchase:

"The level of criminality in the US financial and political systems has reached a threshold where it can no longer be spun into something which [the] Public can ignore and where US drug 'enforcement' efforts are now revealed to be nothing more than a reaction to the imperative of 'managing' the drug trade so as not to lose control of the trillions of dollars at stake. Crime has become, overtly, the largest free enterprise in the world. . . . The move will place Citigroup in control of one of the major—and proven—money laundering institutions in Mexico and allow Citigroup (first time for a US company) to penetrate the Mexican stock market. . . . It doesn't matter anymore whether the American public chooses to notice. The fait accompli is that drug money and criminal money are now out of the closet as the most important determinants of economic success for the US financial system. The careless arrogance of these moves only reveals the utter confidence in Washington, on Wall Street and in the banking system that no voices from the wilderness can stop it."[583]

No doubt, Ruppert's thesis has been confirmed. And if we wonder why this pattern has been allowed to develop, we need only follow the money. Alain Ambrose, editor at Geopolitical Drug Dispatch, estimates that roughly 80 percent of the total drugs economy is laundered by western banks and that for every dollar made by gangsters 75 cent end up with these banks. This is why no one is allowed to interfere with the status quo—and yet we have not seen all.

---

[582] COCKBURN & ST. CLAIR, *WHITEOUT* (1999) 370

[583] Mike Ruppert, *All hell breaks loose*, 2001 http://www.fromthewilderness.com/free/ciadrugs/053101_Citigroupandasa.html.

As Mazur found out when he met Akbar Bilgrami, a BCCI official responsible for Latin American operations, the biggest money launderer was the Federal Reserve. Bilgrami told him:

"The Federal Reserve Bank [is the biggest money launderer in the U.S.]. They are such hypocrites! They know that the Bank of the Republic in Bogotá has a teller window known as 'the sinister window.' Under Colombian rule, any citizen who has huge piles of cash can come to that window and anonymously exchange their U.S. dollars for Colombian pesos—no questions asked. This causes the central bank to accumulate pallet loads of U.S. dollars that are shipped to the Federal Reserve and credited to the account of the Bank of the Republic—again no questions asked.

The people at the Federal Reserve aren't idiots. They see this river of hundreds of millions in U.S. dollars being shipped to them from Colombia. They know what generates that cash. That's drug money that has been smuggled from the U.S. and Europe to Colombia. The Federal Reserve takes that because it's good economics for this country's banking system. The Americans so-called War on Drugs is a sham."[584]

Mazur found out that this information was correct, and Bilgrami's story is supported by the testimony of Al Martin, the Iran-Contra insider. As he said:

"Another way the government 'acquiesced' to these narcotics operations was by effectively allowing them to launder vast sums of money through Iran-Contra sympathetic banks in south Florida. They allowed enormous sums of money to leave these banks for accounts in Central America, the Caribbean, South America, and so on. Banks like Eagle National Bank, which was 80% owned by the Banco de Colombia, the central Bank of Colombia, were allowed to maintain a confidential cable

---

[584] MAZUR, *THE INFILTRATOR* (2009) 339

arrangement with their main bank in Colombia. They were completely unfettered. There were no forms to be filled out. Nothing. . . . I was a substantial client of Eagle National Bank at that time, as was Jeb Bush and all of his minions. "[585]

As we can see, this is all in the open, and it is easy to put two and two together for those who have a look. Indeed, it is for this reason that no one does. After DEA agent Michael Levine's undercover work in the early 1980's implicated top officials in three countries, the DEA and DOJ ensured that future investigations would be blocked long before they reached those at the top. Hence, it was a glitch in the system that made it possible for Mazur to do his work, and when he connected the drugs economy to the central banking system, that was it for law-enforcement. As Mazur said:

"No one in our government or any other country's government wants to test the integrity of the financial community anymore. I continue to interact with and train thousands of law-enforcement officers throughout the U.S. Their hands are tied. Bureaucrats have established regulations obstructing anyone from doing what we did. "[586]

---

[585] MARTIN, *THE CONSPIRATORS* (2002) 165

[586] MAZUR, *THE INFILTRATOR* (2009) 340

11

CONCLUSION

"In our age there is no such thing as 'keeping out politics'. All issues are political issues, and politics itself is a mass of lies, evasions, folly, hatred and schizophrenia."[587]

—George Orwell—

IN THIS PART of the book, we have looked at the shady side of drug policy. As seen, current policies breed not only hypocrisy but intrigue, and if we ever wondered why drug policy continues as it does, we have an answer: Despite all the shortcomings of prohibition, power politics and scapegoating ensure that it still wreaks havoc, and the collective wisdom of humanity has yet to reach a point where we will free ourselves from our burdens.

No doubt, facing that the world is run by gangsters comes at great psychological cost. No doubt, opposing the status quo comes at a great personal expense. In closing our eyes to the bigger picture, however, we continue to give power to the forces that has unleashed hell upon humanity. As Hannah Arenth discovered in researching the Nazi psychology, the ideal subject of tyrannical rule is not the person who is convinced of a totalitarian ideology; it is the person for whom the distinction between fact and fiction, truth and falsehood, is no longer of relevance.[588] Hence, the triumph of totalitarianism resides not in a few rotten apples, but in the common man's eagerness to deny difficult issues. It is a problem of carelessness, plain and simple, and in doing nothing—and in wanting to know nothing—we give power to the darkness.

---

[587] GEORGE ORWELL, *POLITICS AND THE ENGLISH LANGUAGE* (1946)

[588] ARENDT, *THE ORIGINS OF TOTALITARIANISM* (1966) 474

Indeed, it is the cowardice of man that has brought us into this mess. Without the psychological phenomenon of scapegoating and its mass appeal, war profiteers could not flourish. Without it, we would have had the sense to treat drug users as other consumers, and we would have steered away from the destruction of values on a near-cataclysmic scale. Even so, we keep forcing our will upon others without thinking of human rights and we accept lawlessness to govern our institutions. It does not take much to discover that this problem is worldwide. And as society did not learn the lessons from alcohol prohibition, it is difficult to conceive of a more prophetic outcome: In criminalizing products that have been a central part of human experience and tradition for millennia, we have not only provided jerks with the authority of law; we have legitimized arbitrary persecution and prepared for a dynamic where the drugs economy destroys all proper government. "Al Capone" runs the show.

11.1. The Failure of Law and Order

This may be harsh to imagine. Even so, let us not fool ourselves. The concept of law and order no longer makes any sense, and the drug laws have been key to the eradication of a more wholesome morality. One may object, but where is the righteousness of the prohibition quest? How can prohibitionists continue to spin a tale of good guys and bad guys? As we have seen, it is not possible to separate the drugs economy from other economies—its hypocrisy only comes with a more sinister side. Thus, DEA agents like Celerino Castillo have written books on how the DEA is colluding with murderous death squads who use drug laws as a means to frame political opposition and to maintain control.

The duplicity, however, is even more astonishing. As an example, DEA agent Hector Berrellez discovered how the CIA had murdered a DEA agent who did not accept the CIA's centralization of drug markets. In the traditional manner of deception, the torture and death of Enrique "Kiki" Camarena in 1985 became another atrocity that was attributed to the drug lords. His death was used by politicians to escalate the War on Drugs and Camarena retrospectively received the DEAs most esteemed award. He was even on the cover of Time Magazine, but it is difficult to envision the betrayal felt by drug warriors when they discover that the game is rigged.

For "Kiki", it was a tip for a 2,500-acre marijuana plantation called *Rancho Búfalo*, which was owned by Félix Gallardo, Rafael Caro Quintero, and Ernesto Fonseca Carrillo that got him into trouble. The CIA was deeply connected to this farm with an estimated annual production worth $8 billion, but "Kiki" did not care. Thus, after raiding the premises with 450 military men, Camarena was kidnapped to reveal what he knew; he was found one month later, bound, and mutilated in the trunk of a car. His skull, jaw, nose, cheekbones, and windpipe were crushed. His ribs were broken, and a hole had been bored into his skull with a power drill. Amphetamines and other drugs found in his toxicology report suggested that he was forced to remain conscious while being tortured.

Such is the hypocrisy of the drug war.[589] Another CIA contractor, Tosh Plumlee, went on FOX discussing this murder, and its due to such courageous individuals that we have any idea of the corruption of government. After all, government itself will attempt to hide rather than clarify any link between itself and organised crime. This fact alone attests to the power of the criminal enterprise and the corruption of government. We have already seen how bad it was in the 1980s, and things have not improved.

When it comes to more recent corruption, attorney Lin Wood has publicised testimony from an agent of Homeland Security who blows the whistle on Rod Rosenstein, recently retired US Deputy Attorney General, for being involved in the most heinous criminal activity. This network includes Chief Justice John Roberts, who is said to have procured two children from Jeffery Epstein. These are children that the good Judge adopted and who "have been through hell", being used as "gifts" or in schemes of blackmail. Indeed, Lin Woods whistleblower reveals how these people used drugs and child porn to

---

[589] For an excellent story on this murder, see Charles Bowden, *Blood on the Corn* (2014)

spin a network of control. He also informs us that Justice Scalia went to the White House because Roberts had teamed up with Hillary Clinton in a quest to kill off judges. The plan was for her to replace these judges after she won the 2016 election, but the White House would not help. Instead, Scalia was found dead on a ranch owned by John Poindexter of Iran Contra fame and while this level of cynicism may be astonishing, it is a tiny fraction of the problems we are dealing with.[590] After all, the hypocrisy and injustice that follow in the wake of the drug laws is global. We are dealing with evermore centralized patterns of corruption; it is like alcohol prohibition, only a million times worse, and with "enforcers" like this, no one is safe.

Hence, every honourable politician, gangster, banker, and enforcer of law should appreciate the bigger picture. They should respect the integrity of whistleblowers and realize that drug prohibition is a danger to the fabric of society. Recognizing the urgency, they should honour the constitution, abstain from siding with totalitarian principles, and work towards an effective remedy for the persecuted groups. In the interests of society, human rights analysis should be allowed, and truth and reconciliation commissions established. This will be the beginning of a new dawn, as society has been caught in an agonizing spiral, one devised by mechanisms of arbitrary law.

It takes its toll to recognize that we are dealing with its offspring, arbitrary persecution. We have been conditioned into thinking that this phenomenon only exists elsewhere, in third world countries. Nevertheless, the connection between moral panic, scapegoating, and human rights violations remains, and unwholesome laws can only encourage unwholesome values. It does not help that this is seldom understood by the policemen who are dedicated to a system of law and order. No one is served by a culture of needless violence, and cops are frustrated for having to enforce laws that make matters worse. This process has been going on for too long, and the riots of 2018-20 are a sign that events are coming to a head.

---

[590]   https://populist press/wp-content/uploads/2021/03/FULL-Transcript-of-Whistleblower-Interview.pdf

One could argue that the Black Lives Matter and Defund the Police movement represent a healthy opposition to a system that is built on injustice. Many do. In truth, however, our policemen have been betrayed by society. If only one of the many constitutional challenges against the drug laws that were made in the 1960s or 70s had been handled correctly by US courts,[591] the American society would have gone down a different route. Rather than developing into a vehicle for unwarranted incarceration and unjust oppression, the police would have gone on to pursue legitimate police work and they would not have continued to persecute drug users.

Only a system of double standards could maintain the demonization of the drug dealer and the victimization of the drug user. However, on such tales budgets were built. On such tales the enforces would construct their moral platform, and the drug free ideal would continue to guide their ways, justifying any collateral damage.

It is unfortunate that the system did not function and that drug users to this day have been denied an effective remedy. Even so, the harder this war is fought, the more obvious the solution becomes, and a day will come when drug producers are not demonized, nor drug users forced to buy their goods at a market where violence reigns and deceit flourishes. For nearly a century, these people have taken the brunt of our collective folly. And while drug users have been stigmatized, drug dealers have been the supreme culprits, arousing the greatest budgets and authoritarian powers.

In the fight against this perceived evil, society has gone haywire demanding ever greater retribution, when in truth drug dealers are the ultimate scapegoats: They are the ones that vast bureaucracies have preyed upon to justify increasing powers and budgets; they are the ones met with wrath for no good reason. Like in the ancient of days, we have left them outside the gates to be sacrificed by an obscure sense of justice.

This, of course, is taboo. Even so, if we are serious with our justice system, this is its worth. To look in the mirror, drug warriors, politicians, and justices twist the Law of supply and demand into one

---

[591] MIKALSEN, *CONSTITUTIONAL CHALLENGES TO THE DRUG LAW: A CASE STUDY* (2017)

of victim and oppressor—and we are not much better than the ancient Hebrews who offered a goat to create a sense of balance with the world. In fact, as a human's life is said to be of more value than an animal, one could argue that we have regressed. Modern man may not believe in spirits, but his worship of authority is more misplaced than ever. Moreover, our sense of justice has not increased by much, and the short-term winners are the politicians, enforcers, gangsters, and bankers who rely upon the drugs economy and the enemy image of drugs to go to work. These forces combine to play out a greater historical act. In the bigger picture, however, it is a game where everyone loses—except those who seek to arrest healthy progress.

We have seen too many examples of officials with an agenda of their own. A certain percentage of the populace will thrive on selfish schemes, and we cannot ignore that there remains a problem with corruption in government. Historically, the drug law is linked to control-oriented elites who put themselves above the law and it is an ideal tool for sinister intentions. In fact, the enemy image of drugs has been a beloved instrument for those who fancy systems of unjust oppression, and if only for this reason the prohibition law should be abolished. The Iran Contra affair speaks volumes, and as Seth Rich, a Democratic National Committee staffer more recently found out, gangsters and politicians have allied long ago. He was murdered by MS-13 gang members in 2016 after downloading incriminating evidence against Hillary Clinton. And if we continue to ignore the corruptive influence of drug prohibition, thinking that the law defines the proper boundaries between good guys and bad guys, the War on Drugs will continue its destructive course.

It should be noted that we are at that point where corruption can go no further without society openly giving up on the rule of law. It is plain to see that the ideology of prohibition has not only brought untold damage, but that society cannot much longer endure such authority. Because authority must build on deception or truth, false authority will have to use totalitarian means to preserve its powers, and the moral panic that comes with reliance on enemy images has brought our civilization to its knees. Not only have war profiteers taken control of government: The War on Drugs reached its logical conclusion in 2012 when U.S. government operations in Latin- and Central America were outsourced to Academi, the private military contractor formerly known as Blackwater. As its operatives are the modern equivalent of the contras, this could only mean a turn for the worse, as also these contractors have proven "too big to fail".

Having no business but war, however, a notable difference between Blackwater and JP Morgan is the former's willingness to truly play "the bad guy". Its mercenaries would be reviled by international forces in Afghanistan for shooting at anything that moved—and they only got away with their activities in Iraq and elsewhere after lead executives threatened to kill congressional investigators. Amazingly, the American embassy in Baghdad, which was filled with CIA- and contract personnel, sided with Blackwater against the State Department, its own nominal superior, in this affair.[592]

The balance of power, therefore, is not what it was. Since the days of the founders, there has been a shift towards tyranny, and while the Congress in the 1970's would make waves when illegalities was discovered, the weight of power has moved into the darkness where creeps are running the show. No doubt, times were more lenient to politicians when lobbyists used their purse rather than the stick to grease the wheels of Washington DC. Nevertheless, as fascism sooner or later comes home to roost, we should not be surprised that the campaigns against terror and drugs would end in ruin for Americans.

---

[592] LOFGREN, *THE DEEP STATE* (2016) 102

11.2. Accepting Unwholesome Premises

*"Everyone knows nowadays that people 'have complexes.'
What is not so well known, though far more important
theoretically, is that complexes can have us."*[593]

—Carl G. Jung—

We can argue what came first: the hen or the egg. However, only the scapegoating mechanism ensures the continuation of a War on Drugs, and the War on Terror is no different: they both build on lies, and their only effective function is to destroy what is left of a healthy society. Hence, whether these campaigns were promoted to serve despotic tendencies already inherent in the state, or these inherent tendencies ensured fertile grounds for lies to flourish is less important. What is more important is that the dark web which connects these dots would naturally gain a life of its own. Psychology, after all, begets policy, and so the military-industrial complex that President Eisenhower warned against before leaving office continued to increase in scope. The tension between constitutional ground and the powerplay of factions became ever more intolerable, and the assassinations of John F. Kennedy and his brother Robert (and their cover-ups) were symptoms of a malady on the body politic. They were evidence that vigilance had failed, and that the republic had become a tyranny. More war therefore followed, where the U.S military performed globally what the elites' personal hit men could only do locally. Criminal enterprises like the Bushes and the Clintons, who catered to the ambitions of globalist elites, became more powerful than mafia families. Their ties to drug cartels and human trafficking only became more blatant, but there were forces who opposed them.

As we have seen, General Fletcher Prouty, Kennedy's most trusted military man, was a pioneer to expose the operations of this cabal. Together with contemporary generals Michael Flynn, Paul

---

[593] C.G. Jung, *A Review of the Complex Theory* (1934)

Vallely, Thomas McInerney, and some 200 military leaders behind President Trump, he is part of a tradition that has known about the cancer that was praying on America and opposed its influence. Since the assassination of Kennedy, therefore, as the globalists' schemes and deceptions took an increasing toll, this tradition has fought to restore constitutional ground—as they see it. President Trump's "America First" policy is the result of this faction. According to insiders, it is a final stand against the City of London and its bankers who have sought to undermine the American experiment since day one.[594] The founders most certainly warned against their influence, and as even congressmen now are writing books about "the Deep State, the fall of the Constitution, and the rise of a shadow government,"[595] this stuff has finally passed the realm of conspiracy theory.

Indeed, with Trump in office, more and more are waking up to find that a neglect of first principles has made Congress subservient to assassins and child traffickers.[596] It is no coincidence that General Flynn's problems with the Deep State began when he tweeted about Pizzagate and wanted to review long-time misuse of public funds. His lawyer, Sidney Flynn, has fought with him and a historic battle is raging as we speak. It is of course not mentioned in the news. But to those who see past the fake media façade that has been set up to present Washington DC as a place of decency, she has become the nation's Joan of Arc. To this half of the population, conspiracy theory has become real with the stealing of the 2020 election. It is all out in

---

[594] JUAN O. SAVIN, *KID BY THE SIDE OF THE ROAD* (2020)

[595] Ibid.

[596] WikiLeaks published cables exposing that DynCorp, another contractor in the wars on drugs and terror, not only earned $2 billion per year in Afghanistan and Iraq, but that the company was involved in child trafficking. The same charges have been levied against the company in Latin America, as well as elsewhere. Regarding its operations in Bosnia, the whistleblower Kathryn Bolkovac a former employee, has told the story of how DynCorp was involved in human trafficking and forced prostitution of minors; her book documents these allegations, and yet DynCorp executives continue to define policy. KATHRYN BOLKOVAC, *THE WHISTLEBLOWER: SEX TRAFFICKING, MILITARY CONTRACTORS, AND ONE WOMAN'S FIGHT FOR JUSTICE* (2011)

the open.[597] A senile Joe Biden even bragged about being part of the "most extensive and inclusive voter fraud organization in the history of American politics", and the collective psychosis is a fascinating watch as the Democratic Party falls apart.

For the other half of the population, the prophecy of H.L. Mencken has come true. If we are to believe CNN, MSNBC, and other media outlets, the White House is now "adorned by a downright moron."[598] America has never been so divided, but the criticism aimed at the President is a clue that he may be a blessing in disguise. After all, the effort to do away with Trump is what we could expect if the network described in this book felt less secure. These people are used to controlling politics, but President Trump is no ordinary politician: he has no loyalty to Washington DC, which has been a den of corruption for centuries, and those who look at his accomplishments will see that he has done more to protect Americans than most other presidents.

Perhaps that is why he is so despised? Looking back, every politician who put the interests of the American people before the interests of the global elite have been subjected to harassment and evidence abounds that Democrats and the establishment media have joined forces. After all, Hillary Clinton and her crew are guilty of much worse crimes than they have tried to frame on Trump. She even paid for the Steele Dossier, which was used to begin investigations, and it is likely that she did so out of fear that Trump would put her in jail. As one can appreciate, there is much to hide. Patrick M. Byrne, former CEO of Overstock, for example, has gone public that he worked with FBI-agents in a sting to catch Hillary receiving bribes. He personally gave her $18 million, but the FBI did not pursue an investigation. Instead, President Obama and CIA Director John

---

[597] The Navarro Report by Dr Peter K. Navarro speaks volumes. So does the work of Judicial Watch, uncovering millions more votes than eligible voters.

[598] "As democracy is perfected, the office [of president] represents, more and more closely, the inner soul of the people. We move towards a lofty ideal. On some great and glorious day the plain folks of the land will reach their heart's desire at last, and the White House will be adorned by a downright moron." H.L. Mencken, Baltimore Sun, July 26, 1920

Brennan wanted to use this information to control her. This was "Operation Snowglobe", and the plan was to keep Hillary on a leash as president and to replace her with Michelle Obama. This little game of intrigue would be enough for Hillary to be afraid of Trump, but here is also the case of the 33.000 deleted emails on her private server, the Benghazi attack, and the fake Osama Bin laden operation that the FBIs Robert Mueller have shielded from exposure.

We may now appreciate why Washington DC, corrupt to its core, has tried to oust President Trump. To those who look behind the headlines, however, the so-called Russian collusion, the Mueller investigation, Ukrainegate, and the impeachment proceedings were charades to keep us distracted.[599] And while the news will not report on any of this, it is probably Trump's pledge to stop human trafficking that bothers elites the most. Annually, many thousands of children are abused in the United States.[600] Because such abuse has been prevalent in the elite circles, the system has protected such activity, but not anymore. Now, America has a president who (in the eyes of predatory elites) has gone rogue, and this very much explains the current panic. For those who look beyond appearances, therefore, there is a civil war, and if the faction behind Trump can rectify this wrong it will expose corrupt politicians, bureaucrats, industrialists, and other powerbrokers. It will be the beginning of a new dawn for America, one where the concept of human rights may be meaningfully applied—and it is only fitting that facing the evils of drug prohibition should follow.

Perhaps 50 years ago, some sort of innocence could be attributed to the prohibitionist quest, but those days are gone. Young people

---

[599] For more on this, see PATRICK M. BYRNE, *THE DEEP RIG: HOW ELECTION FRAUD COST DONALD J. TRUMP THE WHITE HOUSE, BY A MAN WHO DID NOT VOTE FOR HIM* (2021); DAN BONGINO, *SPYGATE: THE ATTEMPTED SABOTAGE OF DONALD J. TRUMP* (2018) and JEROME R. CORSI, *KILLING THE DEEP STATE* (2018). https://www.newswars.com/overstock-ceo-says-fbi-tapped-him-to-bribe-hillary-clinton-as-part-of-sting-operation-for-obama/

[600] For an exposure, see the International Tribunal of Natural Justice at www.itnj.org. Its Judicial Commission of Inquiry into Human Trafficking and Child Sex Abuse has carefully addressed this problem and it should no longer be ignored.

instinctively reject the propaganda of the state; with the internet, information is no longer controlled, and as the distance between theory and practice becomes more difficult to ignore, our leaders can no longer disregard that they have left constitutional ground. Their credibility, in fact, depends upon adjusting to reality: Nearly half the population are aware that there is something wrong with the management of our affairs, and those who dig will find that the War on Terror and the War on Drugs are both examples of the great big lie—that which rulers will advance, knowing that its impact will shock us into conformity.[601]

If it were not for these campaigns, humanity would have followed an inclination to thrive. As a society, we would have begun the movement towards a healthier expression of human potential, but our leaders have failed. Because our leaders have been a spineless bunch, they have boosted these enemy images to provide cover for the theft of rights and resources. Even so, these campaigns not only fail to make the world a safer place; they are what separates us from a more wholesome morality, and our leaders make matters worse by saluting these crusades. As we have seen, such shallowness can only undermine the authority of state—and so, unless politicians want a violent revolution, they should make way for change.

With or without them, humanity will find a solution. Based on what we have seen, it should be clear that the citizenry no longer can

---

[601] As Hitler would write on the principle of the Big lie: "in the big lie there is always a certain force of credibility; because the broad masses of a nation are always more easily corrupted in the deeper strata of their emotional nature than consciously or voluntarily; and thus in the primitive simplicity of their minds they more readily fall victims to the big lie than the small lie, since they themselves often tell small lies in little matters but would be ashamed to resort to large-scale falsehoods. It would never come into their heads to fabricate colossal untruths, and they would not believe that others could have the impudence to distort the truth so infamously. Even though the facts which prove this to be so may be brought clearly to their minds, they will still doubt and waver and will continue to think that there may be some other explanation. For the grossly impudent lie always leaves traces behind it, even after it has been nailed down, a fact which is known to all expert liars in this world and to all who conspire together in the art of lying." ADOLF HITLER, *MEIN KAMPF*, vol. I (1925) chapter X

afford to ignore the wealth of evidence linking public officials to criminal conspiracies, and as the consciousness of humanity aligns with the spirit of freedom there will come a time when we no longer accept double standards and hypocrisy as the norm. Instead, we will embrace a system of principled rule. We will build on the founders' vision to overcome the false right/left paradigm, and we will reap the benefits of the constitutional charter.

We have discussed this in part one and shall now have more to say on the legal implications.

Part 4
The Legal Perspective

12

THE RULE OF LAW

"There is a kind of reciprocity between government and the citizen with respect to the observance of rules. Government says to the citizen in effect, 'These are the rules we expect you to follow. If you follow them, you have our assurance that they are the rules that will be applied to your conduct.' When this bond of reciprocity is finally and completely ruptured by government, nothing is left on which to ground the citizen's duty to observe the rules."[602]

—Lon Fuller, Professor of Law—

WITH THE FRENCH and American revolution political principles were put in place to ensure that reason, not force, would be the rule of law. Since that day, our Constitution has provided the operative framework of government ensuring a legal framework for the greater morality to be applied. Even so, power politics and our demand for scapegoats ensured the continuation of moral panics, increasingly authoritarian states claimed sovereignty in decisions on morality and the founders' call for "a frequent recurrence to fundamental principles" was ignored.

This resulted in frequent confrontation. Self-absorbed elites effectively kept the Spirit of Freedom at bay, but after the horrors of World War II, a massive popular uprising ensured that human rights were put first on the UN agenda. Freshly reminded of the importance of keeping the subconscious in check, so that the dignity of the individual would not be violated by arbitrary state

---

[602] LON FULLER, *THE MORALITY OF LAW* (1969) 40

power, jurists would build on the American Constitution to create the Universal Declaration of Human Rights (UDHR) in 1948.

The Declaration was the first step in the process of formulating an International Bill of Human Rights, which was completed in 1966 and came into force in 1976, after enough countries had ratified. It would take the next 30 years for most UN member states to accept and put it into force. Even so, as we have seen, most officials suffer from an unconscious drift towards tyranny and even among those who take pride in having acted quickly, signing the UN human rights document was, at best, a gesture of good will. At worst, it was a ruse to have the citizenry believe that their leaders were committed to the rule of law, as reality proved otherwise.

Because world leaders had other desires than to serve humanity—or even their own people—the UN human rights apparatus received no legal status. All the UN Human Rights Committee could do was to recommend a solution, and it was easy for self-asserted sovereign nations to ignore its findings. As "sovereignty", according to the founders' philosophy, still rested with the individual, use of the term was itself more evidence of the unconscious drift from the principles of the Constitution.[603]

---

[603] The term "Sovereign State" is an oxymoron, for according to the founders' vision the only sovereign is *the individual*. The reason is that we are no longer organized from the top-down; beginning with the individual we are organized from the bottom-up, and from being all-powerful under the old system the modern state is a governing body consisting of civil servants whose function is (1) to secure the maximum amount of liberty to each and every person, and (2) to ensure a proper balancing of rights and duties so that the wheels of society operate optimally.

Now, there are scholars who do support the collective conception of popular sovereignty. They say that even though the Constitution explicitly mentions "the consent of the governed" as a prerequisite for legitimate governance, the ideal of individual consent is impossible to attain (being that no government can function should it have to have the expressed consent of every citizen every time it wanted something done). Thus, they reason that the Founding Fathers must have had the collective conception of popular sovereignty in mind as a basis for constitutional order. It does, after all, do outright tyranny one better, and so, in the absence of a possibility of ensuring unanimous consent, they reckon this is a compromise we must learn to live with.

The problem, of course, is that this is a compromise that invites despotism. If we accept the premise posited (that, somehow, the individual has consented to be governed by the will of the collective, and he/she cannot thereafter complain), then our leaders can get away with any action no matter how frightful. On the one hand, despotic regimes will justify their actions in the name of the common good, while democratic regimes can effectively persecute and/or exterminate any group as long as a majority remain too pitiless or complacent to care. Needless to say, this is not what the great minds of the Enlightenment

The term was simply stolen so that elites could bend the system to its will as governments in the 18th-, 19th-, and 20th century were taken over by control-oriented factions. Few intellectuals, however, noticed the deception,[604] and so the system continued its skewed course, preaching wholesome values, while those in power promoted regimes of arbitrary law to maintain a grip on populations.

12.1. Towards a Principled System of Justice

It is easy to see why world leaders wavered in affirmation of principled law. While its principles protect us from the yoke of despotism, a system of arbitrary law will bend any which way

Era had in mind when they articulated the principles upon which the new world order should be built. As we have seen, wrestling power away from such regimes was a prime concern of theirs, and in articulating a principle of popular sovereignty they sought to ensure that such regimes could never again claim legitimacy. A state claiming sovereignty, then, is no less absurd than an organization like the UN claiming world sovereignty, merely because states have joined dedicated to a common purpose.

[604] The formidable Natural law-scholar Lysander Spooner was a notable exception. In his *No Treason: The Constitution of No Authority* (1867), he points out the distance between theory and practice, how bankers control world-affairs, and continues: "Thus it is evident that all these men, who call themselves by the high-sounding names of Emperors, Kings, Sovereigns, Monarchs, Most Christian Majesties, Most Catholic Majesties, High Mightinesses, Most Serene and Potent Princes, and the like, and who claim to rule "by the grace of God," by "Divine Right,"—that is, by special authority from Heaven,—are intrinsically not only the merest miscreants and wretches, engaged solely in plundering, enslaving, and murdering their fellow men, but that they are also the merest hangers on, the servile, obsequious, fawning dependents and tools of these blood-money loan-mongers, on whom they rely for the means to carry on their crimes. These loan-mongers, like the Rothschilds, laugh in their sleeves, and say to themselves: These despicable creatures, who call themselves emperors, and kings, and majesties, and most serene and potent princes; who profess to wear crowns, and sit on thrones; who deck themselves with ribbons, and feathers, and jewels; and surround themselves with hired flatterers and lickspittles; and whom we suffer to strut around, and palm themselves off, upon fools and slaves, as sovereigns and lawgivers specially appointed by Almighty God; and to hold themselves out as the sole fountains of honors, and dignities, and wealth, and power,—all these miscreants and impostors know that we make them, and use them; that in us they live, move, and have their being; that we require them (as the price of their positions) to take upon themselves all the labor, all the danger, and all the odium of all the crimes they commit for our profit; and that we will unmake them, strip them of their gewgaws, and send them out into the world as beggars, or give them over to the vengeance of the people they have enslaved, the moment they refuse to commit any crime we require of them, or to pay over to us such share of the proceeds of their robberies as we see fit to demand."

power wants as there is nothing to anchor truth. Truth, in lawyers' terms, will always be connected to justice, which presumes a union between morality and law. Without this bond, the idea of justice becomes meaningless, and the authority of law suffers. Nevertheless, such a system is the only one to bridge the gap between theory and practice, and so it is the preferred solution.

Even so, failure to reason from first principles makes arbitrary law an easy target. To those not insane, the moral superiority of principled law is plain to see, and while the tension between these legal paradigms has been formative to the evolution of society, we see a gradual unfolding of reason.[605]

Our society has yet to ensure the supremacy of principled law. Instead, human culture represents much the same childlike state that we have seen in the centuries before. We are a nation of "adults" who fear the burden of personal responsibility and who therefore become intent on telling others what to do. However, there is a change in the winds, and recent drug political trends are a sign that more and more begin to value autonomy. This is a clue that the Spirit of Freedom is brewing, and because of its impact on human evolution, the influence of first principles has increased considerably. Excepting America, Europeans were the first to set up their own system of rights protection (the European Court of Human Rights). Since 1959, this model has become popularly embraced as a solution for the rest of the world, and most nations have constitutional courts where citizens can have their rights determined.

---

[605] The concept of rights has evolved as humanity has evolved. It is not only a sign of our growing understanding (and appreciation) of values that are at the very heart of the human experience; it embodies our journey from darkness into the light, for if history is a progressive unfolding of reason then the advancement of human rights is our greatest triumph. Psychologically speaking, it is a testimony of the extent to which we have tamed our fears and conquered our own unconsciousness; legally speaking, it is a moral compass out of our misery, and to the degree we respect each other's natural, inalienable rights a perfect world will come into being.

Now, these courts are not yet the impartial, independent, and competent arbiters that they promise to be.[606] In recent years, however, more and more constitutional courts are doing things right—and when it comes to the constitutionality of the drug law, they are coming down hard on the state.[607] This is another sign that the spirit of freedom is having an effect, as a citizenry who care about their autonomy will have officials that respond in kind. Systemwide, therefore, there is increasing dissonance between those who remain dedicated to psychosis and those who seek honest and working solutions, and a time draws near when those who put convenience before principle will not fare so well.

This is inevitable.[608] As humanity matures, the integrity of law strengthens; the legal system becomes less plagued by arbitrariness and power-political intrigues and aims to ensure conditions more resonant with the calibration of first principles. Translated to our age, we are in the final stages of this historical quest and the mission is simple: Because our constitutional system presents ten givens[609] which have been ignored by most states, we

---

[606] At the very least, in Canada, South Africa, Colombia, Mexico, Germany, Norway, and the United States, drug users have tried their luck, only to be met by a judiciary who thrive on the dictates of arbitrary law.

[607] As the South African Western Cape High Court concluded, March 31, 2017: "The evidence, holistically read together with the arguments presented to this court, suggests that the blunt instrument of the criminal law as employed in the impugned legislation is disproportionate to the harms that the legislation seeks to curb insofar as the personal use and consumption of cannabis is concerned. This conclusion is supported by the importance of the core component of the right to privacy and, further, by the cautious approach that must be taken to the evaluation of the criminalisation of cannabis which, as indicated earlier in this judgment, is certainly characterised by the racist footprints of a disgraceful past." *Prince v Minister of Justice and Constitutional Development and Others; Rubin v National Director of Public Prosecutions and Others; Acton and Others v National Director of Public Prosecutions and Others* (4153/2012) [2017] ZAWCHC 30; [2017] 2 All SA 864 (WCC); 2017 (4) SA 299 (WCC) (31 March 2017) [90]

[608] If this sounds harsh, consider that in representing this legal tradition lawyers are providing validity to all those destructive drives generated by tyrannical governments. Had they known better, they would have embraced principled reasoning, not opposed it, and by Constitutional standards they are guilty of treason. As the Spirit of Freedom is returning, therefore, our officials and magistrates should think twice before aligning themselves with the legal tradition that has brought so much suffering.

[609] The Virginia Declaration of Rights of June 1776 was the first Constitution to contain all ten essentials of modern constitutionalism. These are (1) sovereignty of the people; (2) universal principles; (3) human rights; (4) representative government; (5) the Constitution as paramount law; (6) separation of powers; (7) limited government; (8) responsibility and

must return to basics and a re-evaluation is inevitable. Only in readjusting the body of criminal law into conformity with first principles can Higher law work its magic, and drug prohibition is only one area of reform. It is, however, the most urgently called for. And no matter what future direction of our drug policies, they must be harmonious with fundamental human rights standards such as autonomy, dignity, proportionality, and equality. They must be effective ways of dealing with harms; they must be the least intrusive means available; and they must be evidence-based constructs that reasonable people can agree on. No one in their right mind will claim otherwise. And as doubts exist whether this is currently the case, constitutional courts must treat this issue with the utmost respect.

12.2. THE CONSTITUTION AND THE DRUG LAW

"Keeping faith with the constitutional spirit means interpreting individual rights liberally and enforcing them unflinchingly."[610]

—Louis D. Bilionis, Professor of Law—

To summarize the thinking behind our constitution, there are two basic moralities: one temporary morality, which is provided by earthly standards according to time and place, and one eternal morality from which a system of Higher law is built. Temporary morality more or less corresponds to the higher morality, but in times of moral panic there will be a dissonance that represents a constitutional violation.

---

accountability of government; (9) judicial independence and impartiality; and (10) the right of the people to reform or abolish their own government.

[610] Louis D. Bilionis, *On the Significance of Constitutional Spirit*, North Carolina Law Review Vol. 70:1803 (1992) 1824

This violation can be more or less severe. As seen from the perspective of Higher law, contemporary law will always be short of the ideal, but the more it departs, the worse are the constitutional implications. After all, the more it departs, the more people will be persecuted for no good reason, but due to the psychological/moral climate, this violation will not be recognized by the majority.

It is for this reason that the founders grounded rights in the individual and devised a test to ensure that rights were protected. Liberty demands a rational link between means and ends. This link must be verified, not merely imagined. And to put it shortly, if any citizen contests a prohibition law, the state must demonstrate that its regulation serves a compelling interest, that it is narrowly tailored to serve this interest, and that its objectives could not be met by relying on less restrictive means.

This test ensures a balancing of the rights of the individual versus the interests of society—and it is a principle of law and reason that the more a law infringes the basic right to liberty, the stronger the presumption against it, and the greater the justification required to vindicate its use. According to the culpability principle, criminal sanctions must be proportionate to each offender's blameworthiness. This principle is connected to the constitutional principles of dignity, autonomy, and liberty, and there is no need to look for an explicitly stated right to drugs for them to apply.[611]

As Judge Diarmuid F. O'Scannlain noted, "a discerning constitutional thinker must appreciate the extent to which the constitutional project quintessentially was an effort to codify pre-existing natural law rights."[612] These are first principles, and

---

[611] To quote Roger Errera, a professor of law: "There is no closed list of personality rights, nor is there any need for one. They have, however, a central purpose, a conceptual unity resulting from their common purpose: the protection of the person as such, of his or her integrity, identity, autonomy and dignity." European Commission for Democracy Through Law, *European and U.S. Constitutionalism*, Science and technique of democracy, No. 37 (2003) 35

[612] Hon. Diarmuid F. O'Scannlain, *The Natural Law in the American Tradition*, 79 Fordham Law Review (2011) 1528

numerous articles in every modern Constitution can be drawn upon to invalidate the drug law. Elsewhere, I have shown how this applies to the UN and the American Bill of Rights,[613] and for a law to be just (and therefore binding in conscience), its restrictions must be (1) necessary to protect the rights of others, and (2) proper insofar as they do not violate the pre-existing rights of the persons on whom they are imposed.[614]

While this may seem complicated, it is not. As Professor Douglas Husak noted, "punishments must be justified, and justified punishments must be deserved,"[615] and human rights law is there to ensure that this is the case. Thus, it starts from first principles and proceeds by means of logical argument, and the test of reason is simple.

---

[613] MIKALSEN, *TO END A WAR* (2015); MIKALSEN, *TO RIGHT A WRONG* (2016)

[614] See RANDY E. BARNETT, *RESTORING THE LOST CONSTITUTION: THE PRESUMPTION OF LIBERTY* (2003)

[615] Douglas Husak, *Applying Ultima Ratio: A Skeptical Assessment*, Ohio State Journal of Criminal Law, Vol. 2:535 (2005) 537

12.2.1. The Test of Reason Applied to the Drug Law

"The framers of the Constitution knew, and we should not forget today, that there is no more effective practical guarantee against arbitrary and unreasonable government than to require that the principles of law which officials would impose upon a minority must be imposed generally. Conversely, nothing opens the door to arbitrary action so effectively as to allow those officials to pick and choose only a few to whom they will apply legislation and thus to escape the political retribution that might be visited upon them if larger numbers were affected. Courts can take no better measure to assure that laws will be just than to require that laws be equal in operation."[616]

—Justice Jackson—

To understand how the criteria above invalidate the drug law, we must remember that the fundamental premise from which all else follows is that the individual is to have as much freedom, self-determination, and responsibility as possible. To justify any limitation on our freedom, therefore, officials must demonstrate that the law satisfies the test of legality, necessity, reasonableness, and legitimate purpose. To succeed in this quest, they must show that the separation between licit and illicit drugs makes sense and that they have good reasons for criminalizing illicit drug users. The government must prove that the harm it seeks to prevent is widespread or significant, and the liberty presumption is always to be considered. Hence, common sense dictates that if the harm is slight the government is entitled to little interference, and if the harm caused by the cure is worse than the disease, the government is entitled to no interference.

---

[616] *Railway Express Agency v. New York*, 336 U.S. 106 (1949) 112-13

The only way prohibitionists can deprive drug users of autonomy and liberty rights, therefore, is first demonstrating in specific fashion the precise nature of the problem. Having proved that drugs are the threat they allege, the government must show that the drug law is necessary to combat this threat; that it is effective in doing so; and that it at the same time preserves the interests of the individual and society. Among other measures, this means that the prohibition not only must be effective in curbing the supply and demand, but that it must be *the least intrusive instrument* amongst those which might achieve a protective function. All these criteria must be met, for only in doing so can prohibitionists demonstrate that the law strikes a fair balance between the rights of the individual and the interests of the community.

This is the essence of the test of reason. If the State fails to show that the drug law meets these criteria, we are dealing with an arbitrary, disproportionate, and discriminatory practice—and we have a violation of our catalogue of rights.

12.2.2. ACCEPTING PRINCIPLED REASONING

Now, as this test has been shunned by prohibitionists, it has been difficult to establish competent tribunals. Instead, moral panic has ensured the survival of taboos, and while there is much to suggest that a principled review would invalidate the drug law,[617] prohibitionists continue to evade the rule of law, taking for granted that their policies are compatible with human rights principles. Nevertheless. While this situation persists,

---

[617] See Barrett, Lines, Schleifer, Elliott, & Bewley-Taylor, *Recalibrating the regime: The Need for a Human Rights-based approach to International Drug Policy*, Beckley Foundation (2008); Bewley-Taylor, *Emerging Policy Contradictions between the United Nations Drug Control System and the Core Values of the United Nations*, International Journal of Drug Policy, 16(6) (2005) 423–431; Mena & Hobbs, *Narcophobia: Drugs Prohibition and the Generation of Human Rights Abuses*, Trends in Organised Crime, 13(1) (2010) 60 74; MIKALSEN, *TO END A WAR* (2015); MIKALSEN, *TO RIGHT A WRONG* (2016)

prohibitionist reasoning is refuted by reality as well as experts on law,[618] and evidence abound that they ought to know better.

After a century of embracing the prohibitionist crusade, we have learned (1) that whether we are talking about licit or illicit drugs, there is the same law of supply and demand in effect and the same varying patterns of use; (2) that alcohol and tobacco, each in their own way, are the worst of all drugs (3) that the criminalization has little to no influence on the user population; (4) that the problems generated by prohibition (organized crime, corruption, violence, disease, deaths by overdose, etc.) are worse than the problems caused by the drugs; and (5) that a health-oriented approach, like the one we have for alcohol, is a much more sensible solution.

In other words, as we have wised up, we have learned that the idea of prohibition is built on faulty premises, prejudices that can be traced back to an overblown enemy image and the impact of moral panic. Indeed, there is not even an agreement what "dependency" means,[619] and when we consider that the separation between licit and illicit drugs is nonsensical and that less invasive—and more prudent—means than the law-and-order approach are available, we have a sound basis for arguing that today's policy is incompatible with key human rights standards.

After all, the equality principle protects against discriminatory practices, while the proportionality principle defines criteria that all laws must comply with to be compatible with our catalogue of rights. And as most experts on drug policy agree that the separation between licit and illicit drugs makes no sense, and that

---

[618] In *Drug control, Crime prevention and Criminal Justice: A human Rights Perspective Note by the Executive Director* (2010), Antonio Maria Costa argues that drug prohibition has no problem with human rights. Professor Damon Barrett disputes his reasoning in Barrett, *Security, Development and Human rights: Normative, Legal and Policy Challenges for the International Drug Control System*, International Journal of Drug Policy, 21(3) (2010) 140–144.

[619] "But in fact, today as in the past, even medical authorities have not been able to agree on what drug dependence is. In one recent collection of essays on the subject, twelve psychological theories, eight biological theories, twelve sociological theories, and fifteen mixed theories are offered, all with at least some claim to respectability." BAKALAR & GRINSPOON, *DRUG CONTROL IN A FREE SOCIETY* (1998) 36; see also Dan Lettieri et al., *Theories on Drug Abuse*, NIDA Research Monograph 30, 1980

a health-oriented approach—like the one we grant to the users of alcohol and tobacco—is a much more sensible solution to the drug problem, it seems clear that we are dealing with a violation of the equality principle. Furthermore, because these policy analysts also agree that drug prohibition can never achieve its goal of a drug-free world; that there are less invasive means available, more fit to minimize the harms caused by drug use; and that the harms associated with prohibition far outweigh the harms caused by drug use, it seems clear that drug prohibition is incompatible with the principle of proportionality. This being so, we can conclude that we are dealing with a human rights violation.

Prohibitionists, predictably, will disagree. As we have seen, they build their analyses from the opposite set of premises (totalitarian) and believe that there are good reasons for treating drug users and alcohol users differently. Be that as it may. They are free to prove the superiority of their policy to an independent, impartial, and competent commission—and with all the critique that prohibition has got from the human rights community, they would welcome the opportunity. They simply cannot continue their policies without responding to these allegations—and before going to court, there are questions to consider.

12.2.3. QUESTIONS IN NEED OF ANSWERING

"Possession offenses are wolves in sheep's skin, highly efficient instruments of oppression and discrimination that have been camouflaged as run-of-the-mill criminal offenses, and thereby protected against legal challenges and shielded from public scrutiny."[620]

—Markus D. Dubber, Professor of Law—

With Resolution 57/5, the CND promised to take all measures to ensure an adequate, inclusive, and effective preparatory process for the UNGASS meeting. The UN drug warriors asked the General Assembly to reaffirm that, at this special session on the world drug problem, it would "address substantive issues on the basis of the principle of common and shared responsibility and in full conformity with the purposes and principles of the Charter of the United Nations, international law and the Universal Declaration of Human Rights," and while this can only be done by giving the problematic relationship between drug prohibition and human rights law full attention, the issue ended up being ignored.

This, of course, does not change the fact that officials at the UN and elsewhere have an obligation to ensure that drug users' rights are protected. And to those people interested, important questions are: What exactly is the drug problem? What part of it is prohibition related and what part is pharmacologically related? What is the historical origin of drug prohibition? Is it the result of a proper political process? Did officials back then listen to expert advice and build their policy on facts or could it be the result of a moral panic, brought into being by prejudice and self-serving agendas? What effect has prohibition had on the supply and demand of illicit drugs? Has it proven efficient, or are there fatal

---

[620] Markus D. Dubber, *Policing Possession: The War on Crime and the End of Criminal Law*, The Journal of Criminal Law and Criminology Vol. 91:4 (2001) 918

flaws in the strategy that cannot be amended? To what extent has the drugs economy corrupted our social order? Are the good guys and the bad guys clearly defined groups, or has the illicit economy corrupted society to the point where entire governments are in on it? If so, how realistic is the goal of winning the War on Drugs? Is this war effort necessary, or are there alternatives to prohibition, less intrusive and more efficient at protecting the health and welfare of mankind? Last but not least, how does our catalogue of rights compare to this picture?

So far prohibitionists have not been willing to look into such questions. To this day, they have embraced a policy of fear without giving any consideration as to whether their fear is misplaced—and to maintain a punitive policy, they have ignored all evidence of its failure. We see this clearly in the UN drug control machinery. Rather than objectively evaluating what the problem is, the workings of this machinery have been skewed and biased in favour of the prohibition ideology and its terminology has never admitted to any positive benefits deriving from drug use. On the contrary, to justify a War on Drugs and the goal of a drug-free world, the negative dimensions of drug use have been its sole focus and the message has been that the consumption of illicit drugs (unlike alcohol) is always problematic and must never become accepted as a way of life.

Nevertheless, the drug control conventions establish that all nation's drug laws must be "subject to its constitutional principles and the basic concepts of its legal system."[621] And if prohibition is to remain policy, the task before prohibitionists is to show that the drug war is compatible with a system of principled law. Some of the questions raised by the rights-oriented debate are discussed above, but there are a few more to reflect upon. The evidence, of course, is different depending upon what kind of substance is to be discussed. Nonetheless, the objections from a principled

---

[621] Article 3 (2) of the United Nations Convention against Illicit Traffic in Narcotic Drugs and Psychotropic Substances, 1988.

perspective are the same, and using cannabis as an example can be stated accordingly:

• Whereas all comparisons of the problems associated with cannabis and legal drugs such as alcohol and tobacco demonstrate that the legal ones are more harmful to users' health and more destructive to us as a society, how will you defend the present policies? How can you, without basing your drug policy on a discriminatory practice—and thus violating the principle of equality—argue in favor of a health-oriented approach toward alcohol users and a continued criminalisation of cannabis users?

• Whereas the same supply and demand factors are involved when it comes to cannabis and other drugs such as alcohol and tobacco, and whereas the different groups of drugs also have the same varying patterns of use associated with them, how will you justify the persecution and the demonisation of the drug law violators? What sort of crimes against his fellowmen has a cannabis producer, transporter or seller committed that an alcohol producer, transporter or seller has not?

• Whereas virtually all of the world's leading drug policy scholars agree that the drug laws have had worse consequences for society in general and users in particular than the drug use itself would have had, and whereas more and more organisations and commissions publish reports that confirm the same, how will you, from the growing evidence base that suggests that the cure (cannabis prohibition) is worse than the disease (cannabis use) defend current policies as measured against the principle of proportionality?

• Whereas a majority of drug policy experts agree that there was a moral panic behind the outlawing of cannabis, whereas these professionals acknowledge that its current classification makes no sense, whereas scholarly works such as James Ostrowski's Answering the Critics of Drug Legalisation, Douglas Husak's

Drugs and Rights, and David A.J. Richards' Sex, Drugs, Death, and the Law have thoroughly refuted the traditional arguments in favour of criminalisation, whereas an independent, impartial and competent tribunal (the Cannabis-tribunal in the Hague, 2008) has already qualified the prohibitionist argument as "based on fallacies" and "absolutely worthless", and whereas the drug laws thus seem to build their credibility on a series of faulty premises; Considering the fact that the enemy image of cannabis has proven to be vastly exaggerated, considering that the separation between the licit and illicit substances has proven an arbitrary divide, considering that the evidence is increasingly clear that the drug laws have failed in reducing their supply and demand, considering that American, as well as European decriminalisation experiments have shown a health-oriented approach to be more successful in dealing with the harms caused by drug use, considering that the cure has proven worse than the disease to the degree that the harms caused by prohibition now have become so enormous that they threaten to undermine the very fabric of our society, considering that paternalistic and moralistic arguments have failed, and considering that you can no longer justify prohibition on the basis that (1) it suppresses different types of crime, (2) that it protects our youth and the well-being of society, (3) that drug abuse has substantial economic and social costs, (4) that cannabis use is intrinsically immoral and degrading in nature, (5) that its use is self-destructive and dangerous and may cause a variety of harms, including physical injury, addiction and death, (6) that it is a gateway drug, (7) that its use is not a victimless crime since it causes harm to others, and (8) that we do not know the consequences of legalisation; all this considered, what compelling reasons can there be for prohibition, and in what way are its means tailored towards its explicitly stated ends?[622]

---

[622] Source references and documentation for all these allegations are found in MIKALSEN, *TO END A WAR* (2015)

When it comes to cannabis, such questions indicate the difficulties posed by the rights-oriented debate. If drug prohibition is compatible with human rights, it should be easy to answer, but none have stepped to the challenge. To the contrary, world leaders have ducked these questions for years and the UN censored them from the UNGASS 2016 preparatory process. AROD, the organization who were pursuing these questions, had attempted to get an answer from the Norwegian government for nearly a decade; four ministers of justice had ignored repeated calls and threats of constitutional responsibility, but to no avail.

While the rule of law demands an answer, authority refuses to oblige. Instead, our leaders continue to use the law as an excuse to continue the mistakes of old, and some—like the Norwegian Attorney General—have written to suggest that drug law violators are exempt from human rights. This, of course, is merely tyranny revealing its head, and those among our civil servants who wish to continue this trend must invalidate this chain of reasoning by answering the following question:

• Whereas the fundamental principle from which our system of law follows is that the individual is to have as much freedom, responsibility and self-determination as absolutely possible (that is, as compatible with a similar right and freedom of others); whereas to whatever degree our rights and freedoms shall be restricted weighty societal considerations must necessitate such actions (that is, they must be required for the protection of the general welfare and the purpose of securing due recognition and respect for the rights and freedoms of others); whereas the purpose of human rights law is to see to it that this is so and to protect the individual from undue, unjust and arbitrary interferences; whereas at the core of the human rights conventions we therefore find certain legal principles derived from the Wholeness concept, mirrored in all humanitarian values, and bringing together constitutional law, social contractarian thought and moral theory; whereas the articles of the conventions are the result of these principles and established to promote them so that their light can shine forth as we mature as a society towards greater levels of understanding; whereas these conventions thus are established to ensure to all people, without distinction of any kind, protection against discriminatory, unjust, arbitrary and disproportional practices; whereas this obviously includes the world's 200–300 million drug users, and whereas the objective of human rights law therefore is to secure also to them the rights and protections recognised in the human rights conventions; Considering that you undertake to strive for the advancement and observance of the rights and protections recognised in these conventions; considering that the principles you have a duty to promote and protect establish certain criteria that our system of law must be in accordance with in order to be lawful; considering that the abolitionists have assembled overwhelming evidence that the drug laws, as measured against these criteria, are found wanting; considering that these laws' societal function and consequence has been so devastating that they fulfil the criteria as gross human rights violations and crimes against humanity; considering that the abolitionists have presented documentation that legal scholars and drug policy experts around the world have concluded the same and that former officials of such stature as UN Secretary General and High Commissioner for Human Rights are among the people who have attested to this factual picture; considering that you have been presented with four questions that must be answered to the satisfaction of an independent, impartial and competent tribunal if these scholars' and experts' conclusions are to be refuted; considering that the prohibitionist regime has never been submitted to the test of reason and that our officials hitherto have refused to respond to these questions; considering that the rule of law demands that they be answered, but that every official so far confronted with the matter has flouted his duties and denied us our right to an effective remedy; considering that up to 300 million drug users therefore are without the protection of human rights law and considering that the validity of the social contract and your credibility as civil servants now depends on the degree to which you take the promotion and observance of human rights law seriously; considering that your responsibility not only to the world's drug users but also to humanity at large, the rule of law and the human rights conventions you have a duty to protect and promote is clear; considering that objectively speaking there is no doubt that the abolitionists' concerns are valid and that to protect the integrity of the principles at the heart of the conventions you therefore need to see to it that human rights law rules supreme, that the matter is properly reviewed, and that these questions are satisfactorily answered; considering that if you fail to do so without adequately addressing the issues raised herein—that is, explaining wherein this chain of reasoning you disagree and/or what more corroboration we need to substantiate our contentions—it will become evident that your opposition to drug reform is blind, that it is motivated by ignorance and ignoble ambitions and that you are misusing your authority in an attempt to arrest the development of human rights rather than advancing it; considering that in doing so you are, in effect, an enemy of all things good and decent, standing shoulder to shoulder with gangsters and war profiteers against the rule of law and the interests of the human race, and that you rightfully can be persecuted as a wilful participant in crimes against humanity; All this considered, how will you explain your reasons for maintaining that the principles of human rights law do not apply to our drug laws? How will you explain your position and your rationale that the drug users somehow are exempt from a catalogue of rights that is inherent to every human being and that we are all supposed to enjoy?

Today, this is the challenge facing prohibitionists. Hence, any civil servant in the UN or elsewhere who insist upon maintaining the status quo, must confront the rights-oriented debate and answer these questions to the satisfaction of an independent, impartial, and competent tribunal. The importance that they do cannot be overstated. The rule of law necessitates a response—and, legally speaking, prohibitionists cannot continue to ignore these questions without taking part in crimes against humanity.

13

CHASING THE SCREAM

"Transforming ordinary productive citizens into criminals, for conduct having less measurable harm than tolerated conduct, is a sign of religious zealotry rather than public welfare. In that context, drug laws become a metaphor for pretensions of personal virtue and their repeal a metaphor for confessing the sin of pride. That is one reason anti-drug militants resist legalization; the act would confess error and thereby hinder pride, particularly painful for government officials who have brutalized drug-using citizens for so long. But we are all sinners, and guilt need not be shame unless error persists after it has been recognized."[623]

—Richard Lawrence Miller—

AS WE HAVE seen, there is no doubt that the drug law fails to meet the test of reason.[624] The implications for our system of law is vast, as this not only means that the state is obliged to stop persecuting drug law violators; it means that every person under correctional control for such violation is suffering arbitrary imprisonment and that society has a duty to ensure their release and appropriate compensation.

Hence, it does not take much to see that the refusal to deal with the rights-oriented debate stems from a psychological incentive to ignore reality. As even an apology is too much to ask

---

[623] MILLER, *THE CASE FOR LEGALIZING DRUGS* (1991) 126

[624] The fact that leading UN officials such as Antonio Maria Costa has compared the legalization of drugs to the legalization of pedophilia, human trafficking, and arms smuggling speaks volumes about the perceived drug threat and the flawed reasoning behind the drug war.

from prohibitionists, thinking in terms of restitution seems abhorrent. It is as if the drug dealers—assisted by some legal loophole—found a way to scam their way out of wrath's way. Even so, as seen from the perspective of the greater morality, these violators have been unjustly persecuted by bigots and hypocrites, people who ought to know better, and the prohibitionists should consider themselves lucky to evade prison or vigilante justice.

However, the idea that prohibitionists have been part of one of history's greatest atrocities is difficult to ponder, and it is more comfortable to abide by a fake morality. Most likely, this is why drug users so often have been denied their day in court, while drug dealers are not taken seriously at all when they claim a rights violation. To this day, a collective psychosis has ensured that the disconnect between first principles and contemporary law has not been seen nor understood and despite more and more professors of law calling for the constitutionalization of criminal law,[625] our systems of justice continue to stall progress by demonizing drug users and fabricating reality.

---

[625] Markus D. Dubber, *Toward a Constitutional Law of Crime and Punishment*, Hastings Law Journal Vol. 55 (2004) 45; Sanford H. Kadish, *Fifty Years of Criminal Law: An Opinionated Review*, California Law Review Vol. 87:943 (1999); Claire Finkelstein, *Positivism and the Notion of an Offense*, California Law Review Vol. 88:335 (2000); Michal Buchhandler-Raphael, *Drugs, Dignity, and Danger: Human Dignity as a Constitutional Constraint to Limit Overcriminalization* (2012) 293 ("the broken criminal justice system is in tension with one of the fundamental principles of American constitutional jurisprudence, namely, constitutional protection of individual liberties and freedom from government intrusion into the private lives of individuals.")

13.1. An Orwellian Society

"The goal of nipping every potential threat in the bud, combined with the impossibility of its achievement, sets in motion a continuing expansion of preventive measures, an infinite regress along the causal chain toward the origin of threats, the heart of darkness."[626]

—Markus Dubber, Professor of Law—

The parallels to the Orwellian society are apparent. After all, while the actors and the details vary, the overall plot remains the same; (1) we have the war profiteers, those in power with a vested interest in expanding the powers of government; (2) we have lies, incoherent deceivings, and oversized enemy images that is used to take away civil liberties; (3) we have a massive propaganda apparatus that repeats the war profiteers' lies, prejudices, and misconceptions as if they were God's honest truth; (4) we have a demonized outgroup who must bear the brunt of society's neglect; (5) we have a bureaucratic thrust which ensures that the campaign of oppression will run its course no matter how detrimental its consequences and no matter how defective its reasoning; (6) we have a populace without sufficient integrity to think for themselves, who conform to group pressure and let fear poison their minds; and (7) we have a collective psychosis so powerful that logic and reason is turned on its head.

No matter time and place, these are the ingredients in any of the major afflictions that have befallen humanity. As Orwell noted, persisting in such delusion "necessitates an unending series of victories over our own reason", and so a certain amount of energy will be spent to cover up the obvious. At the state level, therefore, totalitarian tactics will be used to maintain the balance of power, while at the personal level defence mechanisms such as

---

[626] Markus D. Dubber, *Policing Possession: The War on Crime and the End of Criminal Law*, The Journal of Criminal Law and Criminology Vol. 91:4 (2001) 842

projection and denial make it possible to ignore the obvious. Thus, fear grips society, and to the extent that panic prevails those who tell the truth will be ignored, hated, persecuted, or killed. In this way a psychosis is preserved, rooting out integrity wherever it is found, and this dynamic has not changed.

As people are blinded by the morality of their day, humanity has continuously been troubled by the psychology of fear, and our love for scapegoats has ensured that the dream of utopian societies has remained at a distance. Because people want to bridge this gap there will always be those who think that the ends justify the means, not knowing that the means are everything and that the psychology of fear is the problem to begin with. Neglecting this bit, (and the larger framework of which it is part) the human ego has continued its historical rampage, blind to the error of its ways. Prohibition, in these terms, is part of a greater heritage. And while immature minds will want to place the blame elsewhere, on some outside agent in the form of a demonic entity or tyrannical ruler, the truth is that none of our collective hardships would have been possible without the state of unconsciousness that we have welcomed as a release from the burden of autonomy and responsibility.[627]

The fact that humanity is moved by unconsciousness rather than consciousness may be odd to consider. But there it is. Plain to see behind our collective mantra of "freedom for all" is the reality that we do not really want this freedom; that we fear it and its implications. We may salute the ideal of autonomous living, of integrity and responsibility, but the status quo is a more honest mirror. In this regard, a look reveals the same collective pattern of denial that has afflicted humanity in the centuries before—and while a majority of the population, true to their childish ways, will want to blame their leaders, their neighbour, or someone else, the

---

[627] The German psychologist Wilhelm Reich was a keen observer of this dynamic when he observed that rulers like Hitler or Stalin "were only instruments of circumstances." (REICH, *THE MASS PSYCHOLOGY OF FASCISM* (1970) 260) Before the war, with a perception lesser minds would chastise, he pointed out that the success of tyrannical movements like fascism depended "in its pure form [on] the sum total of all the irrational reactions of the average human character." Ibid., xiv.

truth is that we are all to blame. Some more and some less, but the shape of society will be a direct reflection of our average consciousness and we are all responsible for the status quo. Indeed, only our moral lethargy makes the status quo bearable. And if we had understood what Martin Luther King meant when he said that "each man's death diminishes me, because I am involved with mankind", we surely would have recognized the link between the founders' and the prophets' mission, and why integrity—to them—came so easily.

14

REALIZING THE CONSTITUTION

"The whole art of government consists in the art of being honest"[628]

—Thomas Jefferson—

SOCIAL ENGINEERS KNOW that the collective consciousness—i.e., the Nation's psyche—will determine the quality of the social fabric and that there is a correlation between individual integrity, constitutional principles, and state power. They also know that because of this, a people will get exactly the kind of politicians they deserve.

It is, after all, inconceivable that a policy like prohibition would have been allowed to thrive with so much destructive power if it were not for the dynamics between the individual and the state: Of course, the ideology of prohibition, with its promise of budgets, powers, prestige, profits, and eternal warfare would appeal to agents of tyranny. It provided another opportunity to rob the individual of control, and to the extent that officials could exalt the enemy image of drugs their lust for power would be satisfied.

Being a boon to agents of state, we can appreciate why the drug laws have endured to this day unrestrained by checks and balances.[629] In looking at policy from a perspective of self-

---

[628] Thomas Jefferson, *A Summary View of the Rights of British America*, 1774

[629] As Miller noted: "A goal that cannot be achieved, progress that cannot be measured, results for which no one can be held accountable, and billions of dollars to be gained from the whole thing. Such is the strategy that produces more and more drug warriors. Awesome power is wielded by individuals and institutions who would feel harm if the drug problem diminished, who gain by perpetuating policies that strengthen the illicit drug trade." MILLER, *THE CASE FOR LEGALIZING DRUGS* (1991) 107

preservation, however, it is more difficult to understand why we, the public, have found it so appealing. After all, we have grown accustomed to dealing with substances such as alcohol, coffee, sugar, and tobacco without resorting to violence and there is no reason to believe that regulating other substances will make life worse.

In fact, evidence—and reason—suggest the opposite. As seen, policies derived from a morality of love are not only better than those provided by fear but, to the extent that we fall prey to the enemy image of drugs, society will perish in a nightmare of its own making. It is difficult, then, to see why we so willingly have given away our freedoms in exchange for promises of security. Looking at issues of drug policy, an open and reflective mind would quickly have deduced the implications of abiding by any other ethics than that of our Constitution and so, to comprehend the popularity of the prohibition quest, we must look to unconscious factors such as projection and denial. Only these defence mechanisms can explain why we, as a society, have come to accept politicians that put the interests of gangsters and war-profiteers above those of the community; why policemen continue to justify transgressions against fellow citizens; and why parents will report their children's drug habits to authorities, thinking it for their own good.

As seen from the greater perspective, the story of prohibition is merely another testimony of the extent to which irrational fear can make society attack itself, and it is only because of the trauma that comes with being born into lesser-ordered societies that we do not recognize the greater morality of the prophets and the implications of first principles as one. Psychologists, however, recognize that our consciousness spans from a kind of God-like, loving, and all-connected state to the psychosis of fearful, self-serving egos that we know so well. Psychological health is connected to the former while psychological disease is connected to the latter—and psychological growth, the release of trauma, indicates a leap in consciousness where the ego, powered by love, overcomes previously limiting, false, and disserving beliefs.

In a very real sense, such events represent a healing of trauma on the personal and collective level. This is because our identity is deeply entwined with our morality and we cannot thrive in a world where our moral code is confused by cultural prejudice. When a moral panic has engulfed society, our deeper morality, that which sees the world as whole and humanity as one, is broken into one that resonates with the enemy image and those who persecute others believe that they are doing it for the right reasons. With time, they will find that they are not. However, as long as the law is in place, it will infect and corrupt our minds into committing and accepting atrocities, and this creates shame. This shame is, at first, not consciously admitted. Even so, our denial of reality makes us as individuals and society much less than we can be—and because this little detail will continue to bug us until we find the courage to act on the information, a mechanism is in place to ensure that, sooner or later, most people will begin to think about things.

It may be a depression, a psychosis, a jail cell, corruption at the workplace, or something else. What is certain is that the symptoms of living in unjustly ordered societies create psychological as well as political problems, and to overcome these problems we need to expand our understanding. Now, in times of moral panic, the only way to do this is a willingness to question authority and well-established public sympathies. As we find the courage to do so, we build integrity; we gain a better understanding of our place in the world, and this redirects our attention towards constitutional values.

As seen from a mystic's perspective, therefore, the Constitution was a manuscript whose potential would become unleashed over a period of time. It represented our inherent potential, and being intimately connected with the power of love, it would take centuries before the collective consciousness had matured to the point where we could consciously draw upon its powers. For that to happen, we would first have to work through our issues collectively. The level of culturally induced fear would have to be recalibrated so that the ego could readjust to a greater reality, *and then*, when the citizenry cared sufficiently about right and wrong to ensure a kingdom of compassion, reason would have its day. We would finally cohabit in peaceful and autonomy-enriching societies where community spirit prevailed and where the dynamics between the individual and the whole ensured an ever-grander vision of what it means to be alive on God's green earth.

To the founders, much the same thinking was in vogue. They knew that while the morality of the Constitution was built on a foundation of love, integrity was needed to connect—and the world was short on both. Hence, contemporary morality resulted in a lesser state of affairs, one where collective prejudice and irrational fears defined the limits of social interaction. This lesser state of affairs was reflected in our structure. Hierarchical, control-, and competition-oriented societies resulted from less-than-wholesome belief structures, but as humanity wised up the founders expected a better world. The principles of the Constitution, derived from the Wholeness, would recalibrate dysfunctional practices into ever more functional policies and to the extent that humanity abided by their implications, we would experience the bliss of utopian societies.

Now, we have seen how our morality is influenced by enemy images and the similarities between drug prohibition and earlier moral panics are laid bare. Studying the much-ignored connection between psychology and politics, we have found that the condition of society, at any given point, will mirror the collective mind, and just as there is a connection between the psychology of fear, trauma, the rise of moral panics, and totalitarian government, we have unearthed a connection between the psychology of love, healthy cognitive functioning, well-ordered government, and utopian societies.

On the political spectrum, therefore, autonomy and tyranny are mutually exclusive polarities—and while the power of love is connected to the morality of the Constitution, the power of fear makes us abide by a lesser standard. Around and around this circle goes: from moral panic to moral panic, from personal crisis to personal crisis. But when the collective consciousness has matured to the point where the level of integrity is sufficient, the founders and the prophets knew that we would begin to organize according to the dictates of reason rather than passion. That was the thinking behind the Constitution. In the utopian land of the founders, the social contract would be respected, and people would live as free folks in a society that abided by constitutional principles. This would ensure a collective effort to see its values realized to the greatest extent—and this would result in the flourishing of human potential in all its diversity. That was the promise of the Constitution: Utopian societies, once we would care sufficiently about the rule of law to deduce its implications.

The comparison between the founders and the prophets, then, should be recognized: They more than anyone were representatives of that deeper force, the Spirit of Freedom, which unwearyingly were working upon humanity, honing it for consciousness to establish at a higher, more evolved foothold. As seen from this view, the spirit of the 1960's was just a contraction associated with the birth of something much bigger, and the coming revolution will be of biblical proportions. As a matter of fact, millions of people around the world have now attained states of consciousness similar to those which paved the way for organized religion. This book is just one of the many signs that a change is in the air and those who pay attention have every opportunity to see the unfolding of scriptural events.

Not only have sizable portions of humanity begun the process that makes the old consciousness more aligned with the underlying fabric of the cosmos, but the Spirit of Freedom is growing strong within them. Those who care to study these things, therefore, will find that globally a new consciousness is on the rise, and as soon as society wises up to the point where citizens stop looking to the authorities of old to save us from self-inflicted wounds, there will be the long foretold "second coming"—only this time it will not be Jesus.

This great prophet was there to elevate the vision of humanity into something loftier than the vindictive Old Testament God. In showing what love at its most powerful—unconditional—could do, his shining example set a new standard, one for others to attempt, but there was nothing he could do to make rulers submit to a higher reason. Instead, many centuries of pain and suffering would pass before the collective psyche had matured to the point where government pledged to respect the demands of a more wholesome ethics—but they hardly knew what this ethics was.

Indeed, while organized religion was born out of mystical experience, the world proved too infected with fear and prejudice for the greater lessons to be grasped. Organized religion, like the rest of society's power-centres, would end up in the hands of authorities who wished always to be considered authorities. No matter the fallacies upon which their power rested, representatives of the old system would not gleefully empower the lower classes, and as soon as the French and American revolution ended, those in power would demolish their charters of liberty. Thus, while the founders took humanity one step further by having government formally submit to a principled rule, the world would continue askew and God's Kingdom would be just out of reach until humanity en masse was ready to transform.

14.1. THE SECRET DOCTRINE REVEALED

"Fortunately, some are born with spiritual immune systems that sooner or later give rejection to the illusory worldview grafted upon them from birth through social conditioning. They begin sensing that something is amiss, and start looking for answers. Inner knowledge and anomalous outer experiences show them a side of reality others are oblivious to, and so begins their journey of awakening. Each step of the journey is made by following the heart instead of following the crowd and by choosing knowledge over the veils of ignorance."[630]

—Henri Bergson, Philosopher—

According to the founders' line of reasoning, humanity is guided by a Higher law which not only defines the limits of government but the proper expression of human interaction—and as law and morality is eternally bound, it should come as no surprise that the Higher law of the Constitution and the Eternal morality of religion are one and the same.

The principles of the founding were the political equivalent of mystical insight[631] and spiritually, the message of Jesus, Buddha, Mohammed, and the idols of religion was derived from the same enlightened intuition. In short, they represented autonomous living, the idea of taking responsibility for creation and learning to tell the difference between the turmoil inside and outside so that a greater perspective could be found, one that transcended the play of duality. In following the implications of Wholeness and

---

[630] HENRI BERGSON, *ON INTUITION VS. INTELLECT* (1907)

[631] As Alexander Hamilton noted the source of fundamental rights: "[T]he sacred rights of mankind are not to be rummaged for among old parchments or musty records. They are written as with a sunbeam, in the whole volume of human nature, by the hand of Divinity itself and can never be erased or obscured by mortal power." Alexander Hamilton, *The Farmer Refuted* (1775)

trusting that which transcends our understanding, they held that a greater vision would grab hold; that we would overcome the habits of lower-ordered mental faculties and begin to connect with the Ground of Being at ever more refined levels of coherence. Thus, according to these visionaries, fragmentary understanding would give way to integrative wisdom, and as consciousness continued its evolution towards greater levels of value-fulfilment the idea of separation would gradually come to an end.

At first, this summary might sound odd, naïve, or occult. On the one hand, religious people will hail some prophets as godlike while they see others as heretics. Then there is established science which will tell us that there is no God—in fact, no meaning—to be found; that consequently, there is no moral code superior to any other, and that love is merely the sensation of firing neurons—not much different from eating chocolate. Add to this that a great deal of human warfare and persecution has been motivated by religion, and one would assume that this synopsis is pure hogwash and that the prophets were as prone to violence as the Old Testament's God.

Nevertheless, to the extent that the idols of religion deserve their status, this was the message, and those who take a closer look will find that, from religion to religion, the esoteric teachings are all the same: The thread that binds them is the call to inner work, and while the practices and techniques are loaded with cultural differences, their common core is to abide by those values, ideals, and principles that follow from Wholeness. No matter who we are, or what we have done: In following the Law of One, saints, gurus, and prophets held that a greater wisdom would come to permeate our reasoning; we would gradually learn to see beyond the realm of deceptive limitations—and not only become more and more one with the mind of God, but in the process become godlike ourselves.[632]

---

[632] As Jung noted: "The Christ-symbol is of the greatest importance for psychology in so far as it is perhaps the most highly developed and differentiated symbol of the self, apart from the figure of the Buddha." STEIN (ED.), *JUNG ON CHRISTIANITY* (1991) 195

This, then, is the secret doctrine, the one that has been suppressed by authority. Throughout history, we find that the Church has been as opposed to this code of personal enlightenment as the state has been towards liberation movements, which comes as no surprise. We already know that the interests of citizens and rulers are inherently opposed—and while individuals have a vested interest in autonomy, authority has a vested interest in encouraging dependency.

Hence, to those in charge, the founders' and the prophets' true quest has been plain heresy, and so ecclesiastical authorities have fought mystics with the same fervency that political authorities have fought liberation movements. The power of these structures depends upon them maintaining the status quo, and the idea of a direct connection between man and God is no more popular to the priests of organized religion than of abiding by first principles to rulers.

If we are to make progress in this situation, therefore, we cannot trust authority to provide a solution to our problems. All the prophets could do was to point us in the right direction and all the founders could do was to provide us with a set of principles for sound government; it would be up to us to take it from there, and if we are to overcome this shadow that has caused us so much death and suffering, we must follow their example.

14.2. Towards a More Wholesome Psyche

"The great lesson from the true mystics [is that] the sacred is in the ordinary, that it is to be found in one's daily life, in one's neighbours, friends, and family, in one's backyard." [633]

—Abraham Maslow, Professor of Psychology—

We have seen that the ideological ground of the Constitution was that of autonomy enhancement and that its morality proceeded from a foundation of love. We also know that there is a connection between state- and individual power and that the power of the Constitution is intimately bound with our inner constitution. At any given time, the condition of society will mirror that of the collective mind, and if we want a better world the answer is simple: We must confront our secret fears and overcome the habit of dualistic thinking by committing to those values, ideals, and principles that follow from Wholeness.

In following the implications of Wholeness and trusting that which transcends our understanding, we not only begin to connect with the greater morality, but we reorganize our mind in a way that is beneficial for personal growth. The road to salvation, therefore, may be paved politically with principled law, but it is the responsibility of the individual to free him/herself from collectively shared prejudice. Only to the extent that this is done can society move forward. We must deal with the taboos of society and if we accept this responsibility, we find that in questioning authority we build integrity. We begin to see wholes where previously there were portions and divides; this, again, introduces us to a greater reality, and we find that love is what it is all about.

---

[633] MASLOW, *RELIGIONS, VALUES, AND PEAK-EXPERIENCES* (1970) x

This psychological process is well-recognized among initiates of mystery schools from East to the West, including Freemasonry. It is even recognized by the third force of Western psychology, the humanistic movement, and the idea is to reach a state of enlightenment by overcoming fear-based psychological obstacles/responses. It is a method that is empirically validated as it reduces trauma, opening the way for integrity to develop. This ensures a greater appreciation for one's own autonomy and liberty rights, which again results in increased respect for the rights of others. It is a timeworn truth that the more we learn to integrate the connotations of Wholeness, the more we are free of disserving and unduly limiting beliefs—and that the more we are, the more our relationship to our surroundings will also change.

There is, in fact, nothing with our dualistic worldview that is inevitable or objectively correct. Instead, our ideas about good and evil, life and death, left and right politics, and so on, are the result of poor analytical faculties, and those who free their mind will experience a merging where the common man's perception of duality is transcended into understanding of ever higher unity. Thus, the old notion of a conflict between self-interest and community interest disappears and we begin to experience evermore deeply the unity that connects all fabric.

While yet controversial, this psychological process begins to unfold the minute we accept that consciousness truly comes first and that our experience is not merely coloured but created by our beliefs. Matter, as we understand our reality, is therefore better understood as a fixture, a tool for imagination, and we can create the kind of world that we want by the power of thought. As we have seen, love and fear represent the primordial forces that give meaning to the human experience; together the two make up the polarities that inform the human psychology, and the more we understand and learn to separate between these forces the better.

As formerly discussed, while the psychology of love heals trauma, provides for personal growth and results in healthy interaction, the psychology of fear does the opposite: It produces trauma, which again provides for the defence mechanisms that give rise to moral panics and totalitarian government. Moreover, the power of these forces translates to our morality, and we have seen how the prohibition morality is influenced by fear. Prohibitionists, however, are not the only ones to suffer from a confused morality; indeed, it is inherent in the fabric of our time, and once we have found the courage to do away with this great injustice, we should not rest too comfortably. Humanity, after all, is one great consciousness, fragmented into form, and we can evolve only to the extent that we make a conscious effort to overcome the scapegoating phenomenon.[634]

14.2.1. The Rift of Unconsciousness

"God whispers to us in our pleasures, speaks to us in our conscience, but shouts in our pains: It's His megaphone to rouse a deaf world."[635]

—C.S. Lewis—

As we have seen, the War on Drugs is not the only example of the great Big Lie, that which leaders will advance to serve totalitarian agendas. Also the War on Terror awaits reckoning, for as long as these campaigns persist totalitarian forces will push on for greater powers. These campaigns only have validity to those in psychosis, and to those who look closer, "drugs" and "terrorists" are enemy images blown out of proportion to make us trade in our freedom

---

[634] If we are not happy with our experience, it is because we have patterns of thought which have taken us to realms where despair, anguish, loneliness, and insecurity reigns. In these locations of the psyche, only neurosis exist, and to get out, we need to focus on the positive aspects of existence. Only in doing so can our lives again become filled with quality, only in doing so can we step out of victimhood, and only this way can we ensure a movement into a more blissful area of experience. Indeed, as the consciousness of humanity matures, guiding by the lights of mystic intuition becomes as natural as issues of self-doubt to the ordinary ego, and if we only stopped acting as if God seized talking to humans some 2000 years ago, things would run much faster according to plan.

[635] Lewis, *The Problem of Pain* (1962) 83

for promises of security; they are the tools that social engineers of the despotic kind use to succeed, and they count upon the power of trauma to keep us in chains.

If not for these frightening images, the dynamic of society would change. Without them, war profiteers would have to stop building tanks, guns, and bombs, and to find less troublesome ways to stay in business; resources dedicated to death, persecution, and destruction would become available for more constructive work and their divisive effects would come to an end. All, in short, would be recalibrated towards a higher level of health and harmony—but authority does not agree.

It does not matter that their logic is refuted by reason and evidence: According to our leaders, these campaigns are all that stand between us and oblivion, and they ignore the evidence linking organizations such as ISIS and Al Qaeda to secret services. As evinced by the imprisonment of Brad Birkenfeld, a UBS banker who informed the U.S. government that he had solid information on 19,000 bank accounts which were used to finance terrorism, no one wants to look into these things.[636] Nor does authority want to look at the definition of "terrorism" or "drugs," as it is impossible to do so without including acts and substances that the state has legalized. Instead, since the 1930's, our politicians have committed to analyses and intelligence (from the secret services) concluding that "terrorist" organizations have successfully merged with "narcotics" traffickers in a joint effort to destroy our freedom—and because the enemy is not merely at the gates, but can be found among our children, the idea is that even more extreme measures are needed to save society.

The absurdity of this logic is evident to those not caught in society's moral panic. Nevertheless, the media has been keen to support authority, and the defenders of the status quo have managed to hold public inquisitiveness at bay by appealing to our sense of patriotism.

---

[636] For more on this story, see Scott Bennett, *Shell Game: A Whistleblowing Report* (2013)

It is a time-worn truth, however, that political taboos hide a more sinister reality. In this case, it was that Americans, having come to depend on scapegoats to forget the extent to which they have fallen short of the founders' vision, needed an outlet for all that could not be faced—and the war on drugs and terrorism became the solution. It went well for a while: The enemy images of drugs and terrorists could be used to justify any imaginary improvement and those who objected were put on terror lists or removed from positions of influence. Thus, the military-industrial-political complex could continue to expand in scope, feeding on fear and searching out new enemies to attack, even after the collapse of the Soviet Union.

Nevertheless, being built on a lie, politicians should have known better than to let war profiteers define policy. This deal with the devil would come back to haunt them, and in accepting the official version of 9/11-events, public officials would not only estrange themselves from positions of integrity, but they would be struggling ever more with war profiteers who expected these wars to continue into perpetuity. We have seen what the $1 trillion that has been spent on the War on Drugs has done to American liberties. Today, thanks to the War on Terror, national security spending in the United States totals around $1 trillion a year, and this represents a vast milking cow to corporations whose services we would do better without.

Just ask the Afghan or Iraqi people. In Iraq, between 2003 and 2006, the U.S. military spent nearly $1 billion a week paying for these services.[637] Even so, production of oil and electricity remained below pre-war levels and schools, hospitals, cars, and food were less available than before the war. We would do well to remember that Saddam's Iraq was already deeply troubled by sanctions, a country where more than a million people, including 500,000 children, had died because there were no medicines to heal or machine parts to operate basic services. Nevertheless,

---

[637] Robert L. Borosage, Eric Lotke and Robert Gerson, *War Profiteers: Profits Over Patriotism in Iraq*, September 2006

Iraqis enjoyed more electricity, better schools, and better hospitals under a dictatorship shackled by sanctions than under the U.S. occupation.

This, of course, was because money was going elsewhere. Loading up planes directly from the Federal Reserve, the United States had shipped nearly $12 billion in U.S. currency to Iraq between May 2003 and June 2004. After the funds arrived, few records were kept for the Pentagon's Inspector General, but the GAO found evidence of widespread mismanagement, waste, and corruption in the spending and disbursement of over $19.6 billion, most of it going to U.S. corporations.

It comes as no surprise that no one has been held accountable for the widespread failures of contracting in Iraq. Indeed, as the US government hired more private companies than in any previous war, spending at least $138bn on private security, logistics, and reconstruction contractors, who supplied everything from diplomatic security to power plants and toilet paper, everything worked according to plan. After all, the United States government is run by the big corporations, and no one seriously believed its lie that Saddam was threatening the world with weapons of mass-destruction.[638] For those not caught in the brewing war-psychosis, it was plain to see that even Colin Powell, the U.S. Secretary of State, was ashamed when he presented the "evidence" for this at the UN, and as usual it was about keeping the wheels of war running.

As students of power-politics know, the United States got out of the Great Depression by becoming an economy rigged for war, and after World War II the military industrial complex invented the cold war to keep going. As time passed, these war efforts were ever more privatized, and the Iraq War would be the first war where there were more contractors than military personnel on the ground. As the torture scandal at Abu Ghraib and Blackwater's killing of 17 innocent civilians in Nisour Square, Baghdad, would

---

[638] If we really worried about these weapons, the first thing that should have been done was to arrest Mark Thatcher, the son of Margaret Thatcher, the British Prime Minister, who sold them to Saddam in the 1980's. See MENASHE, *PROFITS OF WAR* (1992)

prove, these privateers clearly operated beyond the scope of international law. Even before Blackwater's massacre, the State Department had probed its operations, calling the firm's culture "an environment full of liability and negligence",[639] and yet the company would continue its operations, raking in more than $1bn in contracts.

Contractors such as CACI and Blackwater, however, were not the only representatives of an environment filled with "liability and negligence." We have already seen that DynCorp, a corporation involved with child-trafficking, profited nicely. Indeed, 87 percent of all contracts awarded by the State Department in Afghanistan went to only five corporations, with DynCorp on top. And this company was not only awarded a $2.5 billion contract for reconstruction, but over the next decade would make more than $1bn a year fighting terrorism.

Not merely terrorists, of course. The company is also fighting drugs in Afghanistan and elsewhere, even though lessons from the past suggest that it would be naïve to believe that corporations such as Blackwater/Academi and DynCorp have any intention of winning the drug war. Behind the scenes, there is the "Secret Team" in control of markets, and in 2001, after the Taliban unexpectedly eradicated three-quarters of the world opium crop, experts on power-politics knew that it was only a matter of time before an intervention. It did not take long, and since the invasion of Afghanistan a smooth-running, an ever more centralized network has ensured that the country supplies more than 90 percent of the world heroin market. After seeing what we have seen, this could not have been possible without the drug-fighting machinery looking in the other direction, and whistleblowers such as Sibel Edmonds have revealed that government-orchestrated drug running is abundant, even on NATO bases.[640]

---

[639] LOFGREN, *THE DEEP STATE* (2016) 102

[640] The American Civil Liberties Union called Sibel Edmonds "the most gagged person in the history of the United States of America". Two weeks after 9/11, she began working for the FBI as a translator because of her knowledge of Turkish, Azerbaijani and Farsi. She was translating top-secret material related to terrorist networks in the U.S. and the rest of the

The world, in other words, continue as before. And another massive war profiteer has been Halliburton, the company where Vice President Cheney previously held a CEO position. Only ten days into the Bush administration, Cheney and his friends started to prepare for war, and having successfully lobbied Congress to accept an illegal war, this company (where Cheney still maintained stocks) made a small fortune. Before the Iraq War, it received a no-bid $7 billion contract for oil exploits and over the next decade Halliburton would grab $40 billion's worth of contracts. Many were given at cost-plus terms without any bidding from competing firms. What this means is that the more money these corporations spend, the more money they earn—and make money Halliburton did. At prices up to $600 a gallon, the company drove convoys of empty trucks through the desert, putting drivers and security personnel at risk. Several would die because of this, but Halliburton was paid to run trips and it did not matter if trucks ran empty or were destroyed. As the company got paid according to how much it spent, Halliburton would abandon or destroy $85,000 trucks if they got a flat tire or experienced mechanical problems and they never changed the oil. As an example of its other business practices, the company charged the government $45 for cases of locally produced soda and $100 to

---

world when she discovered that U.S. agencies, like the CIA, are cooperating with terrorist organizations and that the FBI is hiding this information from the public. After raising concerns with her supervisors, she received threats and was ultimately fired. She tried to tell the truth in 2002 and 2004, but the U.S. government forbade her to do so under the "state secret privilege" and "threat to national security" rules. Nevertheless, Edmonds' charge ties in nicely with the rest of the picture discussed in this book: Her main thesis is that "the Pentagon, CIA and State Department kept very intimate contact with al-Qaida terrorists, and are neck-deep in illegal arms and drug trafficking in Central Asia. She spoke openly about this in her 2013 interview with Nafeez Mosaddeq Ahmed, a writer on geopolitics and expert on environment and energy. She pointed out that Osama bin Laden's successor, Ayman al-Zawahiri, had numerous meetings with U.S. military and intelligence activists from 1997 to 2001 in Baku, capital of Azerbaijan, to discuss the goals of an operation called 'Gladio B.' According to her statements, al-Zawahiri, bin Laden's family members and other leading Mujahidin figures were transported by NATO airplanes throughout the 'hot spots' in Central Asia and the Balkans with the goal of supporting the Pentagon's destabilization acts." Vladimir Dimitrijevic/ Gilian Palmer, *All Secrets of Sibel Edmonds, or: Who Manages World Terrorism?* March 16, 2014

wash bags of laundry, while employees were paid 50 cents an hour for laundry work. They were also paid by the government to provide special foods for Filipino and other low-paid workers in Iraq, but Halliburton provided no meals and these workers had to eat trash and leftovers.

Add to this that eight months after the Iraq War began, nearly 50,000 U.S. troops—more than one-third of the total force—lacked modern body armour. The shortage was the result of a broken procurement process. While twenty U.S. companies could make the required vests, Point Blank Body Armor successfully lobbied for a contract to produce all the body armour, even though the company could not possibly manufacture enough to satisfy the order. Nevertheless, while young boys and girls, in a mistaken fit of patriotism, were maimed or killed, U.S. corporations prospered, and Point Blank's CEO David H. Brooks, to celebrate, spent $10 million on a party in New York City's Rainbow Room.[641]

This, then, is the modern warfare state—this is what has become of the founder's vision. It is a monstrosity that feeds on humanity, and we can expect it to continue its destructive course, always preparing for war and looking for enemies, real or imagined.

---

[641] Robert L. Borosage, Eric Lotke and Robert Gerson, *War Profiteers: Profits Over Patriotism in Iraq*, September 2006

14.2.2. The Final Revolution

*"Someday, after mastering the winds, the waves, the tides
and gravity, we shall harness for God the energies of love,
and then, for a second time in the history of the world, man
will have discovered fire."*

—Pierre Teilhard de Chardin—

It goes without saying that no thinking person would consent to the status quo. As we have seen, the only type of government rational minds will agree upon is one dedicated to a just order; a government created for the express purpose of protecting individual rights; that uses its police power to ensure that everyone are equally protected; and that never abuses power by violating pre-existing rights. That is all. The bloated security state, then, as soon as humanity wises up, better prepare for moneys going elsewhere. And as also politicians these days are beginning to feel the impact of the disintegration of the Constitution—their true powerbase—there is a momentum for change.

Every day, public officials are in the grips of a system that expects them to preserve psychosis. Deserters have affirmed the systemic pressure to leave integrity behind, and the horror of the wars on drugs and terrorism does not merely extend to the persecuted. As we have seen, our officials are struggling to maintain the lie that keeps the moral ground beneath their feet. Take this lie away from them and many will experience the abyss that Nietzsche talked about, that from which the old self cannot return. However, as we also have seen, according to mystics, death and resurrection is one and the same, and for those who venture to do the inner work, the reward will be a more wholesome psyche.

Now, Nietzsche's abyss may seem threatening to the ego.[642] Nevertheless, it is a small price to pay when the world is

---

[642] The philosopher Nietzsche is a good example of the kind of ramblings that come out of a fear filled ego, detached from deeper ground. His failure to connect with it would drive

crumbling, and to those who listen our ideals, values, and intuitions remain accessible guideposts, giving us direction to follow. Thus, as in the days of the founders, time has proved ripe for integrity to build among politicians. And as soon as they have found the courage to look at drug prohibition, it is important that we deal with the War on Terror. As long as these campaigns are allowed to continue, it will be a show of unconsciousness, and speaking of the criminal law, there are other areas where government unduly burdens populations.

As society matures, therefore, constitutional courts will honour first principles and government committees will form to look at the implications for society. At some point, we will also recognize that the only viable revolution humanity can have is a revolution of thought and committees will form whose purpose it is to look at the data concerning the nature of consciousness. Erecting an impartial and competent panel, it will be possible to show that consciousness precedes matter, and the implications of recognizing the power of love will be vast. Until our time, humanity has been guided by the dictates of lower-ordered mental faculties and from our fragmented perspective, we have not been able to see the bigger picture. Thus, warfare and control-oriented behaviours abound. Nevertheless, as seen from the higher perspective, a Spirit of Freedom has guided us, ensuring that we learn from our mistakes, and people are more and more connecting with a state of consciousness which swallows Whole the old, granting access to this larger perspective.

What we have before us is, then, is a psychological process, a cleansing of the national psyche even more profound than that of Germany after World War II or South Africa post-Apartheid. What we have before us is a paradigm shift—a leap in consciousness—where humanity lets go of the limiting constrains that comes with accepting deceiving culturally-shared beliefs. In

---

him insane, but he was onto something when he wrote "Beware that, when fighting monsters, you yourself do not become a monster ... for when you gaze long into the abyss. The abyss gazes also into you." FRIEDRICH NIETZSCHE, BEYOND GOOD AND EVIL (1886) 146

following the path of the great mystics, people are stepping into a greater realm, one where their sense of self becomes grounded in the soul of the Cosmos, for according to these visionaries we are all one consciousness fragmented into many forms. It is only at the surface that we appear separate, and at the deeper levels of our psyche our consciousness connects with the psyche of humanity. Beyond this point, we are part of an even larger psyche, that of the Earth and the Cosmos—and while this may seem odd, joining this new paradigm is truly a revelation.

Indeed, according to the travellers in consciousness, throughout all of creation, we find a fabric that is sentient, alive, and curious of itself—and every fragment is an inviolate part of its Being. This Divine Consciousness maintains a balance of the cosmos, ensuring cycles of time and a rich vastness of play. Through a fragmented form we are lost to the bigger picture, but as consciousness evolves, we reconnect with the greater aspects of our psyche and the Ground of Being.

14.2.2.1. THE GREAT PLAY

"Upon my heart fell one drop of Brahmic Bliss, leaving thence forward for always an aftertaste of heaven. Among other things . . . I saw and knew that the Cosmos is not dead matter but a living Presence, that the soul of man is immortal, that the Universe is so built and ordered that without any peradventure all things work together for the good of each and all, that the foundation principle for the world is what we call love and that the happiness of everyone is in the long run absolutely certain. . . . I learned more within the few seconds during which the illumination lasted than in previous months or even years of study, and I learned much that no study could ever have thought. . . . Especially [I] obtained such a conception of THE WHOLE . . . as dwarfs all conception, imagination or speculation, springing from and belonging to ordinary self consciousness, such a conception as makes the old attempts to mentally grasp the Universe and its meaning petty and even ridiculous. . . . A great deal of this is, of course, from the point of view of self consciousness, absurd—[but] it is nevertheless undoubtedly true."[643]

—Richard Maurice Bucke, MD—

That consciousness is everything and that love is the force that opens our eye to the vitality and the play of the cosmos, may be difficult to accept. The world, after all, seems firm enough and so do our troubles. Nevertheless, according to the new paradigm, the cosmos is a sentient entity, and our consciousness is an integral part of this greater being. Thus, it transcends time, space, birth, and death. Time, according to those who have ventured beyond the ordinary state of consciousness, is really a mass-movement

---

[643] Bucke had this experience at 36. It changed his life, making him one of the great pioneers of modern psycology. See R.M. BUCKE, *COSMIC CONSCIOUSNESS: A STUDY IN THE EVOLUTION OF THE HUMAN MIND* (1961) 8,14

towards greater levels of value-fulfilment; history, the result of this universal force's inherent drive towards self-actualization; and this consciousness is not only experienced as another evolutionary leap, but as the universe's self-actualization *through* us.

While this may be much to consider, the new consciousness is essentially a process of remembrance. The universe, being a living entity, organizes itself at different levels of complexity and from atoms to minerals, to plants, to animals, to humans, we see consciousness experiencing its existence at different parameters. Hence, it is only because our senses are focused on the surface that matter is seen as dead and inert. Nonetheless, physicists know that matter is simply light pressed down to a slow vibration[644] and light itself is quite mysterious. What we know is that it is a spectrum of frequency of which we only perceive a tiny fraction— and as it always travels at the same speed, relative to the observer, the mystics may be right.

There is in fact nothing science can produce which proves the mystical perspective wrong. Instead, mysticism has been called the "perennial philosophy" for its timeless appeal. And as Ken Wilber, a modern philosopher, noted: "So overwhelmingly widespread is the perennial philosophy . . . that it is either the single greatest intellectual error ever to appear in human kind's history—an error so colossally widespread as to literally stagger the mind—or it is the single most accurate reflection of reality yet to appear."[645] Indeed, Einstein himself recognized mystical experience as the source of all true science, and the French palaeontologist Pierre Teilhard de Chardin called it "the great

---

[644] For more on how modern science/physics compares to the mystic perspective, see PAUL DAVIES AND JOHN GRIBBIN, *THE MATTER MYTH* (1991); NICK HERBERT, *QUANTUM REALITY* (1985); GARY ZUKAV, *THE DANCING WU LI MASTERS* (1979); AMIT GOSWAMI, *THE SELF-AWARE UNIVERSE* (1993); FRITJOF CAPRA, *THE TAO OF PHYSICS* (2010); MICHAEL TALBOT, *MYSTICISM AND THE NEW PHYSICS* (1981); EDWARD E. CLOSE, *TRANSCENDENTAL PHYSICS* (2000)

[645] KEN WILBER, *THE EYE OF SPIRIT: AN INTEGRAL VISION FOR A WORLD GONE SLIGHTLY MAD* (1998) 39

science and the great art, the only power capable of synthesizing the riches accumulated by other forms of human activity."[646]

We have good reasons, then, to look at their message. Remember that mystical experience is also at the heart of all true religion, and Wilber recognizes Sri Aurobindo (1872 -1950) as the greatest mystic who ever lived. His works summarize the same overall picture as that which is touched upon in this book—and Aurobindo, most definitely, was on to the greater perspective. Tuning in to the cosmic consciousness, he clearly saw the movements of the Whole and concluded thus:

> *"But what after all, behind appearance, is this seeming mystery? We can see that it is the Consciousness which had lost itself returning to itself, emerging out of its giant self-forgetfulness, slowly, painfully, as a Life that is would-be sentient, to be more than sentient, to be again divinely self-conscious, free, infinite, immortal."[647]*

His philosophy would elaborate on this great play.[648] Probably, he was the greatest social engineer that ever lived,[649] and while some have criticized mystics for being navel-gazing introverts who care little for the world, Aurobindo understood the importance of acting against injustice. He did not only theorize about the movement of the Spirit of Freedom in his works; it also moved strong within him, and as India was under British rule, Aurobindo became a force in the liberation-movement. His revolutionary speeches and articles made Lord Minto, the British Governor-

---

[646] TEILHARD DECHARDIN, *LETTERS FROM A TRAVELLER* (1975) 47

[647] SATPREM, *SRI AUROBINDO OR THE ADVENTURE OF CONSCIOUSNESS* (2008) 291

[648] "The step from man towards superman is the next approaching achievement in the earth's evolution. There lies our destiny and the liberating key to our aspiring, but troubled human existence—inevitable because it is at once the intention of the inner Spirit and the logic of Nature's process." AUROBINDO, *THE HOUR OF GOD* (2009) 101

[649] See e.g., SRI AUROBINDO, *THE HUMAN CYCLE, THE IDEAL OF HUMAN UNITY, WAR AND SELF-DETERMINATION* (2012)

General, call him India's "most dangerous man," and even the threat of a death sentence did not bother him.[650]

His integrity, then, was strong—which again comes as no surprise. To those who follow the mystics' road it comes as natural as breathing, as they can feel it in their bones what it means to be an inviolate piece of the Great Architect's play. Having attained an intimate relationship with the force that unites all things, they know that time and space are constructs for consciousness-at-large to experience certain parameters of existence; that the ego has forgot about it, so that it could take life to the extreme; to despair in anguish, and to know all those aspects of existence that is not available on any other level; and that, behind this great play, there are cycles of time, cycles where consciousness spans from its lower to its higher potentialities.

In this manner, the Wholeness is provided with opportunities for growth and understanding, while the fragments—we—have the privilege of rediscovering our true heritage, i.e., the consciousness that pervades all existence. The cosmic fabric is woven so that each part contains the whole, and it is highly sentient, responding to our every call. To the extent humanity, therefore, believes that we doomed for extinction; that the terrorists are threatening to destroy our values; and that the ends justify the means, there are obvious lessons to be learned, and the cosmos will speak louder to its children, providing us with the impetus for growth.

The Human psyche remains in its infancy, as we have yet to discover how our beliefs create reality. Nevertheless, behind this nightmare we have created, there is a deeper calm, a Wake frequency, where the Wholeness—and the fragments—are

---

[650] As he explained to a member of the Viceroy's Executive Council, when he refused to submit a mercy petition to reverse his death sentence to life imprisonment: "[He preferred the death sentence, because] he would be reborn in a few years to fight the Satanic Government, whereas, after a long term of imprisonment, he would be unfit to take part in the war of Independence that would soon break out." In a later statement before the court, he also declared "If it is suggested that I preached the ideal of freedom, which is against the law, I plead guilty. If that is my fault, you can chain me, imprison me, but you will not get out of me a denial of that charge." P. Rajeswar Rao, *The Great Indian Patriots*, Vol. 1 (1991) 208, 209

intimately one. At these deeper layers, fragmentary experience is never lost. Streams of consciousness exist where one can take part in the experience of entire collectives and whether it is the silent, drowsy, yet mighty, quality of minerals and mountains; the hive-mind migration of flocking birds; the will of tyrants to dominate; the revolutionary fervour that inspired communism; or all gardeners' love for their flowers, these streams contain the experience and exist unbound by space and time.

The same, of course, goes for any other fragmented experience—and while this may be of little comfort to the ego, the appearance of time makes its perspective limited. Hence, only a childish ego, irresponsive of its ways, will deny higher reasoning. The ego, most certainly, has its place, but to the extent that it is walled off from the greater reality by clinging to ideas of victimhood it can never experience itself at its full capacity. If we want to experience a different reality, therefore, we should be open to the suggestion that those who have experienced these states of consciousness are on to something and that, perhaps, it is better to guide according to the dictates of more wholesome perspectives/ values than the misgivings of a traumatized inner voice.

To those who have not experienced such states, it is difficult to know what to make of this matter. Even so, it should be noted that direct experience has a way of making believers out of sceptics.[651] It would be wise, then, to withhold judgement until we have met with these realms, and there are tried and reliable means to get there. Different techniques and tools are discussed in previous works,[652] and we can expect science to learn more about this new paradigm as research on psychedelics advance.

---

[651] Stanislav Grof, a leading researcher on psychedelics, noted: "In my experience, everyone who has reached these levels develops convincing insights into the utmost relevance of the spiritual and religious dimensions in the universal scheme of things. Even hardcore materialists, positivistically oriented scientists, sceptics and cynics, and uncompromising atheists and antireligious crusaders such as the Marxist philosophers suddenly become interested in a spiritual search after they confronted these levels in themselves." STANISLAV GROF, *REALMS OF THE HUMAN UNCONSCIOUS: OBSERVATIONS FROM LSD RESEARCH* (1979) 95

[652] MIKALSEN, *REASON IS* (2014)

These substances have been used by shamans, oracles, and truth-seekers for millennia, and they provide the most reliable means to study the phenomenon. This, most likely, is also the real reason for their illegal status. Authority, as we know, does not appreciate a direct connection with God as it makes people difficult to control. Those who experience these dimensions come back without the old idea of limithood, and while they previously may have had a poor concept of self—one where the idea of selfhood relied upon affiliation with a certain race, social class, or culture, and where death was the end of everything—their new identity has traversed these obstacles to growth. In its place, a firmer platform has evolved, one grounded in the cosmos and first principles, and so they will be more prone to revolution than suffering the despotism of fake authority. The example of Aurobindo serves as a reminder. And to the extent that we follow his example, the world will turn for the better.

14.2.2.2. MODERN MYSTICISM

"To be a mystic is simply to participate here and now in that real and eternal life; in the fullest, deepest sense which is possible to man. It is to share, as a free and conscious agent . . . in the joyous travail of the universe: Its mighty onward sweep through pain and glory towards its home in God."[653]

—Evelyn Underhill—

We have learned about the mystics and the insights that can be divined from expanded states of consciousness. They are not that rare; with the increased popularity of psychedelics in the 1960's, many connected with the greater psyche—and while some did not

---

[653] EVELYN UNDERHILL, *MYSTICISM: A STUDY IN THE NATURE AND DEVELOPMENT OF MAN'S SPIRITUAL CONSCIOUSNESS* (1962) 447

know what to make of it, others received great visions. Several studies were done in the 1950-60's, confirming that these were not hallucinations but experiences as valid as any other. Another wave of psychedelic research is beginning to build, and despite a regime of prohibition, every year, more millions get to experience a taste of the "otherworldly."

Now, while such states of consciousness have been available to individuals throughout the centuries, they were considered "peak-experiences",[654] and those who reported them soon went back to a normal state of consciousness. Nevertheless, the more they experienced this state, the more it would bleed through back to their ordinary consciousness, and so it was that a new kind of experience arose—one beyond traditional ideas of good and evil. Instead, to the new consciousness, the play of duality was more refined. From the ordinary, waking perspective, people could still feel the presence of their ego and its fragmentary understanding; hence, they would be happy or sad like before, but there was another layer to this experience, one where the Wholeness would impress its weight upon the old ego.

Because of this pressure from above, the ego was no longer so unsure of its place in the world and as it began to trust in the greater reality managing emotions proved easier. Thus, everything was prepared for an acceleration of growth. While personal issues remained to be resolved, a bridge was crossed, and a more pronounced sharing of information between the ego and the deeper psyche had begun. The more these modern mystics honoured the implications of Wholeness, the better this bridge would be prepared. Not only did the rewards of guiding by the implications of Wholeness appear self-evident; the more people integrated its wisdom, the more their ideas about consciousness would change; as integrity built, depth and significance would follow, and they began to experience more directly the pride and joy that ants collectively derive from their civilization building.

---

[654] MASLOW, *RELIGIONS, VALUES, AND PEAK-EXPERIENCES* (1970)

Indeed, as seen from the greater perspective, the cosmos can be compared to an enormous machinery where we—its fragments—are its spokes. These spokes all have free will and to the extent that we are influenced by fear, tensions will arise. Like sand in the machinery, the idea of separation gains weight and we move deeper into forgetfulness. With love, however, life moves in the other direction. Like oil, love greases the machinery of the cosmos towards greater levels of coherence, self-awareness, and value fulfilment, and to the extent that we strive in this direction, all will be revealed. Incarnation after incarnation, we will elevate our frequency to the point where it resonates with Source—and then another "song" begins.

14.2.2.3. THE ASCENSION PROCESS

"The idea of limit, of the impossible begins to grow a little shadowy and it appears instead that whatever man constantly wills, he must in the end be able to do; for the consciousness in the race eventually finds the means. It is not in the individual that this omnipotence expresses itself, but in the collective will of mankind that works out with the individual as a means. And yet when we look more deeply, it is not any conscious will of the collectivity, but a superconscious Might that uses the individual as a center and a means, the collectivity as a condition and field."[655]

—Sri Aurobindo—

While we are here on earth, we have basically two options. We may move beyond appearances, discover that the inner landscape is really all that is, and start walking the mystic road. Doing so brings integrity and as this is the bridge between us and a greater

---

[655] SRI AUROBINDO, *THE LIFE DIVINE* (1970) 15

form of consciousness, those who venture to play this game go on to find that its rewards are huge. As they balance their ego towards the point where a drop becomes the ocean, they experience creation at its fuller potentials; not only will the Divine be seen in all things, but they meet hive-mind supergods and evolve towards these potentials.

Knowing this, no wonder integrity comes easy to mystics. No wonder they tend to have a calm when there is a storm around them. They know that building integrity is the only game in town, and that for those who do not guide by the lights of Wholeness there remains only living in denial while letting the defence mechanism of projection keep another game going; one built around fragmented understanding, arbitrary moral codes, and subjectively valued observations without ever connecting to the soul of the universe—that fabric which unites everything.

It is a diversion that is common enough and it is the natural result of insufficient analytical power to connect with Wholeness. Thus, because most have not seen the bigger picture, we have had priests who have told us that divinity was different from us; that we were debased, worthless creatures; that Satan would tempt any free thinker; that it was better to accept the authority of clergy, kings, and other authoritarians; that God had blessed these people with authority for a reason; that He therefore wanted us to kill their enemies; and that mystical insight was bullshit because this old mysterious God in the sky long ago stopped talking to humans.

Not only that. As history moved forward, a counterforce arose which objected to the doctrines of organized religion. Hence, on the other side, learned men told us that there was no God, no meaning, no significance, and that the idea of a loving creator was disproved by current affairs. Such were the cries to the universe, the lies that they had come to believe, and collectively speaking the echo of silent despair would ring out loud, resulting in a destructive force—a dissociated, disconnected, and frightful landscape of our own making.

To the extent that the citizenry believed in such ideas, the cultural driftwood that clogged the collective mind could only mount, and the consciousness of humanity would slide deeper into unconsciousness. If we had been wise, we would have understood that only more love for self and others could improve upon events, but because "shit happens" in places where denial and projection rule the ground, people accepted the victim role. This, however, could only further undermine integrity and at the collective level, until today, the organism of humanity would have sufficient issues for most to accept trauma as a way of life. Even so, as we have seen, there is a way out, and the prophets and the founders pointed in this direction.

Among humanity, there have always been those who did not buy into the dictates of fake authority and who broke free of the collective consciousness. Attaining an ability to perceive the world of first principles, they became ambassadors of the future. They became visionaries, and behind the veil of events they saw the Spirit of Freedom honing humanity, and ensuring that we moved forward despite a multitude of egos who embraced despotic means and short-sighted ends.

We could call it a miracle. But lucky for us everyone, even the Universe, wants to be found. As seen from Cosmos' perspective, the ego was a marvel of creation, for in jumping from the animal to the human form it transcended the group-soul and established Mind. Having the ability to reflect back on itself was a huge step for consciousness, and while this new level of self-awareness came with challenges (we would, after all, experience ourselves as adrift, separate from creation and alone) it was written in the sands of time that humanity would prevail. Pressure from above and the pain of living on our knees would provide the necessary correction mechanism. And while we, as individuals, always have had the opportunity to find our way by following the lights of Wholeness, it has got easier with time.

The reason is that this process takes place at the collective and the individual level. There are cycles within cycles, but behind cycles of time we find the universe's exhalation and inhalation process. Outbreath and inbreath, forgetfulness and remembrance, this is the bigger game that is played, and the machinery of the cosmos is ready to take earth to its next level. The ego, therefore, is not the cosmos', nor humanity's crowning achievement. Seen from the greater perspective, it is merely a prerequisite for a larger play, as it makes it possible for the Wholeness—and us—to experience what is not.[656] Thus, free will would take us on a nightmarish ride, but it was always known that the illusion of separation would come to an end. And while history is a testimony to our trials, humanity has matured, and the increasing duality is a sign that change is upon us.

Like I have said, there are cycles within cycles, and we are drawing near to a big event, the end of a great Age. Time being a process of value-fulfilment, the universe has a built-in drive towards ultimate potentials, and the omega point will be when the cosmic consciousness—the galaxy's own consciousness—becomes embodied in man en masse. This will be its crowning achievement! As seen from the higher perspective, the universe, in a slow and painful process that spans ages, has built man as a bridge to realize itself, and there are individuals on this planet who have experienced this dramatic shift. So far, only for a few hours, but time is not the essence. The point is that great possibilities await those who venture beyond the realms of the known psyche, and there is no reason to think that this visionary state will not one day be commonly enjoyed.

As a matter of fact, in the annals of humanity, we have always intuited this process. As discovered by anthropologists, the hero's journey is a common template in narratology around the world;[657] departure (separation), initiation (descent), and return (atonement/

---

[656] Taking part in the play of duality obviously comes with great trials and we have all done stupid stuff. Real stupid. But from the cosmic perspective there are no real taboos; only karmic lessons to be worked out, and this is what we are dealing with. To the short-sighted ego, who does not even see beyond life and death, these karmic lessons appear as injustice and trials it would rather do without. Nevertheless, they are of great service, as they gradually correct our vision. No doubt, there remain plenty of people around who will dedicate their lives to bothering others, simply because they do not want to take responsibility for their own lives. Even so, earth can be seen as a preschool where consciousness learns to walk. After graduation, greater possibilities for enfoldment awaits, but first basic lessons must be learnt.

[657] JOSEPH CAMPBELL, *THE HERO WITH A THOUSAND FACES* (1949)

ascension) are key to any good plot, and the universe seems to think so too. In the history of humanity, therefore, we find many different cultures where this universal play is intuitively grasped, but none summarized it better than the Upanishads. These ancient Sanskrit texts, dating from before 500 BCE, contain some of the central philosophical concepts and ideas of Hinduism. It is no coincidence that they are at the heart of India's wisdom tradition and the story of Vishnu's dream is worth a reminder. Vishnu, according to this myth, is the source of all Creation. He sustains and protects the Universe and is present everywhere—but to experience what he is not this deity must dream. Michael Talbot summarizes the mystic's perspective to this tale:

> *"There is a Hindu myth about the Self of the universe that perceives all of the existence as a form of play. However, since the Self is what there is, and is all that there is, it has no one separate to play with. Thus, according to the Hindu tradition, it plays a cosmic game of hide-and-seek with itself. It assumes a kaleidoscope of faces and facades—a dazzling infinity of masks and forms until it has become the living substance of the entire universe. In this game of hide-and-seek it can experience ten billion lifetimes, see through ten billion eyes, live and die ten billion times. Eventually, however, the Self awakens from its many dreams and remembers its true identity. It is the one and eternal Self of the cosmos. The game begins. The game ends."*[658]

It sure took time to bend the ego into shape so that it was ready to move on to the next level, but here it is: At this time, millions of people have begun to bridge the gap that keeps the ego ignorant of the greater reality and having opened consciousness to incorporate greater areas of the psyche, they know of the possibilities that await. No doubt, then, those who cling on to fake authority will have their hands full in the coming years. Even

---

[658] MICHAEL TALBOT, *MYSTICISM AND THE NEW PHYSICS* (1981) 160

without a war on drugs and terrorism, humanity has got enough problems to deal with. The Covid-19 debacle is another wake up call to a sleeping populace, and to the extent that our leaders continue to abide by mischievous ways, the example of Aurobindo should inspire us all. Indeed, a long-foretold apocalypse is imminent—and no doom-and-gloom is necessarily involved. The apocalypse simply means "the Uncovering", and it is up to us whether we want to give in to fearful fantasies or realign with constitutional ground.

The increasing polarity may be troubling, but as seen from the higher perspective it is merely a testimony to the ploughing of the field. No doubt, there are those who will go into the night with the old ego—and they will follow their path, but it will not be Earth's. For Earth, as the game of duality comes to an end, the idea of a limit is disintegrating; she is moving on to higher frequencies, and to the extent that we make a conscious effort to overcome the darkness within, we will find our way guided by the dictates of first principles. We can see it already has begun. Humanity's greatest hour is upon us, and as more millions every year get to know this new form of consciousness, the collective psyche will seize to be defined by unconsciousness: The human psyche will awaken to its true potential, and there will be a Higher Universal Man rising.

BIBLIOGRAPHY

Ackerman, Bruce, *The Rise of World Constitutionalism*, VIRGINIA LAW REVIEW VOL. 83:771 (1997)

AGEE, PHILIP, *INSIDE THE COMPANY: A CIA DIARY* (Stonehill 1975)

Ahrens, Deborah, *Drug Panics in the Twenty-First Century: Ecstasy, Prescription Drugs, and the Reframing of the War on Drugs*, ALBANY GOVERNMENT LAW REVIEW Vol. 6:397 (2013)

ALEXANDER, MICHELLE, *THE NEW JIM CROW: MASS INCARCERATION IN THE AGE OF COLORBLINDNESS* (New Press 2011)

Alexandre, Michelle, *Sex, Drugs, Rock & Roll and Moral Dirgisme: Toward a Reformation of Drug and Prostitution Regulations*, UMKC LAW REVIEW Vol. 78, No. 1 (2009)

ALEXY, ROBERT, *A THEORY OF CONSTITUTIONAL RIGHTS* (Oxford 2002)

Alexy, Robert, *Constitutional Rights and Proportionality*, JOURNAL FOR CONSTITUTIONAL THEORY AND PHILOSOPHY OF LAW VOL. 22:51 (2014)

AKHIL REED AMAR, *AMERICA'S UNWRITTEN CONSTITUTION: THE PRECEDENTS AND PRINCIPLES WE LIVE BY* (Basic Books 2012)

ANDENÆS, JOHS, *ALMINNELIG STRAFFERETT* (Universitetsforlaget 2004)

ANDENÆS, JOHS., *ETTER OVERVEIELSE: ARTIKLER I UTVALG* (Gyldendal 1992)

ANDENÆS, JOHS, *STRAFFEN SOM PROBLEM* (Exil 1994)

ANDENÆS, MADS & BJØRGE, ERIK, *MENNESKERETTENE OG OSS* (Universitetsforlaget 2012)

Anderson & Rees, *The Legalization of Recreational Marijuana: How Likely Is the Worst-Case Scenario?* JOURNAL OF POLICY ANALYSIS AND MANAGEMENT Vol. 33:221 (2014)

ANDREWS, ANDY, *HOW DO YOU KILL 11 MILLION PEOPLE* (Thomas Nelson 2010)

ANKERBERG, JOHN & WELDON, JOHN, *THE SECRET TEACHINGS OF THE MASONIC LODGE* (Moody 1990)

Araiza, William D., *Deference to Congressional Fact-Finding in Rights-Enforcing and Rights-Limiting Legislation*, NYU LAW REVIEW Vol. 88:878 (2013)

ARENDT, HANNAH, *THE ORIGINS OF TOTALITARIANISM* (Harcourt 1966)

ARKES, HADLEY, *BEYOND THE CONSTITUTION* (Princeton 1990)

ARKES, HADLEY, *CONSTITUTIONAL ILLUSIONS & ANCHORING TRUTHS: THE TOUCHSTONE OF THE NATURAL LAW* (Cambridge 2010)

Ashworth, Andrew, *Is the Criminal Law a Lost Cause?* LAW QUARTERLY REVIEW Vol.116:225 (2000)

ASSAGIOLI, ROBERTO, *TRANSPERSONAL DEVELOPMENT* (Aquarian 1993)

ATTWOOD, SHAUN, *AMERICAN MADE: WHO KILLED BARRY SEAL? PABLO ESCOBAR OR GEORGE H.W. BUSH* (Gadfly 2016)

AUROBINDO, SRI, *THE HOUR OF GOD* (Lotus Press 2009)

AUROBINDO, SRI, *THE HUMAN CYCLE* (Pondicherry 2012)

AUROBINDO, SRI, *THE IDEAL OF HUMAN UNITY* (Pondicherry 2012)

AUROBINDO, SRI, *THE LIFE DIVINE* (Pondicherry 1970)

AUROBINDO, SRI, *ON YOGA: THE SYNTHESIS OF YOGA* (Pondicherry 1957)

AUROBINDO, SRI, *WAR AND SELF-DETERMINATION* (Pondicherry 2012)

BAILYN, BERNARD, *THE IDEOLOGICAL ORIGINS OF THE AMERICAN REVOLUTION* (Harvard 1967)

BAINERMAN, JOEL, *CRIMES OF A PRESIDENT: NEW REVELATIONS ON THE CONSPIRACY AND COVER UP IN THE BUSH AND REAGAN ADMINISTRATION* (S.P.I. books 1992)

BAKALAR, JAMES B. & GRINSPOON, LESTER, *DRUG CONTROL IN A FREE SOCIETY*, (Cambridge 1998)

Balkin, Jack M., *Abortion and Original Meaning*, CONSTITUTIONAL COMMENTARY Vol. 24:291 (2007)

Ball, Carlos A., *Why Liberty Judicial Review is as Legitimate as Equality Review: The Case of Gay Rights Jurisprudence*, JOURNAL OF CONSTITUTIONAL LAW Vol. 14:1 (2011)

Bandow, Doug, *From Fighting the Drug War to Protecting the Right to Use Drugs: Recognizing a Forgotten Liberty*, FRASER INSTITUTE (2012)

Baradaran, Shima, *Drugs and Violence*, UNIVERSITY OF UTAH COLLEGE OF LAW Research Paper No. 75 (2015)

Barnett, Randy E., *An Originalism for Nonoriginalists*, BOSTON UNIVERSITY SCHOOL OF LAW Working Paper No. 99-14 (1999)

Barnett, Randy, *Bad Trip: Drug Prohibition and the Weakness of Public Policy*, YALE LAW JOURNAL Vol. 103:2593 (1994)

Barnett, Randy E., *Constitutional Clichés*, CAPITAL UNIVERSITY LAW REVIEW Vol. 36:493 (2008)

Barnett, Randy E., *From Antislavery Lawyer to Chief Justice: The Remarkable but Forgotten Career of Salmon P. Chase*, CASE WESTERN RESERVE LAW REVIEW Vol. 63:653 (2013)

Barnett, Randy E., *The Golden Mean Between Kurt & Dan: A Moderate Reading of the Ninth Amendment*, DRAKE LAW REVIEW Vol. 56:897 (2008)

Barnett, Randy E., *The Gravitational Force of Originalism*, GEORGETOWN PUBLIC LAW AND LEGAL THEORY Research Paper No. 13-010 (2013)

Barnett, Randy E., *The Harmful Side Effects of Drug Prohibition*, UTAH LAW REVIEW 11-34 (2009)

Barnett, Randy E., *The Imperative of Natural Rights in Today's World,* BOSTON UNIVERSITY SCHOOL OF LAW, Working Paper No. 03-20 (2003)

Barnett, Randy E., *Is the Constitution Libertarian?* GEORGETOWN PUBLIC LAW Research Paper No. 1432854 (2008)

Barnett, Randy E., *Justice Kennedy's Libertarian Revolution: Lawrence v. Texas*, BOSTON UNIVERSITY SCHOOL OF LAW, Working Paper No. 03-13 (2003)

Barnett, Randy E., *The Misconceived Assumption about Constitutional Assumptions*, GEORGETOWN LAW FACULTY Working Papers (2008)

Barnett, Randy E., *The Ninth Amendment: It Means What It Says*, TEXAS LAW REVIEW Vol. 85:1 (2006)

Barnett, Randy E., *The Original Meaning of the Judicial Power*, BOSTON UNIVERSITY SCHOOL OF LAW Working Paper No. 03-18 (2003)

Barnett, Randy E., *The Original Meaning of the Necessary and Proper Clause*, BOSTON UNIVERSITY SCHOOL OF LAW Working Paper No. 03-11 (2003)

Barnett, Randy E., *The People or the State: Chrisholm v. Georgia and Popular Sovereignty* VIRGINIA LAW REVIEW Vol. 93 (2007)

Barnett, Randy E., *The Presumption of Liberty and the Public Interest: Medical Marijuana and Fundamental Rights*, WASHINGTON UNIVERSITY JOURNAL OF LAW AND POLICY Vol. 22:29 (2006)

Barnett, Randy E., *The Proper Scope of the Police Power*, NOTRE DAME LAW REVIEW Vol. 79:429 (2004)

BARNETT, RANDY E., RESTORING THE LOST CONSTITUTION: THE PRESUMPTION OF LIBERTY (Princeton 2014)

Barnett, Randy E., *Scrutiny Land*, MICHIGAN LAW REVIEW Vol. 106:1479 (2008)

BARNETT, RANDY E., THE STRUCTURE OF LIBERTY: JUSTICE AND THE RULE OF LAW (Oxford 2014)

Barnett, Randy E., *We the People: Each and Every One*, YALE LAW JOURNAL Vol. 123:2576 (2014)

Barnett, Randy E., *Who's Afraid of Unenumerated Rights?* JOURNAL OF CONSTITUTIONAL LAW Vol. 9:1 (2006)

Barrett, Damon, *Security, Development and Human Rights: Normative, Legal and Policy Challenges for the International Drug Control System*, INTERNATIONAL JOURNAL OF DRUG POLICY 21 (2010)

BAUM, DAN, SMOKE AND MIRRORS: THE WAR ON DRUGS AND THE POLITICS OF FAILURE (Little Brown 1996)

Beale, Sara Sun, *What's Law Got To Do With It? The Political, Social, Psychological and Other Non-Legal Factors Influencing the Development of (Federal) Criminal Law*, BUFFALO CRIMINAL LAW REVIEW Vol. 1:23 (1997)

BEATTY, DAVID M., THE ULTIMATE RULE OF LAW (Oxford 2004)

BECKER, DEAN, TO END THE WAR ON DRUGS: POLICYMAKERS' EDITION (DTN Media 2014)

BEIEROT, NILS, NARKOTIKA OCH NARKOMANI (Bonniers 1965)

BENNETT, SCOTT, SHELL GAME: A WHISTLEBLOWING REPORT TO THE U.S. CONGRESS (2013) (online book)

Benson, Bruce L., *The War on Drugs: A Public Bad*, NORTHWESTERN UNIVERSITY'S SEARLE CENTER ON LAW (2008)

Bergland, David, *Libertarianism, Natural Rights and the Constitution, A Commentary on Recent Libertarian Literature*, CLEVELAND STATE LAW REVIEW Vol. 44:499 (1996)

BERNAYS, EDWARD, PROPAGANDA (Routledge 1928)

BERTRAM, EVA, ET AL., DRUG WAR POLITICS: THE PRICE OF DENIAL (University of California 1996)

BEWLEY-TAYLOR, DAVID R.., INTERNATIONAL DRUG CONTROL: CONSENSUS FRACTURED (Cambridge 2012)

Bibas, Stephanos & Bierschbach, Richard A., *Constitutionally Tailoring Punishment*, MICHIGAN LAW REVIEW Vol. 112:397 (2013)

Bilionis, Louis D., *The New Scrutiny*, Emory Law Journal Vol. 51:101 (2002)

Bilionis, Louis D., *On the Significance of Constitutional Spirit*, NORTH CAROLINA LAW REVIEW Vol. 70:1803 (1992)

Bilionis, Louis D., *Process, the Constitution, and Substantive Criminal Law,* MICHIGAN LAW REVIEW Vol.96:1269 (1998)

BLACK, CHARLES L., *A NEW BIRTH FOR FREEDOM: HUMAN RIGHTS, NAMED AND UNNAMED* (Yale 1999)

BLACK, EDWIN, *NAZI NEXUS: AMERICA'S CORPORATE CONNECTIONS TO HITLER'S HOLOCAUST* (Dialog 2009).

BLAU, JUDITH & MONCADA, ALBERTO, *JUSTICE IN THE UNITED STATES: HUMAN RIGHTS AND THE U.S. CONSTITUTION* (Rowman & Littlefield 2006)

BLAVATSKY, HELENA, *THE SECRET DOCTRINE: THE SYNTHESIS OF SCIENCE, RELIGION AND PHILOSOPHY* (Kessinger1938)

Blickman & Jelsma, *Drug Policy Reform in Practice: Experiences with Alternatives in Europe and the US*, TRANSNATIONAL INSTITUTE (2009)

Block, Walter, *Drug Prohibition: A Legal and Economic Analysis*, JOURNAL OF BUSINESS ETHICS Vol. 12:689 (1993)

BLUM, WILLIAM, *KILLING HOPE: U.S. MILITARY AND C.I.A. INTERVENTIONS SINCE WORLD WAR II* (Common Courage 2003)

Blumenson, Eric, *Recovering from Drugs and the Drug War: An Achievable Public Health Alternative,* JOURNAL OF GENDER, RACE AND JUSTICE Vol. 6, No. 2 (2002)

Blumenson, Eric & Nilsen, Eva, *Policing for Profit: The Drug War's Hidden Economic Agenda*, UNIVERSITY OF CHICAGO LAW REVIEW Vol. 65:35 (1998)

BOLLINGER, LORENTZ (ED.), *CANNABIS SCIENCE: FROM PROHIBITION TO HUMAN RIGHT* (Peter Lang 1997)

Bollinger, Lorentz, *Recent Developments Regarding Drug Law and Policy in Germany and the European Community: The Evolution of Drug Control in Europe*, JOURNAL OF DRUG ISSUES (2002)

Bomhoff, Jacco, *Genealogies of Balancing as Discourse*, LAW & ETHICS OF HUMAN RIGHTS, Vol. 4, Issue 1, Article 6 (2010)

BONGINO, DAN, *SPYGATE: THE ATTEMPTED SABOTAGE OF DONALD J. TRUMP* (Post Hill 2018)

Bonnie, Richard & Whitebread, Charles, *The Forbidden Fruit and the Tree of Knowledge: An Inquiry into the Legal History of American Marijuana Prohibition*, VIRGINIA LAW REVIEW Vol. 56:971 (1970)

Borgmann, Caitlin E., *Rethinking Judicial Deference to Legislative Fact-Finding*, INDIANA LAW JOURNAL Vol. 81:1 (2009)

BOWARD, JAMES, *LOST RIGHTS: THE DESTRUCTION OF AMERICAN LIBERTY* (St. Martin's Griffin 1995)

Boyd, Graham, *Collateral Damage in the War on Drugs*, VILLANOVA LAW REVIEW Vol. 47:839 (2002)

Brandeis, Jason, *The Continuing Vitality of Ravin v. State: Alaskans Still Have a Constitutional Right to Possess Marijuana in the Privacy of their Homes*, ALASKA LAW REVIEW Vol. 29:2 (2012)

Brashear, Bruce, *Marijuana Prohibition and the Constitutional Right of Privacy: An Examination of Ravin v. State*, TULSA LAW JOURNAL Vol. 11:563 (1975)

BROGAN, HUGH, *LONGMAN HISTORY OF THE UNITED STATES OF AMERICA* (Guild 1987)

Brown, Darryl K., *Can Criminal Law Be Controlled?* MICHIGAN LAW REVIEW Vol. 108:971 (2010)

BROWN, L.D, *CROSSFIRE: WITNESS IN THE CLINTON INVESTIGATION* (Black Forest 1999)

Brown-Nagin, Tomiko, *The Civil Rights Canon: Above and Below*, YALE LAW JOURNAL Vol. 123:2698 (2014)

Brown, Rebecca L., *Liberty, the New Equality*, NYU LAW REVIEW Vol. 77:1491 (2002)

BUCCHI, KENNETH C., *OPERATION PSEUDO MIRANDA: A VETERAN OF THE CIA DRUG WARS TELLS ALL* (Penmarine 2000)

Buchhandler-Raphael, Michal, *Drugs, Dignity, and Danger: Human Dignity as a Constitutional Constraint to Limit Overcriminalization*, TENNESSEE LAW REVIEW, Vol. 80 (2013)

BUCKE, R. M., *COSMIC CONSCIOUSNESS: A STUDY IN THE EVOLUTION OF THE HUMAN MIND* (University Books 1961)

BURDICK, CHARLES K., *THE LAW OF THE AMERICAN CONSTITUTION: ITS ORIGIN AND DEVELOPMENT* (Putnam 1922)

BUTLER, SMEDLEY, *WAR IS A RACKET: THE PROFIT MOTIVE BEHIND WARFARE* (World Library 2010)

CAMPBELL, JOSEPH, *THE HERO WITH A THOUSAND FACES* (Pantheon 1949)

CAPRA, FRITJOF, *THE TAO OF PHYSICS: AN EXPLORATION OF THE PARALLELS BETWEEN MODERN PHYSICS AND EASTERN MYSTICISM* (Shambala 2010)

CAREY, GEORGE WASHINGTON, *GOD-MAN: THE WORD MADE FLESH* (1920)

CASTILLO, CELERINO, *POWDERBURNS: COCAINE, CONTRAS AND THE DRUG WAR* (Sundial 1994)

CHEIN, ISIDORE, ET AL., *THE ROAD TO H: NARCOTICS, DELINQUENCY, AND SOCIAL POLICY* (Basic books 1964)

Chemerinsky, Erwin, *The Constitution and Punishment*, STANFORD LAW REVIEW Vol. 56:1049 (2004)

Chemerinsky, Erwin, *Substantive Due Process*, TOURO LAW REVIEW Vol. 15:1501 (1999)

CHOMSKY, NOAM, *POWER AND TERROR: CONFLICT, HEGEMONY, AND THE RULE OF FORCE* (Pluto 2011)

Christiansen, Matthew A., *A Great Schism: Social Norms and Marijuana Prohibition*, HARVARD LAW & POLICY REVIEW Vol. 4:229 (2010)

CHRISTIE, NILS, *KRIMINALITETSKONTROLL SOM INDUSTRI* (Universitetsforlaget 2000)

CHRISTIE, NILS, & BRUUN, KETIL, *DEN GODE FIENDE* (Universitetsforlaget 1985)

CLOSE, EDWARD R., *TRANSCENDENTAL PHYSICS* (toExcel Press 2000)

Colb, Sherry, *Freedom from Incarceration: Why is This Right Different from All Other Rights?* NYU LAW REVIEW Vol. 69:781 (1994)

COLBY, GERARD, *DU PONT DYNASTY: BEHIND THE NYLON CURTAIN* (Lyle Stuart 1984)

Cole, David, *Formalism, Realism, and the War on Drugs*, SUFFOLK UNIVERSITY LAW REVIEW Vol. 35: 241 (2001)

Conkle, Daniel O., *The Second Death of Substantive Due Process*, INDIANA LAW JOURNAL Vol. 62:215 (1987)

CONRAD, CLAY S., *JURY NULLIFICATION: THE EVOLUTION OF A DOCTRINE* (Carolina 1998)

CONRAD, NORRIS & RESNER, *HUMAN RIGHTS AND THE US DRUG WAR* (Creative Xpressions 2001)

CORSI, JEROME R., *KILLING THE DEEP STATE* (Humanix 2018)

Csete, Joanne, *From the Mountaintops: What the World Can Learn from Drug Policy Change in Switzerland*, OPEN SOCIETY FOUNDATIONS (2010)

Cunnings, Jordan, *Nonserious Marijuana Offenses and Noncitizens: Uncounseled Pleas and Disproportionate Consequences*, UCLA LAW REVIEW Vol. 62:510 (2015)

CURTIS, MICHAEL, *NO STATE SHALL ABRIDGE: THE FOURTEENTH AMENDMENT AND THE BILL OF RIGHTS* (Duke 1986)

D'Amato, Anthony, *Natural Law: A Libertarian View*, FACULTY WORKING PAPERS, Paper 148 (2008)

DAMON, WILLIAM & COLBY, ANNE, *SOME DO CARE: CONTEMPORARY LIVES OF MORAL COMMITMENT* (New York 1992)

Danovitch, Itai, *Sorting Through the Science on Marijuana: Facts, Fallacies, and Implications for Legalization*, MCGEORGE LAW REVIEW Vol. 43:91 (2013)

DALRYMPLE, THEODORE, *ROMANCING OPIATES: PHARMACOLOGICAL LIES AND THE ADDICTION BUREAUCRACY* (Encounter 2008)

DAVIES, PAUL, *THE COSMIC BLUEPRINT: NEW DISCOVERIES IN NATURE'S CREATIVE ABILITY TO ORDER THE UNIVERSE* (Templeton Foundation Press 2004)

DAVIES, PAUL & GRIBBIN, JOHN, *THE MATTER MYTH: DRAMATIC DISCOVERIES THAT CHALLENGE OUR UNDERSTANDING OF PHYSICAL REALITY* (Simon & Schuster 1992)

DEAN, STANLEY R. (ED.), *PSYCHIATRY & MYSTICISM* (Nelson-Hall 1979)

DECAMP, JOHN, *THE FRANKLIN COVER-UP* (AWT. Inc 1992)

DECHARDIN, TEILHARD, *LETTERS FROM A TRAVELLER* (Fontana 1975)

DE GREIFF, PABLO (ED.), *DRUGS AND THE LIMITS OF LIBERALISM* (Cornell 1999)

DICE, MARK, *ILLUMINATI: FACTS AND FICTION* (The Resitance 2009)

Dichter, Mark S., *Marijuana and the Law: The Constitutional Challenges to Marijuana Laws in Light of the Social Aspects of Marijuana Use*, VILLANOVA LAW REVIEW Vol. 13:851 (1968)

Dippel, Horst, *Modern Constitutionalism: An Introduction to a History in the Need of Writing*, **THE LEGAL HISTORY REVIEW** Vol. 73:**153 (2005)**

Domosławski, Artur, *Drug Policy in Portugal: The Benefits of Decriminalizing Drug Use*, OPEN SOCIETY FOUNDATIONS (2011)

Doss, Arden & Doss, Diane, *On Morals, Privacy, and the Constitution*, UNIVERSITY OF MIAMI LAW REVIEW Vol. 25:395 (1971)

DOSSEY, LARRY, *REINVENTING MEDICINE: BEYOND MIND-BODY TO A NEW ERA OF HEALING* (Harper Collins 1999)

Dubber, Markus D., *A Political Theory of Criminal Law: Autonomy and the Legitimacy of State Punishment*, LEGITIMATING CRIMINAL LAW (2004)

Dubber, Markus D., *The Legality Principle in American and German Criminal Law: An Essay in Comparative Legal History* (2010)

Dubber, Markus D., *New Legal Science: Toward Law as a Global Discipline* (2014)

Dubber, Markus D., *The New Police Science and the Police Power Model of the Criminal Process* (2004)

Dubber, Markus D., *Policing Possession: The War on Crime and the End of Criminal Law*, JOURNAL OF CRIMINAL LAW AND CRIMINOLOGY Vol. 91:829 (2001)

Dubber, Markus D., *Toward a Constitutional Law of Crime and Punishment*, HASTINGS LAW JOURNAL Vol. 55 (2004)

Duke, Steven B., *Drug Prohibition: an Unnatural Disaster*, FACULTY SCHOLARSHIP SERIES, paper 812 (1995)

Duke, Steven B., *The Future of Marijuana in the United States,* YALE LAW SCHOOL, Public Law Working Paper No. 299 (2013)

Duke, Steven B., *Mass Imprisonment, Crime Rates, and the Drug War: A Penological and Humanitarian Disgrace,* FACULTY SCHOLARSHIP SERIES, Paper 826 (2010)

DUKE, STEVEN, B. & CROSS, ALBERT C., *AMERICA'S LONGEST WAR: RETHINKING OUR TRAGIC CRUSADE AGAINST DRUGS* (Tarcher/Putnam 1993)

DWORKIN, RONALD, *A MATTER OF PRINCIPLE* (Harvard 1985)

DWORKIN, RONALD, *LAW'S EMPIRE* (Harvard 1986)

DWORKIN, RONALD, *SOVEREIGN VIRTUE: THE THEORY AND PRACTICE OF EQUALITY* (Harvard 2002)

DWORKIN, RONALD, *TAKING RIGHTS SERIOUSLY* (Harvard 1978)

Ely, John Hart, *Legislative and Administrative Motivation in Constitutional Law*, FACULTY SCHOLARSHIP SERIES, paper 4114 (1970)

EPSTEIN, EDWARD J., *AGENCY OF FEAR: OPIATES AND POLITICAL POWER IN AMERICA* (Verso 1990)

Erlinder, Peter, *Mens Rea, Due Process, and the Supreme Court: Toward a Constitutional Doctrine of Substantive Criminal Law*, AMERICAN JOURNAL OF CRIMINAL LAW Vol. 9:163 (1989)

ESCOHOTADO, ANTONIO, *A BRIEF HISTORY OF DRUGS: FROM THE STONE AGE TO THE STONED AGE* (Park Street 1999)

ESKELAND, STÅLE, *DE MEST ALVORLIGE FORBRYTELSER* (Cappelen Damm 2011)

Eskridge, William N., *Destabilizing Due Process and Evolutive Equal Protection*, UCLA LAW REVIEW Vol. 47:1183 (2000)

European Commission for Democracy through Law, *European and U.S. Constitutionalism*, SCIENCE AND TECHNIQUE OF DEMOCRACY, No. 37 (2003)

Eylon & Harel, *The Right to Judicial Review,* VIRGINIA LAW REVIEW Vol. 92, No. 5 (2006)

Fallon, Richard H., *Individual Rights and Governmental Powers*, GEORGIA LAW REVIEW Vol. 27:343 (1993)

Fallon, Richard H., *Legitimacy and the Constitution*, HARVARD LAW REVIEW Vol. 118:1787 (2005)

Farrell, Robert C., *Justice Kennedy's Idiosyncratic Understanding of Equal Protection and Due Process, and its Costs*, QUINNIPIAC LAW REVIEW Vol. 32:439 (2014)

FEINBERG, JOEL, *HARMLESS WRONGDOING: THE MORAL LIMITS OF THE CRIMINAL LAW* (Oxford 1990)

FEINBERG, JOEL, *HARM TO OTHERS: THE MORAL LIMITS OF THE CRIMINAL LAW* (Oxford 1987)

Finer, Joel J., *Psychedelics and Religious Freedom*, HASTINGS LAW JOURNAL Vol. 19:667 (1968)

Finkelstein, Claire, *Positivism and the Notion of an Offense*, CALIFORNIA LAW REVIEW Vol. 88:335 (2000)

FINNEY, CHARLES, *THE CHARACTER, CLAIMS, AND PRACTICAL WORKINGS OF FREEMASONRY* (DAY 1998)

FINNIS, JOHN, *NATURAL LAW AND NATURAL RIGHTS* (Oxford 2011)

FISH, JEFFERSON (ED.), *HOW TO LEGALIZE DRUGS* (Northvale 1998)

FISHER, PAUL A., *BEHIND THE LODGE DOOR* (Shield 1989)

Fiss, Owen M., *Groups and the Equal Protection Clause*, PHILOSOPHY AND PUBLIC AFFAIRS Vol. 5:107 (1976)

FORST, RAINER, *THE RIGHT TO JUSTIFICATION: A CONSTRUCTIVIST THEORY OF JUSTICE* (Columbia 2011)

FORTE, ROBERT (ED.), *ENTHEOGENS AND THE FUTURE OF RELIGION* (Park Street 2012)

FOWLER, JAMES W., *STAGES OF FAITH: THE PSYCHOLOGY OF HUMAN DEVELOPMENT AND THE QUEST FOR MEANING* (Harper 1981)

FOWLER, JAMES W., *WEAVING THE NEW CREATION: STAGES OF FAITH AND THE PUBLIC CHURCH* (Harper 1991)

FULLER, LON, *THE MORALITY OF LAW* (Yale 1969)

Galliher, Keys & Elsner, *Lindesmith v. Anslinger: An Early Government Victory in the Failed War on Drugs*, JOURNAL OF CRIMINAL LAW AND CRIMINOLOGY Vol. 88:681 (1998)

GARLAND, DAVID, *THE CULTURE OF CONTROL: CRIME AND SOCIAL ORDER IN CONTEMPORARY SOCIETY* (Chicago 2001)

GARWOOD, DARRELL, *UNDER COVER: THIRTY-FIVE YEARS OF CIA DECEPTION* (Grove Press 1985)

GEBSER, JEAN, *THE EVER PRESENT ORIGIN* (Ohio 1997)

GERBER, RICHARD, *VIBRATIONAL MEDICINE* (Bear & Co 2001)

GERBER, RUDOLPH J., *LEGALIZING MARIJUANA: DRUG REFORM AND PROHIBITION POLITICS* (Greenwood 2004)

Gerber, Scott D., *Liberal Originalism: The Declaration of Independence and Constitutional Interpretation*, CLEVELAND STATE LAW REVIEW Vol. 63:1 (2014)

GERBER, SCOTT D., *TO SECURE THESE RIGHTS* (New York 1995)

Gershowitz, Adam M., *An Informational Approach to the Mass Imprisonment Problem*, FACULTY PUBLICATIONS, Paper 1264 (2008)

GEWIRTH, ALAN, *THE COMMUNITY OF RIGHTS* (Chicago 1996)

GEWIRTH, ALAN, *REASON AND MORALITY* (Chicago 1981)

GLOVER, JONATHAN, *HUMANITY: A MORAL HISTORY OF THE TWENTIETH CENTURY* (Random House 1999)

Goldberg, Suzanne B., *Equality Without Tiers*, SOUTHERN CALIFORNIA LAW REVIEW Vol. 77:481 (2004)

GONZALEZ, SERVANDO, *PSYCHOLOGICAL WARFARE AND THE NEW WORLD ORDER: THE SECRET WAR AGAINST THE AMERICAN PEOPLE* (Spooks 2010)

GOSWAMI, AMIT, *THE SELF-AWARE UNIVERSE: HOW CONSCIOUSNESS CREATES THE MATERIAL WORLD* (Simon & Schuster 1993)

Gowder, Paul, *Equal Law in an Unequal World*, IOWA LAW REVIEW Vol. 99:1021 (2014)

GRAY, CHRISTOPHER, *THE ACID DIARIES: A PSYCHONAUT'S GUIDE TO THE HISTORY AND USE OF LSD* (Park Street 2010)

GRAY, JAMES P., *WHY OUR DRUG LAWS HAVE FAILED AND WHAT WE CAN DO ABOUT IT: A JUDICIAL INDICTMENT OF THE WAR ON DRUGS* (Temple 2001)

Grey, Thomas C., *The Uses of an Unwritten Constitution*, CHICAGO-KENT LAW REVIEW Vol. 64:211 (1988)

GRIFFIN, DAVID RAY, *9/11 CONTRADICTIONS: AN OPEN LETTER TO CONGRESS AND THE PRESS* (Interlink 2008)

GRIFFIN, G. EDWARD, *THE CREATURE FROM JEKYLL ISLAND* (American Media 2002)

GRINSPOON, LESTER, *MARIJUANA RECONSIDERED* (Harvard 1977)

GRITZ, JAMES BO, *A NATION BETRAYED* (Lazarus 1989)

Grob, Charles et al., *Pilot Study of Psilocybin Treatment for Anxiety in Patients with Advanced-stage Cancer*, ARCHIVES OF GENERAL PSYCHIATRY Vol. 68, no. 1 (2011)

GROF, STANISLAV, *THE COSMIC GAME: EXPLORATIONS OF THE FRONTIERS OF HUMAN CONSCIOUSNESS* (Suny 1998)

GROF, STANISLAV, *LSD: DOORWAY TO THE NUMINOUS* (Park Street 2009)

GROF, STANISLAV, *PSYCHOLOGY OF THE FUTURE* (Suny Press 2000)

GROF, STANISLAV, *REALMS OF THE HUMAN UNCONSCIOUS: OBSERVATIONS FROM LSD RESEARCH* (Souvenir 1979)

GROF, STANISLAV, *WHEN THE IMPOSSIBLE HAPPENS* (Soundstrue 2006)

GROF, STANISLAV & HALIFAX, JOAN, *THE HUMAN ENCOUNTER WITH DEATH* (Dutton 1977)

Grosman, Lucas S., *Drugs under the Constitution*, SELA PAPERS, Paper 108 (2012)

Grund, Jean-Paul & Breeksema, Joost, *Coffee Shops and Compromise: Separated Illicit Drug Markets in the Netherlands*, OPEN SOCIETY FOUNDATIONS (2013)

Gunther, Gerald, Foreword: *In Search of Evolving Doctrine on a Changing Court: A Model for a Newer Equal Protection*, HARVARD LAW REVIEW Vol. 86:1 (1972)

Gur-Arye, Miriam & Weigend, Thomas, *Constitutional Review of Criminal Prohibitions Affecting Human Dignity and Liberty: German and Israeli Perspectives*, ISRAELI LAW REVIEW Vol. 44:63 (2011)

HAGBERG, JANET & GUELICH, ROBERT, *THE CRITICAL JOURNEY: STAGES IN THE LIFE OF FAITH* (Sheffield 2004)

HALL, MANLY P., *THE SECRET DESTINY OF AMERICA* (Philosophical Research Society 1944) (online book)

Hallam, Bewley-Taylor, & Jelsma, *Scheduling in the International Drug Control System*, SERIES ON LEGISLATIVE REFORM OF DRUG POLICIES No. 25 (2014)

Hamburger, Philip A., *Natural Rights, Natural Law & American Constitutions*, YALE LAW JOURNAL Vol. 102: 907 (1993)

HAMEROFF, KASZNIAK & SCOTT (EDS.), *TOWARD A SCIENCE OF CONSCIOUSNESS* (Cambridge 1998)

HANCOCK, GRAHAM (ED.), *THE DIVINE SPARK: PSYCHEDELICS, CONSCIOUSNESS AND THE BIRTH OF CIVILIZATION* (HayHouse 2015)

HART, CARL, *HIGH PRICE* (Harper 2014)

Hart, Henry M., *The Aims of the Criminal Law*, LAW AND CONTEMPORARY PROBLEMS Vol. 23:401 (1958)

HARTSTEIN, MAX, *THE WAR ON DRUGS: THE WORST ADDICTION OF ALL* (iUniverse 2003)

HASKINS, G.L., *LAW AND AUTHORITY IN EARLY MASSACHUSETTS* (Archon1968)

HEINDEL, MAX, *THE ROSICRUCIAN COSMO-CONCEPTION* (Ulan 2012)

HELLMAN, ARTHUR D., *LAWS AGAINST MARIJUANA: THE PRICE WE PAY* (University of Illinois 1975)

HERBERT, NICK, *QUANTUM REALITY: BEYOND THE NEW PHYSICS* (Doubleday 1985)

HERER, JACK, *THE EMPEROR WEARS NO CLOTHES* (Ah Ha publishing 1998)

Hessick, Andrew, *Rethinking the Presumption of Constitutionality*, NOTRE DAME LAW REVIEW Vol. 85:1447 (2010)

Heyman, Steven J., *The First Duty of Government: Protection, Liberty, and the Fourteenth Amendment*, DUKE LAW JOURNAL 41:507 (1991)

Hindes, Thomas L., *Morality Enforcement Through the Criminal Law and the Modern Doctrine of Substantive Due Process*, UNIVERSITY OF PENNSYLVANIA LAW REVIEW Vol. 126:344 (1977)

Hirschl, Ran, *The Rise of Comparative Constitutional Law: Thoughts on substance and Method*, INDIAN JOURNAL OF CONSTITUTIONAL LAW (2008)

HOBBES, THOMAS, *LEVIATHAN* (Penguin 1982)

Holmes, Justice, *Common Carriers and the Common Law*, THE ANGLO-AMERICAN LAW REVIEW Vol. 13:609 (1879)

HOOD, RALPH, *HANDBOOK OF RELIGIOUS EXPERIENCE* (Religious Education Press 1995)

Hughes, Jula, *Restraint and Proliferation in criminal Law*, REVIEW OF CONSTITUTIONAL STUDIES Vol. 15, Issue 1 (2010)

Huhn, Wilson, *The Jurisprudential Revolution: Unlocking Human Potential in Grutter and Lawrence*, WILLIAM & MARY BILL OF RIGHTS JOURNAL Vol. 12:65 (2004)

Husak, Douglas, *Applying Ultima Ratio: A Skeptical Assessment*, OHIO STATE JOURNAL OF CRIMINAL LAW Vol. 2:535 (2005)

HUSAK, DOUGLAS, *DRUGS AND RIGHTS* (Cambridge 1996)

Husak, Douglas, *Four Points about Drug Decriminalization*, CRIMINAL JUSTICE ETHICS Vol. 22, Issue 1 (2003)

HUSAK, DOUGLAS, *LEGALIZE THIS! THE CASE FOR DECRIMINALIZING DRUGS* (Verso 2002)

Husak, Douglas, *Liberal Neutrality, Autonomy, and Drug Prohibitions*, PHILOSOPHY AND PUBLIC AFFAIRS Vol. 29, No. 1 (2000)

HUSAK, DOUGLAS, *OVERCRIMINALIZATION: THE LIMITS OF THE CRIMINAL LAW* (Oxford 2008)

HUSAK, DOUGLAS & DE MARNEFFE, PETER, *THE LEGALIZATION OF DRUGS: FOR AND AGAINST* (Cambridge 2005)

HØSTMÆLINGEN, NJÅL, *HVA ER MENNESKERETTIGHETER?* (Universitetsforlaget 2010)

Jackson, Jeffrey D., *Putting Rationality Back Into the Rational Basis Test: Saving Substantive Due Process and Redeeming the Promise of the Ninth Amendment*, UNIVERSITY OF RICHMOND LAW REVIEW Vol. 45:491 (2011)

Jackson, Vicki C., *Constitutional Law in an Age of Proportionality*, YALE LAW REVIEW Vol. 124:3094 (2015)

JAHN, ROBERT & DUNNE, BRENDA, *MARGINS OF REALITY: THE ROLE OF CONSCIOUSNESS IN THE PHYSICAL WORLD* (Harcourt 1987)

JAMES, WILLIAM, *THE VARIETIES OF RELIGIOUS EXPERIENCE* (Barnes & Noble 2004)

JEFFERSON, THOMAS, *THE ANAS* (Online book)

Jelsma, Martin, *Drugs in the UN system: the Unwritten History of the 1998 United Nations General Assembly Special Session on Drugs*, INTERNATIONAL JOURNAL OF DRUG POLICY Vol. 14 (2003)

Kadish, Sanford H., *The Crisis of Overcriminalization*, AMERICAN CRIMINAL LAW QUARTERLY Vol.7:17 (1968)

Kadish, Sanford H., *Fifty Years of Criminal Law: An Opinionated Review*, CALIFORNIA LAW REVIEW Vol. 87: 943 (1999)

KAPLAN, JOHN, *MARIJUANA: THE NEW PROHIBITION* (Pocket Books 1971)

Kaplan, John, *The Role of Law in Drug Control: Self-Harming Conduct and Society*, DUKE LAW JOURNAL Vol. 1971:1065 (1971)

Karlan, Pamela S., *Equal Protection, Due Process and the Stereoscopic Fourteenth Amendment*, McGeorge Law Review Vol. 33:473 (2002)

Karst, Kenneth L., *The Liberties of Equal Citizens: Groups and the Due Process Clause*, UCLA Law Review Vol. 55:99 (2007)

Kennan, George, *E. H. Harriman: Railroad Czar* (Cosimo 2011)

Kesavan & Stokes, *The Interpretive Force of the Constitution's Secret Drafting History*, Georgia Law Journal Vol. 91:1112 (2003)

King, Rufus, *The Drug Hang Up: America's Fifty-Year Folly* (Norton 1972)

King, Rufus, *Wild Shots in the War on Crime*, Journal of Public Law Vol. 20:85 (1971)

Krishna, Gopi, *Kundalini: The Evolutionary Energy in Man* (Shambala 1997)

Kruger, Henrik, *The Great Heroin Coup: Drugs, Intelligence, and International Fascism* (Trineday 2015)

Krøvel, Roy, *Kokainkrigen: 20 år av en velsignet forbannelse* (Fagbokforlaget 2004)

Kumm, Mattias, *Democracy is not enough: Rights, proportionality and the point of judicial review*, New York University Public Law and Legal Theory Working Papers, Paper 118 (2009)

Kumm, Mattias, *The Idea of Socratic Contestation and the Right to Justification: The Point of Rights-Based Proportionality Review*, Law & Ethics of Human Rights Vol. 4:141 (2010)

Kurland, Philip & Lerner, Ralph, *The Founders' Constitution* (Online book)

Kwitny, Jonathan, *The Crimes of Patriots: A True Tale of Dope, Dirty Money, and the CIA* (Norton 1987)

Langer, Ellen & Alexander, Charles, *Higher Stages of Human Development: Perspectives on Adult Growth* (Oxford 1990)

Laniel, Laurent, *The Relationship between Research and Drug Policy in the United States*, Management of Social Transformations, Discussion Paper No. 44 (1999)

Lanza, Robert, *Biocentricism: How Life and Consciousness are the Keys to Understanding the True Nature of the Universe* (Benbella 2009)

Lash, Kurt, *The Lost History of the Ninth Amendment: The Lost Original Meaning*, Loyola Law School, Research Paper No. 2004-5 (2004)

Lee, Donna, *Resuscitating Proportionality in Noncapital Criminal Sentencing*, Arizona State Law Journal Vol. 40:527 (2008)

Lee, Youngjae, *The Constitutional Right Against Excessive Punishment*, New York University Public Law and Legal Theory Working Papers, Paper 3 (2005)

Lett, Donald G., *Phoenix Rising: The Rise and Fall of the American Republic* (Authorhouse 2008)

Leveritt, Mara, *The Boys on the Tracks: Death, Denial, and a Mother's Crusade to Bring Her Son's Killers to Justice* (Dunne 1999)

Levinson, Daryl J., *Empire-Building Government in Constitutional Law*, NYU Law School Public Law and Legal Theory Working Paper Series, Working Paper No. 84 (2004)

Levinson, Rosalie Berger, *Reining in Abuses of Executive Power through Substantive Due Process*, Florida Law Review Vol. 60:519 (2008)

Lewis, C. S., *The Problem of Pain* (MacMillan 1962)

Lindauer, Susan, *Extreme Prejudice: The Terrifying Story of the Patriot Act and the Cover Ups of 9/11 and Iraq* (Createspace 2010)

Lipton, Bruce H., *The Biology of Belief: Unleashing the Power of Consciousness, Matter and Miracles* (HayHouse 2010)

Locke, John, *Essays on the Law of Nature* (Clarendon 1954)

Locke, John, *Two Treaties of Government and a Letter Concerning Toleration* (Yale 2003)

Lofgren, Mike, *The Deep State: The Fall of the Constitution and the Rise of the Shadow Government* (Penguin 2016)

Loewald, Hans W., *Papers on Psychoanalysis* (Yale 1980)

Loewald, Hans W., *Sublimination: Inquiries into Theoretical Psychoanalysis* (Yale 1988)

Lollini, Andrea, *The South African Constitutional Court Experience: Reasoning Patterns Based on Foreign Law*, Utrecht Law Review Vol. 8, Issue 2 (2012)

Luna, Erik, *The Overcriminalization Phenomenon*, American University Law Review Vol. 54:703 (2005)

LYNCH, TIMOTHY, (ED.), *AFTER PROHIBITION: AN ADULT APPROACH TO DRUG POLICIES IN THE 21ST CENTURY* (2000)

MAAS, PETER, *MANHUNT* (Randomhouse1986)

MACCOUN, ROBERT & REUTER, PETER, *DRUG WAR HERESIES* (Cambridge 2001)

MACKAY, CHARLES, *EXTRAORDINARY POPULAR DELUSIONS AND THE MADNESS OF CROWDS* (Bentley 1841)

MADISON, HAMILTON & JAY, *THE FEDERALIST PAPERS* (Timeless Classics 2010)

Maguire, Sarah A. & Nourse, V.F, *The Lost History of Governance and Equal Protection*, DUKE LAW JOURNAL Vol. 58:955 (2009)

MARTIN, AL, *THE CONSPIRATORS: SECRETS OF AN IRAN-CONTRA INSIDER* (National Liberty 2002)

MASLOW, ABRAHAM, *RELIGIONS, VALUES, AND PEAK-EXPERIENCES* (Penguin 1994)

MASLOW, ABRAHAM, *TOWARD A PSYCHOLOGY OF BEING* (Van Nostrand 1982)

Massey, Calvin, *The New Formalism: Requiem for Tiered Scrutiny?* UNIVERSITY OF PENNSYLVANIA JOURNAL OF CONSTITUTIONAL LAW Vol. 6:945 (2004)

MASTERS, BILL, *DRUG WAR ADDICTION: NOTES FROM THE FRONTLINES OF AMERICA'S NO. 1 POLICY DISASTER* (Accurate 2001)

Materni, Mike C., *The 100-plus Year old Case for a Minimalist Criminal Law*, NEW CRIMINAL LAW REVIEW Vol. 18 issue 3 (2015)

MATHRE, M.L., *CANNABIS IN MEDICAL PRACTICE: A LEGAL, HISTORICAL, AND PHARMACOLOGICAL OVERVIEW OF THE THERAPEUTIC USE OF MARIJUANA* (McFarland 1997)

MATTHEWS, PATRICK, *CANNABIS CULTURE: A JOURNEY THROUGH DISPUTED TERRITORY* (Bloomsbury 1999)

Mazur, Cynthia S., *Marijuana as a Holy Sacrament: Is the Issue of Peyote Constitutionally Distinguishable from That of Marijuana in Bona Fide Religious Ceremonies?* NOTRE DAME LAW REVIEW Vol. 5:693 (1991)

MAZUR, ROBERT, *THE INFILTRATOR* (Little Brown 2009)

McAffee, Thomas B., *The Original Meaning of the Ninth Amendment*, COLOMBIA LAW REVIEW Vol. 90:1215 (1990)

McConnell, Michael W., *Natural Rights and the Ninth Amendment: How Does Lockean Legal Theory Assist in Interpretation?* NYU JOURNAL OF LAW AND LIBERTY Vol. 5:1 (2010)

McCOY, ALFRED W., *THE POLITICS OF HEROIN: CIA COMPLICITY IN THE GLOBAL DRUG TRADE* (Lawrence Hill 1991)

McDONALD, FORREST, *NOVUS ORDO SECLORUM: THE INTELLECTUAL ORIGINS OF THE CONSTITUTION* (Kansas 1985)

McGEHEE, RALPH, *DEADLY DECEITS: MY 25 YEARS IN THE CIA* (Sheridan 1983)

McGinnis, John & Mulaney, Charles, *Judging Facts Like Law: The Courts Versus Congress in Social Fact-Finding*, CONSTITUTIONAL COMMENTARY Vol. 25, Issue 1 (2008)

McTAGGART, LYNNE, *THE FIELD: THE QUEST FOR THE SECRET FORCE OF THE UNIVERSE* (Harper 2008)

McWHIRTER, DARIEN & BIBLE, JON, *PRIVACY AS A CONSTITUTIONAL RIGHT: SEX, DRUGS, AND THE RIGHT TO LIFE* (Quorum 1992)

MELMAN, SEYMOUR, *THE PERMANENT WAR ECONOMY: AMERICAN CAPITALISM IN DECLINE* (Simon & Schuster 1985)

MENASHE, ARI BEN, *PROFITS OF WAR: INSIDE THE SECRET US ISRAELI ARMS NETWORK* (Sheridan 1998)

MIKALSEN, ROAR, *CONSTITUTIONAL CHALLENGES TO THE DRUG LAW: A CASE STUDY* (Createspace 2017)

MIKALSEN, ROAR, *REASON IS: ON THE NATURE OF CONSCIOUSNESS AND HOW EVERYTHING IS CONNECTED TO EVERYTHING* (Createspace 2014)

MIKALSEN, ROAR, *TO END A WAR: A SHORT HISTORY OF HUMAN RIGHTS, THE RULE OF LAW, AND HOW DRUG PROHIBITION VIOLATES THE BILL OF RIGHTS* (Createspace 2015)

MIKALSEN, ROAR, *TO RIGHT A WRONG: A TRANSPERSONAL FRAMEWORK FOR CONSTITUTIONAL CONSTRUCTION* (Createspace 2016)

MILL, JOHN STUART, *ON LIBERTY* (Hackett 1978)

MILLER, RICHARD LAWRENCE, *THE CASE FOR LEGALIZING DRUGS* (Praeger 1991)

MILLER, RICHARD LAWRENCE, *DRUG WARRIORS AND THEIR PREY: FROM POLICE POWER TO POLICE STATE* (Praeger 1996)

MILLER, WILLIAM & C'DEBACA, JANET, *QUANTUM CHANGES: WHEN EPIPHANIES AND SUDDEN INSIGHTS TRANSFORM ORDINARY LIVES* (Guilford 2001)

MILLS, C. WRIGHT, *THE POWER ELITE* (Oxford 1956)

MILLS, JAMES, *THE UNDERGROUND EMPIRE: WHERE CRIME AND GOVERNMENTS EMBRACE* (Doubleday 1986)

MOORJANI, ANITA, *DYING TO BE ME* (Hay House 2014)

MÖLLER, KAI, *THE GLOBAL MODEL OF CONSTITUTIONAL RIGHTS* (Oxford 2012)

Möller, Kai, *Proportionality: Challenging the critics*, I.CON Vol. 10: 709 (2012)

MURPHY, MICHAEL, *THE FUTURE OF THE BODY: EXPLORATIONS INTO THE FURTHER EVOLUTION OF HUMAN NATURE* (Tarcher 1992)

MUSTO, DAVID, *THE AMERICAN DISEASE: ORIGINS OF NARCOTIC CONTROL* (Yale 1973)

Musto, David, *The History of Legislative Control Over Opium, Cocaine, and Their Derivatives* (1987)

Nelson, Caleb, *Judicial Review and Legislative Purpose*, NEW YORK UNIVERSITY LAW REVIEW Vol. 83:1784 (2008)

Nelson, William E., *Changing Conceptions of Judicial Review: The Evolution of Constitutional Theory in the United States 1790-1860,* UNIVERSITY OF PENNSYLVANIA LAW REVIEW Vol. 120:1166 (1972)

Niles, Mark C., *Ninth Amendment Adjudication: An Alternative to Substantive Due Process Analysis of Personal Autonomy Rights*, UCLA LAW REVIEW Vol. 48:85 (2000)

Nilsen, Eva & Blumenson, Eric, *Liberty Lost: the Moral Case for Marijuana Law Reform,* SUFFOLK UNIVERSITY LAW SCHOOL, Research Paper No. 09-20 (2009)

Nilsen, Eva & Blumenson, Eric, *Policing for Profit: The Drug War's Hidden Economic Agenda*, UNIVERSITY OF CHICAGO LAW REVIEW Vol. 65:35 (1998)

NORMAND, ROGER & ZAIDI, SARAH, *HUMAN RIGHTS AT THE UN: THE POLITICAL HISTORY OF UNIVERSAL JUSTICE* (Indiana 2008)

NUTT, DAVID, *DRUGS—WITHOUT THE HOT AIR: MINIMISING THE HARMS OF LEGAL AND ILLEGAL DRUGS* (Cambridge 2012)

O'BRIEN, KATHY, *TRANCE-FORMATION OF AMERICA* (Reality 1995)

Ooyen-Houben, Marianne M. J. van, *The Dutch Coffee shop system: Tension and Benefits,* Michigan State International Law Review Vol. 25:3 (2017)

O'Scannlain, Diarmuid F., *The Natural Law in the American Tradition*, FORDHAM LAW REVIEW Vol. 79:1513 (2011)

Ostrowski, James, *Answering the Critics of Drug Legalization*, NOTRE DAME JOURNAL OF LAW, ETHICS & PUBLIC POLICY Vol. 5:823 (1991)

Ostrowski, James, *The Moral and Practical Case for Drug Legalization,* HOFSTRA LAW REVIEW Vol. 18: Issue 3, Article 5 (1990)

Oteri & Silvergate, *The Pursuit of Pleasure: Constitutional Dimensions of the Marihuana Problem*, SUFFOLK LAW REVIEW Vol. 3:55 (1968)

PACKER, HERBERT L., *THE LIMITS OF THE CRIMINAL SANCTION* (Stanford 1968)

PEIKOFF, LEONARD, *THE OMINOUS PARALLELS* (New American Library 1982)

PAINE, THOMAS, *RIGHTS OF MAN* (WordsWorth 1996)

PAYAN, TONY, *COPS, SOLDIERS, AND DIPLOMATS: EXPLAINING AGENCY BEHAVIOR IN THE WAR ON DRUGS* (Lexington 2006)

PERKINS, JOHN, *CONFESSIONS OF AN ECONOMIC HITMAN* (Berrett-Koehler 2004)

PERT, CANDACE B., *MOLECULES OF EMOTION: WHY YOU FEEL THE WAY YOU FEEL* (Pocket Books 1999)

Preiser, Peter, *Rediscovering a Coherent Rationale for Substantive Due Process*, MARQUETTE LAW REVIEW Vol. 87:1 (2003)

PROUTY, L. FLETCHER, *THE SECRET TEAM: THE CIA AND ITS ALLIES IN CONTROL OF THE UNITED STATES AND THE WORLD* (Skyhorse 2008)

PROVINE, DORIS MARIE, *UNEQUAL UNDER LAW: RACE IN THE WAR ON DRUGS* (Chicago 2007)

PURUCKER, G. DE, *WIND OF THE SPIRIT* (Theosophical 1984)

QUIGLEY, CAROLL, *TRAGEDY AND HOPE: A HISTORY OF THE WORLD IN OUR TIME* (Macmillan 1966)

RAO, P. RAJESWAR, *THE GREAT INDIAN PATRIOTS*, VOL. 1 (Mittal 1991)

RAWLS, JOHN, *A THEORY OF JUSTICE* (Harvard 2003)

RAWLS, JOHN, *JUSTICE AS FAIRNESS: A RESTATEMENT* (Harvard 2003)

REED, TERRY & CUMMINGS, JOHN, *COMPROMISED: CLINTON, BUSH AND THE CIA* (SPI 1994)

REICH, WILHELM, *THE MASS PSYCHOLOGY OF FASCISM* (Ferrar1970)

Reinarman, Craig, Cohen Peter D. A., & Kaal, Hendrien L., *The Limited Relevance of Drug Policy: Cannabis in Amsterdam and in San Francisco*, AMERICAN JOURNAL OF PUBLIC HEALTH Vol. 94:836 (2004)

REUTER, PETER, & MCCOUN, ROBERT, *DRUG WAR HERESIES: LEARNING FROM OTHER VICES, TIMES, AND PLACES* (2005)

Reynolds, Glenn &. Kopel, David, *The Evolving Police Power: Some Observations for a New Century*, HASTINGS CONSTITUTIONAL LAW QUARTERLY Vol. 27:511 (2000)

Richards, David A. J., *Human Rights and the Moral Foundations of the Substantive Criminal Law*, GEORGIA LAW REVIEW 13:1395 (1978)

Richards, David A.J., *Liberalism, Public Morality, and Constitutional Law: Prolegomenon to a Theory of the Constitutional Right to Privacy*, LAW AND CONTEMPORARY PROBLEMS Vol. 51:123 (1988)

RICHARDS, DAVID A.J., *SEX, DRUGS, DEATH, AND THE LAW: AN ESSAY ON HUMAN RIGHTS AND OVERCRIMINALIZATION* (Rowman 1982)

RICHARDS, DAVID A. J., *TOLERATION AND THE CONSTITUTION* (Oxford 1989)

Richards, David A.J., *Unnatural Acts and the Constitutional Right to Privacy: A Moral Theory,* FORDHAM LAW REVIEW Vol. 45:1281 (1977)

Roach, Kent, *The Primacy of Liberty and Proportionality, Not Human Dignity, When Subjecting Criminal Law to Constitutional Control,* ISRAELI LAW REVIEW Vol. 44:91 (2011)

Robinson, Paul H. & Darley, John M., *The Utility of Desert,* NORTHWESTERN UNIVERSITY LAW REVIEW Vol. 91:453 (1997)

ROBINSON, MATTHEW & SCHERLEN, RENEE, *LIES, DAMN LIES, AND DRUG WAR STATISTICS* (SUNY 2007)

ROOM, ROBIN, ET AL., *CANNABIS POLICY: MOVING BEYOND STALEMATE* (Oxford 2010)

Rosenfeld, Michel, *The Rule of Law and the Legitimacy of Constitutional Democracy,* SOUTHERN CALIFORNIA LAW REVIEW Vol. 74:1307 (2001)

ROUSSEAU, JEAN-JACQUES, *THE SOCIAL CONTRACT* (Digireads 2005)

Rubin, Edward L., *Bureaucratic Oppression: It's Causes and Cures,* VANDERBILT UNIVERSITY LAW SCHOOL, Working Paper no. 14-15 (2012)

Rubin, Edward, *Judicial Review and the Right to Resist,* VANDERBILT UNIVERSITY LAW SCHOOL, Working Paper Number 08-11 (2008)

RUBIN, VERA, AND COMITAS, LAMBROS, *GANJA IN JAMAICA: A MEDICAL ANTHROPOLOGICAL STUDY OF CHRONIC MARIHUANA USE* (1975)

RUPPERT, MIKE, *CROSSING THE RUBICON: THE DECLINE OF THE AMERICAN EMPIRE AT THE END OF THE AGE OF OIL* (NEW SOCIETY 2004)

RUSSELL, DAN, *DRUG WAR: COVERT MONEY, POWER AND POLICY* (Kalyx 2000)

RUSSEL, PETER, *THE GLOBAL BRAIN: SPECULATIONS ON THE EVOLUTIONARY LEAP OF PLANETARY CONSCIOUSNESS* (J. P. Tarcher 1983)

Sabo, Michael, *The Higher Law Background of the Constitution: Justice Clarence Thomas and Constitutional Interpretation,* ASHBROOK STATESMANSHIP THESIS (2009)

Sanders, Chase J., *Ninth Life: An Interpretive Theory of the Ninth Amendment,* INDIANA LAW JOURNAL Vol. 69:759 (1994)

Santiago, Miriam Defensor, *The New Equal Protection,* PHILIPPINE LAW JOURNAL Vol. 58:1 (1983)

SATPREM, *SRI AUROBINDO OR THE ADVENTURE OF CONSCIOUSNESS* (Mira Aditi 2008)

SCHALER, JEFFREY (ED.), *DRUGS: SHOULD WE LEGALIZE, DECRIMINALIZE OR DEREGULATE?* (Prometheus 1998)

SCHNOEBELEN, WILLIAM, *MASONRY: BEYOND THE LIGHT* (Chick 1991)

SCHWARTZ, TONY, *WHAT REALLY MATTERS: SEARCHING FOR WISDOM IN AMERICA* (Bantam 1996)

SCOTT, PETER DALE, *AMERICAN WAR MACHINE: DEEP POLITICS, THE CIA GLOBAL DRUG CONNECTION, AND THE ROAD TO AFGHANISTAN* (Rowman 2014

SCOTT, PETER DALE & MARSHALL, JONATHAN, *COCAINE POLITICS: DRUGS, ARMIES AND THE CIA IN CENTRAL AMERICA* (1998)

SCOTT, PETER DALE (ED.), *9/11 AND AMERICAN EMPIRE: INTELLECTUALS SPEAK OUT* (Olive Branch 2006)

SCOTT, PETER DALE, *THE ROAD TO 9/11: WEALTH, EMPIRE, AND THE FUTURE OF AMERICA* (California 2008)

SEAGRAVE, STERLING & SEAGRAVE, PEGGY, *GOLD WARRIORS: AMERICA'S SECRET RECOVERY OF YAMASHITA'S GOLD* (Verso 2005)

SEN, AMARTYA, *THE IDEA OF JUSTICE* (Harvard 2011)

Shedler, Jonathan & Block, Jack, *Adolescent Drug Use and Psychological Health: A Longitudinal Inquiry,* AMERICAN PSYCHOLOGIST Vol. 45 (1990)

SHELDRAKE, RUPERT, *MORPHIC RESONANCE: THE NATURE OF FORMATIVE CAUSATION* (Park Street 2009)

SHELDRAKE RUPERT, *THE PRESENCE OF THE PAST: MORPHIC RESONANCE AND THE HABITS OF NATURE* (Park Street 1995)

Sherry, Suzana, *The Founders' Unwritten Constitution,* UNIVERSITY OF CHICAGO LAW REVIEW Vol. 54:1127 (1987)

Sherry, Suzanna, *The Ninth Amendment: Righting an Unwritten Constitution*, CHICAGO-KENT LAW REVIEW Vol. 64:1001 (1988)

SHULGIN, ALEXANDER, *PIKHAL: A CHEMICAL LOVE STORY* (Transform 1992)

Siegel, Stephen A., *The Origin of the Compelling State Interest Test and Strict Scrutiny*, AMERICAN JOURNAL OF LEGAL HISTORY Vol. 48:355 (2006)

SIMON, STEPHEN A., *HUMAN RIGHTS OR AMERICAN PRIVILEGES? THE SUPREME COURT'S EVOLVING USE OF UNIVERSAL REASONING* (Doctoral dissertation 2007)

Smith, Annaliese, Comment, *Marijuana as a Schedule I Substance: Political Ploy or Accepted Science?* SANTA CLARA LAW REVIEW Vol. 40:1137 (2000)

SMITH, HUSTON, *CLEANSING THE DOORS OF PERCEPTION: THE RELIGIOUS SIGNIFICANCE OF ENTHEOGENIC PLANTS AND CHEMICALS* (Tarcher/Putnam 2000)

SMOLEY, RICHARD, *INNER CHRISTIANITY: A GUIDE TO THE ESOTERIC TRADITION* (Shambala 2002)

Snure, Brian, *A Frequent Recurrence to Fundamental Principles: Individual Rights, Free Government, and the Washington State Constitution*, WASHINGTON LAW REVIEW Vol. 67:669 (1992)

Solum, Lawrence B., *Originalism and the Unwritten Constitution*, UNIVERSITY OF ILLINOIS LAW REVIEW Vol. 2013:1935 (2013)

Spooner, Lysander, *Vices are Not Crimes: a Vindication of Moral Liberty* (1875) (Online book)

Stevens, Alex, *Drug Policy, Harm and Human Rights: A Rationalist Approach*, INTERNATIONAL JOURNAL OF DRUG POLICY 22 (2011)

STICH, RODNEY, *DEFRAUDING AMERICA* (Diablo 1988)

STICH, RODNEY, *EXPLOSIVE SECRETS OF COVERT CIA COMPANIES* (2006)

STILL, WILLIAM T., *NEW WORLD ORDER: THE ANCIENT PLAN OF SECRET SOCIETIES* (Huntington 1990)

STOCKWELL, JOHN, *THE PRAETORIAN GUARD: THE US ROLE IN THE NEW WORLD ORDER* (South End 1991)

STOLAROFF, M.J., *THANATOS TO EROS: THIRTY-FIVE YEARS OF PSYCHEDELIC EXPLORATION* (VWB 1994)

STONE, ROGER, *THE MAN WHO KILLED KENNEDY: THE CASE AGAINST LBJ* (Skyhorse 2013)

STONE, ROGER & HUNT, SAINT JOHN, *THE BUSH CRIME FAMILY: THE INSIDE STORY OF AN AMERICAN DYNASTY* (Skyhorse 2016)

STRASSMAN, RICK, *DMT AND THE SOUL OF PROPHECY: A NEW SCIENCE OF SPIRITUAL REVELATION IN THE HEBREW BIBLE* (Park Street 2014)

Stuart, Susan, *War as Metaphor and the Rule of Law in Crisis: The Lessons We Should Have Learned From the War on Drugs*, VALPARASIO UNIVERSITY SCHOOL OF LAW, Legal Studies Research Paper (2011)

STUNTZ, WILLIAM J., *THE COLLAPSE OF AMERICAN CRIMINAL JUSTICE* (Harvard 2013)

Stuntz, William J., *The Pathological Politics of Criminal Law*, HARVARD LAW SCHOOL Public Law Working Paper No. 22 (2001)

Sun, Tammy W., *Equality by Other Means: The Substantive Foundations of the Vagueness Doctrine*, HARVARD CIVIL RIGHTS-CIVIL LIBERTIES LAW REVIEW Vol. 46:150 (2011)

SULLUM, JACOB, *SAYING YES; IN DEFENCE OF DRUG USE* (Penguin 2004)

SUMMERS, ANTHONY, *THE ARROGANCE OF POWER: THE SECRET WORLD OF RICHARD NIXON* (Avalon 2003)

Sunstein, Cass R., *Homosexuality and the Constitution*, INDIANA LAW JOURNAL Vol. 70:1 (1994)

SUTTON, ANTONY, *AMERICA'S SECRET ESTABLISHMENT: AN INTRODUCTION TO THE ORDER OF SKULL AND BONES* (Liberty House 1986)

Sweet, Alec S., *All Things in Proportion? American Rights Doctrine and the Problem of Balancing*, Faculty Scholarship Series Paper 30 (2010)

SZASZ, THOMAS, *CEREMONIAL CHEMISTRY: THE RITUAL PERSECUTION OF DRUGS, ADDICTS, AND PUSHERS* (Syracuse University 2003)

SZASZ, THOMAS, *OUR RIGHT TO DRUGS: THE CASE FOR A FREE MARKET* (Praeger 1992)

TAILOR, JOHN, *CONSTRUCTION CONSTRUED AND CONSTITUTIONS VINDICATED* (1820) (Online book)

TALBOT, DAVID, *THE DEVIL'S CHESSBOARD: ALLEN DULLES, THE CIA, AND THE RISE OF AMERICA'S SECRET GOVERNMENT* (Harper 2015)

TALBOT, MICHAEL, *THE HOLOGRAPHIC UNIVERSE* (Harper 2011)

TALBOT, MICHAEL, *MYSTICISM AND THE NEW PHYSICS* (Routledge 1981)

TARPLEY, WEBSTER & CHAITKIN, ANTON, *GEORGE BUSH: THE UNAUTHORIZED BIOGRAPHY* (Progressive Press 2004)

TARPLEY, WEBSTER, *911 SYNTHETIC TERROR: MADE IN THE USA* (Progressive 2007)

TART, CHARLES L., *TRANSPERSONAL PSYCHOLOGIES: PERSPECTIVES ON THE MIND FROM SEVEN GREAT SPIRITUAL TRADITIONS* (Harper 1992)

TAYLOR, STEVE, *OUT OF THE DARKNESS: FROM TURMOIL TO TRANSFORMATION* (Hay House 2011)

TEASDALE, WAYNE, *THE MYSTIC HEART: DISCOVERING A UNIVERSAL SPIRITUALITY IN THE WORLD'S RELIGIONS* (New World Library 1999)

Tennen, Eric, *Is the Constitution in Harm's Way? Substantive Due Process and Criminal Law*, BOALT JOURNAL OF CRIMINAL LAW Vol. 8: 3 (2004)

Thomas, Clarence, *Judging*, UNIVERSITY OF KANSAS LAW REVIEW Vol. 45:1 (1996)

Thomas, Clarence, Toward a Plain Reading of the Constitution: The Declaration of Independence in Constitutional Interpretation, HOWARD LAW JOURNAL Vol. 30:691 (1987)

Torke, James W., *the Judicial Process in Equal Protection Cases*, HASTINGS CONSTITUTIONAL LAW QUARTERLY Vol. 9:279 (1982)

TRAVER, HAROLD H. & GAYLORD, MARK S. (ED.), *DRUGS, LAW AND THE STATE: A REEXAMINATION OF THE PHYSICS OF MOTION* (Hong Kong 1992)

Treiman, David M., *Equal Protection and Fundamental Rights—A Judicial Shell Game*, TULSA LAW REVIEW Vol. 15:183 (1979)

TRENTO, JOSEPH, *PRELUDE TO TERROR: EDWIN P. WILSON AND THE LEGACY OF AMERICA'S PRIVATE INTELLIGENCE NETWORK* (Carrol 2005)

TRENTO, JOSEPH, *THE SECRET HISTORY OF THE CIA* (Caroll & Graff 2005)

Tribe, Laurence H., *Lawrence v. Texas: The Fundamental Right that Dare Not Speak its Name*, HARVARD LAW REVIEW Vol. 117:1893 (2004)

Tribe, Laurence H., *On Reading the Constitution*, The Tanner Lectures on Human Values, Delivered at The University of Utah (November 17 and 18, 1986)

Tribe, Laurence H., *Reflections on Unenumerated Rights*, JOURNAL OF CONSTITUTIONAL LAW Vol. 9:483 (2007)

Tribe, Laurence & Dorf, Michael, *Levels of Generality in the Definition of Rights*, UNIVERSITY OF CHICAGO LAW REVIEW Vol. 57:1057 (1990)

Tupper, Kenneth & Labate, Beatriz, *Plants, Psychoactive Substances and the International Narcotics Control Board: The Control of Nature and the Nature of Control*, HUMAN RIGHTS AND DRUGS Vol. 2 No 1 (2012)

Tussman, Jospeh & tenBroek, Jacobus, *The Equal Protection of the Laws*, CALIFORNIA LAW REVIEW Vol. 37:341 (1949)

UNDERHILL, EVELYN, *MYSTICISM: A STUDY IN THE NATURE AND DEVELOPMENT OF MAN'S SPIRITUAL CONSCIOUSNESS* (Methuen 1962)

UNDP, *Perspectives on the Development Dimensions of Drug Control Policy* (March 2015)

VALENTINE, DOUGLAS, *THE STRENGTH OF THE WOLF* (Verso 2004)

VENTURA, JESSE, *THEY KILLED OUR PRESIDENT: 63 REASONS TO BELIEVE THERE WAS A CONSPIRACY TO ASSASSINATE JFK* (Skyhorse 2013)

Vollenweider, Franz X. & Kometer, Michael, *The Neurobiology of Psychedelic Drugs: Implications for the Treatment of Mood Disorders*, NATURE REVIEWS NEUROSCIENCE Vol. 11 (2010)

WAAL, HELGE & PEDERSEN, WILLY, *RUSMIDLER OG VEIVALG* (Cappelen 1996)

WADE, JENNY, *CHANGES OF MIND: A HOLONOMIC THEORY OF THE EVOLUTION OF CONSCIOUSNESS* (State university of New York Press 1996)

WALSH, LAWRENCE E., *FIREWALL: THE IRAN-CONTRA CONSPIRACY AND COVER-UP* (1997)

WALSH, ROGER N., & VAUGHAN, FRANCES, *BEYOND EGO: TRANSPERSONAL DIMENSIONS IN PSYCHOLOGY* (Tarcher 1980)

Ward, Andrew, *The Rational Basis Test Violates Due Process*, NYU JOURNAL OF LAW & LIBERTY Vol. 8:713 (2014)

WATSON, LYALL, *LIFETIDE: A BIOLOGY OF THE UNCONSCIOUS* (Hodder & Stoughton 1979)

WEIL, ANDREW & ROSEN, WINIFRED, *FROM CHOCOLATE TO MORPHINE: EVERYTHING YOU NEED TO KNOW ABOUT MIND-ALTERING DRUGS* (2004)

Werb et al., *Effect of Drug Law Enforcement on Drug-Related Violence: Evidence from a Scientific Review*, INTERNATIONAL CENTRE FOR SCIENCE IN DRUG POLICY (2010)

West, Robin, *The Authoritarian Impulse in Constitutional Law*, UNIVERSITY OF MIAMI LAW REVIEW Vol. 42: 531 (1988)

WHITE, JOHN (ED.), *KUNDALINI: EVOLUTION AND ENLIGHTENMENT* (Paragon 1990)

WILBER, KEN, *THE EYE OF SPIRIT: AN INTEGRAL VISION FOR A WORLD GONE SLIGHTLY MAD* (Shambala 1998).

WILBER, KEN, *EYE TO EYE: THE QUEST FOR THE NEW PARADIGM* (Shambala 1996).

WILBER, KEN, *INTEGRAL SPIRITUALITY: A STARTLING NEW ROLE FOR RELIGION IN THE MODERN AND POSTMODERN WORLD* (Integral Books 2006).

WILBER, KEN, *UP FROM EDEN: A TRANSPERSONAL VIEW OF HUMAN EVOLUTION* (New Science Library 1986).

WILBER, KEN, *QUANTUM QUESTIONS: MYSTICAL WRITINGS OF THE WORLD'S GREATEST PHYSICISTS* (Shambala 2001).

WILCOCK, DAVID, *THE ASCENSION MYSTERIES: REVEALING THE COSMIC BATTLE BETWEEN GOOD AND EVIL* (Dutton 2016)

WILCOCK, DAVID, *THE SOURCE FIELD INVESTIGATIONS: THE HIDDEN SCIENCE AND LOST CIVILIZATIONS BEHIND THE 2012 PROPHECIES* (Dutton 2011)

WILLIAMS, PAUL, *OPERATION GLADIO: THE UNTOLD STORY OF THE UNHOLY ALLIANCE BETWEEN THE VATICAN, THE CIA, AND THE MAFIA* (Prometheus 2015)

WILKINSON, RICHARD & PICKETT, KATE, *THE SPIRIT LEVEL: WHY EQUALITY IS BETTER FOR EVERYONE* (Penguin 2010).

Williams, Ryan C., *The One and Only Substantive Due Process Clause*, THE YALE LAW JOURNAL Vol. 120:408 (2010)

WILSON, WOODROW, *THE NEW FREEDOM* (1913, online book)

WINKELMAN, MICHAEL & ROBERTS, THOMAS (EDS.), *PSYCHEDELIC MEDICINE: NEW EVIDENCE FOR HALLUCINOGENIC SUBSTANCES AS TREATMENTS*, Vol. 2 (Praeger 2007)

Winterbourne, Matt, *United States drug policy: The Scientific, Economic, and Social Issues Surrounding Marijuana* (2012)

Wisotsky, Steven, *A Society of Suspects: The War on Drugs and Civil Liberties*, CATO POLICY ANALYSIS No. 180 (1992)

WISOTSKY, STEVEN, *BEYOND THE WAR ON DRUGS: OVERCOMING A FAILED PUBLIC POLICY* (Prometheus 1990)

Wisotsky, Steven, *Not thinking Like a Lawyer: The Case of Drugs in the Courts*, NOTRE DAME JOURNAL OF LAW, ETHICS AND PUBLIC POLICY, Volume 5, Issue No. 3 (1991)

WOLLSTONECRAFT, MARY, *A VINDICATION OF THE RIGHTS OF MAN* (1792) (Online book)

WOLLSTONECRAFT, MARY, *A VINDICATION OF THE RIGHTS OF WOMAN* (Online Library of Liberty 1790)

WOOD, *WHERE DID THE TOWERS GO? EVIDENCE OF DIRECTED FREE-ENERGY TECHNOLOGY ON 9/11* (New Investigation 2010)

WULFF, DAVID M., *PSYCHOLOGY OF RELIGION: CLASSIC AND CONTEMPORARY VIEWS* (Wiley 1991)

Yankah, Ekow N., *A Paradox in Overcriminalization*, NEW CRIMINAL LAW REVIEW Vol. 14:1 (2011)

Yoshino, Kenji, *The New Equal Protection*, HARVARD LAW REVIEW Vol. 124:747 (2011)

ZIMBARDO, PHILIP, *THE LUCIFER EFFECT: HOW GOOD PEOPLE TURN EVIL* (Rider 2009)

ZUKAV, GARY, *THE DANCING WU LI MASTERS: AN OVERVIEW OF THE NEW PHYSICS* (Morrow & Co 1979)

About the Author

Roar Alexander Mikalsen is the author of six books which are changing the world one at a time. His authorship covers a large area ranging from cosmology, mysticism, self-help, and consciousness research to power politics, human rights law, drug policy, constitutional interpretation, and social engineering.

He is the founder of the Alliance for Rights-Oriented Drug Policies (AROD), an organization which addresses drug policy reform from a perspective of human rights and a nominee of two prestigious human rights awards (Vaclav Havel and Martin Ennals).

A platform for his work is Life Liberty Productions, a publishing house and consulting agency dedicated to the Spirit of Freedom. You will find books that are embraced by professionals and have the potential to bring humanity one step further on the online store lifelibertybooks.com